the book of
islands

Philip Dodd & Ben Donald

PALAZZO
EDITIONS

Contents

INTRODUCTION

"Islomania is a rare affliction of spirit.
There are people who find islands somehow irresistible.
The mere knowledge that they are in a little world surrounded by sea
fills them with an indescribable intoxication."

Lawrence Durrell

Even if, as John Donne's much-quoted line tells us, no man is an island, an awful lot of us would like to be one, or at least be on one. The powerful attraction of an island is the promise of isolation (that word itself derived from the Italian word for "island"), a total escape from the cares and stresses of life on the mainland.

The Book of Islands is a celebration of that appeal, and of the extraordinary diversity, energy and culture of the islands that punctuate our world. This is a spin of the globe by longitude from east to west, following the daily journey of the sun and starting out from 180°, the marker for the International Date Line, that invisible cable ostensibly stretched between the two poles, with a kink here and a loop there to suit political or practical demands. From Tonga and the Chatham Islands, the first places on the planet to greet each new dawn, we travel anti-clockwise, tracking the sun west through the time zones, across the Pacific and Australasia, into Asia and on through Europe, Africa and across to the Americas before the day sets, and the book draws to a close, in Samoa.

It is not difficult to define what an island is – in fact Chambers Dictionary does it rather neatly: "A mass of land (not a continent) surrounded with water." That was a given. But to choose the most compelling islands for this book, the question we asked ourselves was which of them possessed a particular sense of history and culture, an insularity or "islandness" that set them apart from all the rest.

Islands should ideally be approached by boat, at a pinch by plane or helicopter if needs be (which can provide a wonderful overview of a scattered archipelago: the Bahamas dotted in turquoise seas, for example). But we were not so purist as to exclude those islands linked to a mainland by the slender tether of a bridge or causeway, a needless quibble since all islands are joined to the Earth's surface at their root – even the Uros, those bizarre reed islands apparently floating on the surface of Lake Titicaca.

OPPOSITE Huli Wigmen in traditional costumes during the Sing Sing Festival, New Guinea

As we examined the candidates, we found that some of those "masses of land surrounded by water", although technically islands, did not, to us at least, have the necessary sense of "islandness". Size, oddly, was not an issue. Some are vast. Baffin in Canada – not even as large as New Guinea, Borneo or Madagascar – is still bigger than Germany, but definitely felt like an island.

We went by instinct in the end. We found that we did not think of Ireland, for example, as an island (more a state of being perhaps, riven between the identities of North and South), so we included wonderful islands lying near its coastline: the Aran Islands off Galway, quintessentially Irish, and the spiky Skelligs close by County Kerry. New Zealand did seem to possess the necessary island quality, while Australia, as a continent, was out of contention, but offered islands of great character, from Rottnest near Perth in the far west to Fraser Island off Queensland and, of course, Tasmania, home of the screeching devil.

We also wanted to include small islands with big personalities. The tiny Lake Palace, Udaipur, majestic and gracious; Reichenau and Mainau in Lake Constance. Sometimes we chose an entire archipelago – the Maldives, the Seychelles or Cape Verde – rather than trying to select one minor representative. But in the Balearics, each one of Ibiza, Mallorca, Menorca and Formentera were distinctive enough to merit individual focus.

A hundred islands or so were automatic selections – those with global reputations that have inspired our imaginations, as well as literature, the arts, music and movies: Jamaica, the birthplace of reggae, Gauguin's beloved Tahiti, Pablo Neruda's Easter Island and Ithaca, home of Odysseus.

Even within this one hundred, their character embraced the surfing meccas of the Hawaiian islands and the urban chic of the Île St-Louis in Paris, the steamy passion of Sicily and the chilly charms of Iceland, and ranged from the commerce of Hong Kong Island to the 1950s olde-worldiness of the Isle of Wight and the decadence of Cuba. We liked islands far from the madding crowd – Tristan da Cunha way out in the Atlantic, Tierra del Fuego at the tip of South America, Sakhalin on the far northern edge of Russia – or tucked away, like Likoma in the heart of Africa.

Some islands are countries in their own right, others split between powers like Hispaniola, divided between Haiti and the Dominican Republic, or Sint Maarten/St-Martin divvied up in the most amicable of arrangements between France and The Netherlands. Territorial disputes are rife in the history of islands. An island is so much more definable as a target of proprietorial greed than a mainland "country" with its shifting borders.

The nations of the world have expended much time, effort, blood and thunder in battling for control of islands, and capturing and recapturing, incessantly trading and ceding these packages of land so strategic for defence (Saipan) or commerce (the Spice Islands, now known as the Moluccas). Unexpected pockets of empire turned up: the Swedish influence in St Barts, the German pasts of Samoa and Guinea. And usually it was the indigenous population that suffered – Malta, for example, seems to have been owned at some point by everybody other than the Maltese – or in some cases simply were "disappeared" or relocated. In their wake the colonialists left a polyglot legacy, strata of different cultures that affect the islands to this day.

As we went beyond the obvious pleasure playgrounds – the Bahamas, Capri, Santorini, Mauritius, Bali, each a must-have – we found new categories that contrasted with the blue sea/white sand image of the island as a holiday paradise. Wilderness islands: Wrangell, Kerguelen. Mystical islands: Chiloé, Easter Island. City islands: Stockholm's Gamla Stan, Singapore, the serene Venice, pulsating Manhattan.

There were prison islands: Alcatraz, for its inmates almost unbearably within touching distance of the cable cars and switchback hills of San Francisco; Robben Island, where Nelson Mandela was incarcerated; and Devil's Island, made famous by Papillon. Islands of exile like Napoleon's St Helena and Elba; of sanctuary and prayer: Iona or Caldey; and pilgrimage: Ganga Sagar in the mouth of the Ganges. And there were islands that have entered the language: Bikini and Curaçao, the latter a potential ingredient in an islomaniac cocktail with Madeira, Rum and a shot of Islay whisky.

For each entry we have tried to give a snapshot of what is unique about each island or archipelago, a flavour of its individuality, history and character, its language, festivals, cuisine or tribes. The images illuminate an angle of that essence, each an encouragement to start digging out your passport. There are passionate or wry quotes about each location from famous islanders, distinguished travel writers, poets, songwriters and visiting luminaries. And a nugget of essential information includes longitude and latitude, area, highest point, population, main city, and a selection of the great and the good who were born or lived on the islands.

The variety of the 200 islands is astonishing, a diversity and biodiversity so often remarkable precisely because of being self-contained and uncontaminated – Socotra, Madagascar or the Galapagos are precious, fragile sanctuaries. But the changing climate and rising sea levels, and the threat of infection inadvertently brought in by tourists, either eco or non-eco, mean that these islands can not rest easy, and others, like the low-level Maldives or briny Smith Island in Chesapeake Bay, may not be with us for many decades more. We must enjoy them while we can.

Philip Dodd and Ben Donald

Tonga
SOUTH PACIFIC

Half a world away from the Greenwich Meridian lies the International Date Line – an imaginary time warp that in principle allows you to stand with one leg in today and the other in tomorrow (or yesterday depending on which direction you are facing). Unlike the Meridian, however, which scythes unflinchingly along 0° longitude, the International Date Line, ostensibly following 180°, traces a far more erratic route for both practical and political reasons. This is why Tonga, although lying east of 180°, has ended up just west of the Date Line, allowing the island the cheerful claim of being the first land to greet each new dawn, year and millennium.

According to legend, it was around the end of the first millennium AD that the god Tangaloa visited this sprawling Pacific archipelago and, with a little help from 'Ilaheva, a local woman, sired the first in an enduring line of Tongan kings and queens. Tongans have generally – despite a reform movement in the mid-2000s – been diligently respectful towards their monarchs, whether the incumbent King George Tupou V, his predecessor Tupou IV (the world's heaviest monarch according to *Guinness World Records*), or Queen Salote, who placed the previously little-known Tonga firmly into the global consciousness by her gracious appearance at the 1953 coronation of Queen Elizabeth II. It was raining and, to show respect to a higher-ranking person, according to Tongan custom Queen Salote refused to close the top of her carriage.

This sense of tradition, whether royal, religious (ninety-nine per cent of Tongans declare themselves Christian), familial or practical (demonstrated in wonderfully complex *ngatu* bark weaving), lies at the heart of the Tongan psyche. As such, there have to be escape valves and the *fakaleiti* is a posse of male transvestites tolerated, like the *hijras* of India, as an expression of otherness. The national drink, *kava*, a gum- and brain-numbing extract from the root of the kava plant, supplies a quick way of heading off into a different stratum of consciousness. The rugby team, the Sea Eagles, releases a more macho energy – and very nearly upset the odds by putting eventual champions South Africa under pressure in the 2007 World Cup. Unique amongst the competing teams, they had brought a priest along as part of their squad.

Surprisingly perhaps, Tonga is not yet a major tourist destination. There is plenty to explore, some 170 islands covering a total of 7,700 square kilometres (2,972 square miles) – although only 747 of those are actually *terra firma*. Each island group offers a discrete personality, from the volcanic Niuas in the far north to the coral atolls of central H'apai and, down south, the main island of Tongatapu, where waves blast through the natural limestone tunnels of the Mapua'a Vaca blowholes to create briny geysers.

Those tourists who do visit can take full benefit of the tropical climate and renowned welcome. On one of his perambulations across the Pacific waters, Captain Cook dubbed this archipelago the "Friendly Islands". In fact, it was later discovered that the feasting he enjoyed was a trap to capture him and his crew. It seems only a lack of organization – or perhaps too much *kava* – on the part of the natives saved his skin.

RIGHT Mapua'a Vaca blow-holes, Tongatapu Island

Tonga, the Kingdom of Tonga **Longitude:** 174° 30' W **Latitude:** 19° 50' S **Area:** 747 sq km (288 sq mi) **Archipelago area:** 7,700 sq km (2,972 sq mi) **Highest point:** 1,033 m (3,389 ft) Kao Island
Population: 116,000 **Capital:** Nuku'alofa **Natives:** Queen Salote Tupou III, Epi Taione, Lesley Vainikolo

"There is not in the world
a little kingdom like Tonga,
peaceful, contented and happy."

Queen Salote Tupou III of Tonga

Chatham Islands, New Zealand **Local names:** Rekohu, Wharekauri **Longitude:** 176° 40' W **Latitude:** 44° 00' S **Area:** 966 sq km (373 sq mi) **Highest point:** 299 m (981 ft)
Population: 600 **Principal town:** Waitangi **Native:** Tommy Solomon

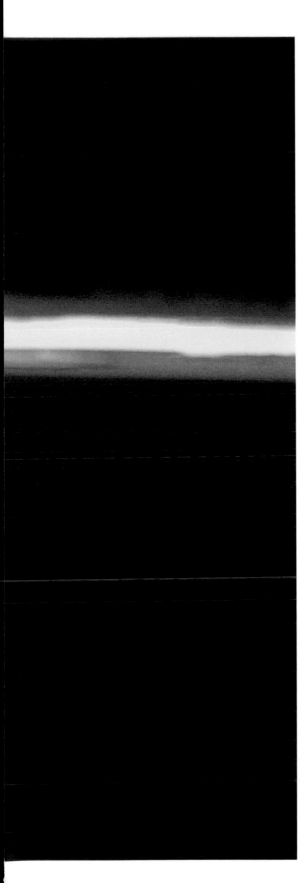

Chatham Islands

SOUTH PACIFIC

In a world of marketing and obsessions with lists of superlatives and firsts, the Chathams were slow to exploit the potential of the first day of the twenty-first century to raise their profile as a destination. For most people, it did not even put them on the map. Lying in their own time zone, forty-five minutes ahead of their owner New Zealand, the islands had a chance to promote themselves as the first place in the world to greet the dawn of the new millennium. In the event they lost out to more PR-conscious Tonga, and thus they remain within a tantalizing glimmer of marking that arbitrary line in the Pacific Ocean known as the International Date Line, at which each new day begins.

That said, if the world were flat, the Chathams would feel like the edge of it, such is their remoteness and isolation from human society. There are just two stores – a grocer and an off-licence – in the main settlement of Waitangi on Chatham, the largest of the ten islands that make up this archipelago. Just two of the islands are inhabited, and those six hundred or so souls are hugely outnumbered by the cows that graze all over the land and account for the near-absence of trees. The original forest cover is gradually being re-established to claim back partially the islands' swathes of rolling farmland, rocky basalt outcrops and red-orange soiled post-volcanic conical hills. In the interior of the T-shaped main island, with bays on both sides and the Te Whanga lagoon in the middle (where strange, fossilized sharks' teeth wash up), copses of *kopi* and *akeake* trees have now taken hold amid the wind-slanted Pacific bush. With this conservation effort, a number of the islands' eighteen unique bird species – including the local black robin and the *taiko* or magenta petrel (formerly a part of the native diet) – have been brought back from the edge of extinction.

The tale of the Chathams is a salutary chapter in the book of man's inhumanity to man. The indigenous Moriori people had made a religion out of non-aggression as a means for self preservation, only to find themselves enslaved, sometimes eaten, and their ancestral home (which they called Rekohu) pillaged by the Maoris, who invaded what they called Wharekauri in their war canoes. The Europeans discovered and settled the Chathams in 1791, and left the two tribes to fight it out while claiming the islands for George III. Captain William Broughton named the islands after his ship, and introduced the civilizing industries of whaling and sealing. It was only in the 1980s that the true fate of the Moriori was discovered, some fifty or so years too late to save them. The last supposed full-blood Moriori, Tommy Solomon, died in 1933. Belated monuments scattered around the islands now act as a sober reminder of the peace the departed natives once so wisely promoted, while other traces of the islands' ancestry can be found in petroglyph and dendroglyph stone- and tree-carvings.

"We peered through the steerage-hatch towards noon & the Chathams were ink stains on the leaden horizon."

David Mitchell, *Cloud Atlas*

LEFT Sunrise greets the new Millennium

Fiji

SOUTH PACIFIC

As a paradise destination, the island nation of Fiji has a longer track record than most. In the 1950s, high-society members including Gary Cooper, Cary Grant, John Wayne and Noël Coward would island-hop the so-called Coral Route in seaplanes. Then Tom Hanks became a Castaway here and Brooke Shields was discovered in a Blue Lagoon. It is no surprise, therefore, that today one in nine visitors is a honeymooner. But there was a time when visitors to these 320 islands around the Koro Sea (of which only a hundred are inhabited) received a very different welcome – as a shoe in Fiji's national museum testifies. It belonged to Reverend Thomas Baker, who came as a missionary to these parts in 1867. He was eaten.

Although independent since 1970, and paradoxically a military republic prone to un-paradise-like military coups, Fiji is an enthusiastic member of the British Commonwealth. The motto is "Fear God and Honour the Queen", and Her Majesty's portrait is widely on display. Religion of all creeds also plays a large role among the inhabitants, who are themselves a blend of Melanesian, Polynesian and Micronesian mixed with Indian, Chinese and European. The Bible exists here in Fijian, and Protestant churches all over the islands ring with singing. In the capital, Suva, stands a magnificent Roman Catholic cathedral and Sre Siva Subramaniya is the largest Hindu temple in the Southern Hemisphere.

The Fijians are a smiling, welcoming and unhurried people, whose lives revolve around the village. Here *bure* thatched buildings resonate to the sound of *bula*, the traditional greeting. *Meke* dances bring to life stories and legends, and the saronged locals fill their hair with flowers,

present each other with gifts and sit around large wooden bowls scooping up coconut shells full of *kava* – a supposedly narcotic substance made from the crushed root of the Polynesian pepper shrub, which numbs the tongue and tastes like washing-up water. Fortunately the rest of the cuisine, including *kokoda* (fish steamed in coconut, lime and any tropical fruit), compensates for the experience.

Fiji's main island is Viti Levu. It is shaped like a rugby ball, which is appropriate for a nation that considers rugby the real and binding secular religion. Over the years – and despite losing the cream of their indigenous talent, such as Joe Rokocoko and Sitiveni Sivivatu, to their richer rugby neighbours New Zealand – these lush rainforest isles, with their mangrove swamps, sand dunes and cloud-wrapped mountains, have produced the world's most successful sevens teams, more than their share of World Cup upsets and a formidable pack of UN peacekeepers.

"Fiji is like the world you thought you'd left behind – full of Australian tourists looking for inexpensive salad bowls (though why anyone would think a race of Queenquegs, proud of their cannibal past, might excel at making salad bowls is not only a cultural mystery, but proof that tourists will believe almost anything)."

Paul Theroux

ABOVE Rugby practice on mudflats near Suva

OPPOSITE Fijian houses, *bures*

Fiji, The Republic of the Fiji Islands **Local name:** Matanitu ko Viti **Longitude:** 179° 00' E **Latitude:** 17° 20' S **Area:** 18,274 sq km (7,056 sq mi) **Archipelago area:** 1,290,000 sq km (497,940 sq mi) **Highest point:** 1,323m (4,340 ft) Mt Tomanivi **Population:** 918,675 **Capital:** Suva **Natives:** Sireli Bobo, Paulini Curuenavuli, Mike Howlett, Cassius Khan, Joe Rokocoko, Waisale Serevi, Vijay Singh, Sitiveni Sivivatu, Lote Tuqiri, Laisa Vulakoro

New Zealand

SOUTHWEST PACIFIC

"New Zealand is not
        a small country but
a large village."

Peter Jackson

Understandably, New Zealanders raise a bemused eyebrow when reminded of the often-repeated notion that New Zealand is merely an antiquated, Antipodean reincarnation of Albion. This image is reinforced by usually anonymous one-liners. "If an English butler and an English nanny sat down to design a country," runs one, "they would come up with New Zealand."

The truth is that the New Zealand of the twenty-first century has moved on considerably. These islands are, like a succulent lamb shank, a hundred per cent pure New Zealand: as distinctive as a Maori tattoo, as determined as Pai, the heroine of *Whale Rider*. Rather than a throwback to the yesteryear of the motherland, this is a youthful, innovative land. In 1893 it became the first nation to enfranchise women, and later the first – and to date, only – country to be run simultaneously by a female monarch (Queen Elizabeth II), governor-general, prime minister, speaker and chief justice.

The very shape of New Zealand has become a brand – the two islands, North and South, touching nose to tail, while Stewart, the much smaller and generally forgotten third island, dangles below. They look like a vertical interpretation of the long white cloud, the *aotearoa* of the Maori name for the islands. The Maori, their first settlers, came from the East Polynesian islands sometime around AD 800. Eight centuries passed before Abel Tasman arrived in 1642. Dutch cartographers first named the islands after Zeeland, and James Cook re-spelled or misspelled it as Zealand. The Europeans brought along their usual baggage: potatoes, disease, muskets and missionaries, but the Treaty of Waitangi of 1840 was a relatively civilized pact between settlers and Maori, although to this day many Maori believe the treaty was slanted and interpreted against their interests.

This casts a lingering shadow across a luminous future. With only four million people on the islands, the country has been able to develop an uncrowded, organic feel that is right for the times. Even its two North Island "big smokes" – Auckland and its rival city, windy Wellington – are low-rise and laid-back. They sit on the fringes of the great natural beauty of New Zealand, which resides in a powerful blend of alpine scenery, glaciers, volcanoes, geysers and forests, the backdrop for the *Lord of the Rings* movies under the guidance of local boy Peter Jackson. Four-fifths of the islands' flora and fauna is unique. The giant moa is now extinct, but New Zealand is home to the flightless kakapo, the kea parrot and, of course, the oddly dumpy kiwi – long-beaked, flightless and nocturnal, an unlikely NZ icon.

The forests are full of lofty timber, standing tall like the All Blacks, who perhaps better represent New Zealand's uniting of Maori determination and British, specifically Scots, grit: chiselled, flinty, unflinching and forward-looking.

OPPOSITE Maori man with *Moko* facial tattoos, Rotorua

LEFT Auckland at dusk

OVERLEAF Mitre Peak reflecting on Milford Sound

New Zealand **Longitude:** 176° 00' E **Latitude:** 40° 00' S **Area:** 267,990 sq km (103,444 sq mi) **Highest point:** 3,754m (12,316 ft) Aoraki aka Mt Cook **Population:** 4,257,000 **Capital:** Wellington
Natives: Zinzan Brooke, Jane Campion, Bob Charles, Russell Crowe, Neil Finn, Sean Fitzpatrick, Richard Hadlee, Edmund Hillary, Keri Hulme, Rachel Hunter, Witi Ihimaera, Peter Jackson, Kiri Te Kanawa, Jonah Lomu, Katherine Mansfield, Ngaio Marsh, Ernest Rutherford, Mark Todd, Hayley Westenra **Residents:** Precious McKenzie, Andrew Mehrtens, Sam Neill, Richard O'Brien, Anna Paquin

Vanuatu
SOUTH PACIFIC

"The land that has always existed."

The meaning of Vanuatu in the local language

ABOVE Vanuatu volcano

OPPOSITE Land diver bungee jumping

Vanuatu, Republic of Vanuatu **Longitude:** 168° 00' E **Latitude:** 15° 00' S **Area:** 12,336 sq km (4,762 sq mi) **Archipelago area:** 860,000 sq km (331,960 sq mi)
Highest point: 1,877 m (6,158 ft) Mt Tabwemasana **Population:** 211,900 **Capital:** Port Vila **Native:** Vanessa Quai

n a recent index created by UK think-tank The New Economics Foundation, Vanuatu emerged as the "happiest place on Earth", based on the criteria of climate, scenery, the islanders' respect for their environment and, maybe not least, the lack of any income or corporate taxation. James Michener said it was the inspiration for Bali Hai in *South Pacific*.

Not everything is hunky dory on Vanuatu, however. Climate change is making itself felt, there are hurricanes and cyclones aplenty, and the archipelago's economy is limited. Although an agriculture based on subsistence crops means there is no desperate poverty or famine, the islands possess little in the way of minerals or petroleum, hence a decision to tap into the less tangible but equally lucrative areas of hi-tech and financial services.

In fact, the parameters of money are relative here. In the north of the archipelago, wealth – mainly in the form of pigs, Vanuatu's original, much-prized currency – is judged by how much of it you can give away. And just as Mammon is not worshipped in the usual way, the islanders (the ni-Vanuatu) look to some unlikely gods: Prince Philip is revered in the village of Yaohnanen on the island of Tanna. Tanna has also deified John Frum, an archetypal American serviceman: when African-American soldiers arrived in the Second World War, they became a new touchstone of empathy and generosity, their ambulance's red crosses adopted as the god's insignia.

Vanuatu lies north-east of Australia, a roughly Y-shaped patchwork of eighty-three often volcanic islands (some still active). It is a proud island nation, although its neighbour to the south, New Caledonia, has territorial claims on two tiny islands, Matthew and Hunter. Vanuatu's Melanesian inhabitants had their first significant encounter with Europeans in the late eighteenth century, and by 1906 the jostling for claims had settled down to the point where France and Britain ran the country jointly as the New Hebrides. This arrangement, called the Condominium, included an aggressive practice of "blackbirding", a euphemism for slavery. Western diseases made inroads into the remaining ni-Vanuatu (the common cold was often fatal). The supply of sandalwood, shipped to China for incense, was swiftly depleted. And the duplication of bureaucracy in two languages was totally inefficient – the system was nicknamed "Pandemonium". At one point in the Second World War, when France fell to the Nazis, the country was technically at war with itself.

Despite the loss of the sandalwood trees, Vanuatu's rainforests have remained relatively untouched. Vulcanologists have plenty to monitor, and divers can enjoy clear waters and blowholes as well as the world's only underwater Post Office on Hideaway Island. The ni-Vanuatu are relaxed. They gather beneath giant banyans on village meeting grounds, or watch the world go by in hibiscus and frangipani-draped Port Vila, the capital on Efate. There they can sit back and listen to the local string-band music – a kind of ni-Vanuatu skiffle-cum-bluegrass. If a pure adrenalin rush is needed, they can join the jumpers of Pentecost Island in the *naghol*, when islanders plummet 30 metres (100 feet) from wooden towers, their ankles attached to springy liana vines – the original bungee jump.

Bikini

MARSHALL ISLANDS, NORTH PACIFIC

> "The main island,
> drawing close on
> the starboard bow,
> was so precisely
> the conventional picture
> of a South Sea
> Island that it might
> have been the
> jacket of a very
> old novel."
>
> James Cameron, journalist

Bikini is a story of twentieth-century madness. It was here, on this seven and a half square miles of Pacific atoll, that the US government carried out twenty nuclear bomb tests between 1946 and 1958. One of them, Operation Bravo, involved the underwater explosion of an H-Bomb one thousand times more powerful than that dropped over either Hiroshima or Nagasaki.

The impact not only conditioned world history, and future life for the islanders, but also in a more frivolous way changed female fashion forever. Far from being inspired by any erotic or exotic associations, the French designer Louis Réard, just days after the atomic tests took place, christened his new two-piece swimsuit the bikini on the grounds that the excitement it would cause would be comparable to the impact of the nuclear device (his rival, Jacques Heim, had just launched the slightly less revealing "atome" swimsuit).

Following its explosive launch on the Paris catwalks in July 1946, Roger Vadim used the bikini to create an ideal of a new and fatal femininity, and to launch the career of Brigitte Bardot in 1957. Bryan Hyland boosted sales by singing about this "itsy bitsy" garment and in 1962 Ursula Andress established the bikini as a truly iconic fashion item, as she rose Venus-like from the sea in *Dr No*, the first James Bond film.

Such sartorial preoccupations would have been lost on the eleven Micronesian families who were duped into leaving their homes. President Harry S. Truman had promised King Jude, chief of the Micronesian community, that the nuclear tests were "for the good of mankind and to end all wars". The king humbly replied: "We will go believing that everything is in the hands of God." The community of 167 inhabitants left their homes and in the next two years underwent three further relocations, each time from one more infertile atoll to another. They finally settled on Kili, where they remain to this day, formally compensated by the US government to the tune of $150 million dollars, an account that the hastily set up and under-funded Nuclear Claims Tribunal has so far been unable to settle in full.

Already a cemetery of scuttled US battleships at the end of Second World War – and therefore a potential divers' paradise – the island remains uninhabited. The promised negligible radiation levels when they were briefly repatriated in the 1970s have long remained too high for the islanders. Tourism to the island is slowly on the rise, however, and with it the profile of the plight of its rightful inhabitants.

OPPOSITE US submarine *Apogon*, sunk in the 1946 atomic bomb test at Bikini Atoll

"Nauro Is. Native Knows Posit. He Can Pilot.
11 Alive. Need Small Boat. Kennedy."

Commander John F. Kennedy

Solomon Islands

SOUTH PACIFIC

The Solomon Islands were discovered in 1568 by the Spanish explorer Alvaro de Mendana de Neira, who was travelling west from Peru. They lie at the outer limit of the drowned Australasian continent, and are born of the geological friction of the Indo-Australasian and Pacific plates. This tectonic activity created a dynamic and brooding ecosphere of both active and dormant volcanoes, jungle-clad peaks, uplifted atolls, creeks, lagoons, waterfalls and misty rainforests that are home to 230 types of orchid. In the swamps lurk crocodiles, skinks, the rare and indigenous grey marsupial known as the cuscus, and all manner of snakes, lizards and frogs.

The Solomons make up the second largest island nation in the South Pacific, covering some 1,500 kilometres (932 miles) from the Shortlands in the west to Anuta in the east. They encompass many island groups, including Choiseul, New Georgia, Florida and Santa Cruz, and every Pacific race from blue-black Papuans and dark-blond Melanesians to fair Polynesians. There are seventy four indigenous languages. It is perhaps no surprise, therefore, that ethnic and territorial tension should surface in such thinly spread land and barely defined nationhood.

In 1943 and thereafter until that fateful day in Dallas, John F. Kennedy, would have reason to be grateful for the wisdom of the Solomon islanders. During the Second World War, while commanding the USS *PT-109*, Kennedy's ship was rammed by a Japanese destroyer. Kennedy swam to the rescue of many of his crew and found himself shipwrecked with ten others on

Plum Pudding Island (so-called for its shape but since renamed Kennedy Island and known locally as Kasolo). They were discovered by two local men, Biuku Gasa and Eroni Kumana. In the absence of any common language, the locals suggested that the stranded navy personnel use a coconut to write an SOS message that could be delivered by dugout canoe. The message in a coconut was duly sent, the commander and future president duly saved, his status as a war hero secured, and the dried shell would come to sit and be treasured on his desk in the Oval Office throughout his tenure.

The islands, which number just a few short of a thousand (though only 347 are inhabited), saw much bitter fighting during the Second World War, in particular the group known as the Guadalcanal, which today are home to the administrative capital Honiara. But this was just a middle chapter in a bloody history dating back to the 1890s, when the Solomons became

one of the last corners of the world to fall under European religious or political control as a British protectorate. The islands' most recent chapters include ethnic violence and civil war that ended in 1998 with the arrival of an Australian peacekeeping force. Although independent since 1978, this Melanesian island nation is formally still part of the British Commonwealth.

Today the islanders' warring is confined to the festival racing of war canoes across 'the slot' the channel so-named during the Second World War – between the thirteen or so main islands, including Munda, Gizo and Uepi, that form the nation's nucleus. The real threat comes from the exploitation of the islands' resources: timber, nickel, lead and gold. With the discovery of the wreck of the *PT-109*, however, and a recent visit by Max Kennedy, JFK's nephew, the islanders – Gasa and Kumana in particular – have received long-overdue national recognition for their wartime support.

OPPOSITE Kennedy Island   ABOVE Spotted Cuscus   OVERLEAF Waiting for the ferry in Honiara

Solomon Islands **Longitude:** 155° 00' E **Latitude:** 6° 00' S **Area:** 27,556 sq km (10,637 sq mi) **Archipelago area:** 725,172 sq km (280,000 sq mi) **Highest point:** 2,332 m (7,651 ft)
Mt Popomanaseu **Population:** 566,800 **Capital:** Honiara, Guadalcanal **Natives:** Biuku Gasa, Eroni Kumana, Francis Manioru, Chris Meke Walasi, Alick Wickham

"Round them shimmered the light,
      the sand, and farther back the darker,
proprietary trees."

Patrick White, *A Fringe of Leaves*

Fraser Island, Queensland, Australia **Alternative name:** K'gari **Longitude:** 153° 10' E **Latitude:** 25° 15' S **Area:** 1,652 sq km (638 sq mi) **Highest point:** 244 m (800 ft)

Fraser Island

QUEENSLAND, AUSTRALIA

Fraser Island is the largest sand island in the world, 140 long kilometres (87 miles) of the stuff, roughly shaped like a platypus jutting north away from the mainland and containing an extraordinary collection of lakes, dunes, trees and streams. Grabbing a 4WD – nothing else can tackle the terrain first impressions are that this island is one tough survivor, standing its ground despite the onslaught of natural forces, and resisting the best efforts of both wind and water, even as they have continually shaped, morphed and sculpted its sand.

Along Fraser's eastern edge runs a splendid beach, called simply the Seventy-Five Mile Beach. It is a dune-buggy enthusiast's dream, with a quick swerve round the carcass of the *Maheno*, a cruise ship that came to grief on these shores in the mid-1930s. It was from the flotsam of an earlier wreck that the island took its name. Almost exactly a century earlier, in 1836, the *Stirling Castle* crashed and the captain's wife Eliza Fraser, whose husband perished in the disaster, was taken in by the aborigines. When she returned to a heroine's welcome in Sydney, she promptly cashed in with a bestselling book (her story was later depicted in fiction by Patrick White as *A Fringe of Leaves* and in paint by Sidney Nolan). Eliza claimed to have suffered at the hands of the aborigines, leaving a sour taste to her story that may have contributed to the disappearance of the K'garis; the final members of the Butchulla tribe left the island in 1904.

The ever-shifting dunes of Fraser, some 240 metres (787 feet) high, have formed inspiring shapes: the Pinnacles and the Cathedrals are self-descriptive, while the Teewah Cliffs present a palette of multicoloured sands. And there are lakes all across the island. Barrage lakes and window lakes. Perched lakes that sit on the sand base, such as Lake Boomanjin. The sublimely heart-shaped Lake McKenzie, forest-bound and sand-rimmed. Along the quietly flowing waters of Eli Creek, wooden walkways offer the chance to go walkabout in the only rainforest built on sand.

Although some of the island's waters are discoloured by minerals – the mining of zircon, monazite, rutile and ilmenite was finally halted in the 1990s – most, filtered by the sand, are full of clean and clear water. But that very purity means there is not much sustenance for low-grade organisms and so there is relatively little in the way of water-based wildlife. There are, however, communities of acid frogs, wild brumbies, birds and dingoes, which patrol the island and are far cooler than the packs of stag weekenders collapsing on the beaches. Any vegetation has to survive in only 10 centimetres (4 inches) of soil. The (now World Heritage-protected) environment of Fraser Island is a fragile construction, as delicate and complex as the leaves of the giant *angiopteris* ferns – a fringe of leaves indeed.

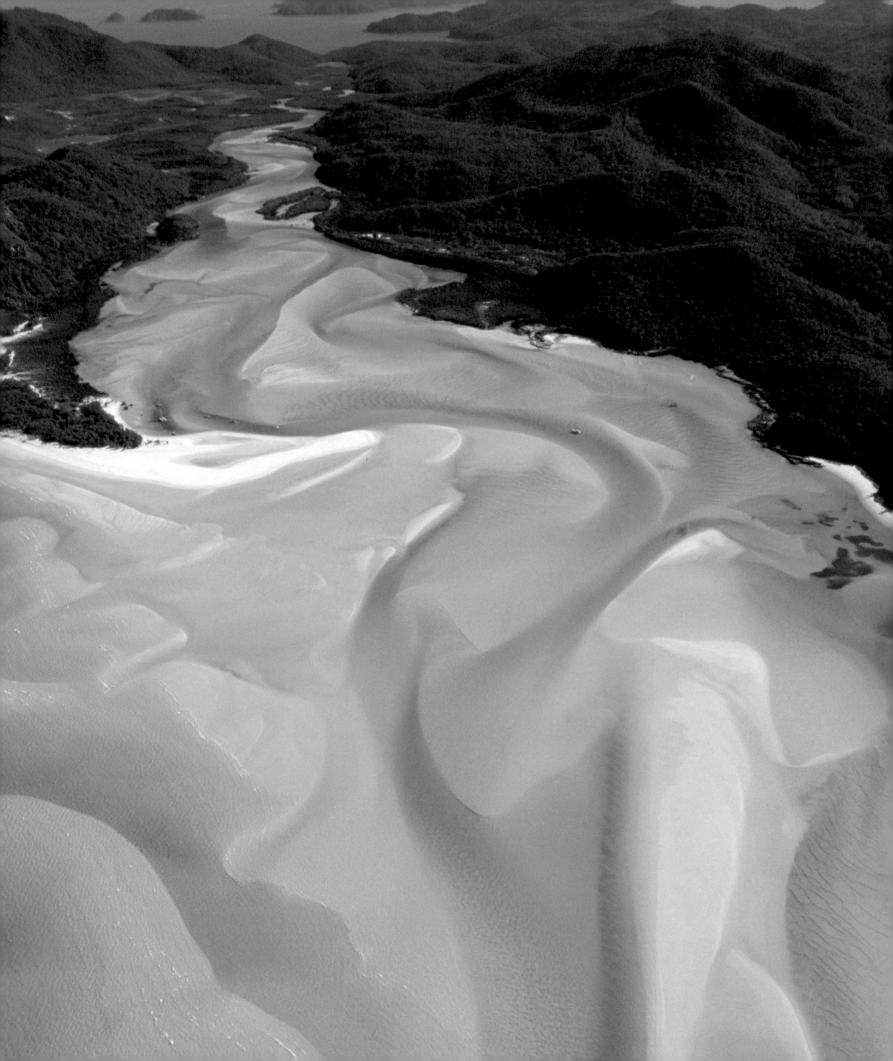

Great Barrier Reef Islands

CORAL SEA

> "I came as a tourist to reef places. I do not know of what I am looking for… But I can accord these places the same respect my own group expects for cathedrals, shrines and cemeteries."
>
> Rosaleen Love, *Reefscape*

Victor Hugo once wrote that dreams are the aquarium of the night; if this is the case then the sea off the coast of Queensland is a 2,000-kilometre (1,243-mile) long revelry. From the guano-caked Lady Elliot Island in the south, via the fine-sanded Keppels, to Hinchinbrook and Dunk in the archipelagos off Cairns in the north and beyond up to New Guinea, the waters are alive with a Technicolor kaleidoscope of fish and sea life. They come in all shapes and sizes and are both peaceful and poisonous: wrasse, parrot fish, mandarin fish, seahorses, box fish, rays, whales, octopuses and sharks. It is a marine safari – the underwater equivalent of the African savannah.

Above the water the famed Aussie lifestyle plays out: an open-air, laid-back, brash and bronzed world of sporting heroes and wraparound shades. Surf and sunshine are perennial. Nowhere else is this more on show than on the shoal of islands that lie off the coast, some of them fragments of continent and others *cays* made from built-up sand

The centrepiece of this lifestyle, lying at the midpoint of the stretch of coast, are the seventy-four Whitsunday Islands, named after the day on which Captain James Cook first discovered them. They emerge like the mountains they were – before rising sea-levels cut them off from the Australian continent – except now they are capped by dense jade-green forest. Their creeks are havens for yachties and cruisers, while on Whitsunday Island itself, those not boat-bound laze on the white-sanded sanctuary of the appropriately named Whitehaven Beach and other stretches of adland sand, such as Dugong Beach.

Further north, through the Tropic of Capricorn, the Great Barrier Reef Islands are scattered under a halo of evocative names, each with its own flora and fauna. On Magnetic Island Cook's compass once ran amok, and now koalas rule their roost of eucalypts and the poisonous but fire-resistant cycad trees. Near Daydream Island in the Molles archipelago, the *Pandora*, the ship sent to capture and enslave the mutineers on Captain Bligh's *Bounty*, was holed and broke up. Here also are Planton, Tancred and Denman – some of the smallest and most isolated landmasses in Australian waters.

Fortunately, thanks to the Marine Parks Authority, the majority of these islands are still undeveloped and uninhabited – especially since the nineteenth-century "dispersals" that uprooted the indigenous aborigine populations. It is the Authority's arduous task to watch over this natural wonder of the world; to preserve it in all its size and variety for future generations against a constant battle with pollution, over-fishing and the irrepressible tide of tourism. Here, life might be a beach, but it takes hard work to keep it intact.

OPPOSITE High tide at Whitehaven Beach

OVERLEAF Great Barrier Reef

Great Barrier Reef Islands, Queensland, Australia **Alternative name:** Whitsunday Islands **Longitude:** 149° 00' E **Latitude:** 20° 15' S **Area:** 37,000 sq km (14,280 sq mi) **Highest point:** 459 m (1,505 ft) Hook Peak **Population:** 15,900 **Principal town:** Airlie Beach, Whitsunday Shire

Tasmania

SOUTHERN OCEAN/TASMAN SEA

A chip off the old block, flicked out from the southern haunch of the Australian continent, Tasmania is a broken-off chunk of rock, mainly dolerite, that formed part of the mainland twelve thousand years ago. Now it guards a more recent past haunted by dark ghosts. By the 1830s, the island's original inhabitants – aboriginals who were here for at least 350 centuries – had been reduced to a fragment of their numbers. The few dozen who remained were forcibly removed 'for their own safety' to Flinders Island, just north of Tasmania, which finally finished them off. In their place had come convicts from England. They and their guards survived as best they could in the harsh, unwelcoming surroundings of penal colonies like the penitentiary at Port Arthur, where in 1996 a deranged gunman massacred tourists and workers. As so often, it was the humans who tainted the land.

For Tasmania was, and to a great extent still is, a natural state; a pioneering Green Party was founded on the island, over one-third of which has "reserve" status. Here roamed the now-extinct Tasmanian tiger (though, like the Loch Ness Monster and the Yeti, sightings persist) and its fellow carnivores do still roam – the cat-like Eastern quoll and the legendary Tasmanian devil. While the Looney Tunes version of this cantankerously screeching marsupial went from strength to strength, the real devil has long been under threat.

The Tasman who gave his name to island, tiger and devil was Abel Tasman, who first landed here on 24 November 1652. He called it Anthoonij van Diemenslandt, after the governor of the Dutch East Indies who had sponsored his journey. The British subsequently shortened it to Van Diemen's Land, before Tasman finally got his enduring name association in 1856. Early European visitors to Tasmania thought that the island represented an image of a pre-Industrial Revolution Britain. The author Anthony Trollope, who stayed there in the 1870s, noted: "Everything in Tasmania is more English than is England herself."

The island is certainly temperate. It is separated from the mainland by the swirling, surging Bass Strait, and is the only Australian state to lie south of the 40th Parallel. Tasmania has become a popular place for retirement away from the grinding heat of the mainland. Far from the unhurried cities of Hobart and Launceston there is a wilderness and a wildness, particularly up north in the glacial landscape beneath the jagged Cradle Mountain, and out to the south-west, where the Franklin-Gordon Wild Rivers Park is a turbulent landscape of rapids, gorges, gullies and waterfalls. The west coast receives the anger of the Roaring Forties, winds unhindered as they blast across the southern seas all the way from Argentina – and which help push any pollution away from the island. Hell's Gate, the mouth to the Macquarie Harbour, is a long way from the genteel green pastures, the hop farms and oast houses upstream on the Derwent River.

RIGHT Aerial view of the Estuary and Blackman Bay

Tasmania, Australia **Longitude:** 146° 30' E **Latitude:** 42° 00' S **Area:** 68,332 sq km (26,376 sq mi) **Highest point:** 1,617 m (5,305 ft) Mt Ossa **Population:** 485,263 **Capital:** Hobart
Natives: David Boon, Richard Flanagan, Errol Flynn, Eileen Joyce, Christopher Koch, C. J. Koch, Edith Lyttleton aka G. B. Lancaster, Crown Princess Mary of Denmark, Ricky Ponting, Jaason Simmons, Mary Augusta Ward **Residents:** Marcus Clarke, Graeme Murphy

"A place of fierce contrasts, of tormenting memories which it contains in its deeply gracious presence."

Andrew Motion, poet

Saipan

NORTHWEST PACIFIC

Along with the thirteen other islands that make up the Commonwealth of the Northern Mariana Islands, the capital Saipan is the peak of what is technically the tallest mountain range in the world. For, 11 kilometres (7 miles) beneath its surface, lie the depths of the lowest point in the Earth's crust – the Mariana Trench.

About the size of the San Francisco peninsula, the islands each have two very distinct and contrasting characteristics. On their west side lie sandy beaches and coral lagoons, with evocative rock formations such as the Old Man by the Sea – a huge limestone boulder whose wind-gnarled surface bears the withered features of a timeless sage. To the east are alluring and precipitous edges, such as those of Suicide Cliffs. At the centre, the limestone mass of Mount Tapotchau surges up like a volcano.

And all around, the island's nature is illuminated by the spear-shaped flecks and flashes of its bright orange-leafed flame trees.

Like many islands, the culture and landscape of the North Marianas betray the bloody attentions of man's wars. They were named by the Spaniards who discovered them, and they then came briefly under German rule as the Kaiser flexed his muscles in the lead-up to the Great War. Later they fell to the Japanese, who established fishing and sugar industries, but also turned the islands into a military base. Their liberation by US forces in the 1944 Battle of Saipan was one of the bloodiest battles of the Pacific in the climax of the Second World War. Pillboxes, burnt-out tanks and cannons can still be seen all over Saipan. Names like Tank Beach and memorials to the dead of both sides also serve as reminders of the conflict.

One positive effect of having had so many owners is Saipan's great cultural diversity. The indigenous *chamorro* language is still spoken by nineteen per cent of the population. The local Austronesian language, Carolinian, can also be heard in many places. A number of the inhabitants are first-generation immigrants from Japan, China and Korea, and the island's most important annual festival is the Saipan Parade of Cultures, a proud showcase of the mixed origins of the settlers held in March. Many of these – up to fifty per cent by some estimates – have come to work in Saipan's principal industry of clothing manufacture.

ABOVE Lagoon near Tank Beach

OPPOSITE "Suicide Cliffs"

"The greenery and blue sky. The silent beach. The absence of noise. Natural whispers of thousands of spirits rising ever so silently over the waters."

Banana Yoshimoto, *Amrita*

Saipan, United States Commonwealth of the Northern Mariana Islands **Longitude:** 145° 45' E **Latitude:** 15° 12' N **Area:** 115 sq km (44 sq mi) **Highest point:** 474 m (1,555 ft) Mt Tapotchau
Population: 62,400 **Principal town:** Saipan **Residents:** Guy Gabaldon, Larry Hillblom

"The wind-driven waves of saltwater
   are lapping on the sandy shore,
And above the bridge to Phillip Island
   the black-backed Pacific gulls soar."

Francis Duggan, "San Remo on an April Evening"

Phillip Island

VICTORIA, AUSTRALIA

If you go down to the dunes at dusk, you are guaranteed a spectacular show. The central focus of every day on Phillip Island takes place just as the sun sets. On Summerland Beach, a perfectly choreographed parade is performed by a cavalcade of smartly attired black-and-white penguins, who emerge from the waters where they have spent the day and trot across the sands towards their burrows hollowed out within the dunes. This daily promenade has become such a fixture that permanent wooden stands have been constructed to improve the vantage points for spectators. And like the Aussie Rules Football stadiums in nearby Melbourne, there are now even prestige-value "boxes" for those willing to spend a few more dollars to get as close as possible to the performers (once called fairy penguins, but now officially known, for politically correct reasons, as little penguins).

Phillip Island lies to the south of Melbourne, that lingering seam of Victoriana on Australia's southern coastline. The island acts as something of a breakwater to the city's Westernport Bay. The crowds that gather to see the penguins in action have generally taken the hour and a half's drive from downtown to swing across the bridge linking the island to San Remo on the mainland.

There are other annual but rather different invasions, as crowds of enthusiasts arrive to watch not bipedal aquatic residents but equally exotic two- and four-wheeled visitors: the motorcycles of the World Superbike Championships and V8 Supercars tearing up Phillip Island's motor circuit, which has existed since the 1920s.

However, the main attraction is the wildlife. Mutton birds, aka short-tailed shearwaters, wheel offshore from the Nobbies headland on the island's western tip, or over Cape Woolamai

at its other end. There is a massive colony, numbering about seven thousand, of fur seals – Australia's largest and one of the most significant in the Southern Hemisphere. And from the island's boardwalks there are neck-cricking views of koalas snoozing high up in the gum trees.

Not much else happens here, although there is an historic homestead on tiny Churchill Island next door. The pace of life, other than when the bikers and petrol-heads are *in situ*, is undemanding, as the names of the main townships suggest – Cowes, Rhyll and Ventnor, good old-world Isle of Wight place names all. Here, the main purpose of existence is to enjoy a moment of escape from the hubbub of the metropolis, and to wonder if life as a penguin, pottering back to your dune to preen and dine, might not be a rather pleasant alternative.

OPOOSITE The Nobbies

RIGHT Little penguins

Phillip Island, Victoria, Australia **Longitude:** 145° 12' E **Latitude:** 38° 30' S **Area:** 103 sq km (40 sq mi) **Highest point:** 110 m (360 ft) **Population:** 7,100 **Principal town:** Cowes

Guam

NORTHWEST PACIFIC

Just as nine-tenths of an iceberg's true size lies hidden, so most of the beauty of Guam lies unseen, both beneath the surface of the Pacific and the surface of first impressions.

The largest island in Micronesia stands in effect atop the highest mountain in the world, and scuba divers from all over the world flock here for the chance to throw themselves off the top of it. At 10,911 metres (35,797 feet) below sea-level, Challenger Deep is the very bottom of the Mariana Trench, just off the south-west coast of Guam. It is officially the deepest point on Earth, and diving on the coral wall at the lip of this abyss is often likened to floating over the summit of Mount Everest. But the reward for feeling the Earth plunge away beneath you is not just the vertigo of an aquatic bungee jumper, but a chance to feast the eyes on a mesmerizing tapestry of oceanic coral teeming with weird and wonderful sea life, ranging from the white spotted boxfish and royal angelfish to rays, reef sharks and eels, all feeding off and darting in and around a huge console of bulbous coral

brains that resemble some vast and sleeping otherworldly intelligence.

Above water the story is not so oneiric. This strategic island has been first ravaged by colonial and world wars and then overwhelmed by commercial tourism. A succession of invasions and occupations – from the 1890s Spanish-American War (the Spanish had first discovered the island in the seventeenth century) to the Japanese occupation in the Second World War – has taken the indigenous Chamorro culture to the brink. Guam is now an unincorporated territory of the United States (and therefore the point where America's day begins), which means duty-free status and a landscape profoundly marked by the trappings of metropolitan life. Often called "America in Asia" (a quarter of the landmass remains under US military jurisdiction), Guam and in particular Tumon Bay and the Pleasure Island district, is a cityscape of hotels, high-rise apartment blocks and shopping malls targeting Japanese tourists, for whom the island is a nearer version of Hawaii and who make up the island's main source of income.

Touchingly the Chamorro culture, itself heavily influenced by over two hundred years of Spanish rule as part of the Spanish East Indies, does still persist, and ensures that the tapestry of mankind's presence on Guam maintains at least a hint of the variety to be found underwater. With their central community notion of *inafa'maolek* (interdependence), the Chamorros provide a sobering counterpoint to the individualism played out in the malls. Guam's capital has recently had its native name, Hagatna, restored, and traditions including games, festivals, cuisine, dance and music have in particular been preserved in the Chamorro village of I Sengsong. Here, and elsewhere in the "boonie" (as the jungle is known in these parts), the descendants of the island's first inhabitants, governed by their *maga'haga* matriarchs, continue to speak their language, weave cloths from pandanus and coconut-tree fibres, and create music from home-made instruments such as the nose flute.

RIGHT Coastline at Umatac

Guam, Territory of Guam (United States) **Local name:** Guåhan **Longitude:** 144° 45' E **Latitude:** 13° 27' N **Area:** 541 sq km (209 sq mi) **Highest point:** 406 m (1,332 ft) Mt Lamlam
Population: 173,450 **Capital:** Hagatna **Natives:** Flora Baza Quan, J. D. Crutch, Daniel De Leon Guerrero, John Hattig **Resident:** James Woods

"I rejoice in the gentle, peaceful life I lead: no storms,
no gales of wind to dread; a sky that is almost
always serene, an air that is pure in spite of the heat."

Rose de Freycinet, explorer

"Separated from the entire world by 10,000 versts …
so remote it would take a hundred years to get home again."

Anton Chekhov

Sakhalin

NORTH PACIFIC

There was a time when being sent to Sakhalin meant exile, a life sentence and almost certain death. People had to be forced to go there and often never came back. At the dawn of the twentieth century, and still decades before Stalin invented the gulag, the last tsars used the island as a penal colony – a Russian version of Britain's Botany Bay in Australia – banishing citizens with inconvenient views to the extremities of their empire. In the new century, Sakhalin the consumer of souls gives life to Russia's energy economy. Lured by the virgin treasures of uranium, oil and silver that lie concealed within her, the island is now at risk of rape by every multinational energy corporation that rushes to dissect and plunder her.

The vast landmass that is domineering Russia is not noted for its islands. Separated from the Russian mainland to the west by the Tatar Strait, on the map Sakhalin looks like an extension of the island nation of Japan, and indeed Japan and Russia disputed the island's ownership for over a century. The Japanese had arrived in the early 1800s, attracted by the fishing prospects of the surrounding sea that, according to one report, "looked as if it was boiling with fish", but the Russians claimed it in 1853 as part of their push to secure the whole eastern Amur region. Both sides embarked on a war that resulted in Japan reclaiming the southern half – where the architectural influence is still very much in evidence. Then

in 1905, in a military chess move, they swapped it for the nearby Kuril Islands, which form a chain to Hokkaido south from the Kamchatka peninsula. Neither side at the time cared about the indigenous culture of *nivkhi*, a pejorative and nondescript term meaning simply "northern peoples". No more than two thousand survive as a curio whose unique culture has been distilled to a national dish, *mos*, of fish mixed with blueberries and roots, and clothes made from pounded fish skin.

In the Soviet era, Sakhalin became the largest and most sensitive militarized zone of that secretive regime. It was a political and military island, a natural battleship whose airspace was even out of bounds – demonstrated to international outrage in 1983, when a Korean passenger jet was gunned down over it, killing all 257 on board.

The north of the island, around Cape Terpeniya, is still littered with the rusting remnants and ghost towns of communism. It was on Sakhalin in 1990 that the Soviets conducted an experiment in capitalism (could the West be right?), only to announce triumphantly that it had failed because it made people poor. Now, however, Sakhalin looks set to make a lot of people very rich, as the island's lakes and pristine taiga of bamboo and grassy mountains are opened up and literally exposed, for better or worse, to the forces of the world's free market.

Sakhalin, Sakhalin Oblast, Russia **Longitude:** 143° 00' E **Latitude:** 51° 00' N **Area:** 76,400 sq km (29,490 sq mi) **Highest point:** 1,609 m (5,729 ft) Mt Lopatin
Population: 673,100 **Principal town:** Yuzhno-Sakhalinsk

> ## "There was a certain tree, or stones, heaps of rock, different trees. They knew exactly where the place was."
>
> Eddie Mabo, Torres Strait Islander

Torres Strait Islands

TORRES STRAIT

Pinioned between Australia and New Guinea in 150 kilometres (93 miles) of ocean – the very strait that gives them their name – the 274 islands that make up the Torres Strait archipelago once formed a solid bridge linking the two larger landmasses. The islands today are the visible tips of a range of mountain peaks; piercing the surface of the sea, they look on the map like a scattered set of stepping stones. Nowadays, Piper Navajo planes ferry mail and do the school run between them.

This geological arrangement, at a vital border between Australasia and Asia, has proved far too tempting for a series of predators – not least the packs of tiger sharks, saltwater crocs and sea snakes that swim offshore. Despite this, the Torres Strait Islanders have, somehow, managed to survive and fiercely protect their identity. The difficult future for the islanders – who come from a Melanesian rather than aboriginal background – was presaged in 1606 when Luis Váez de Torres, a Galician sailor working for the Spanish Crown, landed on what is now Dungeness Island. He and his crew looted supplies, shot an islander trying to run away, abducted three women and then gaily sailed away.

Since then the islands have seen a range of visitors come and go – some welcome, many not. The London Missionary Society arrived a hundred years after Captain James Cook claimed the islands for Great Britain. Pearl divers from Japan followed in the 1860s, lured by potential pickings to Thursday Island, the main island of the group. Many are buried in Thursday's cemetery beneath Green Hill Fort, built to resist potential Russian attack in the First World War. More recently, the islanders have had to cope with the threat of animal diseases trying to island-hop, and the arrival of asylum seekers.

Throughout all this the islanders have drawn on strong tribal instincts, bonded by tradition and music. Each of the Torres Strait Islands – there are five groups, ranging from the swampy far western islands to the volcanic eastern islands – has its distinct dance, often accompanied by gongs or hourglass drums. Even though many islanders have relocated by choice or otherwise to the mainland, to Townsville or Cairns (where singer Christina Anu was born to Torres islanders), they have never lost the bond with their homeland. This is particularly the case with Eddie Mabo, born on the Murray Islands, a trio consisting of Mer, Dauer and Waier Islands, the easternmost of the archipelago. While working as a gardener at the James Cook University in Townsville in the 1970s, he was shocked to learn that the land back home he thought he owned had in fact been sequestered by the British Crown as *terra nullius*, or no-man's land. He became a campaigning pioneer for land rights, and established a test case that was victorious for the islanders. Eddie died before he knew of the success.

Now the islands gear up for a new onslaught: rising sea-levels. It has been pointed out how cruel an irony it would be if the islanders made it through four centuries of colonial pain, only to witness their precious land become submerged.

OVERLEAF Waier Island

Torres Strait Islands, Queensland, Australia **Longitude:** 142° 20' E **Latitude:** 9° 50' S **Archipelago area:** 48,000 sq km (18,528 sq mi) **Highest point:** 230 m (755 ft) Gelam Paser, Murray Island **Population:** 8,100 **Principal town:** Thursday Island **Natives:** Eddie Mabo, The Mills Sisters

New Guinea

PACIFIC

Perhaps unfairly, New Guinea's reputation precedes it in certain parts. The island and its tribes earned notoriety as the last bastion on Earth, an island altar to that ultimate sin of the flesh – cannibalism. New Guinea is sometimes known as a raw land, and that is the way some of its inhabitants used to like it (human flesh, that is), especially the Korowai and Kombai tribes in the southeast of the island, who were the last – as reassuringly recently as the 1970s – to indulge in this form of nutrition.

The initiated, however, have always known that the rawness of New Guinea was a positive attribute, residing in the island's unique and at times fantastical biodiversity. It is thought that between five and ten per cent of the species of animal and plant life on the planet, including many endemic ones, are to be found on the island. It was once part of the Australian continent and consequently shares with Australia many marsupials, or versions of that genus such as the tree kangaroo and other possums and wallabies. Add to that over two hundred thousand species of insect, including the enormous Queen Alexandra birdwing butterfly, innumerable types of bird of paradise, each with its own colourful and dramatic mating dances and rituals, and over twenty thousand species of plant including myriad orchids, and New Guinea can be seen as the residence of a creation and evolution of biblical proportions; the South Pacific Garden of Eden. Its biodiversity rivals that of the United States or Australia, but New Guinea's is located on one relatively small island.

One contributing factor to this richness is the range of unusual island habitats. The highest mountain range in Oceania, a local Himalayas, runs the length of the island, with the peak of Puncak Jaya at 4,884 metres (16,023 feet) – similar to Switzerland's Matterhorn –

OPPOSITE Four Kukukuku women viewing their valley

New Guinea, Indonesia and Papua New Guinea **Longitude:** 141° 36' E **Latitude:** 5° 20' S **Area:** 786,000 sq km (303,400 sq mi) **Highest point:** 4,884 m (16,023 ft) Puncak Jaya aka Mt Carstensz
Population: 8,442,400 **Principal towns:** Jayapura, Manokwari and Port Moresby **Natives:** Geraint Jones, Mal Michael

at its centre. These mountains contain unique equatorial glaciers that in turn water a range of lowland forests, wetlands, grasslands and mangrove swamps where, especially in the World Heritage Lorentz National Park, nature teems in all her variety of shapes and colours.

New Guinea does not only offer rare nature, though; its human inhabitants are also rare. In 1938, Stone Age farmers of the Dani tribe secreted in the Grand Valley of the Balim river were the last people on the planet to come into contact with the Western world. Incredibly,

they had not met the host of nations that over the centuries have claimed and carved up this island. The Portuguese sailors who named it "las ilhas dos papuas" were unknown to them. They were unaware of the Dutch, British, Germans and others who came after, who finally left the island like an uneasy divorce settlement, carved up between the Indonesians of West Papua and the east of Papua New Guinea. All these visitors showed what a mess of so-called civilization humans can make in a haven of so much natural harmonious perfection.

"New Guinea contains more strange and new and beautiful objects than any other part of the globe."

Sir Alfred Russel Wallace, naturalist

Izu Islands, Tokyo, Japan **Local name:** Izu-shoto **Longitude:** 140° 00' E **Latitude:** 34° 30' N **Area:** 250 sq km (97 sq mi) **Highest point:** 764 m (2,506 ft) Mt Mihana, Oshima **Population:** 27,000 **Principal town:** Oshima Town

Izu Islands

NORTHWEST PACIFIC

They have been called one of Japan's best-kept secrets. The Izu Islands seem a million miles away from the hubba hubba, *Lost in Translation*, 24/7 buzz of Tokyo – the teeming crossings and neon flare of the downtown city. Less than an hour by boat out of the metropolis, the Izu islands are a complete contrast, offering an escape for stressed-out salarymen trapped in the grind of daily routine, especially during the humid summer months.

The mood on Izu is almost Californian, with ocean frontages, shoreside cycle rides, camellias and palm trees. Its position to the south of the Japanese capital means that the cherry blossom flowers early each spring, and the camellias are so gorgeous that there is a museum dedicated to them on Oshima-chu. The charcoal of the camellia wood is used for delicate tea flavouring, its oil for cooking or in traditional woodwork.

The islands form part of the Fuki-Hakone-Izu National Park, and all fall within the catchment area of Tokyo. They provide a slice of forest and volcanic outcrops. The volcano on Oshima, Mount Mihana – known locally as Gojinka, "Sacred Fire" – remains active: it last erupted in 1990. An eruption in the 1950s killed thirty-one people. Oshima is the northernmost and largest of the Izu chain, close to the mainland and the

ferry port of Shimoda, a coastal hideaway that has an important role in Japanese history. It was here in 1853 that US Commodore Matthew Perry concluded a deal that opened up the prospect of trade with the previously hermetically sealed Edo shogunate.

Each of the seven islands of Izu has a recognizable character. Hachijojima in the south is straddled by two large volcanoes, the valley between them offering a view of huge chincapin trees. If that sounds pleasantly exotic, then the presence on the island of the Anchor pub is equally unexpected. On Shochu the booze is produced in a more traditional way: barley is distilled into *sake*. Mikurajima is wilder – wildcats on land, dolphins offshore and sightings of ecotourists looking at both. Kozushima is a remote hiker's destination.

Between the barley *sake* and the seafood and shellfish, or the tempura-fried *ashitaba* leaves (grown on Hachijojima and notoriously high in antioxidants and vitamins), and far from the crowds, life seems peaceful. Not all is calm, though. On the side of Mount Mihana is the morbid reminder of a suicide cliff where, in 1933, one high-school student jumped and was followed in a lemming-like hysteria by 128 others. The rush from Tokyo to Izu is thankfully now less dramatic.

"They were from Oshima in the Izu islands... I glanced again at those rich mounds of hair, at the little figure all the more romantic for being from Oshima."

Yasunari Kawabata, *The Dancing Girl of Izu*

LEFT Hachijojima

Palau
PACIFIC

> "W.A.V.E.
> Welcome
> All Visitors
> Enthusiastically"
>
> One of Palau's many signature signpost acronyms

Composed as it is of strings of tiny islands barely big enough to host Robinson Crusoe, Palau must be the loosest definition of nationhood on Earth. In fact, after Tuvalu, it is the smallest nation on Earth and it is also one of the world's youngest, having been released from UN trusteeship in 1994.

Despite its youth and size, it is still a world capital – albeit capital of the underworld. Palau is a Mecca for diving enthusiasts; a Paris of the deep. At the outer edge of the archipelago, of which only eight islands are inhabited, lie the famous and iconic limestone Rock Islands. These excrescences beg but defy simile, looking like giant green mushrooms or the topiary privet hedges of a European formal garden maze transplanted to the Pacific. In Jellyfish Lake, the diaphanous blobs of that rarity, the benign

non-stinging jellyfish, trapped for so long in a limestone pool that they have lost the need and ability to sting, float in an emerald underwater heaven. Kingfisher Lake is shrouded by church-like silence. Clam-planting at Clam City revives the shoreline as part of the Micronesia Challenge conservation project, taken on by the Palau Republic's president. And at Big Drop-Off, the coral reef falls away in a sheer drop of nearly 275 metres (902 feet), beckoning divers into a kaleidoscope escape from a troubled world.

It wasn't always coconut milk and honey on Palau. Claimed by Spain, sold to Germany and then passed to Japan at Versailles, Palau (sometimes known as Belau or the Black Islands) has seen its fair share of a violence that led to the confiscation and redistribution of tribal lands. When the United States invaded these fifty-five islands to flush out secret Japanese garrisons in the closing months of the Second World War, a planned two-day assault turned into a two-month battle resulting in thirteen thousand dead. This length of resistance and volume of casualties contributed to the development of the atomic bombs that would fall on Hiroshima and Nagasaki. The honeymoon beaches belie the bloodshed, while the rusting tanks and vessels act as underwater memorials and attractions for divers and sea life alike.

But the passing owners have also left their mark in a positive way on a culture as sponge-like as the appearance of the limestone formations and brain coral above and below water. The tradition of wood-carving is undoubtedly a legacy of the pre-war Japanese culture, while the residents of Koror, Palau's gateway island and principal settlement, can even boast that they put Elvis on a national postage stamp before the US of A.

LEFT A *bai* – traditional men's house – in Melekeok Village

Palau, Republic of Palau **Local name:** Belau **Longitude:** 134° 30' E **Latitude:** 7° 30' N **Area:** 459 sq km (177 sq mi) **Highest point:** 242 m (794 ft) Mt Ngerchelchuus **Population:** 20,800 **Capital:** Melekeok

OVERLEAF Rock Islands – a chain of over seventy small islets

"We hung for some time over the coral banks. Between the stems of the coral groves, the blue fish shot hither and thither like arrows of the purest lapis lazuli."

Commodore Matthew Perry

ABOVE Hand in hand during the Sea God Festival in Ungami

Okinawa

EAST CHINA SEA/NORTHWEST PACIFIC

Confiscating every weapon in the province is an effective way of restoring peace – or so the sixteenth-century shogun in these parts thought. In doing so, however, he created an art form that trained the human body to become everything it needed for combat; combat "with an empty hand", or "karate" as the martial art whose birthplace is Okinawa is better known. Disciples of the art form still flock to see the *gojos* and *sensei* in action here, but in the main the prefecture of Okinawa and its hundred or so islands have become a tourist destination for mainland Japan.

Collectively named the Ryukyu Shoto, after the Ryukyu royal family that made this their kingdom for four hundred years, and whose rebuilt castle of Shuri-jo still stands as the main architectural link to the past on the island of Okinawa Honto, the islands hang down in a string from the south-west of Japan to within a leap of Taiwan. Japan's only subtropical region, they are warm throughout the year – so far south that they witness the spring cherry blossom in January. Warmed by the Kurshio current up the east coast they also have a virulent wildlife, which includes some endemic species such as the Yamameko lynx, a unique turtle, woodpecker and crested eagle, and the poisonous green and yellow Habu snake. Humans thrive, too, with Okinawans subsisting on a healthy diet of tofu, fish and seaweed making up the highest percentage of Japanese centenarians.

Longevity was not always so, however. Okinawa was the scene of arguably the bloodiest battle at the end of the Pacific War, which left 12,500 Americans but an incredible 200,000 or more islanders dead. The only battle on Japanese soil, it is thought that around thirty per cent of the islands' population committed *hara kiri*, possibly in mass sacrifice to protect the mainland. Memorials litter the south of the main island of Okinawa, but the most controversial memory remains in the form of US military bases that still host nearly thirty thousand US military personnel.

But Ryukyu culture still survives in the distinctive cuisine, characterized by parrot fish. It also survives in the traditions of carved *sake* flaskes, *shiisa* protective lion figurines and woven *bingata* textiles hand-dyed using hibiscus and vegetable pigments. This is most intact in the outer islands – on the sharp and brooding forested Yaeyama group and Miyako, or the Mabuni hills of the mountainous north that show no trace of the American presence past or present. Here is the Okinawa of lush vegetation, coral reefs and hidden beaches and grottos. This is the place where the particular art form to be perfected is that of lying empty-handed and, yes, disarmed (but of material goods) and for a while saying *sayonara* to the world.

ABOVE *Shiisa* Lion Dog statue at the entry bridge to Ikei Island

Okinawa, Okinawa Prefecture, Japan **Local name:** Okinawa-honto, Okinawa-jima **Longitude:** 128° 00' E **Latitude:** 26° 40' N **Area:** 1,199 sq km (463 sq mi)
Highest point: 503 m (1,650 ft) Mt Yonaha **Population:** 1,150,000 **Principal town:** Naha **Natives:** Olivia Lufkin, Shoukichi Kina, Yu Yamada

Moluccas

BANDA SEA

> "The island can be smelled before it can be seen. From more than ten miles out to sea, a fragrance hangs in the air."
>
> Giles Milton, *Nathaniel's Nutmeg*

We knew them once as the Spice Islands, and there still lingers over the Moluccas – or Maluku as they are known locally – that linguistically heady aroma of nutmeg, mace and cloves. There was a time when spices were a currency that outranked gold. Small, light, easy to transport, durable, they were the perfect product for the times, as ships laden with their fragrant cargoes wended their way from this archipelago south of the Philippines to the rest of the world.

The Spice Islands had one huge advantage – they were the only islands in the world where cloves grew wild, mainly on Ternate and Tidore. The Banda Islands towards the south of the group were, uniquely, home to the nutmeg. Valued for their role in flavouring, for preserving food, for perfumes, for relieving pain (cloves are still widely used for easing the trauma of toothache), whoever could lock down this supply source would have a lucrative monopoly. For a while it was the Venetian empire. In the fifteenth century, Tomé Pires, a Portuguese apothecary, astutely observed that, "Whoever is lord of Malacca has his hands on the throat of Venice."

The major European powers began to grapple with increasing fervour. Portugal took control in the 1570s, and started playing off the local sultans against each other. Spain joined in, but both Iberian contenders were finally seen off by the Dutch, who closed their hands around the Spice Islands firmly for a century or more and grew rich upon the proceeds. There was a

significant side-effect to all this: as each empire desperately sought better sea routes to the islands, they often took a wrong turn, ending up in another new world. In one exchange of Spice Island territory the Dutch acquired Run, one of the Bandas; in the swap the British received an apparently undesirable marshy island in the Americas. It was Manhattan.

There is still a strong colonial atmosphere in the Moluccas – an undertone of Portuguese with a high note of Dutch. This widespread sprinkle of hundreds of islands, between which trundle rusting Indonesian ferries, are naturally lush, around the rainforest-covered mountains and the volcanoes that make up their characteristic terrain. But if the spices were once the focus, other wildlife is now just as important. Falling within the biogeographical zone of Wallacea, the Moluccas contain more endemic species of bird by surface area than any other place on Earth. Currently a range of programmes is underway to protect rare birds – the salmon-crested cockatoo, for example – that have been threatened by trappers collecting them for the caged-bird trade.

Now part of Indonesia, the Moluccas are split into two provinces: Ternate dominates the north and Pulau Ambon the south. Predominantly Christian, the latter tried unsuccessfully to secede from the Indonesian republic when it achieved independence; it is now seeking to establish its identity rather than its independence.

RIGHT Spices and dried beans at the market on the island of Ambon

LEFT Salmon-crested cockatoo

OVERLEAF Volcanic island at Tidore

Moluccas, Maluku/North Maluku, Indonesia **Local name:** Maluku **Longitude:** 127° 24' E **Latitude:** 3° 9' S **Area:** 74,505 sq km (28,759 sq mi) **Highest point:** 3,027 m (9,930 ft) Mt Binaiya, Seram **Population:** 1,291,100 **Principal towns:** Ambon, Ternate

"The Hawaii of the Orient."

Korean government

Jeju-do

KOREA STRAIT

When European explorers first arrived on this island, south-west of the Korean peninsula, they pointed at the land and asked the locals what it was called; they were told "Gyulbat". The name was duly brought back to Europe, slightly corrupted to "Quelpart", and for centuries the island would be known as such. It would be a while before they realized that a bunch of local fruit-pickers had inadvertently christened their island, at least in the mind of the West, after the orange mandarin fruit they thought those first invaders had been pointing at.

Today the main invaders of Jeju-do are honeymooners from Japan (the Japanese had already annexed the island once and re-christened it Saishu during the Second World War) and from mainland Korea (a massive sixty per cent of all Korean newlyweds), who come to this Hawaii of the Orient to be photographed amid the rich bright-yellow fields of rape that cover the island in summer. Perhaps they also come to learn a few lessons in marriage from the unusual and unique matriarchal societies and family structures that exist within some sections of the indigenous population. Here, women known as *haenyoes* are the main breadwinners, working as free-divers all year round whatever the temperature of the water, collecting abalones and conches to sell. They might not wear wetsuits, but they definitely wear the trousers in their relationships.

Visitors are also attracted to the natural treasures of an island that has been designated a World Heritage Site, and in particular to the waterfalls of Ch'eon-ji-yeon and Cheong-bang around Sogwip'o. Another draw is the extensive system of spectacular lava-tube formations, including giant organ pipes of a post-volcanic cathedral, that forms some of the largest caves in the world. Lava is a constant feature of the island, not just in natural formations but also as a material for manmade statues and sculptures. Ubiquitous on the island, gnome-like and creating a slightly eerie, watchful atmosphere, are symbolic lava statues called *dol hareubangs*, meaning "stone grandfathers".

At 1,950 metres (6,398 feet), the extinct volcano of Mount Halla-san is Korea's highest mountain and towers over the island like a guardian spirit. It is central to the island's mythology, for it is said that it was from its foot that three divinities arose – Ko, Yang and Pu – to establish the island's founding families by marrying three foreign princesses. Often clothed in swirling mist and forged from explosive magma, the mountain gives to the whole island an elemental air. Thus it speaks to the Korean visitor with the magnetism of a pilgrimage. Koreans are a people obsessed with nature and the natural order of the elements, as if their very fate – in a region where autonomy from giant neighbours has always come at a cost – was bound up with the island's explosive geology.

OPPOSITE A child with a statue of the native god Harubang

Jeju-do, South Korea **Longitude:** 126° 34' E **Latitude:** 33° 29' N **Area:** 1,846 sq km (713 sq mi) **Highest point:** 1,950 m (6,398 ft) Mt Halla-san **Population:** 560,000 **Principal town:** Jeju City **Native:** Byun Shi Ji

Timor

BANDA SEA/TIMOR SEA

News stories were dominated by East Timor for so long that West Timor was left to one side. Timor is the whole island: within the sprawling straggle of Indonesia, it is the easternmost point of the long tentacle of islands that swings away from the Malaysian peninsula and points towards New Guinea. The very name Timor is derived from *timur*, the Malay word for "east", giving rise to a period when East Timor was called Timor Timur after Indonesia annexed it in 1975.

The island's east-west split was brought to world attention through the struggles of East Timor to establish itself as a nation independent from Indonesia. The campaign lasted a long, bitter, painful quarter of a century and cost many lives, but in May 2002 East Timor succeeded in joining the ranks of independent nations.

The divisions on the island dated back to the trading confrontation between the old European colonial powers. While the Moluccas were a rich source of spices, Timor was a fertile grove for the sandalwood tree. The Portuguese arrived first, but – just as on the Spice Islands – the great clout of the Dutch was hot on their heels and they established a base in Kupang, now the capital of West Timor. The Portuguese retreated to the east of the island, and through a series of agreements the island was divided up: the west for the Dutch, as part of the Dutch East Indies, and the east for the Portuguese. The foreigners stayed there long after Indonesia gained independence in 1949 – leaving in 1975, having promised the East Timorese the chance to vote on whether they wanted to stay separate. They voted in favour, whereupon Indonesia promptly invaded.

Much of the traditional colonial architecture, particularly in the east, was lost during the struggles between Jakarta-backed militia groups, the Indonesian army and the local separatist movement, but there are still traditional houses standing on stilts, constructed from bamboo, grass and palm leaves. In the interior of the island, up on the high range that soars from the sea and runs along the spine of the island, there are villages of onion-domed beehive huts. These are home to the original Tetum, the largest ethnic group. Dili, the capital of East Timor, has a pleasantly laid-back feel, at odds with the horrors of the torture rooms that one of its main hotels once housed. Its western equivalent, Kupang, is all hustle and commerce – the horns and sound systems of the three-wheeled *bemo* pickups punctuating the air. Dili too is now noisy once more, with the sound of construction as it rebuilds a life – and the beginnings of a tourist business – for itself.

"Timor, tomb of a soul that did not perish in the mists of a history lost in the distance of legend."

Xanana Gusmão, president of Timor-Leste

Timor, West Timor, Indonesia and East Timor **Longitude:** 125° 00' E **Latitude:** 9° 00' S **Area:** 30,777 sq km (11,880 sq mi) **Highest point:** 2,963 m (9,721 ft) Mt Tatamailau **Population:** 2,900,000 **Capitals:** Dili (East Timor), Kupang (West Timor) **Natives:** Bishop Carlos Filipe Ximenes Belo, Martinho da Costa Lopes, José "Xanana" Gusmão, José Ramos-Horta, Fernando Sylvan

ABOVE East Timorese Muslim women pray at Ramadan's end

Cebu, The Philippines **Longitude:** 123º 45' E **Latitude:** 10º 18' N **Area:** 4,408 sq km (1,702 sq mi) **Highest point:** 1,006 m (3,300 ft) Mt Osmena **Population:** 3,356,100 **Capital:** Cebu City
Natives: Amapola Cabase, Mahnee Cabase, Leonilo Estimo, Ernesto Lariosa, Vicente Sotto

Cebu

PHILIPPINE SEA

> "This place was making me so stupid-happy that I couldn't wipe the big, ridiculous mango grin off my face. Why was I in such a state of delirium? What was it about Cebu?"
>
> George Estrada, *I Have Tasted the Sweet Mangoes of Cebu*

Cebu's place in the hall of fame of twenty-first century pop culture was sealed in 2007 by Byron Garcia, the enterprising warden of the island's Provincial Detention and Rehabilitation Centre. Recognizing the positive power of music to harness the body and mind to enable inmates to forget anger, violence and thoughts of escape, he decided to incorporate dance routines to famous pop songs into their daily workout. And so, in a bizarre modern day interpretation of "Jailhouse Rock", he had the whole community of inmates dancing to Michael Jackson's "Thriller". He videoed one of the sessions in order to show his superiors the beneficial effects, but the video found its way on to YouTube. In no time, more than 100,000 subscribers had tuned in to watch the tightly choreographed inmates, in orange convict uniforms, grooving in unison and reaching paroxysms of zombied delirium in tune to Vincent Price's climax. The Internet age thus brought a new generation to Cebu – virtually.

This is all very far removed from the daring exploits of the Portuguese explorer and navigator Ferdinand Magellan, who first set foot on this island province of the Visayas archipelago en route to the Spice Islands, and whose fate is inextricably linked with this corner of the world. It was in 1521 that he first set eyes on Cebu (at the time known as Zubu). He subsequently formed a rare friendship and alliance with the island's chief, Raja Humabon, and anointed him and his wife, with permission from the king of Spain, King Carlos and Queen Juana of Cebu. It was a successful alliance, resulting in the installation of Roman Catholicism as the dominant religion and veneration of Magellan, a rare courtesy extended to Europe's colonizers. Every year at the festival of Sinulog, the Cebuanos celebrate Magellan's gift to Raja Humabon of a statue of the black infant Jesus. With much dancing and drum-beating they advance slowly through the streets of Cebu City, recreating the slow flow of the river that gives the festival its name. Magellan himself is remembered in a cross at Punta Engano, where he lost his life to the warring chief of the neighbouring island of Mactan.

Elsewhere the Spanish influence lives on in the fortifications built by Magellan's successor, Lagazpi, in Cebu's relaxed *mañana* attitude, in the island's fertile tradition of literature and poetry, and in the pidgin Hispanic names given to the cuisine of *puto* (roast pork) and *buwad* (dried fish) served with the ubiquitous *budbod* or mango. Now consistently praised by the travel literati for its beaches, diving and beautiful landscape of rolling hills and rugged cliffs, this island – in the midst of a nation with more islands than the fabled shoe collection of its former first lady, Imelda Marcos – is no longer, as she once said, "really hamburgered geographically" and "neither here nor there", but seems (whether via the Internet or old-fashioned exploration) to have arrived.

LEFT Palawan's limestone hills and lagoons

OVERLEAF Village of Batad

"There are two sides to everything. Yin and Yang.
When I went out of Taiwan I got to know the place
a lot better because I could see it from the outside."

Ang Lee

Taiwan

EAST CHINA SEA

Taiwan is an Asian Tiger that has spent six decades punching and clawing above its weight. Curled up off the east coast of its giant neighbour, China, it has proved to be stubborn, intransigent and as rugged as the mountains at its core – amongst which is Mount Yu Shan, East Asia's highest peak.

On the fringes of the interior, twenty-three million inhabitants are squeezed into any available space, and – their eyes and minds ever looking upward – they continue to aim high. In 2004 that ambition was made unmistakably tangible when the Taipei 101 building clinched the title of the world's tallest skyscraper from Kuala Lumpur's Petronas twin towers. Here was a blatant expression of panache, a building insolently resisting the typhoons and earthquakes of its location, reflecting its cultural foundations through a segmented design that hinted at pagodas or bamboo, full of symbolism and meaning. (As is the way in the field of skyscraper design, the 101 was soon forced to relinquish its crown as the Burj Dubai prepared to go one better.)

Hi-tech is still a byword in Taiwan; cutting-edge computer businesses thrive in Hsinchu. "Made in Taiwan" remains a ubiquitous tag. The Taiwanese still scoot hither and thither within the confines of their realm. But there are some oases of calm: in Tainan, the old imperial capital in the south where Taoist and Buddhist temples abound; in the peace of Sun Moon Lake deep in the interior of the island;

and on the hiking trails of the nearby Shei-Pa reserve. After all, the Portuguese who sailed past Taiwan in 1544 called it Formosa – "the beautiful island".

Taiwan's position just off mainland China and to the south-west of Japan made it a valuable and strategic crossroads. The Portuguese, surprisingly, did not stop to colonize it, but in 1624 the Dutch did. China took over the island forty years later, and by the end of the century it had been annexed by the Qing Dynasty.

However, the Japanese had always cast a covetous eye over the island, and in the 1890s the Sino-Japanese wars resulted in its cession to Japan. The Japanese set about giving it an industrial infrastructure, building railways, installing sanitation systems and establishing educational institutions. At the end of the Second World War, however, Japan lost its hold and Taiwan entered a period of estrangement from China. The worst side-effects for the rejected motherland was the brain, cash and cultural drain that followed. Some estimate that the National Palace Museum contains one-tenth of China's treasures, crated over from the mainland in the 1940s.

During the Cold War, this outcrop of anti-communism received kudos and support from the West, and it prospered despite a virtual one-state martial law. The result is that many of its resources have been depleted and pollution is a problem, particularly in the industrial belt of this sweet-potato-shaped island.

LEFT Tai Chi on Elephant Mountain near Taipei 101

Taiwan, Republic of China **Longitude:** 121° 00' E **Latitude:** 23° 30' N **Area:** 35,800 sq km (13,819 sq mi) **Highest point:** 3,952 m (12,966 ft) Yu Shan **Population:** 22,858,900
Principal town: Taipei **Natives:** A-mei, Wu Bai, Winston Chao, Chang Chen, Jay Chou, David Ho, Cho-liang Lin, Yen-Hsun Lu, Kaku Morin, Shu Qi, Lin Qiang, Teresa Teng, Jolin Tsai, Chien-Ming Wang, Cyndi Wang, Joey Wang, Jerry Yang, Tsai Hsiao Yüch **Residents:** Chiang Kai-Shek, Ang Lee, Soong May-ling, Liu Mingchuan, Lin Yutang

"The tethered dinghies nod in a row. There is fresh-baked bread nearby. Golden stone walls of cottages glow against pale blue of morning sea and sky. Gulls line the sea-wall, late wallabies lollop to the cover of low bushes."

Hal Colebatch, "Rottnest Island Morning II"

Rottnest, Western Australia, Australia **Longitude:** 115º 27' E **Latitude:** 32º 00' S **Area:** 19 sq km (7 sq mi) **Highest point:** 45 m (148 ft) **Population:** 300 **Principal settlement:** Thomson Bay

Rottnest

WESTERN AUSTRALIA

Lying just a few kilometres off the coast of Australia, Rottnest has become a day-trip destination for beach bums and year-end party student revellers from Perth, on the mainland. However, the island also stands as testament to an ignominious chapter in the history of Australia. Although originally inhabited by aboriginals, the island remained uninhabited for several thousand years until the Europeans arrived in the seventeenth century. Then through a steady campaign of land dispossession and physical annihilation, Rottnest was transformed into a penal colony and a concentration camp for the aborigines.

Today, Perth is a city where Australians come to retire. They appreciate the isolation and the desert landscape that separates them from civilization and the more populated cities on the other edges of the continent. But this area is already a cemetery for Australia's indigenous population and despite much apparent soul-seeking and fanfare surrounding flag-bearers such as Olympic champion Kathy Freeman, the First Australians still live in squalor on the fringes of society in Western Australia – the country's most mineral-rich and affluent state.

Not unlike other former penal-colony islands, including Gorée and Robben, Rottnest – or "Rotto" in Australian colloquial style – is making a comeback and living off its obvious natural charms. Discovered originally by the Dutch, who initially dismissed this barren, desiccated coastline of Western Australia as uninhabitable, the island was named after its unique beaver-like indigenous marsupial, the quokka, that the Dutch mistook for a rat. It was not until the early nineteenth-century scramble for Australia that the British staked a timely pre-Gold Rush claim to this part of the continent and founded the settlement at the mouth of the Swan River now known as Perth.

Not much happens on Rotto, but that is its charm and why it attracts huge numbers of Australian holidaymakers, especially over New Year. They are seduced by the timelessness and stillness, the eleven kilometres (seven miles) of pristine heathland, the inland salt lakes, the clear scalloped bays and the offshore reefs interrupted by just one human settlement on the east side – Thompson Bay.

From Oliver Hill, charmed by the Fremantle Doctor westerly breeze that bewitches batsmen at the Waca cricket ground, sun-worshippers can gaze west out over the ironically named bucolic West End and across the Indian Ocean. Or they can turn eastwards to the forested Darling mountain range that rises behind the shoreline, and the beaches of Cottesloe and Scarborough that lie before it, and reflect on the island's troubled past.

"Bali is one of the few cultures with origins in one of the great ancient cultures which is still alive in our times. All other great cultures are in stasis or abandoned."

Arthur Erickson, architect

ABOVE Playing a trompong in a Gamelan orchestra

Bali, Indonesia **Longitude:** 115° 00' E **Latitude:** 8° 20' S **Area:** 5,633 sq km (2,174 sq mi) **Highest point:** 3,142 m (10,308 ft) Mt Agung **Population:** 3,156,300 **Capital:** Denpasar
Natives: I Gusti Nyoman Lempad, Desak Nyoman Suarti, I Nyoman Sumandhi **Residents:** Antonio Blanco, Arie Smit, Hans Snel, Walter Spies

Bali

MALAY ARCHIPELAGO

Bali is one of the most – if not *the* most – recognized place names in Indonesia. The island delivers on the preconceptions: the surrounding coral reefs, a wide choice of beaches (white sand in the south, black in the north and west) and a lifestyle as harmonious as the colours in a *batik* pattern. But most visitors are surprised to discover quite how lush, calm and spiritual Bali is: the westernmost of the Lesser Sunda Islands, it is predominantly Hindu, more than ninety per cent of the island population, in a country where they are a minority.

Offerings to the gods are gently placed across the island, and ceremonies solemnly observed. Nyepi, the Balinese New Year's Day in early April, is the "day of absolute stillness", when tourists are corralled inside their hotels to avoid breaking the silence, as the islanders hold their breath and hope to fool the demons – who have been woken the night before by drums, fireworks and the *ogoh ogoh*, raucous wood and papier mâché giants – into moving on and creating havoc elsewhere. A different kind of silence was deafening immediately following the terrorist bombs of October 2002. The bombs ripped through the resort of Kuta and shattered not only lives – mainly of young Australian partygoers – but also the aura of blissful hedonism that had grown up around the island and which has since been painstakingly rebuilt.

Positioned along with its Indonesian neighbours above the Sunda shelf, Bali inherited half a dozen major volcanoes, including the great peaks of Gunung Agung and Gunung Batur. Three thousand years ago, the eruption of Mount Batur was one of the greatest volcanic events in history. The slopes were embraced by the Balinese. The terraced rice paddies they constructed, clinging to the hillsides, fed by a sophisticated system of irrigation, provided an abundant self-sufficiency that underpinned the islanders' quest for freedom.

The Balinese have always preferred self-imposed introspection and isolation – they are afraid of the sea and suspicious of outsiders. The Dutch landed in the 1590s but never quite dominated the islanders, and for much of the sixteenth century onwards, their separateness allowed them to evolve an intricate pattern of religious ceremony, ritual, healing, arts and music, which was polished, honed and refined in the centuries before they were forced to face the outside world again. It is this that gives Bali much of its intriguing character. The art and handicrafts of Ubud are renowned, and there is dance and music everywhere – so much that Noël Coward could not resist writing: "As I said this morning to Charlie, there is far too much music in Bali. And although as a place it is entrancing, there is also a thought too much dancing." Bali-lovers disagree.

OVERLEAF Pura Ulun Temple on the shore of Lake Bratan

Hong Kong Island

SOUTH CHINA SEA

For almost a century Hong Kong itself was a figurative island – a remnant of the British Empire and scion of the Western free-market economy bolted on to the bottom of communist China. It straddles the mainland peninsula of Kowloon and a number of islands, the greatest of which – and the focus of the city-state's history, as well as its commercial and political life – is Hong Kong Island.

The forest of concrete, steel and glass imposed upon this outcrop in Victoria Harbour is a monument to man's irrepressible urge to tame and triumph over nature. Through the addition of land reclaimed solely at the service of augmenting this temple to Mammon, the island is larger now than the undeveloped rock originally claimed by the British in 1841 at the height of the Opium Wars. The colonial seafront now sits several blocks back from the water's edge, and above it rises a host of signature skyscrapers. In recent years Hong Kong Island has come to display a who's who of modern architects – from Norman Foster's extravagant temple to the Hong Kong Shanghai Bank, to Ming Pei's angular Bank of China building, whose positioning is deemed by acolytes to cast negative *feng shui*.

At the feet of these glittering office blocks thrives a city pulsating with the frenetic rhythm of unrestrained hedonism. Besides money-making, Hong Kong Island's malls and boutiques, especially those south of Hollywood Road (inevitably named SoHo), attract shopaholics like any other affluent world city. Gourmets flock to the cobbled Lan Kwai Fong district, packed with glamorous restaurants. A post-colonial world of tea time and "G'n'T time" plays out at the island's cricket and polo clubs and at the race track at Happy Valley. The island's elite then retire to their desirable residences in Repulse and Stanley bays.

To gaze down from Victoria Peak (tamed by both funicular and the world's longest elevator) on the result of five thousand years of Chinese history merged with a century and a half of British rule is a giddying sight – especially from the cliff-edge rollercoaster. It is disturbingly hypnotic to behold and for many, magnetic. Despite the fears of Chinese rule the show most definitely goes on. But at night, when the island becomes a dazzling spectacle of neon – and despite the knowledge that, incredibly, seventy per cent of it is still composed of countryside, parks and forest – it is impossible not to feel a greater sense of *feng-shui* misalignment. There exists a sense that man's triumphs here may not include mastery of his own irrepressible nature, evidenced by the electricity drain and the street markets of Wing Lok, which sell birds' nest soup and a myriad animal-based Chinese remedies that are extinguishing the species and habitats of Sumatra and Siberia. If one ever wondered where all the world's resources were going, to be used, traded or consumed in a way so disconnected from their provenance, the answer could be here.

LEFT Traditional pharmacies in Schung Wan

OPPOSITE Sampans in Hong Kong Harbour

OVERLEAF Hong Kong at night

Hong Kong Island, Hong Kong, China **Longitude:** 114° 14' E **Latitude:** 22° 11' N **Area:** 78 sq km (30 sq mi) **Highest point:** 554 m (1,818 ft) Victoria Peak **Population:** 1,268,100
Natives: Jackie Chan, Maggie Cheung, Marco Fu, Karen Mok, Fiona Rae, John Rocha, David Tang, Nicholas Tse **Residents:** Wong Kar-Wei, I. M. Pei, John Woo, Martin Yan

"If you can't buy something
in Hong Kong then
it probably doesn't exist."
Michael Palin

"One great wild untidy luxuriant hothouse
made by nature for herself."

Charles Darwin

Borneo

MALAY ARCHIPELAGO

The Sultan of Brunei (a kingdom on the world's third-largest island), is often fabled for his extreme monetary riches, but it is Borneo itself that deserves acclaim for its still greater riches of the natural kind. For it is here, incredibly, that since 1996 more than three hundred previously unseen and undocumented species of animal and plant have been discovered. These include a new species of cloudy leopard, a small red cat with a strong bushy tail, and a chameleon mudsnake. In this age of presumed finite knowledge of the depth and breadth of our planet, revelations from this island are both incredible and humbling.

Ensuring the survival of such natural richness and uncharted diversity is both a race against time and a battle against mankind. The natural habitat of many of these animals is slowly but surely being destroyed. The logging industry, fuelled by the Malaysian need for banal plywood, is encroaching on the lowland rainforests. Fifty per cent of the annual tropical timber trade comes from Borneo.

The rainforest is being replaced by mangroves, planted for the palm oil so essential in the biofuels needed desperately by the booming Asian economies ironically to reduce their carbon-dioxide emissions at the service of the environment. Fires and droughts in recent years have only served to exacerbate the situation. Meanwhile, the nests of swiftlets in Borneo's vast, unique and guano-piled cave systems are sought after as delicacies and aphrodisiacs by the Chinese, fuelling a billion-dollar wildlife industry.

Chief among the animals under threat is the the orang-utan, joined in its fight for survival by the Sumatran rhino and the Bornean clouded leopard. And there are signs that a world in need of such majestic symbols as catalysts is beginning to wake up – with national parks such as the Tanjung Puting being established, inside whose borders no further logging is permissible. Although it still occurs.

The cost of failing to recognize the need for immediate action would not only be the loss of flora and fauna, but also of its human inhabitants. Across the disputed modern-day divisions of Indonesian and Malay territory inherited from the Anglo-Dutch ownership of the island in the eighteenth and nineteenth centuries, the island is home to more than thirty ethnic groups, including the Kayan, Keniah or Penan. Some of these, numbering as few as thirty individuals, have yet to be anthropologically documented and are, like the orang-utans, on the verge of extinction.

Mystical, uncharted and teeming with the croaks, calls and song of a jungle book of animals, Borneo – the island in the clouds – stands as a symbol both of the riches of the Earth and potentially of the poverty of man.

Borneo, Indonesia, Malaysia and Brunei **Longitude:** 114° 00' E **Latitude:** 1° 00' N **Area:** 743,330 sq km (286,925 sq mi) **Highest point:** 4,101 m (13,455 ft) Mt Kinabalu **Population:** 16,000,000
Principal towns: Bandar Seri Begawan (Brunei), Kota Kinabalu (Malaysian Borneo), Pontianek (Indonesian Brunei)

Java

MALAY ARCHIPELAGO

"A world in which Man coaxes Nature with inexhaustible love and labour, instead of coercing her… In Java I am in the same world as in Lombardy or in Holland."

Arnold Toynbee, historian

Wake up and smell the coffee. It will get you in the mood for a bracing visit to the top of Java's potentially eruptive Mount Bromo, where the view of the sunrise will be further stimulating – that is, if you can stop your teeth chattering in the morning chill. If this doesn't wake you up, pick up on the seismic energy of the island: an earthquake in 2006 rattled more than teeth; a spine of volcanic peaks runs down the back of Java.

Java is the battery that energizes Indonesia; the vast majority of Indonesians, some 120 million of them, live on this long island. Ten million of them can be found in Jakarta,

the capital on the far northwestern tip of Java, where tight control is exerted over the rest of Indonesia's islands. Jakarta, a city blissfully unaware of the concept of urban planning, was thrown up apparently at random. It is a heaving mishmash of a metropolis, with so little in the way of attractive sites that the Dutch-style waterfronts of the Kota district come as a real shock, because of their order and homogeneity rather than their Dutchness (the Dutch East India Company reigned here for three centuries). Amsterdam, conversely, has its own Java Island, home of raves and art installations.

There is history to spare here. In the 1890s one of the earliest examples of a hominid outside of Europe was discovered: Java Man. The truly memorable sites on the island are both natural and manmade. Gunung Bromo and its sister volcanoes always impress, but more remarkable, because of the sheer vision and manpower involved, are the temples of Borobudur and Prambanan. Borobudur is a Buddhist *stupa* - the world's largest, and an unmovable relic on an island swayed by Islam from the fifteenth century onwards. It was abandoned and then rediscovered beneath layers of ash, dust and debris by a British officer while Napoleon was rampaging through Europe, and it has now been reassembled courtesy of UNESCO. Prambanan is its smaller Hindu neighbour.

Despite such treasures, Java has never been a priority tourist destination, though it has always been popular with Chinese visitors. The rough seas that lash its southern shore have limited its beach resorts. Pangdaran is one of the exceptions: a black-sand resort lying on the south edge of West Java. If tourist-driven exploitation is not an issue, Java does have significant environmental concerns – from persistent flooding, landslips and the pressure that the sheer numbers of its population are putting on the available land. Forests are over two-thirds down on the ideal size. Like the *wayang* puppets, this issue casts a shadow over the dreams of the Javanese – unless they are merely clouds in their coffee.

LEFT Buddha at Borobudur temple

Java, Indonesia **Local name:** Jawa **Longitude:** 110° 00' E **Latitude:** 7° 00' S **Area:** 126,700 sq km (48,900 sq mi) **Highest point:** 3,676 m (12,060 ft) Semeru **Population:** 124,000,000
Principal town: Jakarta **Natives:** Sarah Azhari, Lil Dagover, Anthony Fokker, Idjah Hadidjah, Ki Nartosabdho, Mpu Prapancha

LEFT Madakaripura Falls

OVERLEAF Java's volcanic landscape

Hainan

SOUTH CHINA SEA

"The foot of the Earth,
and the corner of the sky."

Literal meaning of Tianya Haijiao, Hainan Island

Hainan, Hainan Province, China **Longitude:** 109° 30' E **Latitude:** 19° 00' N **Area:** 33,920 sq km (13,090 sq mi) **Highest point:** 1,867 m (6,125 ft) Wuzhi Shan **Population:** 8,180,000
Capital: Haikou City **Natives:** Soong May-ling, Hai Rui, Charlie Soong **Resident:** Su Shi

I t still seems odd to Westerners that the swaying palms and sandy beaches of Hainan are part of the People's Republic of China. Dangling only 50 kilometres (31 miles) from that vast country's southern shore, Hainan lies on the same latitude as Antigua and Hawaii, and enjoys all the benefits of its tropical location.

The madding crowds of Western tourists have yet to find their way to Hainan, but for those Chinese who can afford it – and that is an ever-increasing number as the burgeoning middle class sees the return of old money from their expatriate families – it has become their luxury seaside resort. The island they visit to chill out, soak up the sun and lounge by the pool was not always such a sought-after destination. Once upon a dynastic time, it was where those who were unwise enough to incur the wrath of the emperor's officials might find themselves. Here they enjoyed not so much rest and

recuperation as rejection and recrimination, in exile at the furthest corner of the empire – hence Hainan's nickname, "tropical Siberia".

Hainan (the name means "southern sea") is China's second-largest island and its smallest province, off the coast of Vietnam. Like all good tropical destinations, it is particularly appealing during the harshest winter months. Its mildness, coconut groves and coral-studded blue seas are obvious attractions, and work their charm as expected – although out of season the island can be lashed by typhoons swinging in from Taiwan.

This is an island busy building its profile. It already possesses its own sad legend: at Tianya Haijiao, in a Chinese version of Romeo and Juliet, two star-cross'd lovers from rival clans, unable to bear the prospect of being parted, jumped into the sea. The two huge rocks that remain are, it is said, their departed souls.

A more contemporary piece of publicity was provided when the laid-back city of Sanya hosted Miss World 2004 (now, like those earlier visitors, banished to the outposts of empire for having brought opprobrium upon itself). What visitors notice is that Sanya is a city that has not yet settled into its new identity, with buildings sprouting up here, there and everywhere. The heart of the town is down on the beaches of Ya Long Wan and Da Dong Hai, where wooden fishing boats lay up during the day. These beaches come alive after dark, when barbecue stalls offering fresh king prawns light up along the sands. An attraction for those who do not tan easily: this is a land where fair skin on the beach is eminently fashionable.

OPPOSITE Ya Long Beach
BELOW Sanya Harbour

Christmas Island

INDIAN OCEAN

Between October and December every year, the local rules of golf on Christmas Island have to be adapted. For this is the season when, guided by the moon, the island's thousand million endemic red crabs appear from the undergrowth and advance ponderously but inexorably, like wind-up toys, towards the sea to lay eggs for the males to fertilize. The whole island, including every house, car, handbag and shoe, is covered in a moving crimson carpet of crab in what has been hailed as one of the most wondrous animal migrations on the planet – and one of the wonders of the natural world. For three months Christmas Island becomes, in David Attenborough's words, the Kingdom of the Crab. But life must go on, and so the outnumbered residents incorporate the crabs into their life. If a crab on the eighteenth accidentally knocks your ball into the hole you can count it. Not a birdie or an eagle, but a crab, you might say.

The indigenous red crab is just one of a myriad endemic species that have evolved in isolation on Christmas Island, leading it to be dubbed the Galapagos of the Indian Ocean. Among them are the red-footed booby, the endangered Abbot's booby, majestic frigates, bosuns, relatives of the tropic bird, and the giant coconut crab, the largest invertebrate on Earth, capable of cleaving open whole coconuts with its giant claws.

The secret of nature's success on Christmas Island is simply the absence of mankind. For many centuries its almost-continuous cliff-edged coastline proved to be its saviour from the clutches of man. The island was first sighted and named by Captain William Mynors on Christmas Day in 1643, but he was unable to moor safely and so sailed by. Many subsequent captains, explorers and naturalists tried to tame the island, but found its fringes and mountainous interior impassable. Until 1887, that is, when a British vessel – the HMS *Flying Fish* – found an anchorage at the cove that now takes that name. The following year, after various naturalists had examined the treasures available there, phosphate was discovered and the island promptly annexed. Phosphate mines whose booty could be used in fertilizers around the world were, until their closure in 1987 by the Australian government, a constant threat to Christmas Island's fragile ecosphere. While sixty-five per cent of the island is now given over to untouched national park, the remainder bears the scars of open mines.

The mining industry in turn accounts for the unique ethnic make-up of an island so close to Australia – a majority of Chinese, descendants of the coolie labourers brought in to mine the phosphate. Asylum seekers from Indonesia and the Middle East thought it was Christmas when they landed here in the 1980s and 1990s in an attempt to crab Australian residency. But the Australian government excised the island from its migration zone. It seems the only permitted migration on Christmas Island is for real red crabs.

Christmas Island, Territory of Australia **Longitude:** 105º 40' E **Latitude:** 10º 30' S **Area:** 135 sq km (52 sq mi) **Highest point:** 361 m (1,184 ft), Murray Hill **Population:** 1,500
Capital: The Settlement

"It's November, the moon is in its third quarter,
and the sun is just setting. And in a few hours from now,
on this very shore, a thousand million lives will be launched."

Sir David Attenborough

Krakatoa

SUNDA STRAIT

Krakatoa, Lampung Province, Indonesia **Local name:** Krakatau **Longitude:** 105° 20' E **Latitude:** 6° 10' S **Area:** 17.5 sq km (7 sq mi) **Highest point:** 960m (3,150 ft) **Population:** None

It is a toponym that has come to mean just one thing: apocalyptic explosion. Throughout the spring and early summer months of 1883, huge quantities of steam built up in the magma chambers that lay beneath the volcanic island of Krakatoa, in the Sunda strait between Java and Sumatra, about 50 kilometres (31 miles) from each. The pressure grew to the point where the terrestrial chains of the Earth above could no longer contain its insistent demands, and on 27 August 1883, thar she blew...

In the immediate aftermath, 36,000 people died, most on neighbouring islands where the scalding, suffocating ash of the fallout landed. But the impact stretched worldwide. In Perth, on Australia's western coast, the best part of 3,000 kilometres (1,864 miles) away, the residents thought they were hearing the distant rumble of gunfire. In Poughkeepsie, New York, the sunsets were so vivid that firefighters were called out to tackle the illusory blaze. Moons turned blue, and many believe the dramatic effect on sunsets gave Edvard Munch inspiration for the striated skies in the background of *The Scream*. Priests of Islam in nearby Java turned it to their political advantage. This was God demonstrating displeasure, they said – we have to attack the Dutch colonialists whose fault it must be.

The island had ripped itself in two and subsided into simmering intensity. Forty years later, in the 1920s, it gave birth to a small new volcano, known as Arak Krakatau, or Baby K. The islands still lie over the intersection of the Eurasian and Indo-Australian plates: Krakatoa's offspring may – in fact probably will – blow again. Hollywood produced a movie version in 1969, *Krakatoa: East of Java* – vulcanologists and pedants delighted in pointing out that the island actually lies to the west of Java, but the name was re-plugged into popular culture nonetheless.

In the twenty-first century, a trip to Krakatoa (this spelling believed to be a slip of a British clerk's pen or telegraph key, since the local name is Krakatau) offers a chance to view and to participate in a piece of authentic volcanic history. After a three-hour fishing-boat ride from Carita in West Java, tourists are able to land, but the spooky surroundings makes them chary the mystic light, the whiff of sulphur, the bubbling seas, the black sand. The islands are virtually barren, but Arak Krakatau comes alive at night as its lava flow glows bright, and from the two remnants of Krakatoa's sheer cliffs, it is easy to imagine the original shape and size of the great volcano and shudder at the memory of its awesome power.

"The word Krakatoa, despite being a word misspelled and mangled by the imperfect arts of Victorian telegraphy and journalism, became in one awful ear-splitting moment a byname for cataclysm, paroxysm, death and disaster."

Simon Winchester, *Krakatoa: The Day the World Exploded*

LEFT Krakatoa became two islands in the eruption of 1883

Tioman

SOUTH CHINA SEA

Tioman was premiered to the rest of the world in the 1958 movie version of *South Pacific*. Director Joshua Logan and his team chose this small island off the east coast of Malaysia as one of the locations for the fictional Bali Hai. Few people had heard of the place at the time. It was densely forested and sparsely populated, but its beaches and lace-like white coral reefs encapsulated the preconceptions of an audience who did not know – but did not need to know – that the island was a long way from the intended location.

A decade or so later, *Time* projected the notoriety of Tioman to a new level, by picking it as one of the world's most beautiful islands. Few would have quibbled then, or now, as

the island has consistently delivered all the requisite elements of a tropical island: stunning white sandy beaches, azure waters, set against rainforests and soaring mountains: a place to laze, to dive, to chill, clad in a sarong.

The origins of the island lie in legend. It is said that a dragon princess, travelling to her wedding, fell asleep and was transmogrified into the pear-shaped island: the dragon's back solidified into the range of peaks along its spine, and her head into Chula Naga, the Dragon's Horns – the twin peaks that have become the island's icon.

Sailors in transit used the island as a convenient landmark, a sign advising them to hang a northeasterly tack and head onwards to Cambodia. Traders came for betel nuts, sandalwood and camphor. It was a monsoon haven for merchants and pirates. The latter raided the island – and as a result Tioman was abandoned for fifteen years in the 1830s and

1840s. But the fisher families returned, and eked out an existence in obscurity until the media machine took notice.

Thanks to a lack of any great infrastructure – footpaths rather than roads, boat travel around the coves and beaches (although a new marina is due to up the ante), relatively low-key telecommunications – visitors are free to trek the jungle, spotting flying squirrels, macaques, porcupines and snakes, take a dip in clear waterfalls, or, above all to plunge into the waters and take a snorkeller's-eye view of the unique walking catfish and soft-shelled turtle, and the fish flitting through the wartime wrecks of the HMS *Repulse* and *Prince of Wales*, while trying not to step on the frequent, spikily painful sea urchins underfoot as they reach shallow waters. For now – and time is ticking as the coral inevitably suffers damage and bleaching from human activity – Tioman still offers an at-one-with-nature experience.

Tioman, Pahang, Malaysia **Longitude:** 104° 10' E **Latitude:** 2° 50' N **Area:** 134 sq km (52 sq mi) **Highest point:** 690 m (2,264 ft) Gunung Nenek Semukut **Population:** 2,700
Principal town: Kampung Tekek

"Island of
the Sleeping Dragon."
Local legend

Singapore

SINGAPORE STRAIT

For many travellers, Singapore – that punctuation point at the bottom of the Malay Peninsula – is a brief stopping-off airport on the way to or from Australasia, a last chance to refuel before crossing the Equator and heading on to the final leg of the seemingly endless journey. Few passengers escape the transit lounge at Changi Airport. If they do, they arrive with an excess baggage allowance of preconceptions about an ultra-efficient island city locked into excessive rules and regulations, or thinking about William Gibson's tart remark that Singapore was "Disneyland with the death penalty". The received view was that control here was too tight, squeezing out the self-thought and liberties of the Singaporeans (the rest of the world, as it happened, would follow suit, smoking bans in places as anti-establishment as Ireland or Italy merely following in Singapore's footsteps).

Perhaps the contrast with a colonial past of opium dens and smugglers was too great, as the new buildings of this city-state – one of the world's few, alongside Monaco and Vatican City – have pushed away a highly rose-bespectacled past. But the Singapore-ness is still there. There might not be much room for it in the compact downtown central business district, but it's there, in mansions just off the shopping mecca of Orchard Road, in the hymns emanating from St Andrew's Cathedral and in more patches of green than anyone ever expects.

The hub of Singapore on the waterfront was where Thomas Stamford Raffles arrived in 1819 to establish a trading post in what had previously been a low-key Malay fishing village. It was called Singapur by the Malays, from the Sanskrit *singa* ("lion") and *puray* ("city"), because a visiting fourteenth-century prince had allegedly seen a lion here (it was probably a tiger). A treaty with one of the local sultans turned the island into a handy *entrepôt* for the British – "It is all and everything I could wish," wrote Raffles in 1820, "and, if no untimely fate awaits it, promises to become the Emporium and the pride of the East." As with the Raj, the British stamped

their parliamentary system on the colony, but following the loss of the island to the Japanese in 1942 (Winston Churchill said it was their worst defeat of the war), their presence thereafter was diminished, and by 1965 Singapore was independent.

But Raffles' influence can still be felt, and not just at the bars of the Raffles Hotel with a Singapore Sling to hand. He divided the city into subdivisions that reflect the diverse mix of the Singaporeans: Little India (mainly Tamils and Keralan Hindus) and Chinatown, although the Straits Chinese are no minority, but make up three-quarters of the population. Throw the Malays into the mix and you also have a recipe for the deep-flavoured cuisine of the place: drunken prawns and chilli crab are just two of the island's classic dishes.

"As a vision from the sea, Singapore is still exciting. I seem to see a signpost here – a fantasy, of course – reading, 'From here on is the East – behind you, the Rest of the World'."

Gavin Young, *Slow Boats to China*

OPPOSITE Sri Veeramakaliamman Temple

ABOVE Raffles Hotel

Singapore, Republic of Singapore **Local name:** Singapura **Longitude:** 103° 51' E **Latitude:** 1° 17' N **Area:** 655 sq km (253 sq mi) **Highest point:** 175m (574 ft) Bukit Timah **Population:** 4,362,000 **Principal town:** Singapore City **Natives:** Fiona Bruce, Kit Chan, Leslie Charteris, Annabel Chong, Tanya Chua, Erik Khoo, Dick Lee, Lee Hui Min, Jack Neo, Stefanie Sun, Melvyn Tan, Vanessa-Mae, Arthur Yap, Robert Yeo, Huang Yida **Residents:** Munshi Abdullah, William Farquhar, C. Northcote Parkinson, Thomas Stanford Raffles

Sumatra

MALAY ARCHIPELAGO

Sumatra is the largest fully owned island in the chain of 17,508 that make up the scattered nation of Indonesia. Sitting astride the Equator, it is a wild, rugged, humid island of misty rainforests clinging on to dramatic mountains, the last surviving habitat of creatures great and small, including many weird and wonderful endemic species in uneasy cohabitation with man.

The name Sumatra is thought to be an evolution of the Sanskrit *Swama Daipa*, meaning "Isle of Gold". Gold was found and has been mined here since ancient times, and between gold, coal, palm oil and petroleum, the plundering of Sumatra's resources has scarcely abated. Much of the tropical rainforest that used to cover the island has been illegally logged – even within the ten protected national parks here – and turned into pulp to feed the world paper industry. Many of Sumatra's exotic plants are harvested for the perfume industry, their essence distilled into the new season's fashionable fragrance. And Sumatran coffee beans are among the most prized ingredients feeding the twenty-first century coffee revolution.

Inevitably there is a threat to some of the rare flora and fauna, such as the Sumatran pine tree, the *Rafflesia arnoldii* (the world's largest flower), the Sumatran tiger, elephant and rhino and, probably most notable of all, the original "man of the forest" the orang-utan. All the key environmental organizations – Greenpeace, the Worldwide Fund for Nature, the RSPB – are involved in trying to preserve Sumatra's natural assets, but it is a task as mammoth as the daunting Barisan mountain range, topped by the 3,800-metre (12,467-foot) Mount Kerinci, that defines the west of the island.

At the centre of this range lies a caldera formed by what is thought to be the largest volcanic explosion ever to have taken place on Earth, the ash of which would have spread as far as parts of India. The crater is now filled by the waters of the magnificent Lake Toba, home to the Batak ethnic group, with their distinctive wooden houses topped by winged roofs like the hulls of boats.

If not for the diminishing prospects of its wildlife, Sumatra was put on the map on 26 December 2004, when the world awoke to the name of Banda Aceh, a town and region that is both the epicentre of Islam in Southeast Asia and of the seismic movement, created by the continental fault that lies underneath the island, that caused the giant tsunami which devastated the coastal civilization. The relief effort was disrupted by a massive earthquake that shook the region again the following year. Recovery since has been slow but steady. However, for its geological, ethnic and environmental tensions Sumatra continues to be one of the most volatile parts of the world. It is a paradise not yet lost – but on the brink.

"The view of Lake Tawar was extreme charm – enclosed in a coronet of low, pointed mountains which were mantled as if in velvet of the deepest green."
Norman Lewis

OPPOSITE Batak children and long houses
LEFT Gunung Kerinci volcano

Sumatra, Indonesia **Longitude:** 102° 00' E **Latitude:** 0° 40' N **Area:** 470,000 sq km (181,420 sq mi) **Highest point:** 3,800 m (12,467 ft) Mt Kerinci **Population:** 43,309,700
Principal town: Medan **Natives:** Buya Hamka, Rasuna Said, Rizaldi Siagian

Langkawi
ANDAMAN SEA

> "Give me the paradise of the end of spring ... and I'll wrap for you an endless summer."
>
> Inscription in Ibrahim Hussein Museum and Cultural Foundation

The many paradise islands throughout Oceania are sublime expressions of so much flour-like sand, crystal-blue water and endemic flora and fauna that they almost cancel each other out through their surplus of superlatives. Not many, however, are also so rich in tales of myth, magic and legend – and these wonders single out the ninety-nine islands of Langkawi in the Andaman Sea. They are idyllic portals to the realms of fantasy.

Amid the clear emerald waters of the freshwater lake in the heart of The Island of the Pregnant Maiden, for instance, lives a legendary monstrous white crocodile. It is Langkawi's equivalent to the many legendary beasts that have become fearfully associated with other lakes in the world – except that here the fate of any woman daring enough to dip in its waters is not death but a predicted life of infertility. So far there has been no direct evidence or sightings of the albino crocodile, and most intrepid bathers only attest to the presence of curious shoals of ticklish catfish.

At Makan Matsui stands the shrine to a woman accused two hundred years ago of adultery. She was tied to a tree and stabbed, but the white blood she shed was considered proof of her innocence.

The names of places all over the islands are forged from one common and unusually gentle creation myth that tells of two giants who had an argument at one of their daughter's wedding and knocked over a pot of gravy. This christened the capital town of Kuah ("gravy" in Malay) and gave several others their names: Ayer Hangat ("hot water") and Gelanga Pecah ("broken crockery"). The two giants apologized to the populace and agreed as atonement to be turned into stone. They stand as the two peaks Gunung Mat Cincang – its summit now assailed by a popular cable-car – and Gunung Raya, the higher of the two, whose flanks are washed by a spectacular fourteen-tier waterfall.

On the east side of the largest island, Pulau Langkawi, lies a lagoon called the Hole in the Wall, a once-secret anchorage whose entrance is obscured from the sea. But duty-free Langkawi now stands on the brink of discovery by the Sunsail crew and the honeymoon industry. Most of the islands are uninhabited and the free-sailing visitor can lay claim to a whole island for the day. Fortunately, since being returned to British and then Malay rule under the Anglo-Siamese treaty of 1909, Langkawi has been designated a UNESCO geopark, offering protection for its flora and fauna, among them macaque monkeys, flying lizards and giant squirrels, and the giant sea eagles (*helang* in Malay) that give the archipelago its old name of Eagle Island (*kawi*, meaning marble or rock).

OPPOSITE Rock Island

Langkawi, Kedah, Malaysia **Longitude:** 99° 45' E **Latitude:** 6° 25' N **Area:** 479 sq km (185 sq mi) **Highest point:** 890 m (2,920 ft) Gunung Raya **Population:** 45,000 **Principal town:** Kuah
Resident: Ibrahim Hussein

Koh Phi Phi

ANDAMAN SEA

"If you're looking for authentic Asia,
and having a hard time locating it,
don't blame your guidebook.
Blame your own imagination."

Joe Cummings, author of Lonely Planet guide to Thailand

The much-travelled Khao San Road through Thailand has been turned by its foot soldiers into some mythical post-hippy oriental imitation of the original Istanbul-to-Kathmandu beatnik trail. This, and the sandy isthmuses, mushroom-shaped limestone excrescences and hidden pristine lagoons of the tiny Koh Phi Phi archipelago off the island of Phuket, were the focus of *The Beach*, Alex Garland's Generation-X-defining novel. The book showcases a backpacker world of drugs, raves and sex, superficially exotic but unpacked as principally one of inertia and alienation lived out in dirty hostels. At the core of the book is the search – in a world in which "off the beaten track" is the holy grail of travel – for the ultimate undiscovered destination, in this case a beach, that the protagonist can keep a secret just for himself and a private group of the initiated.

Garland's visual and geographical reference point for the book was actually the Philippines, based on the time he lived there, but he transposed it to Thailand specifically to address a particular type of tourism, a sample-hungry tourism of exploitation, selfishness, indifference and lack of open-mindedness and curiosity. When Richard, the main character, pronounced the oft-quoted line "There's no way you can keep it out of *Lonely Planet*, and once that happens it's countdown to doomsday", Garland is not attacking the travel-guide industry. Rather he is deriding the lack of imagination of travellers who depend only on such guides.

In the event, ironically, the film version of the book encouraged even more faux-hippy backpackers to go and "find themselves" in the footsteps of Leonardo DiCaprio and to gaze at the supposed earthly paradise of Ao Maya beach amid polemics that the shooting of the film (the palm trees were all imported for the set) had destroyed the environment. In actual fact the waters of these pristine bays had long since suffered from Thai fishermen using dynamite.

The 2004 Boxing Day tsunami all but wiped the population of the islands and their livelihoods off the map, and brought to an end any luxurious Western debates over travel snobbishness that might have kept people away. These destitute but infinitely hospitable island communities needed the *farang*'s (foreigner's) dollar and simple, unabashed tourism more than ever. And happily, since the muddy waters withdrew the simple if brittle Arcadian serenity of a life lived out in *dhows* and sarongs, amid white sands and turquoise waters and wicker huts and measured out in bread, bountiful seafood and coconuts has been as simple to reassert as it was quick to be washed away. Tourists and travellers alike now return to their full-moon parties here with a greater sense of community.

Koh Phi Phi, Krabi, Thailand **Longitude:** 98° 46' E **Latitude:** 7° 45' N **Area:** 35 sq km (14 sq mi) **Principal settlement:** Ton Sai

Phuket

ANDAMAN SEA

"Crabs, shrimps,
prawns and
dragons wander about
wagging their tails
amidst the waves."

Nai Mi, poet

Most people come for the beaches, since Phuket is one of those must-visit tropical islands. But if they can prise themselves from their sybaritic stupor and head across the island, they will catch a glimpse of what was here before the holiday industry. At the island's main crossroads at Ban Tha Rua stand bronze statues of Khunying Jan and her sister Mook, celebrating their heroic and successful resistance to Burmese invasion in 1785. And in Phuket City, the ornate Chinese *wats* of Jui Tui and Put Jaw are testament to the island's economic history. For tin was once the primary source of wealth for Phuket, and from the sixteenth century onwards, *Hakka* Chinese entrepreneurs and their workforces came down to exploit the mines. When the price of tin dropped, the island shifted its efforts into rubber and pineapple plantations and then, in the mid-1970s, turned its attention to tapping into an inexhaustible seam of tourists.

And why not? Between the headlands, particularly on Phuket's west coast, are the sandy beaches opening on to the Andaman Sea (yes, Phuket is "the pearl of the Andaman"), against the little-explored interior of heavily forested mountains – Phuket derives from *bukit*, a Malay word for mountain or hill.

Chief amongst the beaches is Patong, the eternally busy repository of most of Phuket's noise output, where the hawkers hawk, touts tout and the *kathoey* lady-boys bamboozle Tiger beer-sodden lads in the bars of Soi Bangla. In the 2004 tsunami Patong's many hotel developments suffered badly, though Hat Kamala slightly further north bore the full brunt.

If the pace of life in Patong is taking its toll, if the prospect of yet another karaoke evening out seems simply too demanding, there are a number of alternatives. After all, Phuket is really quite a large island – getting on for the size of Singapore – so the options are hardly restrictive. For quieter beaches, the best route is to head up to the northern end of the island, where its largest beach, Hat Mai Khao, remains relatively unvisited. Just round the corner of Phuket's southern tip is Rawai beach, which (by virtue of its east-coast location) offers fabulous sunset views. Away from the waters and the ribbon developments there are the interior's national park and reserves, and the pineapple and rubber plantations. If the soul is soothed by these restful surroundings, the body can also enjoy its own vacation during the nine-day vegetarian festival that falls each October, at the end of the cool season – a perfect detox.

RIGHT *Kathoey* lady-boy at Patong Beach

Phuket, Thailand **Longitude:** 98° 22' E **Latitude:** 8° 00' N **Area:** 543 sq km (210 sq mi) **Highest point:** 529 m (1,736 ft) Radar Hill **Population:** 315,500 **Principal town:** Phuket City

"This is our hope: that children born today have in twenty years' time
a bit of grass under their bare feet, a gust of pure air to breathe, a stretch
of blue water to navigate and a whale on the horizon to make them dream."

Anon, written on a wooden plaque in the Bay Island marine hill hotel in Port Blair

Andaman Islands

ANDAMAN SEA

When relief helicopters servicing the local salvage operation after the 2004 tsunami flew over the Northern Sentinel island group in the Andaman archipelago, they were greeted by arrows fired by the local tribesmen. Suffice to say the world's last surviving Palaeolithic people, the oldest ethnic group on the planet, have a fairly ancient fear of alien metal things that fly and make lots of noise.

The North Sentinels and, until recently the Jarawa tribe in particular, are known for their hostility; Marco Polo called them "dog-faced cannibals" and Arthur Conan Doyle gave his Andaman villain in *The Sign of Four* "hideous distorted features". There are around nine hundred indigenous tribesmen left – the rest disappeared through disease, encroachment or massacre – comprising five groups. They are dispersed across the inhabited twenty-six islands of the 576-island string of forested pearls, which include the forbidden Nicobar isles, that drops down through the Bay of Bengal from the lobe of Burma.

But if these peoples are preserved and isolated from the modern world through some sense of ethnic conservation, they are also protected out of a sense of paranoia from their Indian landlords, who feel a need to regulate an uneasy yet potentially porous area of their border. All of this – be it the bureaucracy that limits the number of places foreigners can visit or stay overnight, the slings and arrows of outrageous tribesmen, or the saltwater crocodiles that lurk in the island's coastal swamps and limestone caves – combines to make the Andamans enticingly mysterious, dangerous and exotic.

By the time the Raj colonial administration of India decided to make the Andamans a penal colony in the nineteenth century, the islands had already attracted the nickname of the Black Waters. This was due to the cannibalism of the natives, and attacks that resulted in too many a ship wrecked or invading crew member missing. This initially caused the powers that were to review the idea of occupation, but they eventually established a headquarters on Ross Island, and with it a replica of the home counties in the tropics. This came complete with the aptly named Port Blair, whose ruins – those that survived the earthquake of 1941 – remain, eerily overgrown and intertwined with banyan trees.

The tsunami put the Andamans, described by Jacques Cousteau as the "invisible islands", on the map, and for better or worse the Indian government has started to open them up for tourism as a rival to Mauritius and the Seychelles. But only one island, Havelock, has anything approaching the facilities demanded by travellers let alone honeymooners, and it is rather nice to think that amid these fierce tribesmen and the bats, monitor lizards and geckoes of their jungle, perhaps the ideal of a lonely planet might just exist.

ABOVE Phangnga Bay

Andaman Islands, Andaman and Nicobar Islands Union Territory of India **Longitude:** 92° 45' E **Latitude:** 12° 30' N **Area:** 6,340 sq km (2,447 sq mi) **Highest point:** 732 m (2,400 ft) Saddle Peak
Population: 304,800 **Principal town:** Port Blair **Resident:** Vinayak Damodar Savarkar

"The islands are the trailing threads of India's fabric,
the ragged fringe of her sari."

Amitav Ghosh, *The Hungry Tide*

Ganga Sagar

BAY OF BENGAL

I n the middle of January, as the sun moves from Sagittarius into Capricorn, Hindus celebrate Makar Sankranti, the festival of the new harvest, which marks the beginning of an auspicious six-month period. The island of Sagar, in the delta at the mouth of the Ganges, becomes the venue for one of the largest regular gatherings of humans on Earth – the Gangasagar *mela* or fair. As one observer put it: "No invitation is given. No propaganda is carried out. No authority exists for carrying out the *mela*."

To arrive here, the pilgrims will have journeyed from the Bengal countryside and far beyond, massing first in Kolkata, and then overloading a whole wagon trail of crowded buses and ferries, followed by yet more buses to bring them to the island of Ganga Sagar. There

will be two hundred thousand or more, each of them looking to wash away their earthly sins.

They are here because in the epic *Ramayana*, the legend runs that Bhagiratha, king of Kosala, brought the sacred Ganga (Ganges) down to Earth and led her to establish the river's course, rising in the glaciers of the Himalaya at Gomukh, wending its way through the plains of Haridwat, past the equally holy place of Varanasi, and down on to the Bay of Bengal. At its junction with the river Hooghly, the largest of the Sundarban Islands was formed from the Ganges silt. Here Ganga washed the mortal remains of Bhagiratha's sixty thousand ancestors and absolved their sins. For the pilgrims of the twenty-first century, sins will not only be absolved, but on Makar Sankranti day, after a dip in the waters, girls will find handsome

grooms, and vice versa. The same girls can also "marry" the sea, assuring they will never be abandoned or widowed.

As the crowds arrive on the island's southern tip, saffron and red flags flutter. Conch shells are blown. Devotional chants are voiced: *Kapil Muni ki jai*. There is often a heady gust of ganja snaking out of the huts where the naked Naga Sadhu priests sit. It is January, so the climate is often cold and windy as a priest announces, pre-dawn, that it is time for the annual dip, before a walk to the Kapil Muni Ashram to worship again. Between *melas*, the island reverts to a quiet life for its villagers, and the Royal Bengal tigers that stalk its mangrove swamps.

OPPOSITE A Holy dip on Makar Sankranti day

BELOW Processing to the Sangam for evening prayers

Ganga Sagar, West Bengal, India **Longitude:** 88° 05' E **Latitude:** 21° 38' N **Area:** 247 sq km (95 sq mi) **Highest point:** 20 m (66 ft) **Population:** 185,600 **Principal town:** Sagar Town

Sri Lanka

INDIAN OCEAN

Throughout its history, the island we now call Sri Lanka has been blessed with or burdened by many names. For the Greeks it was Taprobane ("copper-coloured"), to the Arabs Serendib and the Persians Serendip (from which Horace Walpole coined the word "serendipity" in the 1750s). *Sinha*, the Sanskrit for lion (the same root as the first part of Singapore's name) led to the Portuguese Ceilão, and thence the British Ceylon. Since independence from Britain it has reverted to Lanka, Sanskrit for "resplendent land" – the name it was known by in the *Ramayana* – preceded by an honorific *Sri*.

That the island has appeared under so many identities is the result of its desirability as a staging post between West and Southeast Asia. Even though the legendary limestone causeway that was once believed to have joined the island to the sub-continent 30 kilometres (19 miles) north no longer exists, Sri Lanka has always been umbilically connected to its big sister, India – although Sri Lankans confess to being rather snooty about their neighbours, and consider themselves a cut above them.

From Orissa and Bengal came the Sinhalese, who now represent the largest ethnic group, primarily Buddhist and rooted in the south and west of Sri Lanka. The island's recent history has been dominated by the relationship between the Sinhalese and the Tamils, imported from India by the British, Dutch and Portuguese to work the rubber and tea plantations. The Tamils, encamped up in the north, and their militant front, the Liberation Tigers of Tamil Eelan, have waged a long and costly battle for separation. Rajiv Gandhi, assassinated in 1991 by an LTTE female suicide bomber, was perhaps the most high-profile victim.

A ceasefire in 2002 promised a calmer, less violent future but recent bombings have stirred up distrust once more. Not for nothing has Sri Lanka been called a teardrop falling from the cheeks of India.

Many people expect Sri Lanka – with its tea, its cricket, its British colonial past – to be nothing more than a rather diluted version of India. In fact, it is quite separate, as quirky and unreadable as one of Murali's most fiendish deliveries. But don't let a Sri Lankan hear you say that. The differences are self-evident in its religion, culture and attitude. Buddhism is everywhere: in the great sites of the island's medieval capital, Polonnaruwa; the mid-jungle rock-top palace of Sigiriya; the tooth supposedly retrieved from Buddha's funeral pyre and enshrined in the hill station of Kandy. Culturally, it has a strong dose of Portuguese and Dutch influence, the latter especially evident in the fortified port town of Galle on the south coast and the Pettah quarter of the capital Colombo. The restful pace of life – bombings aside – is a million miles away from the unceasing energy of a Mumbai or a Delhi. Marco Polo, who had a few stamps in his passport, always said it was the finest island of its size he had ever seen…

> "Ceylon falls on a map and its outline
> is the shape of a tear."
>
> Michael Ondaatje, *Running in the Family*

OPPOSITE Tea plantation in the Hill Country

OVERLEAF On the beach in Colombo's Galle Face

Sri Lanka, Democratic Socialist Republic of Sri Lanka **Longitude:** 80° 50' E **Latitude:** 7° 30' N **Area:** 65,610 sq km (25,325 sq mi) **Highest point:** 2,524 m (8,281 ft) Pidurutalagala aka Mt Pedro **Population:** 20,926,300 **Capital:** Colombo **Natives:** W. D. Amaradeva, Sirimavo Bandaranaike, Aravinda de Silva, Desmond de Silva, Sunil Edirisinghe, Sanith Jayasuriya, Mahela Jayawardene, Lilamani Kapoor, Annesley Malewana, Nanda Malini, Michael Ondaatje, Nadeeka Perera, Ananda Samarakone, Victor Ratnayake, Martin Wikramasinghe **Resident:** Arthur C. Clarke

Lake Palace, Udaipur

LAKE PICHOLA

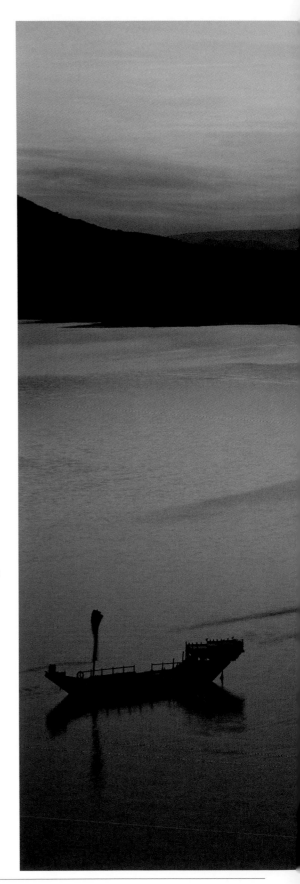

A slice of romance floating in the middle of Rajasthan's Lake Pichola, outlined against the Aravali mountains, the Lake Palace of Udaipur is a fantasy cruise-boat clad in white marble, decorated with mosaic tiles, cast adrift in the name of luxurious indulgence.

The creative force behind the palace was Maharana Jagat Singh II. In Rajasthan, where Maharajahs are two a rupee, the Maharana was the "great warrior" and a successor to the dynasty of Mewar, who believed themselves to be directly descended from the sun god. Despite such noble and divine antecedents, Jagat Singh was confronted by a rather more mundane problem – he needed somewhere to dally. This playboy prince of the 1740s was under pressure from his parents over his habit of organizing late-night meetings with young ladies of his acquaintance. Although the family had a palace in Udaipur, the lake city perched in the red Rajasthani earth, as well as a monsoon palace high up in the Aravali mountains and a separate summer palace, none of these offered sufficient privacy. In order to escape the prying eyes of his mother, father and their servants, he constructed his personal pleasure ground. He chose a four-acre rocky island – Jagniwas Island – in the middle of the lake, and built Lake Palace.

The palace building had fallen into disrepair by the early part of the twentieth century, and for some time it served as a city museum. In the 1960s, however, it was painstakingly restored and reopened as a hotel in 1963. The butlers, they say, are descendants of the original palace retainers. The level of detailing that was inspired by Shah Jahan's Taj Mahal has been copied in each one of its mirrors, ivory carvings and glass inlays. It was not long before James Bond came to stay, when Roger Moore paid court to Maud Adams' Octopussy in the palace (the villain, Kamal Khan, was sequestered in Udaipur's Summer Palace, overlooking the lake).

The old royal barge, the suites and private terraces, wood fires and Rajasthani cuisine, served for a dinner à deux on a floating platform, together create tableaux that shimmer like mirages and do their best to transport the hotel's guests back to the moonlit dates of the Maharana two and a half centuries ago. As they stand on the balconies, brushed by the gentle zephyrs, they offer a silent prayer to the sun gods to send them thanks for not drying out the lake as it did during the drought of 2005. During this period, visitors were forced to access the Lake Palace by means of a somewhat less romantic jeep.

"We used the Lake Palace, a very romantic place, for the interiors of Octopussy's hideaway. The unit slept, ate and relaxed there – it was the shortest travelling time to any location I've ever been on: you just rolled out of bed and you were on the set!"

John Glen, director of *Octopussy*

Lake Palace, Udaipur, Rajasthan, India **Longitude:** 73° 44' E **Latitude:** 24° 36' N **Area:** 1.6 hectares (4 acres) **Altitude:** 577 m (187 ft)

"Each little islet was a separate gem set in
a ring of golden beach sand and with another
wider ring of glass-green water outside where
the coral reef approached the surface, rising like
giant mushrooms from the bottomless blue."

Thor Heyerdahl

ABOVE Maldivian *dhow*

OVERLEAF Low Earth orbit view of the atolls Ari, Malé, Felidu, Nilande, Mulaku and Kolumadulu

Maldives, The Republic of the Maldives **Longitude:** 73° 00' E **Latitude:** 3° 15' N **Area:** 298 sq km (115 sq mi) **Highest point:** 2.3 m (8 ft) **Population:** 369,031 **Capital:** Malé

Maldives

INDIAN OCEAN

The Maldives are the original atolls. The word comes from the local *atholhu* in the islanders' *dhivehi* language: fragmented islets of coral that accreted around the peaks of ancient, long-departed volcanoes, and which remained after their hosts had crumbled in ring-shaped clusters surrounding lagoons. They lie draped across the Equator like a necklace of exotic diamonds – and the name Maldives may itself come from the Sanskrit *maldvipa*, or "garland of islands".

These twenty atolls, made up of a thousand tiny islands, swim together in the Indian Ocean, to the south-west of India and Sri Lanka. Rising sea-levels concern any forward-thinking humanitarian, but for the inhabitants of the Maldives, whose highest point is no more than three metres above sea-level, it is a question of survival. The islets are frighteningly exposed, and weak to resist: although away from the epicentre of the 2004 tsunami, only nine of the islands were not swamped by the fallout of rising waters, and over a hundred people died.

While they do resist, they have done their best to respect the environment that threatens them. The government has kept a careful control of tourist development. Of the 1,190 islands, two hundred are inhabited, and a further eighty are resorts reserved for visitors. On these, only twenty per cent of the land can be covered by buildings, none of which can be higher than the surrounding vegetation; only wood and thatch may be used for construction. Since the Maldives are a Sunni Muslim nation, alcohol is reserved for the resorts. Litter ... billboards ... ugliness ... all have been gently swept away, discreet and thoughtful service provided as standard.

Consequently, the resorts are something of a cocoon. Critics say a stay here is too perfect, too boring. But that's why most people come: to recharge and forget the urgencies of their daily lives. They don't want to move – an Ayurvedic massage is activity enough. There is a little island-hopping on the *dhoni* water-taxis or the occasional seaplane. There's a kind of town-and-gown separation between the tourists and the Maldivians. If they do mingle it is in Malé, the capital on the atoll of Kaafu, where the islands' Islamic status is reinforced by two mosques – the Grand Friday, whose golden dome lights up the skyline, and the centuries-old Hukuru Miski. The Islamic influence dates back to 1153 and survived the interference of Portuguese, Dutch and British colonialists before independence from Britain in 1965.

A high birth-rate provides a separate challenge to the islands' restricted resources. The turquoise waters, white sand and thatched villas may offer a paradigm of paradise, but Eden's problems will have to be addressed.

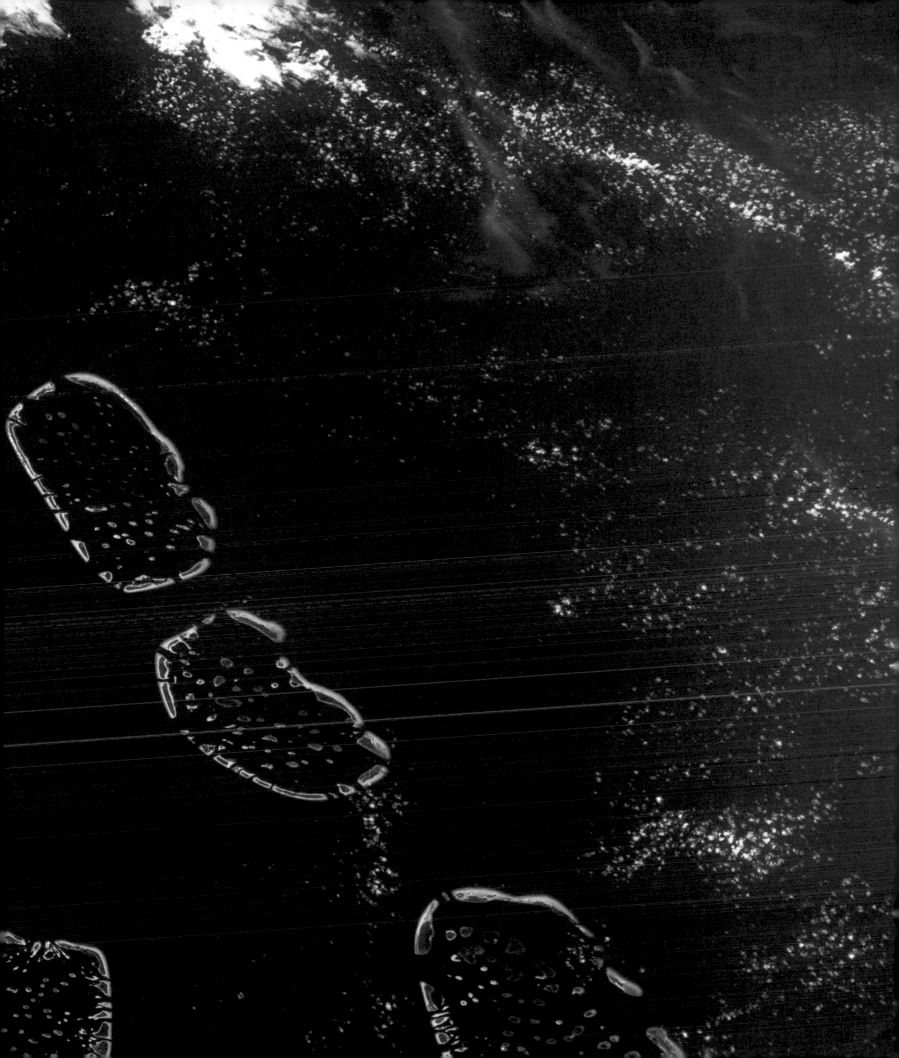

Lakshadweep

ARABIAN SEA

In recent years the southern Indian state of Kerala has adopted the mantle held for so long by Goa as the destination of choice for the generation of would-be hippies who still see the subcontinent as the place for people in search of themselves. But lying just far enough beyond the surf of Kovalam beach off the Malabar coast, the islands of Lakshadweep – also still known by their Dutch name, the Laccadives – require just that little extra imagination and energy, and this ensures their continued isolation.

The exotic name, which seems so apt for these green islands, actually means "a hundred thousand islands". Although scattered like emeralds in the Arabian Sea and suggestive of some insular version of the *1001 Nights*, there are in fact only thirty-six of them, from the Amindivi group in the north to Minicoy in the south, plus twelve various atolls, reefs and submerged banks.

Together they form the tiniest Union Territory of India, although a peculiarly Hindi and enlightened form of Islam is practised on many of the islands. This found its way here in the eighth century, when the Muslim Saint Ubaidullah was shipwrecked and allegedly acted out a vision of the Prophet Mohammed to bring the word of the Qur'an to these parts. After passing by on his travels, Marco Polo referred to the Laccadives, and in particular Minicoy, as "the island of females". Perhaps he was referring to the fact that here property passes down the female line, and women can divorce and remarry without discredit.

After Polo came the Portuguese, who coveted for their ships the finely spun coir matting that is still made here. The Portuguese attempted to establish forts but were summarily expelled. The islands fell under British control in the nineteenth century, after accepting a loan from that imperial island. The loan was intended to repair damage caused by a cyclone, but the Keralese Raja – the only Muslim royal family of India – found it could not keep up the repayments, and so the islands passed to the British East India Company.

Built on ancient volcanic formations, the islands together form one vast coconut garden. Each island typically has a lagoon on one side and a reef on the other, the green and blue ocean separated by a fine white spit of sand. With the deposition of windward sand on the leeward side, the islands are slowly advancing eastwards. Just ten of them are inhabited, subsisting on coconut and tuna-fishing, with Kavaratti the administrative centre. The lighthouse at Minicoy is the only sign of human settlement that can rank as a sight. Thus the indigenous population is largely outnumbered by the shoals of butterfly fish, the manta rays and the odd whale shark – and the Indian honeymooners – that increasingly come to feed on their shores.

"The Indian Ultima Thule."

Tim Mackintosh-Smith, travel writer

Lakshadweep, Union Territory of India **Alternative name:** Laccadive Islands **Longitude:** 72° 30' E **Latitude:** 10° 57' N **Area:** 32 sq km (12 sq mi) **Archipelago area:** 77,700 sq km (29,990 sq mi) **Highest point:** 6 m (20 ft) **Population:** 60,600 **Capital:** Kavaratti **Natives:** Ali Raja of Cannanore, Rajiv Gandhi **Resident:** St Ubaidullah

"On Kerguelen, weather is not
a backdrop but a foreground to
your life: a rogue variable, wrecker
of plans. Man proposes here;
the wind disposes. It has blown
a score of human dreams away."

Matthew Parris, *journalist*

Kerguelen

SOUTH INDIAN OCEAN

Among the obvious destination islands, there are others that appeal precisely because of their extreme locations, exotic in their own way. One such is Kerguelen, hurled by some centrifugal force way out into the sub-Antarctic reaches of the South Indian Ocean. For the tropical island-hopper whose idea of a major expedition is to flip-flop across to the poolside bar and back, the prospect of Kerguelen might seem unattractive. But what draws potential visitors to try to secure a berth on the one ship that visits twice a year is its very isolation – an elemental reality and the chance to see some rare and endangered wildlife.

The archipelago is named after Yves-Joseph de Kerguelen-Trémarec. After sailing to these islands in 1772, but unable to land on them, he returned to France and promptly announced to his sponsor, Louis XV, with a certain amount of licence, that he had discovered a wonderful new territory, "La France australe". The king sent him back to claim it. Once again Kerguelen could not land, but this time he and everyone on board could see this was definitely not the promised land of bounty (when Captain James Cook sailed past he had called it Desolation Island). Although Kerguelen incurred Louis XV's displeasure, the islands remained French, as a TAAF, one of the Terres Australes et Antarctiques Françaises: the territory in total is about the size of Corsica.

On Grande Terre, the main island, a cluster of hardy scientists lives all year round; these *hivernants*, or winterers, live in a clutch of bases, some, like Port Jeanne d'Arc, a Norwegian whaler base, now abandoned. Port-aux-Français, the main base, is a collection of fifty buildings, quarters, labs, workshops with a gym, cinema, library and bar for light relief. Kerguelen is sub-Antarctic, and therefore not ferociously cold, but it is constantly windy, in the path of the Furious Fifties, winds of above 150 kilometres (93 miles) per hour: the only chapel on the island is called Notre Dame Des Vents. With rain or sleet forecast for three hundred days of the year, Kerguelen is definitively not on the package-holiday radar, and for many that is a point in its favour.

The landscape of fjords and inlets around Mount Ross and the Cook Glacier may be treeless, but there is wildlife. Teams from the base go out to study the Kerguelen cabbage, *Pringlea antiscorbutica*, good for fighting off scurvy as the name suggests (a population of imported rabbits enjoys nibbling them). Thankfully the fur and elephant seals – once hunted to the point of depletion – are back in force. And albatross parents leave their chicks in Kerguelen's care while they sweep hundreds of kilometres afield looking for food, bringing it back to their tiny offspring by using their extraordinary inbuilt satellite navigation.

BELOW An Elephant Seal with Royal Penguin chicks

Kerguelen, Terres Australes et Antarctiques Françaises **Alternative names:** Îles Kerguelen, Desolation Island **Longitude:** 69° 10' E **Latitude:** 49° 15' S **Area:** 7,215 sq km (2,785 sq mi)
Highest point: 1,850 m (6,070 ft) Mt Ross **Population:** 75 **Principal town:** Port-aux-Français

Mauritius

INDIAN OCEAN

The tourist industry of Mauritius recycles the quote about the island and heaven as though it had been written by Mark Twain. The truth is that Twain – in his book *Following the Equator* – merely credited it to a nameless citizen to prove how high an opinion Mauritians had of their home. The author himself was rather more sardonic, commenting that Mauritius possessed all the superficial appeal of a park or garden: all show and no depth.

Indeed, the Mauritius that greets the visitor can seem banal: the landscape is often unremarkable – characterized by the endless fields of sugar cane that has long provided the island's main income, not to mention some local rum with a healthy kick.

Each new crop of tourists is spun centrifugally to the resorts, at Flic-en-Flac or le Saint-Géran, that ring the coastline within now sadly dilapidated coral reefs, and where the waters of the Indian Ocean, white sands and coconut palms create a self-contained but undeniably pleasant tropical holiday world.

The authentic charms of Mauritius emerge more subtly. Inland, there is a spicy blend of France, England and India – the last thanks to the dominant immigrant influx. Brightly coloured hand-painted signs, frangipani and bougainvillea suggest Goa or Kerala. French influence, from the days when Paris controlled this critical staging post, remains strong, especially in the Creole language. Traces of the British (who ran the place for the best part of two hundred years) are far less frequent, and the occasional graffiti supporting West Ham FC comes as a shock.

The capital, Port Louis, a hubbub of markets and US-style malls, has a colonial centre where taxis loiter beneath baobab trees, as their passengers penetrate the rundown Natural History Museum to see a reconstruction of the dodo, that slow-moving spoon-billed turkey hunted to extinction on the island by colonial rifles. Incredibly rare, but at least still extant, the Mauritius Blue stamp in the postal museum gives philatelists a frisson.

Away from Port Louis's hustle, some civilized calm is offered by the verdant alleyways of the Pamplemousses botanical gardens or at tea on the verandah of Eureka, an elegantly preserved plantation house in the shadow of one of the islands' rocky crags. The moods of Mauritius flit and change, just as the clouds that scurry from the central massif out to the coast never linger, scudding on to reveal a patch of dazzling sunshine. Eventually the island's subtle charms become as insidious as the pulse of the *ravane* – a large goatskin *bodhrán* that provides the seductive beat for the *sega* dance created by homesick slaves, and which is now performed for the enjoyment of tourists in the flickering light of beachside bonfires.

OPPOSITE The Trois Mamelles mountains overlooking Tamarin Bay

Mauritius, The Republic of Mauritius **Alternative names:** Île Maurice, Moris **Longitude:** 57° 33' E **Latitude:** 20° 17' S **Area:** 1,865 sq km (720 sq mi) **Highest point:** 828 m (2,712 ft) Piton de la Petite Rivière Noire **Population:** 1,250,800 **Capital:** Port Louis **Natives:** Malcolm de Chazal, Marie-José Coutonne, Ti Frere, Robert-Edward Hart, Xavier Le Juge, Hervé Masson, Loys Masson, Edouard J. Maunick, Seewoosagur Ramgoolam, Joseph "Kaya" Topize, Khal Torabully, Jean Uranie **Resident:** Bertrand-François Mahé de la Bourdonnais

"Mauritius was made first,
    and then heaven.
Heaven was copied after Mauritius."

Local saying, quoted by Mark Twain

Réunion

INDIAN OCEAN

Despite being 9,000 kilometres (5,592 miles) from Paris, Réunion island (once known as Île Bourbon after the ruling house when it was taken over in 1649) is politically part of France. It is an overseas *departement*, a county like the Dordogne sitting in the Indian Ocean, rather than a colony – only without the English second home-owners – and enjoying the same rights as "la metropole", as mainland France is known to locals.

To the eyes, nose and taste buds, Réunion (renamed in 1792 after the union of two French regiments) seems superficially at least very much a little corner of France. The smells of freshly baked baguettes, cheeses and patés waft out from boulangeries and charcuteries in Saint Paul and Saint Benoit. The currency is the euro (supported more unanimously than by the mainlanders and the first place in France for the currency to be used when the mayor of the capital, Saint Denis, bought a bag of lychees in the market). The EU flag flies fervently atop the county's administrative buildings. The

paradoxically named village of Hell-Bourg was recently recognized as one of France's most beautiful villages, and it is only the prevalence of painted wooden houses and banana leaves here that betray a more island-like, rickety, rural lifestyle. That and its location east of Madagascar.

Réunion is not an island of beaches and relaxation, however. Sculpted by volcanic eruptions and erosion it is a steep and mountainous place, a paradise for hiking and *l'escalade* – mountaineering; the Nepal of islands. At 3,069 metres (10,069 feet), the extinct giant Piton des Neiges towers above the island next to the very-much-alive Piton de la Fournaise, circled by a trio of magnificent volcanic amphitheatres with the exotic names of Cirques de Cilaos, Salazie and Malafate. The last is now a much-needed national park. Beneath and surrounding these, thriving in the fertile volcanic earth, lie meadows like the Nez du Boeuf, seemingly transported from the Auvergne, the sandy red Plaine des Sables reminiscent

of *Close Encounters*, and dense and untamed forests such as the Belouve-Bebour, more often than not infused with swirling mist. Beneath its fronds grows a multitude of herbs and medicinal plants much sought-after by the island's tisaneurs: liquorice, vanilla, cinnamon and the local cannabis – *zamal*.

Despite the French veneer, Réunion is very much Creole at heart, a fusion of African, Indian and European, Catholic, Hindu and Islam. Once *les marrons* forced to work on the sugar plantations escaped, forging pathways through the interior and seeking refuge from bullets in the îlets or hamlets that still bear their haunting names. Now, however, the ethnic magma of this island is set and lives happily together in a model that is decades ahead of the mainland. Hindu temples are scattered around the island, the air is thick with the scent of *cari* and *rougail* (spicy tomato salsa) and resounds to a common patois lilt, African-style rituals celebrating the dead, and the rhythms of *meloya* and *sega* Afro-European fusion music.

"Do you remember, my beloved Nenere
The little bouquet you gave me
It faded a long time ago
And reminds me how far away you are
Little faded flower
Little beloved flower
Tell me always."

Georges Fourcade, "P'tite fleur aimée", national song of Réunion

RIGHT La Poste

Réunion, Département d'Outre-Mer, France **Alternative name:** La Réunion **Longitude:** 55° 32' E **Latitude:** 21° 07' S **Area:** 2,511 sq km (969 sq mi) **Highest point:** 3,069 m (10,069 ft) Piton des Neiges **Population:** 753,812 **Capital:** Saint Denis **Natives:** Jean Albany, Raymond Barre, Valérie Bègue, Antoine Bertin, Léon Dierx, Georges Fourcade, Axel Gauvin, Roland Garros, Michel Houellebecq, Auguste Lacaussade, Charles-Marie-René Leconte de Lisle, Granmoun Lélé, Évariste de Parny, Blanche Pierson, Jackson Richardson, Jeanne-François Samlong, Firmin Viry

Seychelles

INDIAN OCEAN

With an indigenous and emblematic coconut the shape of the female bottom, and flowers with moist white petals protecting a snow-white bud called clitoria, Fregate, Praslin, Cousine and the rest of the Seychelles seem bent on ensuring the fourth ingredient after sun, sand and sea in the litany of traditional guaranteed delights of island paradises. Even Queen Victoria – a statue of whom stands in the gardens of the high court in the capital Victoria on the main island, Mahe – is there not as the head of an empire but as a symbol of fertility.

And fertile these islands surely are, a mini Madagascar of exotic animal life. Here the giant tank-like aldabra tortoises roam the golf courses of Fregate (there are rumoured to be more tortoises on these islands than people). Here also are hawksbill turtles nesting on a migratory pit-stop on Cousine, giant hairy millipedes and armoured beetles, the rare magpie robin, geckoes and myriad sea life from dolphins to visiting whale sharks and manta rays. Here is where vanilla, cinnamon and cashew nuts grow wild in a lush green jungle of towering sandragon and frangipani trees. And on Praslin, in the World Heritage Site of Vallée de Mai, grows the famed love nut and world's largest seed.

In these isles nature has hewn some of her most wondrous work, be it the polished boulders like *menhirs* or Brancusi sculptures on Fregate, the muscovado sugar sand of Anse Victoria beach, or the pink granite formation of Les Trois Frères that sits above the capital and announces the islands from afar. It has been suggested that the Seychelles are the sunken utopian continent of Lemuria; unlike any *arriviste* atoll or volcanic *parvenu*, they are islands that have a history dating back to when the continents of India and Africa were wrenched apart.

History is something the Seychelles has much to celebrate of as well. For while twin otters ferry honeymooners between the isles of Curieuse, Bijoutier, Silhouette and Alphonse, they perhaps miss the story told in Victoria's Bel Air cemetery. This new French settlement is reportedly where Louis XVII was buried after fleeing the French Revolution. In the nineteenth century, the British brought the freed African slaves whose Creole descendants make up most of the population. In between there were pirates and in 1977 a socialist revolution that chased out jet-set real-estate owners such as Peter Sellers and George Harrison before democracy was restored to the islands in the 1990s. And what better symbol of that democracy than the silver-faced replica of Big Ben that looks over the wigged barristers of a tropical Westminster in Victoria, thousands of kilometres but only four hours away from London; and of course the fact that they drive on the left.

OPPOSITE Coco De Mer Palm seed

Seychelles, The Republic of Seychelles **Local name:** République des Seychelles, Repiblik Sesel **Longitude:** 55° 27' E **Latitude:** 4° 35' S **Area:** 453 sq km (175 sq mi)
Archipelago area: 400,000 sq km (154,400 sq mi) **Highest point:** 905 m (2,970 ft) Morne Seychellois **Population:** 80,650 **Capital:** Victoria **Natives:** Patrick Victor, Jean-Marc Volcy

"'Admiralty are having trouble with their new fleet base in the Maldives. Communists creeping in from Ceylon. Strikes, sabotage – the usual picture. May have to cut their losses and fall back on the Seychelles… Just go and have a look.' M glanced out of the window at the driving March sleet. 'Don't get sunstroke.'"

Ian Fleming, *For Your Eyes Only*

> "It takes a man of wisdom
> to write on water."
>
> Sheikh Mohammed bin Rashid al Makhtoum

Palm Jebel Ali

PERSIAN GULF

Thus spake the man whose vision lay behind the Palm Trilogy, the set of extraordinary real-estate projects intended to create three date-palm tree-shaped island archipelagos – Jebel Ali, Jumeirah and Deira – from reclaimed land off the coast of Dubai. In case anyone be in any doubt of the conviction that underpins the sheikh's Joseph-like dream, these words are also one of four verses spelt out by the boardwalks around each palm frond, to be read from the air: "Take wisdom from the wise", "Not everyone who rides a horse is a jockey" and "Great men rise to greater challenges". One of the key lessons of the Christian Bible was that wise men didn't build their houses upon the sand. But in Dubai it seems the sheikh – descended from a line of humble Bedouin chiefs and now the omnipotent prime mover and poet of this tiny Arab emirate thanks to some clever Dutch engineering – has been able to prove that parable wrong. Most definitely not a case of "any dream will do".

But is it all folly, or is it in fact good, forward-thinking business sense? The sheikh is ensuring Dubai's future for a time when the oil that has secured the emirate's wealth thus far runs out. The three island projects combined will quadruple Dubai's coastline and enable it to attract overseas investors in Dubai real-estate. Meanwhile, the coastline of this burgeoning city will be filled with marinas, water theme parks, hotels and, further inland, Dubailand – a Las Vegas-meets-Disney style leisure park including indoor skiing in the desert and an ersatz distillation of the best of the world's founding cultures from Europe to the Orient. The latest highest building in the world will be here, at 800 metres (2,623 feet) standing taller than the iconic Burj hotel that already seems a historic building in this city of the new. One hundred and thirty-five million cubic metres of rock, sand and limestone will have been dredged up from the Persian Gulf (by imported Indian workers on a pittance) to realize a dream that will be visible from outer space and be a self-styled Eighth Wonder of the World.

The sheikh has been inspired to recognize that beyond the old world of oil, there is the possibility of attracting fifteen million tourists a year to such delights and to redress the image of Islam in the post 9/11 world. In establishing the emirate as a financial, communications and tourism hub, he wants not only to replace what the Lebanon once was for the Arab world, but also to rival London and New York, and put the Arab world at the heart of the modern world.

Socotra

INDIA OCEAN

Like a time capsule dropped into the Indian Ocean a couple of hundred kilometres from the Horn of Africa, Socotra is, for botanists in particular, a living reliquary of plants that have disappeared from great swathes of the world. The reason is simple: isolation. Having broken away from the mainland of Africa 250 million years ago, and by virtue of the surrounding roughness of the seas and demanding swirls of the winds, it is rarely available for visitors. With access slightly improved by the construction of an airport in 1999 (but only slightly, since the monsoons restrict access between June and September), ecotourists are able to discover the thrill of seeing a virtually prehistoric landscape intact.

Prime among the botanical lures is the dragon's blood tree, *Dracaena cinnabari*, its unmistakable inverted canopy described variously as an inside-out umbrella or a verdant mushroom. Created, so the tale goes, from the blood spilt in a heavyweight title clash between a dragon and an elephant, its sap is a source of cinnabar, which in times past served as a bright scarlet dye (vermilion) used in stained glass and to colour the wood of violins, and as a stomach medicine and a fixative for wobbly teeth. The Socotrans still use cinnabar for stomach ache, to colour wool and glue pots, and as a lipstick.

Socotra also produced frankincense, myrrh and the bitter aloe, which is why on an island where the infrastructure is still simple, where Bedouin tents are set up under star-laden skies beneath mist-covered mountain ranges, the feel of the place is positively Old Testament. The clouds around the tops of the granite Haghier mountains supply moisture to the high-living plants – a third of Socotra's eight hundred plant species are unique to the island – while down on the limestone plateaus, succulents including giant cucumber trees give the landscape there the look of the southwestern United States.

Once called "a forgotten footnote of Arabia", this former British protectorate (now part of Yemen, although Somalia has a claim on the island) is surrounded by coral reefs and rich fishing stocks, although the local fishermen have to battle the tempestuous ocean to land any catch. Modernization in Socotra is arriving at creeping pace. The low stone houses of the main town, Hadiboh, are safe from gentrification just yet. Even the building of some new roads, however, has had an impact on the wildlife, making it easier for illegal bird collectors to snare rare falcons. UNESCO and both international and local environmentalists are working hard to ensure that Socotra's extraordinary and natural gene pool is preserved for centuries to come.

OPPOSITE A grove of dragon's blood trees

Socotra, 'Adan Governate, Republic of Yemen **Local name:** Suqutra **Longitude:** 53° 54' E **Latitude:** 12° 30' N **Area:** 3,625 sq km (1,334 sq mi) **Highest point:** 1,525 m (5,000 ft) Haghier mountains
Population: 65,000 **Principal town:** Hadiboh

"It was the plants that fascinated us most.
Whatever the Darwinian equations in force here,
they had produced fantastical results. It was the
botanical equivalent of Dictionary Land, the semantic jungle."

Tim Mackintosh-Smith, travel writer

Bahrain

PERSIAN GULF

A veiled Muslim culture and the smallest Arab state – in the shadow of the tourist cult of Dubai and to most a tedious stopover and refuelling point for Pacific-bound jumbos – the Kingdom of Bahrain was perhaps a logical hiding place for the reclusive and erstwhile King of Pop, Michael Jackson. Never happy in his own skin Jacko, a sometime resident since 2005, was once reported by friends as "feeling increasingly Bahraini". Certainly the multi-million dollar contract handed to him by Prince Abdulla of the reigning royal family to make two albums for his Two Seas record label was a source of encouragement.

Two Seas is also the meaning of the word "Bah-rain", describing as it does Bahrain's landscape of freshwater springs surrounded by the salt water of the Persian Gulf. Site of the ancient civilization of Dilmun, central to the Sumerian creation myth, Bahrain is thought by some to be the Biblical Garden of Eden, but there is little nowadays among its largely flat and featureless landscape to evoke such lushness and abundance. Nevertheless, Bahrain was always regarded as the Pearl of the Persian Gulf – no doubt because of the considerable pearl-diving industry on which its fame and economy were built right up to the early twentieth century.

Because of its position, Bahrain has always been fought over – by Assyrians and Babylonians, Greeks and Persians, as well as Iranians, who until recently still contested the sovereignty of her thirty-three islands. Under the local Abbasid dynasty, the Kingdom of Bahrain had power enough, with land stretching from modern-day Basra in Iraq to Oman, to sack Mecca and Medina and bring back the sacred "black stone" from these shrines of Islam.

Bahrain truly became an Eden again in 1932 – certainly as far as Henry Ford and the local Arab capitalists-in-waiting were concerned – when the first oil in the Middle East was struck

there. This became an ingredient of mass addiction that initiated the West's dependency on Arab resources; it also caused, justified and sustained all the politics, conflicts and peace processes that ensued in the region.

No Arab state is truly an island, and indeed Bahrain is conjoined to both its neighbours. It connects to Saudi Arabia via the King Fahd causeway, while the planned Qatar-Bahrain Friendship Bridge is set to be the largest fixed-link in the world. Bahrain has built on the riches that came, after the British withdrew in 1971, from being the open-minded financial hub of the Middle East while Beirut was burning in civil war. The island is now reaping the benefits as the centre of Formula One racing in the region, complete with her own grand prix, and a port in a storm for an unlikely musical patron.

> "The land of Dilmun is holy, the land of Dilmun is pure. In Dilmun no cry the raven utters. Nor does the bird of ill-omen foretell calamity. The lion kills not, nor the ravening wolf snatch away the defenceless lamb!"
>
> *The Epic of Gilgamesh*

OPPOSITE Al Fateh Mosque

RIGHT A creation by Bahrain fashion designer Maryam Wadiee

Bahrain, The Kingdom of Bahrain **Longitude:** 50° 35' E **Latitude:** 26° 00' N **Area:** 665 sq km (257 sq mi) **Highest point:** 122m (400 ft) Jabal ad Dukhan **Population:** 738,800
Capital: Al Manamah **Natives:** Layla Al-Sayed, Ali Mohammed Falah aka Dboy, Qassim Haddad

"May I announce to you that Madagascar is the naturalist's promised land?
Nature seems to have retreated there into a private sanctuary."

Philippe de Commerson, explorer

OPPOSITE Walking home near a baobab tree

Madagascar, Republic of Madagascar **Local name:** Madagasikara **Longitude:** 47° 00' E **Latitude:** 20° 00' S **Area:** 592,000 sq km (228,500 sq mi) **Highest point:** 2,876 m (9,436 ft)
Maromokotro **Population:** 19,448,800 **Capital:** Antananarivo **Natives:** D'Gary, Régis Gizavo, Jaojoby, Dama Mahaleo, Paul Bert Rahasiman aka Rossy, Etienne Rambotiana aka Bouboul,
Ricky Randimbiarison, Justin Vali

Madagascar

INDIAN OCEAN

Far too few people have experienced the impact of Madagascar, a huge island (the fourth largest in the world) with remarkable natural bounty. Should visitor numbers begin to rise, as long as it is in a controlled, managed, orderly fashion, then some much-needed currency will reach the Malagasy people. This is a very poor island. Only a third of the islanders have drinking water. Life expectancy is low, the birth rate sky high. In Antananarivo, the capital set in the highlands, there are posh hotels in former French colonial chateaux that sadly contrast with the quality of life outside the gates.

Both the islanders and the wildlife on Madagascar are simply trying to survive, but the ages-old practice of *tavy*, a technique of "slash-and-burn" farming in the forests, imported from Polynesia by the earliest settlers, does little to protect vital vegetation and soil quality. They are destroying the very forests that house the mammals – the lemur in particular – which are all indigenous to Madagascar, home to five per cent of the world's plant and animal species, including seven species of baobab tree. The trademark silhouette of the baobab is a symbol of survival: a standard-sized tree on top of a gargantuan trunk, which acts as a reservoir – clever design, beautiful execution, vital supplies.

One area of the island that has escaped the incursions of *tavy* is the northern tip of Madagascar: it is too difficult to access other than by boat or light plane, so amongst the *tsingy*, the limestone pinnacles or karsts, the rarer birds and animals have a moment of peace.

They only encountered humans perhaps as recently as two thousand years ago. Those first settlers were followed by a trail of Polynesians, Arab traders, Portuguese, pirates, British and, for seventy-odd years from the 1880s, a French protectorate (the island was swapped by the British in exchange for Zanzibar), whose officials were fond of relaxing in the hot springs of the interior. Now Madagascar requires a different kind of protectorate: a humanitarian and environmental one.

When DreamWorks launched *Madagascar*, the animated story of four urbanite animals from New York's Central Park Zoo learning to survive amongst their wild cousins, it felt obliged to explain exactly where Madagascar is – way down off the southeastern coast of Africa. If a generation of kids also learnt not only the island's location, but something about its history, culture and wildlife, then that was no bad thing: they may be the ecotourists of the future.

"This is the finest place I have known in all of Africa
to rest before starting my final journey.
It is an illusive place where nothing is as it seems.
I am mesmerised."

Dr David Livingstone

Zanzibar

INDIAN OCEAN

If it hadn't been for the Heligoland treaty in 1890, this island-byword for paradise and exotic Proustian residence of dreams might have been German. Exchanging balmy and aromatic East African assets for a cold, largely barren but strategic rock in the North Sea, the Germans relinquished all claims on the Zanzibar archipelago. This ensured the islands remained British long enough at least for its famous native, Farrokh Bulsara, to claim British citizenship and bequeath a musical legacy in English. Otherwise Freddie Mercury, whose father was a middle-ranking cashier in the British Colonial Office from a family of Parsis from British India, might have ended up going the synthesizer route along with Kraftwerk or singing Nena-style post-war rock.

Zanzibar's fame is now more exotic, as it vies with neighbouring Lamu to be the *de rigueur* destination for wealthy honeymooners seeking luxurious isolation on its many smaller islands. However, it was once – as its name, thought to be from the Persian "coast of blacks", suggests – far more nefarious. A rich trading centre whose wealth was founded on cloves, nutmeg, cinnamon and pepper, Zanzibar was also the centre of the East African slave trade, an industry that contributed to the state's affluence. Livingstone and the British eventually stamped out the slave trade, and an Anglican cathedral now stands on the site of the former slave market. But the winding alleys of Stone Town, the World Heritage Centre of Zanzibar Town on Unguja island, with its bustling bazaars, and the grand Arab mansions with their carved and brass-studded wooden doors, echo with the guilt of these evil profits.

Zanzibar was first discovered by Vasco da Gama and until 1698 it was owned by the Portuguese. It was then briefly the capital of the sultanate of Oman – to which time dates the incongruous grandiosity of Sultan Bagkash's 1883 House of Wonder. In 1963 Zanzibar gained independence before becoming officially part of Tanzania. Since then it has lurched precariously towards fundamentalism, banning homosexuality and even prohibiting celebrations of what would have been Queen Freddie's sixtieth year. The king of rock, however, would be pleased to know that the *taarab* wedding music and love songs of his first homeland, played on Arabian flutes and zithers, is beginning to ride the wave of Western popularity that has carried on its crest music from Buena Vista in Cuba to the sounds of Mali and Bamako. And he would surely have spearheaded the full-moon parties that take place among the *dhows* out on the beaches at Kendae Rocks.

OVERLEAF Women fishing off Nungwi Beach

Zanzibar, Tanzania **Longitude:** 39° 12' E **Latitude:** 6° 12' S **Area:** 1,660 sq km (641 sq mi) **Highest point:** 120 m (492 ft) **Population:** 984,600 **Capital:** Zanzibar City
Natives: Abdulrazak Gurnah, Freddie Mercury, Ali Hassan Mwinyi, Emily Ruete

"Cerulean lake, let this thy mission be."

Chauncy Maples, first Bishop of Likoma

Likoma

LAKE NYASA

The name of the East African Rift Valley lake in which Likoma sits is a matter of dispute. The nation of Malawi calls it, with obvious territorial pride, Lake Malawi, while most of the rest of the world has opted for Lake Nyasa. The island itself belongs to Malawi, but it is actually within Mozambique's territorial waters and so is known as an "exclave" (Tanzania also has some as-yet unresolved claims over parts of the lake).

That Malawi secured the island was due to proselytizing British missionaries heading east from what was then Nyasaland and reaching the island before the Portuguese colonists of Mozambique thought to expand westward. The British arrived in the 1880s, led by Chauncy Maples, a Middlesex-born Old Carthusian and Oxford theological student, driven by a zeal to convert Africa to Christianity. He and his friend Will Johnson were part of the explorer David Livingstone's University Mission to Central Africa, and it was through their energy and zest that Likoma became the centre of Anglicanism in the country.

Chauncy Maples was made Bishop of Likoma, but in 1895 he drowned in a boating accident on the lake. (With a surface area larger than Wales, the lake is as unpredictable as the open sea.) His legacy remains in two wonderful objects. In his memory the other missionaries commissioned a steamboat, built on the Clyde and shipped to Likoma in kit form: the two-year journey of its eleven-tonne boiler alone was the stuff of *Fitzcarraldo*, lugged over the rapids, waterfalls and boulders of the Zambesi. The steamboat is still in active service.

The second legacy is truly extraordinary. St Peter's Cathedral was built on the island in the 1900s, modelled on and the same size as Winchester. The magnificence of its carved sandstone and stained glass stands in stark contrast to the impoverished rocky granite island, with its eucalyptus, mangoes and baobab trees, and thatched cottages. The crucifix above the altar was created out of wood from the *mvula* tree at Chitambo in Zambia, under which Livingstone's heart was buried. Like the steamer, the cathedral, in a state of constant restoration, is working still, with a small but loyal congregation.

For non-believers, Likoma – with no roads, a handful of cars, no running water (but no malaria) – is an offbeat backpacker and occasional honeymoon destination. There are trips on a *dhow* over to the nearby island of Chizumulu, or steamer crossings to Malawi over the clear waters of the lake, which are full of rare perch-like cichlid fish, and offer excellent snorkelling and diving as long as you keep an eye out for cruising crocs.

ABOVE St Peter's Cathedral

Likoma, Malawi **Longitude:** 34° 45' E **Latitude:** 12° 03' S **Area:** 17 sq km (7 sq mi) **Altitude:** 470 m (1,542 ft) **Population:** 9,000 **Principal town:** Likoma
Residents: Will Johnson, Chauncy Maples

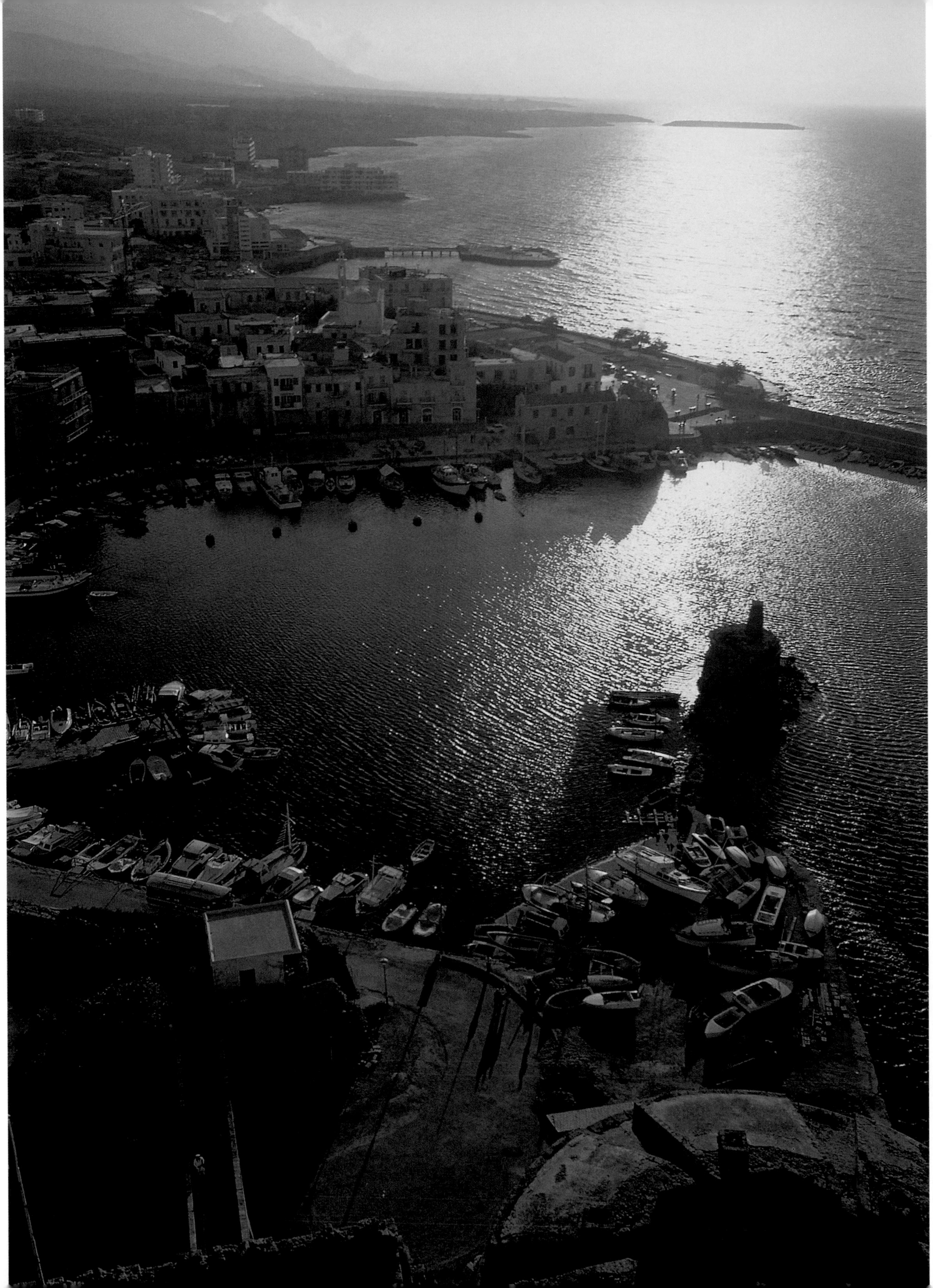

Cyprus

MEDITERRANEAN

"Full of goddesses and mineral springs; ancient castles and monasteries; fruit and grain and verdant grasslands; priests, gypsies and brigands..."

Lawrence Durrell, *Bitter Lemons*

Unlike the other Greek islands, which despite their distinctive characteristics are satellites of Greece, Cyprus is a nation all of its own – a status it shares with Malta alone of all the islands in the Mediterranean. An immense national pride and a sense of autonomous identity lies near the surface of life on this guitar-shaped island, the haloumi-flavoured easternmost outpost of the West in the Med. This pride finds an outlet in the lashings of overwhelming *meze* and *zivania* firewater-fuelled hospitality bestowed upon the visitor, and in the loquacious tales of their homeland expounded by the Cypriot diaspora that seems to make up most of the hairdressing population of London.

Delight in this treasure-bedecked rock is justified. To Cypriots, when it comes to comparing antiquities, Greece is a young upstart rival. Cyprus was, after all, the fair isle where Aphrodite was born – at the Petra tou Romiou near Paphos to be precise – spawning numerous tavernas in her name. She reputedly bathed on the northern shores of the otherwise undeveloped and fragrant cyclamen and juniper-studded Akama peninsula, where loggerhead turtles still come to breed. Another beauty, Cleopatra, was given the island by Mark Anthony, and Richard the Lionheart took time out from the Crusades to marry Berengaria of Navarre in northern Kyrenia. In Cyprus the aura of absolute romance hangs heavy in the air over the scattered ruins of immense cultural achievement. Here lie the necropolis of the kings at Paphos, the Roman amphitheatre and gymnasium at Salamos, a cathedral modelled on Rheims in the northern trading port of Famagusta, and any number of sumptuous and affluent monasteries that cloister the island's interior and which, away from the capitalism of the coast, reveal the real roots and traditions of a mountain-bound monastic people – none finer that the monastery at Kykkos in the Troodos mountains. This is the island where amid the Lebanon cedars of 1,951-metre (6,401-foot) Mount Olympus you can even ski.

Cyprus is also still something of a divided nation – one of the few left in the world – partitioned in 1974, when the Turks invaded to protect the Turkish minority in the north following a Greek coup. The two halves of the island lived apart for decades until, in 2004, the Anatolian-Hellenic cold war was brought to a blurred end. The Green Line can now be passed freely, although the church spires and minarets of the capital, Nicosia, remain bizarrely separated by watchtowers and sandbags. The bisected city has the charged energy of transition (not least thanks to the Russians treating it as an offshore banking haven). This energy reverberates across the island, belying Lawrence Durrell's mulberry "tree of idleness". As Greek and Turkish Cypriots offer one another an uneasy welcome, the once-desultory and old-fashioned Turkish north of Famagusta, Bellapais and the Kapas panhandle or guitar fret, is catching up with the easy tourism and entrepreneurialism of its southern cousins and newly rediscovered compatriots.

OPPOSITE Kyrenia Harbour

LEFT A Greek-Cypriot boy in front of posters supporting reunification

---

Cyprus, The Republic of Cyprus **Longitude:** 33° 28' E **Latitude:** 35° 08' N **Area:** 9,250 sq km (3,571 sq mi) **Highest point:** 1,951 m (6,401 ft) Mt Olympus **Population:** 788,500
Principal town: Nicosia/Lefkosia **Natives:** Marcos Baghdatis, Hussein Chalayan, Archbishop Makarios III, Asil Nadir, Osman Türkay, Anna Vissi, Zeno of Citium **Resident:** Lawrence Durrell

Rhodes

DODECANESE, AEGEAN

The famous knights so often connected with Malta were originally the Knights of the Hospital of St John and Jerusalem – and they came from Rhodes. Here they held out against siege by the Ottomans for two hundred years, before surrendering and being granted safe passage off the island. They chose Malta as their new home. The Knights of St John are celebrated on Rhodes in the name of the cobbled main street – Street of the Knights – in the island's old town. Little remains of the Grand Masters' palace, destroyed in 1856 by an accidental gunpowder explosion, but vestiges remain of the mansions that once stood for each of the Inns – more like Masonic lodges than taverns – which represented each of the countries participating in the Order. There were the Inns of Provence and Auvergne, the Inn of the Spanish and the Inn of the English. The Inn of the Germans existed but has never been traced, although this Masonic order is reminiscent of the fencing Heidelberg Burschenschaft representing the state of Germany that Mark Twain wrote about so amusingly in *A Tramp Abroad*.

When the Knights came together in the fourteenth century their intention was to create a protective union against the evil and advancing Ottoman Empire. It worked well until the knights were simply outnumbered. Mosques, minarets, Christian watchtowers, a Jewish quarter, a hammam, libraries, art galleries and Orthodox churches can still be seen scattered among the honey-coloured stone alleyways. Six hundred years on, the modern incarnations of the knights – the European Union and NATO – have a lot to learn from the prototype of Rhodes.

Perhaps the resolve of the European Union has yet to be tested, and it is too busy revelling in times of peace that instead of marauding conquerors have brought equally invasive and impossibly large cruise ships – incongruous against the medieval proportions – to these shores. Down the east coast at Faliraki, England's finest used to parade, turning the town and in particular "Bar Street" into a pleasure dome of happy hours, yards of beer, screaming karaoke, wet T-shirt competitions and binge drinking. This was a bacchanalian orgy of which the ancient Greek God of alcopops Dionysus would surely have approved, until a British teenager was killed in a nightclub brawl in 2003, causing the tourists to stay away.

Rhodes Town and Faliraki are all most will have seen of the island, forsaking the pleasures locals keep for themselves, including the ruined castle at Kristinia, the beach at Fourni, the slumbering villages of the foothills and Attaviros mountains that form the island's spine, right down to the moorlands and hippy commune of surfers and Westfalia campervans on the southern tip of Prasonisi.

ABOVE Street of the Knights (Ippoton Street), Rhodes Town

OVERLEAF Mandriki Harbour

Rhodes, Dodecanese, Greece **Local name:** Rhodos **Longitude:** 28° 10' E **Latitude:** 36° 15' N **Area:** 1,400 sq km (540 sq mi) **Highest point:** 1,215 m (3,986 ft) Mt Attavyros
Population: 117,000 **Principal town:** Rhodes City **Residents:** Apollonius of Rhodes, Hipparchus, Dionysus Thrax, Tiberius

"Rhodes, where history lies sleeping."

Freya Stark

Kos

DODECANESE, AEGEAN

The father of modern medicine, creator of the oath that doctors traditionally swore, Hippocrates was the most enduringly famous of a clutch of celebrated sons of Kos: the poet Philitas and the painter Apelles were also born on this Dodecanese island – the group's second largest, nosing up like an inquisitive dolphin to the coastline of Turkey. The legacy of Hippocrates continues to resonate on Kos. In the principal centre, Kos Town, stands the antique plane tree on Plateía Platanou, planted by Hippocrates himself in 400 BC or thereabouts, according to local lore. The fact that the tree has been dated at only half a millennium old does not diminish the myth. Southwest of Kos Town stand the columns of the fourth century BC ruins of Asklepieíon, a hugely significant site in Greek history, built to continue Hippocrates' practices, and dedicated to Asclepius, the god of healing (one of whose daughters rejoiced in the name Panacea).

The island of Kos is fertile and lush – it is sometimes called "the Floating Garden": aficionados of the classic Caesar salad will be familiar with the texture of the Kos or cos lettuce (also known as romaine). In keeping with the mild climate, a sense of verdant and holistic harmony imbues Kos. Although its location tight in to Asia Minor gave it an importance both as a fortification and a trading post, the history of Kos has been relatively calm, interrupted only by a relatively infrequent earthquake – Kos Town had to be rebuilt after one in 1933 – or corsair attack, thankfully a rarity today. Kos seems untroubled and unruffled by the past occupation by Alexander the Great, the Romans, the Ptolemies, the Knights of St John and four centuries of Turkish rule. Kos Town's avenues are wide and green, lined with palms and garlanded in hibiscus or jasmine.

Around Mount Dikaíos, on the central ridge of the island, the traditional Asfendíou villages are whitewashed and narrow-alleyed. A short distance away, the craggy Byzantine fortress of Palaió Pyli protects a church built by Christodoulos shortly before he headed to Patmos to found the Monastery of St John. These are a far cry – and a distant bassline – away from Kardámaina, the resort to the south where the nightlife is pumping. Kos Town straddles the two faces of the island. The 1933 earthquake brought to light extensive archaeological treats, including the Casa Romana and its theatre, but the town is crowded and its harbour, high on yachtie activity, nestles beneath the Castle of the Knights, designed to protect the island against the Ottomans.

> "Healing is a matter of time, but it is sometimes also a matter of opportunity."
>
> Hippocrates

OPPOSITE The palm-lined beach below the Castle of the Knights

LEFT The plane tree of Hippocrates shading an old sarcophagus

Kos, Dodecanese, Greece **Alternative name:** Cos **Longitude:** 27° 15' E **Latitude:** 36° 50' N **Area:** 290 sq km (112 sq mi) **Highest point:** 846 m (2,776 ft) Mt Dikaíos **Population:** 30,900
Principal town: Kos Town **Natives:** Apelles, Hippocrates, Philitas **Resident:** Notis Sfakianakis

Samos

NORTH AEGEAN

"Fill high the cup with Samian wine! Leave battles to the Turkish hordes."

Lord Byron, "The Isles of Greece"

I f Kos, a couple of hundred kilometres south in the Dodecanese, can claim a number of notable offspring, not least Hippocrates, Samos – part of the North Aegean group – can reel out an impressive roster of its own. Its star name is that of Pythagoras, the philosopher and mathematician whose hypotenuse theorem ($a^2 + b^2 = c^2$) has been drummed into generations of schoolchildren. Among his fellow Samiots are the astronomer Aristarchus, a pioneer of belief in a sun-centred universe, and the philosopher Epicurus, the original epicure.

Aesop lived here, and Hera, the goddess of fertility and nature, was believed to have been born on Samos. She would be an appropriate native, since the island – "the green pearl of the Aegean" – is rich in vegetation. The Samian wine of which Byron wrote was already being consumed in 1200 BC, made from the Muscat grape, which has a sweet, intense nectar. Olive trees are plentiful, and if you drive the road encircling the island, hugging the cliffs and following the indents of the coastline, the overwhelming fragrance is that of herbs and cypress.

Although the island, bereft of nightlife and hotspots, is quiet and its villages undeveloped, Samos was not always a sleepy backwater. In the 530s and 520s BC, its majestic fifty-oared triremes, the fastest of their kind, helped the benevolent tyrant Polycrates wield an impressive naval power. When eventually its maritime strength was reduced, however – and after the collapse of the Byzantine Empire – the island imploded and was as good as abandoned during the sixteenth century, until the Ottomans came along and restored it to health by attracting back the descendants of the diaspora.

There is great antiquity on Samos. At the Heraion, Polycrates' vast temple for Hera, a solitary reconstructed column remains to hint at how impressive the site must have been. The extraordinary tunnel of Eupalinos is a thousand-metre-long aqueduct built to channel deliveries of Samos's famously clear water, a piece of construction that Herodotus declared one of ancient Greece's most astonishing achievements (Eupalinos, a hydraulics expert, was so good in his surveying that the two ends of the aqueduct met precisely at the first attempt).

However, the main town of Vathy is relatively young: its harbour area dates only from the 1830s. In 1955 the ancient capital Tigani had its own makeover and was renamed Pythagóreio. A new generation of arrivals is now trying to make the journey across the few kilometres that separate Samos from Turkey, as a rapidly increasing number of African migrants set out on what they see as a short (though sometimes a fatal) journey to a land of freedom.

Samos, North Aegean, Greece **Longitude:** 26° 50' E **Latitude:** 37° 45' N **Area:** 477 sq km (184 sq mi) **Highest point:** 1,434 m (4,705 ft) Mt Kerkis **Population:** 33,800 **Principal town:** Vathy
Natives: Aristarchus, Epicurus, Polycrates, Pythagoras, Rhoecus, Theodorus **Residents:** Aesop, Herodotus

ABOVE Statue of Pythagoras

Leros

DODECANESE, AEGEAN

Leros is unique among Greek islands for reversing the stereotypical image of higgledy-piggeldy arrangements of cuboid whitewashed houses with blue wooden shutters, cobbled streets and rickety tavernas. Instead it is home to possibly the only piece of urban planning on any of Greece's myriad islands.

The port town of Lakki on the western coast was once the Greek outpost (then known as Port Lagos) of Mussolini's expanding Mediterranean empire, built by occupying Italians in a manner that reflected their dictator's imperial ambition and a debased classical style. Lakki has the deepest and therefore safest harbour in the Mediterranean, and ownership of the island also gave the Italians a strategic stranglehold on sea-trade routes between Europe and Africa. It was for this reason that Mussolini hailed the island as the equivalent of the Allied island bastion against the Japanese invasion of the Philippines.

They bulldozed whole swathes of muscatel vineyard together with the existing homesteads, then inhabited by a mere four thousand souls, to make way for a garrison town that could hold thirty thousand. They planted eucalyptus to drain the marshland waterfront, and on it they built an avenue fit for military parades, complete with lamp posts bearing the *fasces* emblem of branches and axe heads. This they lined with unique *palacinos* – one or two-storey detached houses built for navy personnel – and a series of public buildings that are strangely urban for a location so rustic and remote.

These include the tall cylindrical tower of their town-hall headquarters, a primary school with circular open-air meeting area and sweeping staircase, the theatre, now a cinema, with its Art Deco lobby and original popcorn machine, and the strange stark vertical shaft of St Nikolaos Church, now Orthodox but originally Catholic for the Italian invaders.

These buildings all share distinctly un-Hellenic clean lines and plain façades, with rounded balconies, portholes, tall thin windows and features such as wooden shutters that fold up into the walls. It is as though Le Corbusier or Mies van der Rohe had pioneered their ideas here. Lakki claims to have the highest concentration of Art Deco buildings outside Miami, but this is not exactly Miami Beach. Nor is it candy-coloured. Or even technically Art Deco. It is rather something in between that has been described as rationalism or "ignored internationalism". Whatever name it takes, however, it is a startling example of a pioneering twentieth-century architecture only replicated outside Lakki in Sabaudia north of Rome.

The Italians always had a unique concept of war – more inclined to fall in love and integrate than occupy, as depicted in the film *Mediterraneo*. It seems they left many friends among the Lerians, many of whom still speak fluent Italian and who are very grateful and even proud of the unique cultural real-estate their former *maestri* left behind. This is just as well, since every August Italian holidaymakers undertake a modern-day invasion of their Italianate former outpost in the Dodecanese.

Leros, Dodecanese, Greece **Longitude:** 26° 50' E **Latitude:** 37° 10' N **Area:** 53 sq km (20 sq mi) **Highest point:** 320 m (1,050 ft) Kleidi **Population:** 8,200 **Principal town:** Agia Marina

"Leros is the Corregidor of the Mediterranean."
Benito Mussolini

Patmos

DODECANESE, AEGEAN

Above the white cube houses of Chora – a village on Patmos dotted by multiple chapels and churches – rises a somewhat dour, highly imposing fortress. This citadel is in fact a building of deep religiosity and faith: the Monastery of St John. Fortified to repel unbelieving marauders, the monastery was founded in 1088 by the Blessed Christodoulos, a monk who had travelled to Patmos to honour St John the Divine. This northern Dodecanese island was where, after being exiled in AD 95, St John wrote the Book of Revelation. The outpouring of writing followed a series of visions, which appeared to him in a cave that is now part of the Agia Anna church. God's voice issued from the rock. John recorded the visions by dictating them to his pupil and amanuensis Prohoros, and created the final book of the Bible. Revelation 1:9 runs: "I John, who also am your brother, and companion in tribulation, and in the kingdom and patience of Jesus Christ, was in the Isle that is called Patmos, for the word of God, and for the testimony of Jesus Christ."

For the best part of a millennium Patmos has been a focus for pilgrims. The monastery itself displays relics of Christodoulos (who was elevated to sainthood), a treasury full of jewels and icons, a rare sixth-century codex and a hallowed twelfth-century icon of St John himself. Because Patmos is somewhat off the main tourist track, visiting the monastery can be hard work – adding to the requisite feeling of arduous travel. The final hike up cobbled pathways and steps adds a tiny coda of effort.

It is said that in ancient times, Patmos sat on the floor of the sea and could only be seen when Selene, the goddess of the moon, shone her beams on it. Artemis caught sight of the island and decided she would like to have it. As Artemis's father was Zeus, ruler of all the gods, it was a done deal. Zeus merely had to sort out the small print with Poseidon.

You might wonder why Artemis made such a fuss, as Selene's half-light made it look substantially more attractive than the reality. This is a rocky island of barren hills, with frankly little of note outside St John. Skala, the port that lies on the shore below Chora and the monastery, is a typical Greek marina, and there are a couple of beach destinations among the inlets and isthmuses that make up Patmos's coastline. The only oddity is Kalikatsou, a column of rock jutting up from the bay of Grikos, which was used by hermits, and to which there was rumoured to be a tunnel that ran all the way from the monastery in Chora.

> "Patmos was a double monastery: a natural monastery whose landscape and life was dominated by an actual one, and therefore doubly hospitable to miracles and visions."
>
> Thurston Clarke, historian and writer

OPPOSITE The Monastery of St John

Patmos, Dodecanese, Greece **Longitude:** 26° 36' E **Latitude:** 37° 21' N **Area:** 34 sq km (13 sq mi) **Highest point:** 269 m (883 ft) Profitis Ilias **Population:** 3,100
Principal town: Chora/Patmos Town **Natives:** Konstantin Lahanas, Emmanuel Xanthos **Residents:** Hosios Christodoulos, St John the Divine, Prohoros

Lesbos

NORTH AEGEAN

Fertile, with a vulva-shaped lagoon penetrating to its core and the two adjacent, breast-like peaks of Lepetymnos and Olympus, the island Lesbos has the topography to justify its passage into common parlance – at least as an epithet – to describe the presumed sexual persuasion of its most famous native and resident. A paradise for bird-watching, Lesbos does not only provoke classroom sniggers; in a bizarre attempt to re-enact some ancient myth and turn the island into a lesbian shrine, it is actively promoted by some tour operators as a destination for women-only holidays.

It is true that the female Greek poet Sappho was born at Eresos on the island, and that although much of her poetry was lost it was seemingly enjoyed for its powerful emotional content directed at women. But Sappho was no precursor to feminism. Her verse has been distilled for the purposes of headlines and pigeonholed into something far simpler and more carnal, so that even her name has passed into common language as a synonym for lesbianism.

In fact, Lesbos was the name of the ancient Greek patron god of this island tucked up by the coast of modern-day Turkey. Lesbos is sometimes referred to as the Emerald Isle because of the estimated eleven million olive trees that cloak her surface in a dark green. The fortress and capital of Mytilene, in particular, stands on seven verdant pine-clad hills, with the imposing outsized dome of the St Therapou church towering over the port, whose depths the Greeks deliberately cobbled so no invading ship could drop anchor. This is where Aristotle lived when he first began his systematic studies in the field of zoology, together with Theophrastus, the father of botany, and the great historian Theophanes, who chronicled the campaigns of Pompey. Mythology would have it that here also are strewn the dismembered head and limbs of Orpheus and the lyre given to him by Apollo.

Nowadays the riches of Lesbos are founded on the more prosaic industries of olive oil, soap and ouzo, and the island remains unspoilt and among the lesser-visited of the Greek archipelago. Its name and fame, however, have long been secured as unwanted as the slur of easy virtue.

Lesbos, North Aegean, Greece **Alternative name:** Lesvos **Longitude:** 26° 20' E **Latitude:** 39° 10' N **Area:** 1,632 sq km (630 sq mi) **Highest point:** 968 m (3,176 ft) Mts Olympus and Lepetymnos
Population: 90,600 **Principal town:** Mytilene **Natives:** Arion, Doukas, Sappho, Terpander, Theophanes of Mytilene, Theophrastus **Residents:** Aristotle, Epicurus

"Some say an army of horsemen,
an army of infantry,
Or a fleet of ships is the fairest thing
On the face of this black earth;
but I say
It is whatever one loves."

Sappho

ABOVE The shops in Paleohori

TOP The statue of Sappho in Mytilene

Santorini

CYCLADES, AEGEAN

"The Pompeii of the Aegean."

Ferdinand Fouqué, geologist

They are truly picture-postcard views. The photographs of the panorama from high up in Santorini, overlooking the bay, are frequently selected by the Greek tourist office as one of the seminal images of their country, and have been reproduced so often that they are seared into our communal travel consciousness.

In fact, Santorini (the name was given by the Venetians in the thirteenth century in tribute to St Irene) is an atypical Greek island, since the island it was once has disappeared. It was ripped apart in 1450 BC by a volcanic eruption, leaving bits and pieces of the volcano's outer rim still standing as five islands around the central, vast and now Aegean-filled caldera. Santorini's beaches – Perissa, Kamari and Vlichada – are black, red and ash-grey, so hot underfoot that flip-flops are essential wear; the cliffs are vertiginous. The eruption also left a deposit of white fragments, or tephra, that still coat parts of the islands. Fumes continue to hover; there is a sulphurous after-taste.

But this very sense of destruction, this awareness of the fragility of the Earth's crust, has its own attraction, and Santorini has become one of the most romantic destinations in Greece – the overall harshness of the landscape offset by the clutter of ochre, white and blue buildings, domed churches and barrel-roofed houses, that ripple along the top of the cliffs in Thira or Oía. And there are wonderful sunsets courtesy of the lingering haze.

This mini-archipelago, the southernmost of the Cyclades group, was originally one island called Stroggli until the volcano let rip. One theory holds that the debris and fall-out descended on Crete and wiped out that island's Minoan civilization. On Santorini life was eradicated for three centuries. Now the ruins of Akrotiri – not to be confused with the RAF base in Cyprus – are the most celebrated Minoan site outside Crete. They were first discovered in 1866, then rediscovered in 1966 and its houses, storerooms, staircases, storage jars and frescoes delicately uncovered by a team under the Greek archaeologist Spyridon Marinatos (the ruins took his life, as he was killed by a fall of stones on the site).

Santorini is vibrant. It has not tried to preserve or protect itself from modern life. The caldera is always full of massive ships transporting liner-loads of Mediterranean cruise-goers to Skalá Firón, the port below Thira, accessible by *télépherique*. Appropriately for this volcanically created location, Santorini has also become a different kind of hotspot, with plenty of bubbling nightlife, which takes over once the last evening cocktail has been dispatched on the terrace bars of Thira.

OPPOSITE Orthodox church in Imerovigli

OVERLEAF The village of Oía

Santorini, Cyclades, Greece **Longitude:** 25° 27' E **Latitude:** 36° 23' N **Area:** 73 sq km (28 sq mi) **Highest point:** 566 m (1,857 ft) Profitis Ilias **Population:** 11,900 **Principal town:** Thira

Mykonos

CYCLADES, AEGEAN

"That's right Millandra, I'm going to Greece
for the sex! Sex for breakfast! Sex for dinner!
Sex for tea! And sex for supper!"

Willy Russell, *Shirley Valentine*

In the 1980s and 1990s Mykonos symbolized the grubby package-tour face of charter flights, unfinished apartment blocks and a diet of ropey **retsina** and meatballs or all-day English breakfasts that the Greek islands presented to the holidaying public. The island's more upmarket Cycladic partner across the water, Santorini, never fell out of grace or favour in the same way, but perhaps the Greeks in the know (and in particular the Athenians) never stayed away. Now Mykonos has regained its former status as an expensive magnet for the *beau monde*, complete with designer shops, boutique hotels and restaurants where *kleftikos* and *dolmades* are rarely on the menu.

Jackie Onassis set the trend first time round, buying a villa here in the 1960s and attracting a multitude of Greek shipping magnates in her wake. For a time Mykonos was to Greece what St Tropez and the Amalfi coast were to France and Italy. A villa on Mykonos was one of the must-haves of the Athens social scene. The fact that the island then slipped off the radar saved it from high-rise development, so when Willy Russell's disenchanted housewife Shirley Valentine arrived from Liverpool in 1989, she fell in love with rosé sundowners against a still-idyllic backdrop of the whitewashed sugarcube houses with turquoise wooden shutters, ubiquitous cats and pink geraniums in olive-oil cans of popular imagination. The precise location where Shirley spent her sunsets is overlooking the gritty shale beaches of Agios Ioannis. It was enough to send a new wave of holidaymakers and real-estate hunters to Mykonos in search of a place in the sun and a photo opportunity in front of the island's corn windmills, which stand like sentinels on the crescent-shaped harbour front.

At the same time, Mykonos opened its arms to the gay community and the flock of ravers and deejays that had made the Balearics their home. Mykonos became a Greek Ibiza. The iconic 1960s Theoxenia hotel, designed before the word "hip" existed, was reborn. In the summer it still grooves to a Café del Mar beat, and even if Pierros and other bars have been surpassed by the haunts of Spain's Sitges as gay destinations of choice, down on beaches such as Super Paradise the pink pound is one the island embraces. Meanwhile, in downtown Hora or Mykonos Town and in the artist communities such as Little Venice, with its pastel-shaded, overhanging Ottoman-style wooden balconies, there is an atmosphere of theatrical campness. For all this surface and sophistication, however, in the maze-like alleyways and little squares you are just as likely to come across lines of pegged washing and timeless tavernas as art galleries.

OVERLEAF Mykonos Harbour and waterfront

Mykonos, Cyclades, Greece **Longitude:** 25° 25' E **Latitude:** 37° 30' N **Area:** 87 sq km (34 sq mi) **Highest point:** 364 m (1,194 ft) **Population:** 6,600 **Principal town:** Mykonos Town
Resident: Manto Mavrogenous

Lauttasaari, Helsinki, Finland **Longitude:** 24º 52' E **Latitude:** 60º 10' N **Area:** 3 sq km (1 sq mi) **Population:** 19,000 **Resident:** Keijo Pctäjä

Lauttasaari

GULF OF FINLAND, HELSINKI

Lying not quite in the heart of Helsinki, but only a few kilometres west of the Finnish capital's centre, the island of Lauttasaari is a somewhat quirky miniature city within a city, home to nineteen thousand residents Its name means "ferry island", but Lauttasaari, its apartments and cottages a popular option for urbanites wanting a break, is now linked to the motherland by causeways and a bridge favoured by fishermen trying to land a batch of local Baltic herring.

This has been called "Helsinki's Manhattan", but although it is a sort of downtown island, there are no skyscrapers, yellow cabs or subway entrances here. Around the island's 10-kilometre (6-mile) perimeter, a footpath links the Baltic-pounded coastal south side with a gentler meadowed western shore scattered with woods of grey alder. At its northern end are odd bunker-style constructions – remnants of fortifications built, just in case, by the Russians during the Crimean War of the 1850s A century later Lauttasaari's dominant piece of architecture, its white concrete church, was designed by local resident Keijo Petäjä and built on Myllykallio Hill. Its high, slender, modernist belfry is the island's landmark, but it also symbolizes Finnish design innovation and Helsinki's urban expansion in the 1950s: at the same time, an industrial zone was established in the south of the island.

By far the most intriguing aspect of Lauttasaari is its saunas. In 1937 the Finnish Sauna Society was founded, its mission to protect the nation's heritage. The organization chose Lauttasaari as a base for four examples of traditional saunas, including the ultimate Finnish version, the smoke sauna. In the Middle Ages saunas were common across Europe, but without the steely Scandinavian determination

to enjoy the pure pleasures of dry heat, the majority of them lapsed into brothels. Up here in Lauttasaari, however, the received opinion is that you should behave in a sauna as you would in church. And there is a positively religious experience on offer. The smoke of the spruce-fired stoves rises like heady incense. The blend of the hot rooms and cold water plunge (off a jetty and into the bracing seawater for the truly brave), or the rigorous use of the loofah in the scrub rooms, is the sauna equivalent of a test of faith after the spirit has been immersed in *löyly*, the all-enveloping cocoon of cleansing steam and heat.

> "Share your tobacco and tinderbox, but not your sauna or your woman."
>
> Finnish saying

"He loved Crete like a living, warm creature
with a speaking mouth and weeping eyes;
a Crete that consisted not of rocks and clods
and roots but of thousands of forefathers
and foremothers who never died."

Nikos Kazantzakis, *Freedom and Death*

Crete

MEDITERRANEAN

Far south from the myriad Greek islands, the broad east west sweep of Crete looks like a barrier dam for the Aegean. It is the largest of the Greek islands, and the southernmost other than the sparsely populated dot of Gavdos between Crete and Egypt. Crete is a world apart, isolated and fiercely independent. The Cretans, proud of and ensconced within their mountains and gorges, have weathered the attentions and persecutions of successive waves of invaders and occupiers. In 1204 the Venetians took hold of the island and remained there until 1669. No sooner had that set of long-term house guests departed than the Ottoman Turks dropped in for another two centuries.

It was only in the 1890s, following a string of rebellions, that an independent Crete, inspired by Eleftherios Venizelos, achieved autonomy, and then became part of Greece in 1913. Three decades later Nazi paratroopers landed near Chania and successfully captured the island – although the German occupation was resisted all the way, as olive grove-shaded cemeteries testify. It is unsurprising, therefore, that there is a flinty, feisty, gnarly, individual quality to the Cretan character, but also a dramatic, life-embracing joy.

Although there are high-density holiday-destination strips on the coastal edges, no time spent in Crete should exclude a visit to the mountain ranges, plateaus, caves and gorges of the interior, clinging on for dear life as an apparently kamikaze taxi driver rides the hairpins with complete nonchalance. Any hypertension can be worked off by a hike down along the Samaria Gorge slicing down to the southwest coast, squeezing through the Iron Gates, just 3 metres (10 feet) wide, watching out for a sight of the kri-kri, Crete's wild goat, or the lammergeier vulture, before emerging onto, and even better into, the soothing sea water near Agia Roumeli.

There are thirty-four million olive trees in Crete, some a couple of millennia old. In fact, there is all the history you could wish for, from the Venetian fortress and harbour of Chania to the old Ottoman Nerantzes Mosque in Rethymno. No history is more specific to Crete than the Minoan remains, in ruined splendour at Phaestos or Gournia, or reborn in the Palace of Knossos restored by Arthur Evans. He was just one of the archaeologists amazed by what they discovered as they unravelled the mystery of the Minoan civilization, like Theseus following the yarn that led him out of the Minotaur's labyrinth.

ABOVE A row of *pithoi* at Knossos

OPPOSITE Samaria Gorge

Crete, Greece **Local name:** Kríti **Longitude:** 24° 52' E **Latitude:** 35° 15' N **Area:** 8,336 sq km (3,218 sq mi) **Highest point:** 2,456 m (8,058 ft) Mt Ida **Population:** 623,700
Principal town: Heraklion **Natives:** Pope Alexander V, Gianna Angelopoulos-Daskalaki, Francesco Barozzi, Odysseus Elytis, Epimenides, El Greco, Nikos Kazantzakis, Rena Kyriakou, Nana Mouskouri, Notis Sfakianakis, Maria Spiridaki, St Titus, Eleftherios Venizelos

Skiathos

SPORADES, AEGEAN

"There on the earth
of his small island,
atop the sea-throttled
cliffs, where the
waves seem to sing a
mysterious lullaby."

Alexandros Papadiamantis, writer

Beaches have been both the godsend and scourge of Skiathos. In a nation of islands whose coastline pleasures are generally of the rocky kind and where a sliver of sand is a rarity, Skiathos is blessed with beaches in abundance. Over the years their fine sand and travel-brochure blue sea has secured the patronage of those seeking a more bucket-and-spade holiday than the secretive pleasures of creeks and alcoves. This has, in turn, tarred the island with the brush of mass tourism and given it what Emperor Dionysius once called its "goat-trodden" air.

Another more eloquent and erudite ancient great, Sophocles, referred to the Sporades Islands as "the stormy, windswept home of valiant men". Skiathos is the most westerly of this group, which lies opposite the Pelion peninsula in northeastern Greece and whence Jason and his Argonauts reputedly set sail. It also incorporates the more virgin lands of Skyros, Skopelos and Alonissos.

Most photographed and vaunted of the beaches – arguably the most famous in all Greece and sold as a sort of Heaven in Hellas – is the golden crescent of Koukounaries (pine cone) beach. More recently, however, Skiathos has risen in popularity as a haven for nudists, and visitors to beaches such as the aptly named Banana, and even more aptly perhaps, Little Banana, are encouraged to bare all.

The beaches were not what attracted the Venetians to this "island in the shade of Mount Athos", the peak that towers over the northeast. They conquered this corridor in the thirteenth century and left behind the island's most interesting architectural relic, the Bourtzi – a small Venetian-style fortress mounted on an islet adjacent to the main settlement of Skiathos town, or Chora. After the Venetians left the locals weren't too impressed with the town and so moved their capital to Kastro, a fourteenth-century settlement that now lies atmospherically deserted. Like most of Greece, the island then fell under Turkish occupation, and Skiathos played a vital part in the rise of Greek nationalism. It was in the monastery of Evangelistria that patriots hiding from the Turks designed the white and blue pattern of the Greek flag – a standard that not only came to symbolize Greece's rebirth as a nation but whose colours are the whitewash and wooden-shutter livery of the entire Aegean landscape and of the Greece of popular imagination.

Skiathos, Thessaly, Greece **Longitude:** 23° 30' E **Latitude:** 39° 12' N **Area:** 48 sq km (19 sq mi) **Highest point:** 438 m (1,436 ft) **Population:** 6,200 **Principal town:** Skiathos Town
Natives: Alexandros Moraitidis, Alexandros Papadiamantis

ABOVE Mandraki Beach

Aígina

SARONIC ISLANDS, SARONIC GULF

The Saronic Islands, of which Aígina is the second largest, stretch south from Athens, and this makes the islands nearest to the Greek capital popular for weekend getaways or second homes. These islands in close proximity to Athens are virtually sea-bound suburbs, whereas the furthest-flung and least-known of the region's islands, Kythira, is way down south, just off the bottom edge of the Peloponnese.

Situated less than an hour by hydrofoil from Piraeus, Aígina offers an enticing relief from the Athenian smog, along with its smaller, nearby siblings Moni and Agkistri. Escaping here is hardly a recent habit. According to the mythological origins of the island, this was where Aígina, the nymph daughter of the river god Asopus and Metope, was installed as a mistress by the great Zeus, an all-powerful sugar-daddy who had already spotted the potential of Aígina as a handy love-nest.

The island once rivalled Athens for power and wealth. Relying on their nautical and trading skills, the islanders became extremely prosperous during the seventh century BC and were one of the first peoples to mint their own coins as currency. Athens' nose was put severely out of joint, to the extent that the Athenians conquered Aígina in 456 BC – the ancient-world equivalent of a hostile takeover.

In Aígina Town, known simply as *hora*, or "capital", there is a hint of metropolitan sophistication in the cafés and bars around the harbour, and there is a touch of Central Park tweeness in the horse-drawn carriages touting for business. Sponges and fresh octopus are on sale alongside fish, vegetables and pistachios from the orchards that grow in the stony but fertile plains in the island's northwest. By contrast, the south is quite barren, volcanic and mountainous.

There is a strong religious presence on Aígina. Part of the island's soundtrack is what seems to be the constant clack of worry-beads, and in the main town there is a host of churches, including the pure-white chapel dedicated to St Nicholas, patron saint of sailors, right on the perfect Greek island harbourside. Further inland pilgrims head to the Agios Nektarios, a huge Greek Orthodox cathedral – almost as large as Istanbul's Agia Sofia. It was built by and dedicated to Archbishop Nektarios, a Thracian who established a convent on the island and was canonized after his death in 1920 due to the healing powers of his relics. A much earlier religious site is the Temple of Aphaia – a gloriously preserved Doric example – dating from 490 BC and set up among pine trees in the northeast. Originally believed to be dedicated to Athena, in 1901 the German archaeologist Adolf Furtwängler found an inscription that determined this as a sanctuary of the local goddess Aphaia. It was a small, belated victory for Aígina over its Athenian neighbours.

> "On a clear day you can pick out the Parthenon from here with the naked eye. Way down below the sea is full of tiny crawling ships streaking the blue with their white wakes."
>
> Lawrence Durrell

BELOW The Temple of Aphaia

Aígina, Attica, Greece **Alternative names:** Aegina, Egina **Longitude:** 23° 28' E **Latitude:** 37° 45' N **Area:** 87 sq km (34 sq mi) **Highest point:** 532 m (1,745 ft) Mt Oros **Population:** 13,600
Principal town: Aígina Town **Natives:** Paulus Aeginetas, Onatas, Ptolichus **Residents:** Nikos Kazantzakis, St Nektarios

"You'd see three guys with their arms around each other,
stumbling up the stairs and singing these impeccable thirds."

Leonard Cohen

Hydra, Attica, Greece **Alternative name:** Ydra **Longitude:** 23° 27' E **Latitude:** 37° 20' N **Area:** 52 sq km (20 sq mi) **Highest point:** 590 m (1,936 ft) Mt Vlichos **Population:** 2,700
Principal town: Hydra **Native:** Panayiotis Tetsis **Resident:** Leonard Cohen

Hydra

ARGO-SARONIC GULF

While the 1960s' Athenian high society and international jet-set flocked in the wake of Jackie O to the newfound glamour of Mykonos, another, much smaller and overlooked Greek island quietly became a haven for a bohemian community of ex-pat artists. This second group shunned the material and superficial world and were drawn by the very simplicity of life on Hydra (meaning 'water') – albeit an exotic simplicity in the shapely form of Sophia Loren, who had played a voluptuous sponge-diver here in the 1957 film *Boy on a Dolphin*. In fact, so simple was life here in the 1960s that there were no telephones, no electricity and no plumbing; the main form of transport – as it still is today – was donkey or, in the absence of a four-footed parody, shanks's pony.

Most notable among those artists drawn to Hydra was the Canadian poet turned singer, Leonard Cohen. He moved here to escape the bustle of life in London, but was horrified to discover telephone poles and wires being erected. He would stare endlessly at these wires, in meditative depression at the thought that civilization had caught up with him and he was not after all going to be able to live the medieval life he had sought on Hydra. However, his spirits were raised when he saw that birds came to the wires – and that is how one of his most famous songs, "Bird on a Wire", first came to him. Then came the tuneful drunk locals by whom he was adopted and with whom he often caroused. The rest of the song flowed out. "Like a bird on a wire, Like a drunk in some midnight choir, I have tried in my way to be free." As Kris Kristofferson once said, this was "a good epitaph to have".

Today Hydra is a fashionable weekend retreat for wealthy Athenians – just 65 kilometres (40 miles) across the Hydra Gulf – and there are many places on the island anxious to claim a part in the Cohen heritage (a mini-industry he would no doubt deplore). The lugubrious and gravel-voiced "grocer of despair" met with other artists in a grocer's set back from the picturesque harbour of Hydra. This is the only settlement on this one-horse island, with its cannons, original battlements, and elegant eighteenth and nineteenth-century sea captains' mansions overlooked by the twin belfries of the monastiri church. The grocer's is now a baker's, but the wooden tables are still there, along with the faintest of echoes of Cohen's first formal concert.

The multi-headed snake of tourism has not yet overtaken the island, and it is still something of a hip hangout and a place for real philhellenes in Cohen's mould. The ancient springs from which the island takes its name have long since dried up, but as Cohen wrote of his chosen residence: "You can taste the molecules dancing in the mountains."

Ithaca

IONIAN SEA

"When you set out
    on your journey to
Ithaca, pray that
        the road is long,
full of adventure,
        full of knowledge."

Constantine Cavafy, poet

Ithaca has long been hailed as the birthplace of Odysseus. His long and difficult journey, his odyssey, no less – trying to return home from Troy to relieve his wife and family, but having to avoid Cyclops, Circe and Calypso along the way – was the inspiration for Homer's epic. "My home is under the clear skies of Ithaca," Odysseus says. "It is a rough land, but nurtures fine men." Now, however, we find that new academic research suggests that Odysseus's Ithaca might in reality have been Cephalonia, the adjacent island. For good measure, Homer's authorship has come under scrutiny – he may have been a talented editor who collated an existing oral history.

Homer called Ithaca "good for goats", and although that might seem a little dismissive, it is absolutely accurate. This Ionian island, one of the group along mainland Greece's western edge, is full of mountain passes and steep hillsides, and there are goats all over the place, nudging their way into deserted monasteries or gently tiptoeing across the coastal roads. A series of switchbacks leads up to the Monastery of the Archangels at Perahori, one of the highest points on Ithaca, from which the island's shape is revealed. It is long and slender, and virtually bisected by the bay of the largest town Vathi, with its immensely deep natural harbour. The name Vathi comes from *bathys*, meaning "deep" – as in bathos and bathysphere.

Outside Vathi, small red-roofed villages line the steep wooded inlets of the island's coastline. In Kioni, on the east coast, yachting flotillas stop off for supper (maybe the delicious local onion pie) before continuing their sailing holiday down through the Ionian Islands. These villages are also the starting point for mini-odysseys to the local bays via wooden motorboat, to pebbled beaches beneath terraced olive groves. Nobody else will disturb you – if another motorboat putters into view it will keep going to find its own quiet oasis. Water is the element of Ithaca, once the capital of all the Cephalonian states, and its islanders have always been admired for their navigational expertise and exploring mentality.

Many of Ithaca's mountain villages are now depopulated – their young journeying once again to find work – but Stavros, the northern capital, is still alive and well. And since they have a terracotta mask dedicated to Odysseus, and a bust of him in the town gardens, it might be wise to concur with the locals that they can keep on proudly claiming him as a native Ithacan.

Ithaca, Ionian Islands, Greece **Local name:** Ithaki **Longitude:** 20° 40' E **Latitude:** 38° 25' N **Area:** 117 sq km (45 sq mi) **Highest point:** 806 m (2,644 ft) Mt Nirito **Population:** 3,100
Principal town: Vathi **Natives:** Odysseas Androutsos, Anthony JJ & Marino Lucas, Ioannis Metaxas

The Åland Islands

BALTIC SEA

"People who live on islands are always letting their eyes glide along the horizon. They see the lines and curves of the familiar skerries, and the channel markers that have always stood in the same spots, and they are strengthened in their calm awareness that the view is clear and everything is in its place."

Tove Jansson, *The Summer Book*

The Åland Islands are spread across the Gulf of Bothnia in the Baltic, commanding a strategic position both into the Gulf of Stockholm and further north into the Gulf of Finland. They form part of the wider Archipelago Sea. This triangular apron of landmasses numbers between twenty thousand and fifty thousand islands, ranging from clumps and outcrops to sizeable human dwellings depending on your definition of an island. They are part of an ongoing process known by scientists as post-glacial rebounding.

The Åland Islands were the first test of the laws and resolve set out by the League of Nations formed after the First World War to intervene and promote peace in international conflicts. Ethnically Swedish but owned by Finland, the islanders had been torn between fear of russification at the hands of Finland and contempt at the rather feckless manner of their treatment by their supposed mother Sweden. They were veering towards independence when the League intervened in this custody battle and brokered a curious form of autonomy whereby the kids have the same passport as the mother – and she sees them at weekends and for holidays – but on a day-to-day basis they live with the father, Finland, who doesn't even speak their language.

There are a lot of children to look after. There is not just the main island of Fasta, home to half the population, but also six thousand other islands and skerries, of which about eighty are inhabited. A startling feature of the wider Åland family is the high number of twins. This is thought to be due to the presence of a uniquely strong twins gene among the population, exaggerated by a protein-strong diet of fish and a tendency to intermarry between cousins.

On many of the Åland Islands can be found just a solitary austere medieval church or Viking burial mound as the sole sign of human settlement – an idyll of meditation and man's closeness to nature. On other outposts of this "land of water" (from the original Germanic *ahvaland*) nature flourishes, be it flocks of migratory birds or rare northern orchids. It is really only on Fasta and in the capital of Mariehamm, or on Sund, Kokar and Kastelholm, that the accumulation of a long history of a proud seafaring people is visible. This can be found in the maritime museums, complete with beautifully restored four-master clippers, in the great fortress of Bomarsund, built by the Russians when they were first handed the islands by Sweden in 1809 and then bombed all but to smithereens by the British in the Crimean War, and in the proud spoils of the Island Games.

Åland Islands, Finland **Alternative name:** Ahvenanmaa **Longitude:** 20° 00' E **Latitude:** 60° 15' N **Area:** 1,512 sq km (584 sq mi) **Archipelago area:** 13,517 sq km (5,217 sq mi)
Highest point: 128 m (420 ft) Orddalsklint **Population:** 26,700 **Capital:** Mariehamn **Natives:** Anni Blomqvist, Sally Salminen

Corfu

IONIAN SEA

I t has often been said that Corfu is the least Greek of all the Greek islands. Location, location, location has much to do with that – the island is a backheel away from Italy's Salento peninsula, and its northern tip is a gnat's whisper from the coast of Albania.

Over the centuries, Corfu has absorbed a range of diverse influences: Byzantine, Goth, Angevin and Norman. The Venetians lingered for four centuries, and their mark is indelible, but they were also followed by the French and the British. The cricket ground, in the heart of Corfu Old Town, a one-time Venetian firing-range, was more safely reserved for explosive outswingers. Prince Philip, Corfu-born (on a kitchen table, according to his biographies), has of course been at the very heart of the British

establishment for more than half a century. Corfu residents point out that he has never been seen tucking into *gyros*, the local meat, chip and *tzatziki*-filled pitta bread. The British also came up with the name Corfu, as their traditionally bungled attempt to pronounce Kérkyra (how many place names in the world are the utterances of linguistically challenged sons of empire?).

Korkyra – like Aígina of the Argo-Saronic islands – was a daughter of Asopus and Metope. While Aígina flirted with Zeus, her sister Korkyra was enjoying a dalliance with Poseidon, who offered her the island. His gift was shaped a little like a sickle, with a northern third of limestone massif, a midriff of undulating hills, its south low and sloping and home to Benitses, the party capital of the island. Even in the winter months Corfu is a verdant palette of olives and cypress trees. Among the most famously wooded spots is Palaiokastritsa, on the northwest coastline, with its three coves. It is a view that prompted Lawrence Durrell to write: "The little bay lies in a trance, drugged with its own extraordinary perfection – a conspiracy of light, air, blue sea and cypresses." (His brother Gerald reminisced at length about the family's stay on the island in the 1930s.) Other literary figures were regular visitors and Edward Lear painted here.

Various European visitors have left their traces in Corfu Old Town. Its network of narrow tiled and cobbled alleys leads variously to two Venetian citadels and The Liston, a terrace of cafés straight out of the rue de Rivoli in Paris. They overlook the Esplanade, a little corner of Britain, complete with bandstand and until recently the cricket pitch (it was relocated after too many balls broke the windscreens of the cars parked nearby). Alas, the ancient marketplace, the Agora, and the Ionian Academy in the Hotel della Venezia were lost during Axis bombing in the Second World War.

OPPOSITE The Monastery of Palaiokastritsa

Corfu, Ionian Islands, Greece **Local name:** Kerkyra **Longitude:** 19° 50' E **Latitude:** 39° 38' N **Area:** 592 sq km (229 sq mi) **Highest point:** 906 m (2,972 ft) Pandokratoras **Population:** 109,500 **Principal town:** Corfu Town **Natives:** Felice Beato, Vicky Leandros, Prince Philip Duke of Edinburgh, Edith Somerville, Spyridon Xyndas **Residents:** Giacomo Casanova, Elizabeth Empress of Bavaria, Gerald and Lawrence Durrell, William Ewart Gladstone

"'Here in Corfu,' said Theodore, his eyes
twinkling with pride, '*anything* can happen.'"

Gerald Durrell, *My Family and Other Animals*

Gotland

BALTIC SEA

Less than a minute by longitude west of Corfu, by virtue of its northern latitude Gotland offers a completely different proposition, although it is equally European-influenced. During the thirteenth and fourteenth centuries – before it was conquered by the Danes – the capital Visby was the walled and fortified town at the centre of the Baltic trading alliance known as the Hanseatic League. The heritage of that long-ago mercantile power is still extant in the two hundred preserved buildings along the narrow winding streets of Visby, a rare and fine collection of early Gothic architecture.

Visby is known as "the city of roses and ruins", after the prolific red roses adorning the stone houses and the ruins, especially those of Visby's ninety-four medieval churches, which were left in tatters after the place was sacked. The Cathedral of St Mary, funded by levies on German merchants, dates from the twelfth century. Fiskargränd, one of the most popular of the rose-lined streets, provided a suitably imaginative location for the film versions of Astrid Lindgren's *Pippi Longstocking* stories.

Fictional versions of Gotland's history abound. The *Gutasaga*, or "Gotland's tale", recounts how this magical island would rise from the sea each evening and sink back down at dawn. Contemporary imagineers drawn by its slow-paced enchantments included the filmmaker Ingmar Bergman, who made his home on the tiny island of Faro just off Gotland's northern tip.

Like Chile's Easter Island, Gotland is working hard to maintain all aspects of its past, not just the medieval buildings of Visby, but also the burial cairns of the Vikings, who used Gotland as a handy stash for the bounty they acquired on their long-range raids. Among the coins and precious metals recovered by archaeologists is silver from as far afield as Baghdad.

Gotland is the largest island not only in Sweden (of which it became a part in 1645), but also the whole of the Baltic. The geology is limestone dominated. The stone is either covered with meadow plants – Gotland is renowned for its wildflowers, including wild orchids, vetch, poppies, harebells, dropwort – or thrusting up in the battered karst stacks called *rauks* along the coast. The beaches are full of shale and pebbles, ideal for building your own miniature cairn, and Gotland's southern location makes it a tempting summer vacation for the Swedes. They can relax with a game or two of *kubb*, one of Gotland's local pastimes, also known as "Viking chess", in which players try to knock over wooden blocks by throwing batons. Gotlanders are proud of their island's distinctive features, whether their offbeat sports, *gutnich*, their traditional language, or the herd of semi-wild Gotland ponies on Lojsta Moor.

"His astonishment was beyond words.
The blue sky lay before him, on the shore
a town with walls and towers, churches and
gabled houses, quite black against the blue sky."

Selma Lagerlöf, *The Wonderful Adventures of Nils*

ABOVE The city walls of Visby

Gotland, Sweden **Longitude:** 18° 33' E **Latitude:** 57° 30' N **Area:** 3,145 sq km (1,214 sq mi) **Highest point:** 84 m (276 ft) Lojsta Hed **Population:** 58,000 **Capital:** Visby
Natives: Susanne Alfvengren, Christopher Polhem **Resident:** Lennart Eriksson

"It is true that Robben Island was once a place of darkness, but out of that darkness has come a wonderful brightness, a light so powerful that it could not be hidden behind prison walls."

Nelson Mandela

Robben Island

TABLE BAY, CAPE TOWN

Flat, windswept and featureless, Robben Island lies just a few kilometres and a short hydrofoil-ride off South Africa's torrid coast at the point where two oceans – Atlantic and Indian, hot and cold – meet and crash against the Cape of Good Hope. Looking back, it is an appropriate vantage point for this land of keenly felt contrasts slowly coming to terms with a human playing field that is not quite but almost as level as its monumental Table Mountain backdrop. On the mainland, in the buzzing hub of Cape Town, commerce thrives: rocketing and desirable waterfront real-estate, a burgeoning film industry, liberated communities of artists and homosexuals, and shopping malls interspersed with aromatic cafés and gourmet restaurants. All of this can justify its existence because just off the coast lies a preserved yet needling and necessary reminder of the ghost that haunts South Africa's past, as sure as the tablecloth cloud that often shrouds its most famous mountain. Robben Island is South Africa's conscience.

The island was used as a penal colony long before its most famous inmate arrived. Under Jan van Riebeeck of the Dutch East India Company, the future founding fathers of the South African nation christened it "island of sins (robben)" and sent there anyone whose sin was to oppose colonial rule. Thus the first prisoner was the leader of the Khoikhoi tribe, Autshumato. When the British took over the Dutch East India Company they continued the tradition and treated the island much as they did Australia – as a home fit only for convicts, lepers, prostitutes, the mentally disturbed and, increasingly, marginalized ethnic groups. The only positive architectural feature of the island – a church designed by Rhodes' favourite architect, Herbert Baker – dates back to this period in the nineteenth century.

By 1963, shortly after the Afrikaners took over, it was noticeable that none of the inmates was white. Robben Island was supposed to be where Vorster and his cohorts could hide apartheid. Instead, however, the two square metres of his cell in B-Section became the most notorious patch of land on the planet. Until his release in 1990 the cause of ANC leader Nelson Mandela was taken up by freedom fighters and defenders of democracy across the world. The island became the cemetery of apartheid. It is testament to both his intellect and humanity – and to how much of a university the island was – that after twenty-seven years of mining the blinding stone of the lime quarry in cold winds, Mandela was able to utter the words "My country is rich in the minerals and gems that lie beneath its soil, but I have always known that its greatest wealth is its people, finer and truer than the purest diamond."

OPPOSITE Prisoner number 46664 revisiting his cell on Robben Island

OVERLEAF View of Table Mountain from the Island

Robben Island, Cape Town, Western Cape South Africa **Longitude:** 18° 22' E **Latitude:** 33° 48' S **Area:** 5 sq km (2 sq mi) **Highest point:** 30 m (98 ft) Minto Hill **Population:** None
Residents: Autshumato, Dennis Brutus, Makhanda, Nelson Mandela, Govan Mbeki, Tokyo Sexwale, Walter Sisulu, Robert Sobukwe, Jacob Zuma

Vaxholm
STOCKHOLM ARCHIPELAGO

"Neither the Alps of Switzerland nor the olive groves
of the Mediterranean nor the chalk cliffs of Normandy
could ever force aside this rival."

August Strindberg on the Stockholm archipelago

Vaxholm, Sweden **Longitude:** 18° 20' E **Latitude:** 59° 25' N **Highest point:** 112 m (367 ft) **Population:** 4,900 **Principal town:** Vaxholm

Go down to the Strömkajen quayside in Stockholm, next to the National Museum, the redbrick City Hall where the Nobel Prizes are doled out each year, and in the mornings there is a flotilla of steamboats, with all the clatter, clangs, fluttering flags, smoking chimneystacks and frantic activity that steam travel involves. The passenger boats are puffing themselves up in preparation for departure, just as they have for a century and more. All of them are ready to head out into the archipelago of islands that lies east of the Swedish capital: a total of twenty-four thousand, of every conceivable shape and size.

Vaxholm is the capital of the archipelago, 25 kilometres (16 miles) as the crow flies north-east of Stockholm. To get there the ferry has to wend a long and winding route, initially nosing out past the building that contains the almost perfectly restored seventeenth-century royal warship *Vasa*. This was the jewel of the Swedish navy but on its maiden voyage in August 1628 – en route to a naval base in the southern part of the archipelago – it sank ingloriously after less than a kilometre. The Vaxholm steamboat putters on for an hour and a quarter, past tiny skerries with a wooden shack and a flagpole flying the blue and yellow cross, past larger wooded islands with the lawns of luxury summer villas sweeping down to boathouses and jetties.

Vaxholm's little neighbour Vaxholmen was chosen as the location for a blockhouse fortification built in 1548 by the king, Gustav Vasa, as a defence against enemy invasion from the east. Later a citadel was raised on Vaxholm itself, and this still squats aggressively to the east of the island's small town, now a military museum. Until the 1880s there was little else here, but the island began to develop as a spa and became a popular destination for the older sisters of today's steamboats.

At the harbour the sense of a nautical existence continues: a gas station, ready to refuel the boats, rubs shoulders with cafés and hotels, including the elegant Hotel Vaxholm, dating from 1899. This is an easily walkable island – around small lanes, past wooden houses (a decree was passed that only permitted wooden buildings, which could quickly be burnt in case of siege). Around each corner there are green fields and sea views, and small businesses: art galleries, design boutiques, and a tearoom with – according to some of its habitués – the world's best vanilla bun.

Gamla Stan

STOCKHOLM

Gamla Stan, "the old town", sits right at the very heart of Stockholm, rich with the city and the Swedish nation's history, a living heritage centre that has nothing of the theme park about it. The streets, lanes and runnels are often narrow, none more so than the Mårten Trotzigs Gränd, which is less than a metre wide. An amble around Gamla Stan will touch on the past and present manifestations of Sweden's royalty, religion and parliament, alongside thirteenth-century cellars converted into jazz bars, and seventeenth-century houses purveying often (though not always) rather tasteful souvenirs: cute hand-painted clogs, miniature wooden models of the archipelago steamboats and warm winter woollies.

In fact, the island is not the oldest part of Stockholm. That honour goes to the adjacent islet Helgeandsholmen, site of the Swedish parliament. But Gamla Stan is old enough; it was first settled in medieval times and has been inhabited ever since. Despite all the proud mercantile mansions and public buildings, the island steadily fell into shabby disrepair for about a hundred years up to the 1950s, but in recent decades it has revived itself completely.

The royal palace stands on a quite steep slope rising up from the quayside of Skeppsbron, looking out over the central harbour area. The current building – still very much a working palace, with all the attendant uniformed guards, pomp and ceremony – was built at the beginning of the eighteenth century to replace the Vasa kings' palace, which had been razed by fire in 1697. The architect Nicodemus Tessin (who also completed his father's design for the enchanting Drottningholm palace west of the city) opted for an Italianate exterior. Gamla Stan is characterized by a mixture of styles in its great buildings, made oddly homogenous by all the russet, yellow and ochre townhouses along its streets. On the main square, Stortorget, the cathedral, Storkyrkan, has an Italian Baroque façade and a Gothic interior; the Axel Ostestiernhaus Palace is in the style known as Roman Mannerism; another palace, the stunning seventeenth-century Riddarhuset could have been transplanted from the Netherlands.

There is no better way to explore Gamla Stan than with a *flâneur*'s mentality, open to what lies around each corner: a museum (medieval, postal, numismatic, Nobel, one of each is here) or a long-running gastronomic treat: Den Gyldene Freden ("Golden Peace") first opened for business in 1722. Prepare to be pleasantly surprised by bumping into oddities like the statue of Stockholm's twentieth-century troubadour and balladeer Evert Taube, which stands in a corner of the small square Järntorget. He wears a beret and sunglasses, looking for all the world as if Jean-Paul Sartre were in town, though a gust of bracing Baltic air would clear any lingering existential nausea.

LEFT Guards at the royal palace

OPPOSITE Stortorget Square

Gamla Stan, Stockholm, Sweden **Longitude:** 18° 04' E **Latitude:** 59° 20' N **Area:** 1 sq km (0.4 sq mi) **Population:** 2,990 **Resident:** Emanuel Swedenborg

"Stockholm contains this secret of the North, mystery…
Episodes which touch on things beyond the world."

Hilaire Belloc

Korcula

ADRIATIC SEA

From the sublime city of Dubrovnik, the Dalmatian mainland slithers outwards and north into the Adriatic along the grey massif of the Peljesac peninsula. The peninsula's undulating body resembles a partially submerged Loch Ness Monster and creates a calm and protective channel on the mainland side. As the first significant island at the entrance to this channel, Korcula was a coveted guardian that for centuries invited attention and attack, and exchanged hands many times.

On one of these occasions, when the Republic of Genoa defeated its future Italian compatriots the Venetians, it took prisoner Korcula's most famous (claimed) native and sent him back to the Ligurian capital. There, in captivity, he penned one of the first travel books and secured his renown as one of the earliest and greatest explorers. His name was Marco Polo. Whether or not Polo was born on Korcula, in the thirteenth century house locals celebrate as his birthplace, it is easy to imagine a young seafaring islander inspired to explore the horizon by the magnificent view afforded from the top of the oval mound on whose flanks is built the essentially Venetian creation of Korcula town.

Though autonomous and never part of the Venetian Republic, the town was built at the zenith of Venetian culture, and despite their indubitable ferocity in conquering the Adriatic their cultural legacy means that history, and the locals, remember them kindly. This cultural bequest is symbolized most aptly by the magnificent cathedral of St Mark's, complete with gothic cornices, gargoyles and rose window, which took 150 years to complete. The town is accessed via a grand gate with triumphal arch, and many of the streets are lined with baroque villas from the seventeenth and eighteenth centuries. Not for nothing is Korcula sometimes referred to as "Little Dubrovnik".

The town's sinister switchback herringbone lanes and narrow, secretive and steep alleyways – as well as the densely wooded interior that inspired the Greeks to name the island "Black Corfu" – gave Korcula a pivotal role in the closing stages of the Second World War. Croatia was aligned with Nazi Germany and the Ustase, Croatia's Gestapo, had given the island to fascist Italy. However, the partisan resistance movement under the future Yugoslav president Josip Tito, numbering Churchill's envoy, the swashbuckling Fitzroy Maclean among them, found this secretive and shrouded island a useful base for covert operations and for preparing the land assault that eventually led over the massif into Bosnia and then on to a triumphal march on Belgrade.

The island found itself embroiled in the civil war that shook the Balkans at the disintegration of Yugoslavia, but it is now a peaceful and langorous museum of Venetian achievement set against a landscape of lazy lime groves, vineyards and Tuscan-style cypresses.

> "The wooded hills of Korcula stood out black against the pale sky."
>
> Fitzroy Maclean, *Eastern Approaches*

OPPOSITE The Good Friday procession

OVERLEAF Korcula town and cathedral

Korcula, Dalmatia, Croatia **Alternative name:** Cúrzola **Longitude:** 16° 57' E **Latitude:** 42° 56' N **Area:** 276 sq km (107 sq mi) **Highest point:** 568 m (1,863 ft) Klupka **Population:** 16,200
Principal town: Korcula **Natives:** Frano Krsinic

"In the midst of the empty, endless hall of snow was a frozen lake; it was cracked in a thousand pieces, but each piece was so like the other that the whole seemed a perfect work of art. In the middle of this lake sat the Snow Queen when she was at home."

Hans Christian Andersen, *The Snow Queen*

Spitsbergen

ARCTIC OCEAN

If there is one island that has come to symbolize the fight against climate change it is Spitsbergen, in the Svalbard archipelago. For it is to here that politicians, natural history documentary-makers and other opinion formers go to see glaciers calving at an alarming rate and grasp photo opportunities in order to brand themselves the green good guy. Spitsbergen is political currency, a quotable *cause celebre* – the Tibet of islands.

It is ironic, therefore, that until the 1920s Spitsbergen was a no man's land that nobody cared about or even claimed. Dutchman Willy Barents first discovered the island in 1596 while looking for the northern sea route; he christened it "jagged peaks". In the eighteenth and nineteenth centuries, the Russians and Norwegians had been the only interested parties, establishing coal-mining communities on three of the islands so far-flung that over decades of mingling and interdependency they established a strange *russenorsk* pidgin dialect of their own. Vestiges of these communities still persist at Longyearbyen, named after the Norwegian businessman John Munro Longyear, and its Russian counterpart Barentburg. Longyearbyen is where the cruisers full of rich retiree tourists put in so they, too, can say they have set foot in the Arctic Circle and buy legitimate fur clothes. It is also the northernmost destination for any regular scheduled flight, and the only place in these parts where human civilization has taken hold enough for people to walk around armed for fear of an encounter with a polar bear. Meanwhile, the other smaller mining communities, their huts, railways and crumpled gondola pylons ruined and abandoned, cast a forlorn and ghostly atmosphere across this windswept land of rushing mist.

As if to bring Spitsbergen's role at the ice edge of mankind's most daunting challenge into focus, plans are underway to preserve here the elements essential for human survival in case of nuclear war or catastrophic climate change. Built 120 metres (394 feet) into a mountain, the Norwegian Seed Bank is to be a five-million dollar "doomsday vault", containing the frozen seeds of three million plant-types essential for mankind's post-apocalyptic regeneration. It seems a design from the world of fantasy, as illusory as the local Fata Morgana mirage effect, but an acknowledgement of the figurative polar night that casts its shadow across human post-industrial achievements. It is appropriate that Spitsbergen should be the location of Hans Christian Anderson's Snow Queen (and battleground of Philip Pullman's *Northern Lights*), but of little relevance to the polar bears of the Edgeoya nature reserve and their dwindling kingdom of ice.

Spitsbergen, Svalbard, Norway **Alternative name:** Spitzbergen **Longitude:** 16° 30' E **Latitude:** 78° 15' N **Area:** 39,044 sq km (15,071 sq mi) **Highest point:** 1,717 m (5,633 ft) Newtontoppen
Population: 2,200 **Principal town:** Longyearbyen **Resident:** John Munroe Longyear

Hvar

ADRIATIC SEA

> "He began to speak of their main street,
> which was broad and paved with marble
> and lined with fifteenth-century palaces
> weathered to warm gold."
>
> Rebecca West, *Black Lamb and Grey Falcon*

Purple is the colour of Hvar. At the height of summer the island's interior appears to stretch for kilometres in a purple haze of gently rolling farmland cloaked in lavender, and also rosemary, sage and thyme. It is a fragrant island that appears and smells as if it has been wafted down from Provence, and which produces the most exquisite honey.

At the edges of Hvar, away from the rural idyll of its scented interior, lies an island of great culture and sophistication, passed down a line of illustrious civilizations – among them Greek, Roman (the Romans gave the island its name, "Pharia"), Byzantine and Venetian – that have at one time or other laid claim to its limestone shores.

Hvar was a centre for Croatian literature during the Renaissance and it is thus central to the Croatian identity. But of the subsequent occupiers it is the Venetians who left the greatest mark; in the fifteenth century they incorporated Hvar into their republic as part of a drive to colonize the Adriatic. The main towns of Stari Grad and Jelsa, and even Hvar itself, seem to be miniature versions of Venice, with a long, elongated central square evocative of San Marco, elegant merchant villas and the rising spire of St Stephen's cathedral, the campanile with its delicate rounded arches of the Franciscan monastery to the south of the main harbour and the overall sense of symmetry and a focal point amid the horizontal and vertical planes. The island's churches abound with works by Tintoretto, Veronese and Bellini. And in the evening the whole town has the golden glow of pale sandstone, picked up by the cobbles polished by centuries of evening *passeggiatas*. Atop and tumbling down the town's sheltering cliff stand the impressive fort and fortified walls of the citadel, built as a refuge against the attentions of marauding corsairs. From here, along the crenellated defensive walks and overlooking the terracotta roofs of Hvar town, centuries of culture lie spread out beneath, but also the echoes of much bloody history that tainted even the islands of this part of the world right up to the eve of the new millennium.

Since the end of the Balkan wars, Hvar has returned to its former position as one of the most fashionable and desirable resorts on the Dalmatian coast. It is a party island for the youth of Split, which lies opposite on the mainland, who come to unfold tall, languid shapes through this Venetian theatre, sip on an aperitif of *prosek* wine before moving on to a feast of *dingac* wine and squid-ink risotto.

Hvar, Dalmatia, Croatia **Alternative name:** Lesina **Longitude:** 16° 28' E **Latitude:** 43° 11' N **Area:** 299 sq km (115 sq mi) **Highest point:** 628 m (2,060 ft) Sveti Nicola **Population:** 11,500
Principal town: Hvar **Natives:** Martin Benetovic, Petar Hektorovic, Hanibal Lucic, Ivan Vucetic **Resident:** Marin Gazarovic

"Raging island, raging passions."

Tag line for *Stromboli*

Stromboli

AEOLIAN ISLANDS, TYRRHENIAN SEA

Stromboli is the northernmost of the Aeolians, a group of seven islands, including Lipari, the main centre, and the appropriately named Vulcano, best known for its hot springs and mud baths. When Roberto Rossellini and Ingrid Bergman arrived on Stromboli to film the movie of the same name, there were volcanic rumbles all round. The two, both married to others at the time, were in the early stages of an affair, she was already pregnant with their child, and a scandal was about to erupt whose fallout would spread across Hollywood and beyond. Shortly after the movie's release in 1950, Senator Edwin C. Johnson fulminated that the Swedish actress was a "free-love cultist, a powerful influence for evil".

If the pair had flicked through Homer's *Odyssey* beforehand, they would have found a harbinger of this in its pages. Odysseus stops off at the Aeolians, just off the north coast of Sicily, and his host Aeolus, god of the winds, gives him a leaving present – an oxhide bag containing strong winds. Odysseus is instructed never to open the bag, but when he settles down for a nap in sight of his home island of Ithaca, his crew can't resist taking a peek inside the bag. They are blown all the way back, much to Aeolus's disgruntlement.

Thanks not least to Bergman and Rossellini, although the film was a commercial flop, Stromboli, like Krakatoa, became a catchphrase for volcanic fireworks. Stromboli is still active – its most recent eruption occurred in 2007, temporarily closing off access to the summit of the volcano. The island's relative accessibility and its flow of lava down to the sea – what the locals call the *sciara del fuoco* or stream of fire – has put it on the tourist trail. Approaching the small island by boat, there is a wild beauty about the place, full of prickly pears, caper bushes and olive trees. There is a powerful palette of colours: orange lava, black sand and rock beaches, white houses covered with fuchsia and bougainvillea. The two main villages, Ginestra and Stromboli, are as yet car, streetlight and development free.

From sea-level visitors can walk up the slopes unattended until they are 400 metres (1,312 feet) from the top, after which they must follow a guide. So, like ants scuttling up the side of a fiery anthill, teams of the curious march up the volcano's sides to stand and marvel. Back down on *terra* relatively *firma* there is time to visit the house where the illicit lovers stayed – an elegant plaque marks the atypically red-fronted building where the seismic emotional tremors of nearly sixty years ago are now quiescent.

OVERLEAF At anchor near Stomboli and the Basiluzzo Islands

Stromboli, Messina, Italy **Longitude:** 15° 13' E **Latitude:** 38° 47' N **Area:** 12 sq km (5 sq mi) **Highest point:** 926 m (3,038 ft) Serra Vancori **Population:** 575

> "The light – so matterly, always broken, always reminding that light is colour – all colour. Potentially. I guess this is a special island-light…"
>
> Aidan Higgins, *Bornholm Night-Ferry*

Bornholm

BALTIC SEA

Had General Gerhard von Kamptz, head of the occupying Nazi forces at the end of the Second World War, not resisted for so long surrender to the Allies instead of the Red Army (for so far east in the Baltic does this Danish island lie), Bornholm might well have been on the list of spoils whose subsequent division on a napkin at Yalta meant either western prosperity or decades of communism. In the event the island became Danish, but its size and strategic importance in the heart of the Baltic resulted in a demilitarized zone in which any mention of posting non-Danish troops will always be greeted with great sensitivity.

Despite being on the eastern front and having its beaches indented with military installations, never a shot was fired in anger on Bornholm. Only a cement-filled head of a Nazi prototype V-rocket once landed on the island, alerting British intelligence to the development of the doodlebugs that were about to be launched on London.

Nowadays, in more frivolous times, Bornholm is the self-styled Mykonos of the Baltic – a summer treat for Copenhagen's chic set, who come here for the most guaranteed sun in the Baltic, pristine beaches such as Dueodde and the golden strip between Hasle and Nekso on the southern coast. Here, one can walk among Denmark's only real mountains or live an idyllic bucolic life of bicycling bliss among ochre, mustard and cerise-coloured wooden and half-timbered houses, and enjoy the unique light that has inspired many painters and the bohemian musical community in the island's cultural hub at Gudhjem ("God's Home").

Windmills are a feature of Bornholm, but even more characteristic are the fifteen medieval churches and especially the four architectural curiosities at Osterlars, Nylars, Olsker and Nyker. Tall, circular, with pointed roofs and flying buttresses, they resemble something from a fairytale. Inside they are laid out on many floors and each has an armoury in which the congregation left its weapons before praying – presumably to Thor. The reference to fantasy is not casual, as by their position and geometry there is also a school of thought that relates these churches to the work of the Knights Templar.

The sagas of warring mythology loom large on an island that has been a bone of contention since the tussles between Sweden and the Hanseatic League of Luebeck. Nothing better evokes such bearded and swashbuckling times as the ruins and huge uneven boulders of the fortress at Hammershus on Bornholm's northwestern tip. This was once the largest medieval fortification in northern Europe.

OPPOSITE A round church in Nyker

Bornholm, Denmark **Longitude:** 14° 55' E **Latitude:** 55° 08' N **Area:** 587 sq km (227 sq mi) **Highest point:** 162 m (531 ft) Rytterknaegten **Population:** 42,800 **Principal town:** Rønne
Native: Oluf Høst **Residents:** Karl Isaksson, Gustaf Munch-Petersen, Martin Andersen Nexø, Olaf Rude

Lofoten Islands
NORWEGIAN SEA

"Arctic light, archaic rock.
The book of the land of
the Lofoten Islands presents
one page of rough ice after another."

Kenneth White, *Letters From Lofoten*

The Lofoten Islands, up into the ring of the Arctic Circle by Norway's northern coast, are home to the original maelstrom: the Mosktraumen, one of the globe's strongest tidal currents, which tugs, surges and swells around the archipelago. The ancient Greek geographer and pioneering travel-writer Pytheas wrote about their power, as did Edgar Allan Poe and Jules Verne. Their strength is awesome and mythical, like the enigmatic three-millennia-old images quite recently discovered in the Refsvikhula sea caves on Moskenesøy, the most southerly of the four main Lofoten Islands.

The tides provide the Lofoten Islands with their *raison d'être*: fish. Every year from the end of January onwards cod arrive to spawn, attracted by the warmish waters on offer, by virtue of the Gulf Stream and its afterburn, the North Atlantic Drift. Given its high northerly latitude, the sea off the Lofotens is remarkably mild. As the cod arrive the fishing season takes off. Much of the fish caught is dried by the natural combination of wind and sun on racks, and the resulting high-in-protein stockfish is exported back south, especially to Italy where the Lofoten variety of *stoccafisso* is considered a gastronomic delicacy.

For anyone wanting to delve more deeply into the history and culture of stockfish, there is an entire museum devoted to the subject in a fishing village with the wonderfully truncated name of Å. The rust-coloured museum juts out into the seawater on stilts, a traditional form of building in Lofoten, known as a *rorbu*, from the words for "row" and "live". Constructed originally as accommodation for the thousands of fisherman who came to Lofoten to catch the cod, they now serve as guesthouses and hostels, sitting on the shoreline framed against the granite mountain peaks.

Despite the mild temperatures, in winter a layer of ice and snow, shaded with subtle tints of colour, settles on Lofoten. After the thaw, and during the summer of virtually twenty-four-hour light, there is a chance to explore the islands more widely by hiking or mountaineering. Vägar, on the easterly Austvagøya, is one of the oldest settlements in northern Norway. Leknes, one of the main towns on the chain, is unusually, for these islands, located inland, though it has a nearby harbour that contains the usual row of wooden houses and which has become a regular stop-off for cruise liners. Wilder life than the daytrippers also roam the islands, including reindeer, bear, beaver and lynx. Lofoten means "lynx foot", the name originally given to just one of the islands, Vestvagøya, because of its shape as seen from the mainland.

Lofoten Islands, Nordland, Norway **Longitude:** 14° 35' E **Latitude:** 68° 28' N **Area:** 4,044 sq km (1,560 sq mi) **Highest point:** 1,161 m (3,809 ft) Higravstinden, Austvågøy **Population:** 24,000 **Principal towns:** Leknes, Svolvaer

Malta

MEDITERRANEAN

The rock of Malta is like a Rosetta Stone, a tablet unlocking in one vertical slice a history and timeline of European civilization. It is a disproportionately influential island, owned and ruled until 1964 by just about everyone – Phoenicians (who gave the island its name "malet", meaning "harbour", Carthaginians, Romans, Arabs, Normans, Angevins, Hohenstaufens, Aragons, French and British – except itself.

History is writ large all over Malta's seven islands, which include Gozo, Comino, Filfla, Cominotto and the Islands of St Paul, where the apostle was shipwrecked in AD 60, bequeathing Christianity to the locals. Re-enacting that history on film among its amphitheatres, Renaissance cathedrals and Baroque palaces, and a versatile landscape that can turn itself to anything from biblical, to Arab to Napoleonic and modern-day Turkey, is largely what sustains the island now. In downtown Valletta there is a bar called simply The Pub, scene of the last pint

of actor Oliver Reed (after a drinking and arm-wrestling competition with six British sailors, according to the barman), who was living on the island during the 1999 filming of *Gladiator*. The area behind Fort St Elmo is familiar from *Midnight Express*.

The fortifications of Valletta itself evoke the proudest moment of Maltese home-grown history. The town was fortified by the Grand Master Jean de Valette, who successfully defended both Valletta and Christendom against Ottoman siege. Valette was a member of the order of the Knights of Malta, an aristocratic title transferred from the Knights of St John and Jerusalem, who had been expelled by the Ottomans from Rhodes, and conferred on Maltese nobility by Charles V of Spain.

Malta had its finest hour during the Second World War, as a vital way-station for the British fleet. For this the islands and her citizens earned the George Cross, and with its red phone and pillar boxes, vintage cars and old crimson and yellow buses, there can be no more British and pro-British corner of the former empire in the Mediterranean. As a mark of affection for the island, Queen Elizabeth chose Malta as the destination for her diamond-wedding holiday.

Beneath the post-imperial veneer, however, lurks a fascinating polyglot culture that mixes maghrebi Arabic, Italian (the official tongue until the 1930s) and Sicilian in a language that contains many unique letters. This is also reflected in the melting-pot cuisine, which encompasses such oddities as dolphin fish pie and delicacies like the popular *torta-tal-lampuki* fish pie.

Package tours and unchecked high-rise developments may have given Malta a bad name, but such modern concerns as beaches, hotels and nightlife miss the point. From megalithic temples and catacombs to the site of the 1989 Bush-Gorbachev summit that signalled the end of the Cold War, Malta is one big open-air museum, the best classroom in the world for learning and reliving the history of Europe.

"Malta had the culture of South London
in a landscape like Lebanon."

Paul Theroux, *The Pillars of Hercules*

OPPOSITE An old-style British postbox in Valletta

ABOVE Fort St Elmo in Valletta

Malta, The Republic of Malta **Longitude:** 14° 26' E **Latitude:** 35° 55' N **Area:** 316 sq km (122 sq mi) **Highest point:** 253m (830 ft) Ta'Dmejrek **Population:** 401,900
Capital: Valletta **Natives:** Gerald Brenan, Ruzar Briffa, Charles Camilleri, Edward de Bono, Luke Dimech, Tony Drago, Michael Mifsud, David Millar, Dom Mintoff, Suzanne Mizzi, Carmelo Pace, Dun Karm Psaila, Joe Sacco

"I knew that if only one small blade of grass
of this gentle, wonderful place
could belong to me, I would be happy."
Gracie Fields

Capri

GULF OF NAPLES

Long before the term *la dolce vita* was invented, the ancient Greek poet Homer spoke of Capri as the "land of sweet idleness", and perhaps this island off the Amalfi coast encapsulates Italian obsessions and the Italian way of life more than any other place in the country.

Orson Welles once opined that everyone in Italy was an actor or actress, and that the only bad ones were to be found in films or on the stage. He would surely have agreed that the very best of them are found on Capri, especially in the height of summer, when the sense of Italian *fare bella figura* – the need to be seen as immaculate and beautiful, in the right place and in the company of *bella gente* (both beautiful and socially acceptable) – has been turned into an art form of the highest theatre.

Capri (from the Greek *kapros*, meaning "wild boar") has been attracting *bella gente* since the "discovery" (at least as far as the nascent nineteenth-century tourist industry was concerned) of the island's famous blue grotto. This coastal aperture in the limestone rock, where sunlight shines up through an underwater opening to produce an alchemical blue, is believed to be the place where Roman emperors such as Tiberius took their private baths.

The Romans were perhaps the first to make Capri a celebrity retreat, building a series of grandiose private villas around the island. Tiberius set up a summer seat of power at the magnificent Villa Jovis. They were followed by Neapolitan, Angevin and Spanish Bourbon aristocracy, who built the many Renaissance and Baroque mansions, churches and convents in the towns of Capri and Anacapri that contribute to the island's architectural and oddly metropolitan majesty. The twentieth century brought painters, writers, artists and eccentrics such as Sargent, Gorky, Modigliani, d'Adelsward Fersen and Axel Muenthe. Today, Capri is haunted by tourists desperate to see how the celebrity half live. People flock to the Villa Fersen to hear the echoes of Versace parties or to the Belvedere di Tragara to spot a VIP or two for themselves.

Capri still manages to mix high fashion with rusticity. For every chic café in the Piazza Umberto there can still be found bucolic scenes of locals picking olives. The one-seater chairlift to Monte Solaro offers superb views of fluted limestone cliffs, soaring reefs, arches and pinnacles such as the Faraglioni needles. It is still an island that Italians, and especially the locals, consider the most beautiful in the world.

OPPOSITE The Faraglioni needles

Capri, Campania, Italy **Longitude:** 14° 14' E **Latitude:** 40° 33' N **Area:** 11 sq km (4 sq mi) **Highest point:** 589 m (1,932 ft) Monte Solaro **Population:** 12,200 **Principal town:** Capri
Native: Edwin Cerio **Residents:** Norman Douglas, Jacques d'Adelsward Fersen, Gracie Fields, Maxim Gorky, Graham Greene, Shirley Hazzard, Friedrich Krupp, Compton Mackenzie, Thomas Mann, Axel Munthe, Pablo Neruda

> "This, however, was the Sicily the inspector liked best: harsh, spare in vegetation, on whose soil it seemed impossible to live, and where he could still run across a man in gaiters and cap, rifle on shoulder." Andrea Camilleri, *The Voice of the Violin*

Sicily

MEDITERRANEAN

Once upon a time there was a country called Sicily. It was a bad land with a bad reputation where people disappeared or woke up with horses' heads in their bed, where the powers that be would watch your every move. It was also a place where your neighbour had never seen anything, never heard anything and never said anything to incriminate anyone else. It was the country of *omerta*, *cosa nostra* and the tentacles of *la piovra*; a wild west of deserted whitewashed villages with diffident old ladies in black. It was the original homeland of the mafia and Mario Puzo's *Godfather*.

For years those who dared to visit found that much of this was true. Separated from Italy by the Straits of Messina, the largest island in the Mediterranean was – and to a certain extent still is – a different country, more African than European and with its own dialect made popular through Andrea Camilleri's fictional Inspector Montalbano. The mafia country of Partinico, Castellammare del Golfo, Castelvetrano and in particular the town of Corleone from where mafia boss Toto Riina controlled his empire were no-go areas.

How paradoxical, therefore, that the island is home to more antiquities and founding moments of European history than Athens: the temples of Zeus and Venus at Erice; the site of the Athenian fleet's destruction at Syracuse; the Byzantine ruins of Taormina; and the old bastion at Ortygia, where Archimedes leapt out of this bath shouting "Eureka!" As much as Sicily's history is rich, the island's landscape – from salt pans and Sancho Panza-esque windmills to, at its heart, the ever-present threat of Mount Etna where Persephone was dragged down to Hades – is also dramatic and photogenic, celebrated by directors from Rossellini to Coppola and, in particular, beautifully showcased in azure in scenes from *Le Grand Bleu*.

In 1992 came operation Mani Pulite ("clean hands") which despite the death of two judges, Falcone and Borsellino, set about an outing of *pentiti* (grasses) and *tangenti* (bribes) culminating in Riina's tame arrest while out driving his car. In came an EU-funded facelift, correcting the island's famously poor infrastructure, and *la vita* on Sicily became as *dolce* as its syrupy yet still mysterious Marsala wine. The Sicily of vendetta is now well and truly sleeping with the fishes, with the blue-bottle-sunglassed youths of this island-home to the fratelli Dolce and Gabbana more likely to succumb to that other Italian malaise – fashion: a case of *dolce et gabbana est pro moda mori*.

OPPOSITE Marettimo Harbour

OVERLEAF The Roman amphitheatre with Mount Etna

Sicily, Italy **Local name:** Sicilia **Longitude:** 14° 11' E **Latitude:** 37° 38' N **Area:** 25,700 sq km (9,920 sq mi) **Highest point:** 3,320m (10,892 ft) Mt Etna **Population:** 5,245,800 **Capital:** Palermo
Natives: St Agatha, Archimedes, Vincenzo Bellini, Count Alessandro di Cagliostro, Andrea Camilleri, Stanislao Cannizzaro, Frank Capra, Maria Grazia Cucinotta, Giovanni Gentile, Natalia Ginzburg, **Giuseppe Tomasi di Lampedusa**, **Pope Leo II**, **Luigi Pirandello**, Salvatore Quasimodo, Alessandro Scarlatti, Totò Schillaci, Salvatore Sciarrino, Leonardo Sciascia, Giovanni Verga

Ischia

TYRRRHENIAN SEA

"At a glance
it was plain
Ischia was no place
for the rush of hours.
Islands never are."

Truman Capote

What is it about Italian islands, volcanoes and Hollywood love affairs? A decade after Stromboli had played host to Bergman and Rossellini, Richard Burton and Elizabeth Taylor tried to escape the ravening press pack in Ischia, an island they had visited while filming *Cleopatra* – the movie that threw them together. Ischia was enjoying its moment as a celebrity magnet. In 1952, a luxurious spa hotel had been built overlooking the bay in Lacca Ameno; its owner was Angelo Rizzoli, founder of the publishers and bookstores that still bear his name. Charlie Chaplin attended the opening party for the Regina Isabella, and the stars who arrived in his wake included Maria Callas, Burt Lancaster and Ava Gardner. In a neat twist, the island itself, especially the main town Ischia Porto, later featured in the movie version of *The Talented Mr Ripley*, as the location for Patricia Highsmith's fictional Mongibello.

The island, the largest in the azure bay of Naples, lies 30 kilometres (100 miles) from that cunning, lawless city. Apart from its great heyday, Ischia has generally taken an understudy's role to Capri, although it has a hefty influx of holidaymakers, including the Neapolitans, each summer. Perhaps that suits it, as it provides a lazy sun-lounger mood, where a face pack of mud from its seemingly ubiquitous

thermal springs – the highest point, Mount Epomeo, was a volcano, but is now dormant – requires enforced immobility, perhaps soothed with a *granita* flavoured with the exquisite lemons from the next-door island of Procida. At Succhivo, the spring on the shoreline offers an all-in-one beauty treatment and suntan.

Ischia has had its moments of drama. The island – known to Virgil as Inarima, to the Romans as Aenaria, and to the Greeks as Pithekoussai after its ceramic clay – has been fought over by the Angevin and the local Durazzo dynasties, assorted pirate chiefs and the Bourbons. Horatio Nelson unleashed a broadside at the castle above Lacco Ameno during a brief rebellion on the island.

Calm now prevails, and one of the most frequently visited spots on Ischia is La Mortella, the villa where the composer Sir William Walton and his Argentinean wife Susana set up house in the early 1950s. A memorial containing his ashes overlooks the gardens Susana created and nurtured in a former quarry – rare Mediterranean plants set against a stern stone background, featuring a gingko biloba tree, a greenhouse with a giant Brazilian water lily and an amphitheatre for *al fresco* concerts. There must be something artistic on the breeze: Henrik Ibsen worked on *Peer Gynt* while staying in another villa on the island, near Casamicciola.

OPPOSITE La Mortella gardens

Ischia, Campania, Italy **Longitude:** 13° 57' E **Latitude:** 40° 44' N **Area:** 46 sq km (18 sq mi) **Highest point:** 788 m (2,585 ft) Mt Epomeo **Population:** 60,300 **Principal town:** Ischia Porto
Native: St John Joseph of the Cross **Residents:** Henrik Ibsen, William and Susanna Walton

Ruegen

BALTIC SEA

When the painter Caspar David Friedrich returned to Dresden in 1818, after a trip to his Heimat in these parts (he was a native of nearby Greifswald on the Pomeranian mainland), he painted a picture of Ruegen island that became one of the iconic works of the German-born Romantic movement. Over time this piece has come to symbolize German culture and Germans' sense of themselves. As a result of this, Ruegen holds a unique almost sacred place in the German psyche.

The painting, *Kreidefelsen auf Ruegen*, depicted three felt-coated Wanderers – early tourists – two men and a woman, looking down over the wild and craggy chalk cliffs of Ruegen known as the Stubbenkammer. According to Friedrich, "the painter should not just paint what he sees in front of him, but also what he sees within himself". In this case he saw awesome wildness, God-given order in nature and man's insignificance in the immensity of the universe, all wrapped up in a sense of *Sehnsucht*, or longing for a greater understanding of the world. It was a bleak vision, but for a nation of philosophers and angst-ridden thinkers it was perhaps the very symbol of the Romanticism that would become the much-devalued banner of decades of loner artists around the world.

Even during the decades of communist rule, Ruegen – Germany's largest island – was one of the country's most popular holiday destinations. Always torn between Danish and Swedish rule, the dukes of Pomerania and the Prussian kaisers nevertheless managed to build here a number of attractive resorts: neoclassical Puttbus is a distinctly un-German, almost *pueblo blanco* town complete with a central circular circus and orangerie like an eighteenth-century English formal garden; while Binz is a Kaisersbad or imperial Kurort (health resort) with a neoclassical seafront. The two are connected – as so often in this land of the model railway – by the imperial narrow gauge railway or Rasender Roland as the train is now known.

However, it was Hitler who put the most indelible stamp on the island, with the monolithic holiday camp at Prora, built by the Kraft durch Freude ("Strength through Joy") movement that provided the often-forgotten socialist side of the Nazi equation. Four kilometres (2.5 miles) of continuous concrete blocks provided one-size-fits-all apartments for holidaying Nazi workers. The camp was never used and is crumbling into disuse, but it is still too big for anyone to know what to do with it.

The building contributes to the eerie and possessed atmosphere that lurks on this romantic, magnetic and spiritual island: among the ancient burial mounds in the forest, in the rippling corn of the rolling golden fields and in the primordial or post-apocalyptic calm that reigns on the adjacent island spit of Hiddensee.

"The wood casts long shadows over the fields.
Birds call with sudden uncanny violence,
like alarm-clocks going off.
The birch-trees hang down laden over
the rutted, sandy earth of the country road.
A soft bar of cloud is moving up from
the line of trees along the lake."

Christopher Isherwood, *On Ruegen Island*

OPPOSITE The chalk cliffs in the Stubbenkammer Nature Reserve

Ruegen, Germany **Local name:** Rügen **Longitude:** 13° 24' E **Latitude:** 54° 22' N **Area:** 926 sq km (357 sq mi) **Highest point:** 161 m (528 ft) Piekberg **Population:** 71,700
Principal town: Bergen auf Rügen **Natives:** George C. Boldt, Ernst Moritz Arndt **Resident:** Gerhart Hauptmann

Lampedusa

PELAGIE ISLANDS, MEDITERRANEAN

On Lampedusa, two cultures and climates meet with the clash of tectonic plates. This is Italy's southernmost outpost, 200 kilometres (124 miles) from Sicily but closer to the coast of Tunisia. In the summer months, the arrival of the tourists boosts not only the population, from four to ten thousand, but also the fun factor of living on the island. Locals say that the winter months are suicidally dull. The first step outside the plane on to the tarmac at Lampedusa delivers a hot blast of desert air imported direct from North Africa.

In fact the island itself is quite desert-like: its soil bleached white, stony and dry, with no agriculture to speak of – an elemental grittiness captured by director Emanuele Crialese in his 2003 film *Respiro*. The terrain is a mixture of cliffs and inlets, but this is not what the planeloads of new arrivals have come for. They want the guaranteed hot weather, the white sand beaches and the diving.

Given Lampedusa's arid nature, It has become an upmarket destination, in keeping, perhaps, with its former aristocratic owners. For two centuries from the 1630s, the island was the property of the Tomasi family – whose most celebrated scion was Giuseppe Tomasi di Lampedusa, author of *The Leopard*. Nobody else had seemed particularly interested in inhabiting it because of corsair attacks, and the family retained its control until the island became part of the newly created Kingdom of Italy in 1860, along with the two other islands of the Pelagic, Linosa and Lampione.

If the majority of holidaymakers have headed south from Italy, there are two other groups of visitors, both of which require special treatment. Each September the Spiaggi dei Conigli, or Rabbit Beach, which connects Lampedusa to the Isola dei Conigli, acts like a maternity ward for endangered Mediterranean loggerhead turtles, drawing comparison with the Galapagos. The loggerhead mothers bury their eggs in the dunes and then head back out to sea, leaving their offspring to fend for themselves. A team of volunteers is on standby to oversee the eggs while they hatch; their vigilance is required to protect eggs and hatchlings from illegal hunters, birds and over-curious tourists.

The second group is a more recent phenomenon: the *clandestini*, North Africans without papers trying to make their way to the European Union via one of its outer fragments, in the same way that Samos in the Aegean has become a potential gateway. There is a constant battle between the migrants and the *carabinieri*, and the regular rounding-up of a new batch of illegal arrivals has sadly become a fixture of daily life on Lampedusa.

"It's not cute. Actually it's rough.
But after a while it's gorgeous."

Valeria Golino, star of *Respiro*

LEFT View of the eastern side of the island, from the Italian Custom Police helicopter

Lampedusa, Agrigento, Italy **Local name:** Isola di Lampedusa **Longitude:** 12° 36' E **Latitude:** 35° 30' N **Area:** 21 sq km (8 sq mi) **Highest point:** 133 m (436 ft) Albero del Sole **Population:** 6,100 **Principal town:** Lampedusa **Resident:** Domenico Modugno

Venice

VENETIAN LAGOON/ADRIATIC

To post-industrial mankind Venice is the city we would no longer have either the art, the wit or the stupidity to build. So much does La Serenissima's beauty seem to belong not only to another time but also to another branch of creation than that of human hand, that she is to the modern eye a part of nature – a uniquely rare, precious and yet threatened creation among manmade objects.

Despite the weight of expectation, even the most world-weary of the millions of tourists that swell the city's population two-hundredfold each year must be chastened from cynicism by the first sight of the only city in the world built on water. "Streets full of water. Please advise," was Robert Benchley's Algonquin-inspired understated quip. For that magician of muddled time and space, Marcel Proust, it was nothing less than the residence of his dreams.

Of course, no such whimsy inspired the opulence with which in its heyday most of its architectural achievements, among them the Palazzo Ducale and the Basilica di San Marco, were first constructed and then decorated by the finest hands of the time – Tintoretto, Titian, Tiepolo and the original Bellini. Originally home to a community of fishermen, these mud flats that make up Venice's 118 islands became increasingly important in the religious conflict between east and west that followed the break-up of Byzantium. Venice is a story of opportunism, profiting both in riches and territory from the 1204 sacking of Constantinople and various Crusades the Venetians decided not to get involved in other than for money, so that at one time, the Venetian thalassocracy controlled a string of ports as far afield as the Black Sea and, were it not for their rivals the Genoese, all but ruled the Med.

Once Vasco de Gama rounded the Cape, however, Venice lost its monopoly. By the time Napoleon arrived he was happy to hand "the finest drawing-room in Europe" (Piazza San Marco) over to the Habsburgs. Obscured by Trieste, Venice could only welcome the whimsy and dollar of tourism. It became a playground of casinos, a lido health resort known to those few who have not visited it through the film of Thomas Mann's novel *Death in Venice*, and a film set or stage for festivals and the yearly masked Carnevale.

It is a reality as fetid as the smell that overtakes the narrow alleys and waterways of the city's *sestieri* (six districts) from San Marco to Castello in summer, as thousands photograph and pile over the Rialto bridge and carve the waters in the myriad *vaporetti* and *motoscafi* of an age the city was not built for. The Lion of St Mark may have long since lost its roar and the city become a postcard ghetto, but the romantic, meditative pleasure of water still washes over all who come to lose themselves in the city's brittle and mystical labyrinth of ancient glory.

OPPOSITE St Mark's Square   ABOVE Renaissance Lord and Lady at the Carnevale   OVERLEAF Gondolas out of season

Venice, Italy **Local name:** Venezia **Longitude:** 12° 21' E **Latitude:** 45° 27' N **Area:** 412 sq km (159 sq mi) **Highest point:** 2 m (7 ft) **Population:** 271,000 **Natives:** Tomaso Albinoni, Giovanni Bellini, Giacomo Casanova, Luigi Enrico Ferro, Carlo Goldoni, Marco Polo, Giovanni Battista Tiepolo, Jacopo Tintoretto, Antonio Vivaldi, Ermanno Wolf-Ferrari **Residents:** Peggy Guggenheim, Donna Leon, Maria Taglioni, Titian, Paolo Veronese

"It is a gnarled but gorgeous city …
the whole scene seems to shimmer –
with pinkness, with age, with self-satisfaction,
with sadness, with delight."

Jan Morris

> "The sea here is more blue than anywhere else, the air is more pure and heady with fragrance. I fell in love, I suppose, but with that intensity of feeling that comes from loving someone for their faults."
>
> Giorgio Armani

Pantellaria

STRAIT OF SICILY

Pantellaria is far in every sense from the Italy of popular imagination. In fact, were it not for being recently dragged into the limelight and favour of Italy's fashion industry, it would not seem Italian at all. A striking hilly black rock floating in the Strait of Sicily, Pantellaria is by its geography, history and whole atmosphere nearer North Africa.

The winds that rise off the coast of North Africa gave this "daughter of the wind" its name, so christened by the Iberians and Ligurians who first settled here. In AD 700, after a spell under Carthage – whose presence survives in punic tombs and the rectangular blocks of their acropolis on the hills of San Marco and Santa Teresa – and a time in exile as a Roman penal colony, the Arabs arrived and created a *tabula rasa* on which to engrave their own culture. Indeed it is the Arabian culture that has left the strongest mark on the island, in its architecture, gardens and spirit of hospitality. The insular Italian population is very proud of this, in a young country where regional differences are keenly felt.

Bright white cuboid *dammuso* houses pepper the island. They are home to Italy's fashion deities Armani and the brothers Dolce and Gabbana, whose sunglasses and immaculate sartorial conceptions have brought the fashion circus here in their wake. All but empty for eleven months of the year, in August it seems the whole of Italy's monopolic media industry retires to its holiday home to grab a piece of *bella figura* and to discuss the contracts and resulting spoils of the forthcoming television season over a glass or two of the famous sweet *passito* wine from the Piano Ghiraldia vineyards.

They eschew the Baroque and Renaissance civilization, the blue grotto of Capri and the established glitz and emerald-green waters of the Aga Khan's Sardinia in favour of the beachless black volcanic rock, hot mineral springs and fumaroles of this island as monochrome as an Armani suit itself. They bathe in the stark beauty of the Specchio di Venere ("Venus's Mirror") caldera lake, or bask in the thermal pools of the seaside hamlet of Gadir, or in the caves of Santaria, where legend has it Calypso and Odysseus had their secret love nest. With the moody inertia of an Antonioni film, it seems a strangely, oddly fertile, other-worldly place to be so popular. But Capri is obviously so yesterday.

LEFT Mud baths at Lake Venere

Pantellaria, Trapani, Italy **Alternative names:** Pantalaria, Pantalleria **Longitude:** 11° 57' E **Latitude:** 36° 50' N **Area:** 117 sq km (45 sq mi) **Highest point:** 836m (2,743 ft) Montagna Grande
Population: 7,700 **Principal town:** Pantellaria **Residents:** Giorgio Armani, Domenico Dolce and Stefano Gabbana

Djerba

GULF OF GABES

Djerba, a large island just off the coast of Tunisia and one of the few islands along the long North African coastline, was another of the Mediterranean islands that acted as stepping stones on Odysseus's circuitous journey home. Here, he and his fellow-travellers met the Lotus Eaters – an encounter that left these early tourists a little dazed. As Tennyson wrote about their visit, "They came unto a land, in which it always seemed like afternoon. All round the coast the languid air did swoon." If the lotus the islanders shared with their visitors was *zizyphus*, which has hallucinogenic qualities, it seems as if Odysseus and his companions were enjoying a pleasant high.

No lotus grows on Djerba today. Some who visit describe it as a mirage floating in the sea, an oasis of palm trees and olives, attuned to the traditional Tunisian description of the island as "La Douce", "the sweet". Others find much of it rather dry, like ageing parchment, and its individual qualities and characteristics less overt, but nonetheless worth seeking out.

A distinctive feature of the generally flat Djerban landscape are the *menzel* farms dotted across the countryside, with blue ironwork and domed towers, part residence and part fortress to defend the residents against raiders, just as the island itself has contended with Spanish crusaders, Ottomans, Carthaginians and Romans. The Romans built a causeway joining Djerba to the mainland, which (rebuilt) still acts as an umbilical cord to Tunisia.

Across this causeway have come the blend of Berbers, Kharadjite Muslims and Jews that make up the island's demographic profile. The El Ghriba ("marvellous") synagogue in the town of Hara Sghira is a major centrepoint for all North African Jews; of the many mosques on Djerba, that of the Turkish Mother in El May, is particularly striking, not because of its size (it is rather small, in fact) or its elaborateness, but because it looks as if it has been sculpted out of white icing.

In Houmt Souq, the main town whose name means "marketplace", the mood is strongly Tunisian. Fez-wearing gents buy and sell. And there is a hint of the Ottoman in the *funduq* hotels, like the *caravanserai* of Turkey, with rooms set off round a central courtyard. Most of the non-local guests – there is a preponderance of French, Italian, Czech and German visitors – are parcelled off into a handful of *zones touristiques* on the north coast, where they can indulge in a little lotus-eating of their own. For a legitimate extra out-of-body experience, a liberal dose of *harissa* on an evening couscous will supply the necessary kick.

ABOVE Playing draughts Tunisian style

ABOVE The Fortress Mosque at El May

Djerba, Medenine, Tunisia **Alternative names:** Jerba, Jarbah, Girba **Longitude:** 10° 48' E **Latitude:** 33° 50' N **Area:** 514 sq km (198 sq mi) **Highest point:** 50m (164 ft) **Population:** 120,000
Principal town: Houmt Souq **Native:** Meni Mazuz **Resident:** Hayreddin Barbarossa

"White silhouettes, white cupolas of the mosques
like upturned breasts against the desert.
They gave an air of freshness, air to aspirate, not this windy,
clawing climate – Djerba is a part of the Sahara."

Carol Drinkwater, actress

Elba

LIGURIAN/TYRRHENIAN SEA

Many of those who have been seduced by the charms of the Tuscan island of Elba have wondered in retrospect whether Napoleon Bonaparte, had he known what lay in store for him – defeat at Waterloo followed by exile on the South Atlantic island of Saint Helena – might have reconsidered his decision to escape from Elba.

Napoleon had been placed under a kind of insular house arrest there in 1814 by the allied might of Britain, Austria, Russia and Prussia. This was not solitary confinement. He had brought along a regiment of *chasseurs* from his personal guard. He was given the title Emperor of Elba as part of the terms of the deal. And initially he kept busy: while he was on the island he made significant improvements to its roads, law courts, its wine business and its agricultural industry. After just three hundred days, however, he could not fight off his empire-building instincts any longer.

He stayed at the Villa dei Mulini near Elba's capital, Portoferraio, where Bonaparte buffs can view a collection of memorabilia or stand on the terrace and imagine their hero's thoughts while studying the fine views over the bay and the mineral-rich hills and mountains. Along with his tweaks to the local economy, Napoleon had revitalized the iron mines that had funded Elba for four thousand years, since the Ligurian and Etruscan eras. So fierce was the glow from the smelters and furnaces that the Greeks called the island Aethalia, or "flame", and passing sailors said it was the fire god Vulcan making weapons for his bellicose colleague Mars. The importance of metal lives on in the names both of Portoferraio (port of iron) and the mainland town of Piombino (lead), from which ferries ply across to Elba.

Although it is the third largest Italian island, after Sicily and Sardinia, and the largest of the seven islands in the Tuscan archipelago, Elba is only 30 kilometres (18 miles) or so in length and easily explored by scooter (there is an annual gathering of Vespa and Lambretta owners on the island). The herbs, olives, rocky cliffs, mountains and villages have something of le Petit Caporal's native Corsica about them – visible to the west on a clear day – and there is a similar mix of hill towns, such as Capioliveri, buzzing ports and beachside resorts.

There is also some excellent wine to soothe a parched throat after a day on the Vespa. The local wine is Aleatico, fortified and aromatic and good enough for Pliny the Elder to recommend it. Napoleon was reportedly fond of a glass or two during his stay, and one of the vineyards on the island inspired John Le Carré to include it as a location in his novel *The Constant Gardener*.

"Lucky Napoleon!"

Dylan Thomas

OPPOSITE The Sanctuary of Madonna di Monserrato

RIGHT The view from the terrace of Napoleon's villa

Elba, Tuscany, Italy **Longitude:** 10° 17' E **Latitude:** 42° 46' N **Area:** 223 sq km (86 sq mi) **Highest point:** 1,018 m (3,340 ft) Monte Capanne **Population:** 31,100 **Principal town:** Portoferraio
Resident: Napoleon Bonaparte

Reichenau and Mainau

LAKE CONSTANCE

"She is a coquettish little lady, Mainau, who demands great attention, to be more loved and above all, and incessantly, new clothes."

Count Lennart Bernadotte

Lapping the southern border of Germany at the confluence of the waters draining from the Swiss and Austrian Alps above, Lake Constance (or in German the Bodensee) is home to a unique, balmy, almost tropical microclimate all of its own. On the northern side of the lake rise two islands, Reichanau and Mainau, whose fertile soil yields a startling variety of exotic fruit and vegetables and which have earned a special place in German hearts and history. If southern Germany is sometimes called the most northern state of Italy, the sun-drenched climate of these fragrant and floral islands could convince you that they were Mediterranean.

More than two-thirds of Reichenau is given over to market-gardening and the cultivation of fruit and vegetables. Few nations take to things with such zest and systematic organization as the Germans and here – under the tutelage of the Swedish Count Lennart Bernadotte, a descendant of the dukes of Baden-Württemburg who own the island and enjoy the Baroque centrepiece Schloss as their family residence – they have taken to gardening with all the Germanic love of nature, sense of environmental friendliness and all-round *Gesundheit*. At the peak of spring, the sight of such extensive carpets of varying but always abundant colour is reminiscent of the tulip season in the Netherlands. On neighbouring Mainau, a combination of the climate and technology contrives to keep most of the Italian gardens, home to many rare species of orchid as well as dripping banana and citrus trees, in bloom all year round, ensuring a constant flow of visitors over the two causeways linking both islands to mainland Germany. Reichenau's name is thought to stem from the old alemanic meaning "rich island". Even the earliest settlers must have been aware of the island's fecundity.

The larder of Germany, Reichenau can also be considered part of the cradle of German civilization. There had been monks here since AD 724, but with the coronation of Charlemagne at Aachen in north Germany, and the birth of the Holy Roman Empire, they found themselves a vital link between the newfound German First Reich and Rome. The three monasteries of Reichenau, St Georg in Oberzell (a wonderful example of Carolingian architecture), at Niederzell and the largest and most important, the Münster at Mittzell, became centres of scholarship, literature, painting and manuscript illumination. The scholarship performed here continued to influence a land soon to be rocked by the birth of Protestantism and a turbulent relationship with the Church right up until its dissolution at the hands of Napoleon.

OPPOSITE The gardener's tower and paths lined with tulips on Mainau Island

ABOVE Aiguilles de Bavella and Zonza village

OVERLEAF The cliff town of Bonifacio

Corsica, France **Alternative name:** Corse **Longitude:** 9° 03' E **Latitude:** 42° 10' N **Area:** 8,680 sq km (3,350 sq mi) **Highest point:** 2,706 m (8,878 ft) Monte Cinto **Population:** 281,000
Principal town: Ajaccio **Natives:** Napoleon Bonaparte, François Coty, Cardinal Joseph Fesch, Alizée Jacotey, Pasquale Paoli, Marie-Claude Pietragalla, Angelo Rinaldi, Tino Rossi, César Vezzani
Resident: Dorothy Carrington

Corsica

MEDITERRANEAN

"A French island basking in the Italian sun."

Honoré de Balzac

There is a beautiful Corsican music called *paghjella*, a polyphonic choral chanting, CDs of which are usually on sale in the souvenir shops alongside the pocket knives, ewe's cheese, wild boar pâté and bottles of Cap Corse apéritif. The haunting male-voice choirs relay chants handed down from generations past, and the music's contrapuntal nature reflects the core of Corsica's history and character: oral tradition, complexity and togetherness. Polyphony is the epitome of Corsican solidarity.

Balanced on the tip of Sardinia's nose, Corsica has (apart from a couple of interruptions) been part of France since 1768, when the island was sold by Genoa to Louis XV. It is a tempestuous relationship: Corsica tries to remain ruggedly independent. The Corsican language, with its distinctive "u" endings – like the polyphony transmitted orally and for long periods never notated – is easily visible throughout the island. One of the great local heroes, Pasquale Paoli, tried to set up a Corsican republic in 1755, but was quashed by the French army. The political struggles continue: between summer visits holiday cottages are blown up – *sauté* – by the separatist movement. Ironic then that one of France's most celebrated leaders, Napoleon Bonaparte, was born into a noble family in the island's capital, Ajaccio.

Under threat, Corsicans retreat into the mountains and the forests of cork oak and pine, or the scented thickets of scrub known as the *maquis*, from the Italian for "mesh". Napoleon always said he could sense the smell of the *maquis* from the sea; now the herbs are used to scent honey. These mountains were once inaccessible other than on foot or by mule. Trekking routes like the demanding GR20 mountain path recreate that difficulty, although an alternative is to take the quaint single-track railway from Ajaccio or Bastia on the other side of the island, which creeps its way up either side of the central ridge to meet in Corte, the old capital and soul of the island.

In the hills, the unwritten law of vendetta prevailed among the tight-lipped, introspective towns like Sartène in the south, which the short-story writer Prosper Mérimée called "the most Corsican of Corsican towns". The great irony was that the men always wanted the land in the hills, and the supposedly worthless seafront land was given to the women, who have benefited from selling off their plots for holiday apartments and second homes. From the megalithic site at Filitosa near Sartène to the cliff town of Bonifacio overlooking Sardinia, or the chic harbour activity in northern Calvi (besieging which Nelson lost his right eye), Corsica has learnt to relax its once guarded welcome – but only so much.

> "Strange how this coast-country
> does not belong to our present world."
>
> D. H. Lawrence

Sardinia

MEDITERRANEAN

As if the rest of the island did not exist, what is most commonly celebrated about the second largest island in the Mediterranean concerns just its north-eastern corner. In the 1960s, overlooking the emerald-green waters of this stretch of coastline, the Aga Khan set up a consortium to build a playboy's summer paradise – the kind of thing that nowadays ought to send a shudder down the spine of true islophiles. He developed the shorelines between Golfo d'Arzachena and the Golfo Aranci with hotels, villas and clubs and, with the copywriting eye of an estate agent, christened the place the Costa Smeralda. Since then it has attracted a coterie of stars, would-be stars and their political equivalents. In August a good portion of the Italian mainland is attracted to a luxurious interpretation of camping (complete with washing machines and satellite television) and clubs where entry to all but the *racommendati* (those with connections) is forbidden, but where it is just as cool to queue outside.

Away from this urban palimpsest lies a pastoral island in a capsule of time and space that Lawrence deemed "lost between Europe and North Africa and belonging to nowhere". Sardinia never submitted to Roman rule. Like Sicily, its enigmatic culture – dating back to mystic pre-Phoenician times as the *nuraghi* stone cairns and ancient monuments strewn across the

hillside testify – its macabre and frenetic masked carnivals such as the sacrifice of the half-man half-goat S'Urthu at Samugheo; and its many-faceted dialect (with the preponderance of words ending in "-ddu") – betray greater influence from other sources such as Catalonia, Spain and Arabia. Like the Corsicans above them, the Sardinians are a fiercely independent-minded people, with a pirate-like fire (bullet-strafed village signposts show that the locals look after themselves) and known to other Italians for their diminutive stature. However the locals maintain that *nella botte piccolo c'e il vino buono* – "small bottles contain the best wine"; in this instance the wine made in their Monte Corrasi vineyards.

Climbing back from the dramatic cliffs, sand dunes, marshes and long golden strips that form Sardinia's coastline is a rugged interior of plateaus, plains and mountains such as Punta Sos Nidos. The Punta la Marmora, in the Gennargentu massif, reaches 1,834 metres (6,017 feet) – as high as many Alpine ski resorts. Amid a landscape of cork oaks, olives, pine trees and myrtles live three sheep for every Sardinian, most of them wild moufflon and the others guided for the seasonal transhumance down ancient shepherds' trails. They are prized as the source of Sardinia's famous pecorino cheese, best enjoyed smoked over myrtle wood, scooped up on a slice of crispy *pane casasau* and downed with *mirto* myrtle-based *grappa*.

ABOVE La Sartiglia Festival

OVERLEAF A Sardinian shepherd with his flock

Sardinia, Italy **Local names:** Sardegna, Sardignia **Longitude:** 8° 59' E **Latitude:** 40° 07' N **Area:** 24,090 sq km (9,300 sq mi) **Highest point:** 1,834 m (6,017 ft) Punta la Mamora
Population: 1,655,600 **Principal town:** Cagliari **Natives:** Pier Angeli, Enrico Berlinguer, Enzo Calzaghe, Elisabetta Canalis, Maria Carta, Francesco Cossiga, Grazia Deledda, Gianluca Festa,
Paolo Fresu, Antonio Gramsci, Elena Ledda, Antonio Marras, Caterina Murino, Renato Soru, Gianfanco Zola **Resident:** Goffredo Mameli

Bioco

GULF OF GUINEA

> "Its moods of beauty are infinite;
> for the most part gentle and gorgeous,
> but I have seen it silhouetted hard against
> tornado clouds and grandly grim."
>
> Mary Kingsley

For most countries, their capital city lies at the fulcrum of the nation's life, a repository of culture and history. For others, a new capital has been created for political or geographical reasons, like Brasilia and Madrid. Equatorial Guinea is very much an exception to the norm. The capital of this small parcel of West African land, tucked in between Cameroon and Gabon, is on the island of Bioco, 200 kilometres (124 miles) northwest of the northern edge of Equatorial Guinea.

The arrangement is the result of the merger of two former Spanish colonies, the island and the mainland Rio Muni. The latter had been of little interest to the Spanish, whereas Bioco – which they called Fernando Po – was rich in cocoa plantations. Come the merger, the main town on the island was the only city of any decent size for the newly created country.

Bioco's first inhabitants – from the pre-Christian era – were the Bubi, a Bantu tribe from the mainland, who were "discovered" by the Portuguese explorer Fernaõ do Pó. He called the island Formosa Flora, "beautiful flower", but it was later named after him. In the 1770s an exchange of territory saw the island pass from Portuguese to Spanish hands. The Spanish in turn leased it to the British, who based an anti-slavery fleet there; Spanish influence then lasted through to the twentieth century.

After independence in the 1960s Equatorial Guinea endured a painful period of internal strife, particularly under the 1970s regime of President Nguema (a cleansing campaign against the Bubi saw him compared to Pol Pot). He of course threw out the old colonial names. The island of Fernando Po became Masie Nguema Biyogo, and thence Bioco; the capital Santa Isabel emerged as Malabo.

The ghosts of the past linger on in Bioco. The cocoa plantations that once thrived are now deserted, including the Art Nouveau mansion of La Barcelonesa. Malabo is full of Spanish plazas and colonial houses, although there are only a few restaurants, where expats gather, and fewer hotels. There is a small stream of visitors, however, drawn by the natural beauty of the rainforest, the volcanic peak of Pico Malabo, and some beaches on the west coast and round the second town, Luba. Anyone having a sundowner on the balcony of the Hotel Bahia in Malabo can feel the ominous presence of the mercenaries and arms traders captured by Frederick Forsyth, who wrote *The Dogs of War* right here.

Today it is the wildlife of Bioco under threat of extinction rather than its Bubi people. In the extensive tropical rainforests that cover the island, a whole range of rare primates, including colobus monkeys, bush babies and guenons, are fighting for survival.

OPPOSITE The tropical rainforest vegetation at the Bay of Luba

ABOVE Guenon monkey

Bioco, Equatorial Guinea **Alternative name:** Bioko **Longitude:** 8° 40' E **Latitude:** 3° 30' N **Area:** 2,017 sq km (779 sq mi) **Highest point:** 3,012 m (9,882 ft) Pico de Basilé **Population:** 130,000
Principal town: Malabo **Natives:** Piruchi Apo Botupa and Paloma Loribo Apo (Las Hijas del Sol) **Residents:** Richard Burton, Desmali, James Holman, Elvis Romero

"However fanciful and fantastic
the Isola Bella may be, and is, it still is beautiful."

Charles Dickens

Isole Borromee

LAKE MAGGIORE

A thin snake of a lake, the northern head of Lago Maggiore peers into Switzerland, but its body is all Italian – the most westerly of the great Italian lakes. Along with Como and Garda, the area has long been a desirable getaway, a Grand Tour stopover with a little splash of Mediterranean light in the foothills of the Alps, for the great and the good (most recently George Clooney, who acquired a villa on Lake Como and introduced a new wave of owners).

There is a handful of islands on Lake Maggiore known as the Isole Borromee, after the Borromeo family who owned them – Tuscan aristocrats who relocated after their antecedents had led a failed uprising in Florence in the fourteenth century. Successful businessmen and ecclesiasts (the family produced cardinals, popes and one saint), they established a mini-fiefdom and dynasty. In 1632 Carlos III – by

now the family had acquired quasi-regal status – took a barren island in the lake, extended it with soil from the mainland, and over decades built a palace as a wedding present for his wife Isabella. The Borromeo's equivalent of the Lake Palace in Udaipur, the island was named Isola Bella. To design the interior of this sumptuous Baroque palace (part of it is still unfinished, and some might call it an over-artificial folly) a swathe of artists and architects were brought in. The ornate frescoes, Gobelin tapestries and Genoese and Florentine furniture have been preserved intact, as have the stepped terraces, grottos and themed gardens. Napoleon stayed in the palace, and in 1935 it hosted the Stresa conference, when Ramsey MacDonald, Pierre Laval and Benito Mussolini met to guarantee peace in Europe.

If Isola Bella is all deliberate show, the gardens on Isola Madre, in the centre of the Bay

of Pallanza, are discreetly enchanting, designed to have a more organic, more natural "English" feel. Like botanical gardens, the exotic shrubs and trees have space to breathe, and pheasants and white peacocks strut and parrots squawk between cypress and palm trees, and camellia, azalea and rhododendron bushes. Gustave Flaubert, visiting in the 1840s, wrote: "Isola Madre is the most sensual place that I have ever seen in the world."

Of the three main Borromee islands, the most natural is known as Isola dei Pescatori. As its name suggests, this is a straightforward working fishing village, and the only one that is permanently inhabited. Near the mish-mash of pink, yellow and brown fishing cottages on its eastern side, a haul of restaurants serves daytrippers who come to enjoy the surroundings. The atmosphere here is very like Burano in the Venetian archipelago.

OPPOSITE Isola dei Pescatori

Isole Borromee, Verbano-Cusio-Ossola, Italy **Longitude:** 8° 31′ E **Latitude:** 45° 54′ N **Area:** 18 hectares (45 acres) **Altitude:** 193 m (633 ft) **Population:** 200

Sylt
NORTH SEA

"You don't have to look anywhere else. Sylt's beaches and bathing remain unrivalled. On Sylt, one single gorgeous day compensates for seven miserable ones."

Hans Albers, actor

While the sailors and modern-day descendants of the old Hamburg Seebaeren (sea dogs) head to Kiel for some real sailing, the well-heeled society of southern cities such as Munich, estranged from the sea, flock to this appropriately named T-shaped sand bar in the North Sea off the west coast of Denmark for their fresh air and fun. They are attracted by its ethereal light, shifting sand dunes and wind-silvered dune grass. They are enchanted by the local Soel'ring dialect and the sentinel lighthouses of places such as List, which the brooding atmosphere imbues with spiritual presence. They are drawn to the gourmet restaurants of Kampen – some of Germany's most famous – and the cute reed-thatched former fishermen's cottages of Westerland, which now house all manner of designer boutiques from Hugo Boss to Louis Vuitton. Or alternatively to a round of the local game of *bosseln*, a lawless form of boules that takes players off all over the countryside while they pull behind them a trolley of *Zielwasser* ("water to help you aim") – which is, needless to say, usually beer. These are all attributes that over the years have made Sylt something of a Teutonic Martha's Vineyard, especially during the communist decades that closed off the Baltic coast and made the North Friesian coast Germany's only seaside.

Come summer, Christmas or Easter, Sylt is jam-packed with Germans huddling up against the wind in the shelter of *Strandkoerbe*, strange-looking solid wood and wicker, ice-cream seller-striped beach baskets in the shape of canopied 1920s vintage cars. Of course, these have to be booked months in advance. And of course where there is a German beach there is likely to be a German practising some beloved *Freikoerperkultur* (FKK), the free-body culture the Germans consider a philosophy but which, in reality, amounts to nudity. Sylt is covered in beaches, quieter family ones on the calmer east side and surf paradises on the west, categorized between FKK Strand (beach) and Textilstrand, the most famous of which is Buhne 16, where of a summer Germans flock to let it all hang out.

Joined to the Friesian mainland by a rail causeway, Sylt's dunes are creeping nearer the coast and shrinking due to erosion by the North Sea. In this most environmentally friendly of lands, internal tourism is on the rise and on Sylt the two-wheeled man is king. No Mercedes or Audis are allowed and a not uncommon sight on Sylt might be that of a Schiffer or a Schumacher on a bike, swapping the limo or the Ferrari for some wholesome eco-friendly exercise and free-wheeling.

LEFT The lighthouse at the Lister Ellenbogen

OPPOSITE *Strandkoerbe*

Sylt, Nordfriesland, Schleswig-Holstein, Germany **Alternative names:** Sild, Söl **Longitude:** 8° 22' E **Latitude:** 54° 54' N **Area:** 99 sq km (38 sq mi) **Highest point:** 52 m (171 ft) Uwe Düne
Population: 21,000 **Principal town:** Westerland

São Tomé

GULF OF GUINEA

In April 1974 half a century of fascist rule in Portugal was overturned, the dictatorship of António Salazar and his successor Marcello Caetano swept away. On São Tomé, the island in the Gulf of Guinea where the Portuguese had overseen plantations of coffee and cocoa for centuries, the collapse of the regime back home had an immediate impact. All the colonial officers and administrators cleared their desks, shut up shop and went back to Portugal, leaving São Tomé adrift, rudderless, its infrastructure extant but inanimate. Those who visit the island today say that little has changed.

This is equatorial territory. The nation of São Tomé and Principé – São Tomé's sister island, a 20-kilometre (12-mile) speck an hour's flight to the north – straddles the Equator, which crosses the islet of Ilhéu das Rôlas off São Tomé's southern coast. These are volcanic islands and the combination of the soil and climate provided fertile ground first for sugar and then coffee and cocoa. The Portuguese, who had found the islands uninhabited, settled them around 1500 and used them initially as a dumping ground for whichever section of Portuguese society was deemed undesirable at the time.

As the lucrative possibilities of São Tomé became apparent, the lack of an indigenous population was solved by the simple expedient of shipping in slaves from the Cape Verde islands or the African mainland. Conditions in the plantations were geared towards high productivity, and the welfare of the workers was at the bottom of the gang-masters' agenda. There were constant struggles, and an independence movement was in full flow even before the abrupt departure of the Portuguese in the mid-1970s.

A few of the plantations, known here as *roças*, continue to be operated by the descendants of those former slaves, and São Tomé chocolate in particular is highly sought-after. There is now a chocolate tour for the handful of visitors who make it out here, who have realized that São Tomé is a tropical paradise, with little in the way of traditional options but superb beaches on the southern coast, and a main town, also called São Tomé, with parks and gardens and great views. A bonus is the local music: a coming together of African and Portuguese rhythms and sounds. *Ussua* is a plantation dance inspired by old-world minuets and *pas de lanciers*, performed to accordion and drums; *socopé* is syncopated, sensuous, Brazilian-influenced; and the *danço-congo* a free-for-all that allowed the plantation workers to get rid of their frustrations.

"It is extraordinary to find a whole country
still living like a hermit crab
in the shell left by its former masters."

Nigel Tisdall, travel writer

OPPOSITE Rio Do Ouro plantation

São Tomé, The Democratic Republic of São Tomé and Principé **Longitude:** 6° 39' E **Latitude:** 0° 10' N **Area:** 854 sq km (327 sq mi) **Highest point:** 2,024 m (6,640 ft) Pico de São Tomé
Population: 133,360 **Principal town:** São Tomé **Natives:** Açoreano, Gilberto Gil Umbelina

Porquerolles, Var, France **Longitude**: 6° 13' E **Latitude**: 43° 00' N **Area**: 13 sq km (5 sq mi) **Highest point**: 142m (466 ft) **Population**: 350 **Principal town**: Porquerolles
Resident: Georges Simenon

Porquerolles

ÎLES D'OR, GOLFE D'HYÈRES

To cross the water to the Îles d'Hyère from the glitz and glamour of the French Riviera at Toulon is to be transported back in time, to a black-and-white, silver-screen age of Bardot and Belmondo, or perhaps something even more rural and idyllic. As a bell tolls in the midday sun, accompanied only by the clink of a game of boules on the sandy village square at Porquerolles, surrounded by statuesque eucalyptus trees, or maybe that of a pre-prandial glass of Ricard, you might expect Monsieur Hulot to come around the corner into the Place d'Armes on a wobbly push-bike or disturbing the peace in a back-firing old Citroën.

It requires just that little extra bit of effort and imagination to go to Porquerolles and her sister islands, Port Clos and Le Levent (together sometimes also known as the Îles d'Or). Consequently they have the air of a private club only for those in the know; a place to escape the hedonism and freneticism of the mainland and instead bathe in the mingling aromas of mulberry, almond, fig, olive and peach groves that cover the island. It is as if the French wanted to keep Porquerolles a secret. Impressive layers of bureaucracy protect the island, limiting development to just a handful of hotels, restricting the number of visitors on the islands at any one time and most recently asserting a summer ban on smoking. No cars are allowed and so time passes at bicycle or walking pace, which allows the small resident population to ensure the atmosphere of this hinterland remains *toujours provence*.

Things were not always so peaceful, as the ruins of forts bear testimony. Back in medieval times the Saracens devastated the islands – all but emptying them of their inhabitants – before handing them over to centuries of pirate misrule by the likes of Barbarossa and his cut-throat Barbary friends. In their assault on the empire of Napoleon, the British blew up the fortifications built to defend mainland France before finally a blanket of peace was allowed to descend. In the nineteenth century Hyère became first a place for convalescing soldiers and subsequently a fashionable health resort, whose curative powers were enjoyed by the likes of Robert Louis Stevenson (though Porquerolles did not, as some claim, inspire *Treasure Island*). Europe's first nudist resort, Heliopolis, was opened on Le Levent and Europe's first nature reserve covers the island of Port Clos in a magic garden of overland and underwater signposted nature trails.

With the slow pace of a French colonial town in North Africa, its bountiful seafood, Côtes de Provence vineyards and the translucent water of its paradigms of beaches at Nôtre Dame and Place d'Argent, Porquerolles has become a refuge for those who appreciate the quiet enjoyment of the good things in life served up with that effortless French mix of simplicity and sophistication.

" 'Do you know the island of Porquerolles?',
he said, finally getting his pipe to light.
'It's apparently very beautiful, as beautiful
as Capri and the Greek islands.'"

Georges Simenon, *Mon Ami Maigret*

> "This gloomy fortress, which for more than three hundred years furnished food for so many wild legends, seemed to Dantès like a scaffold to a malefactor."
>
> Alexandre Dumas, *The Count of Monte Cristo*

Île d'If

MARSEILLES

It is odd that an island characterized by bleak concrete structures should owe its fame, notoriety and subsequent magnetism to the romance of fiction. Île d'If's most famous resident, wrongly imprisoned in the island's fortress through the treachery of his friends, was Dantès, a nineteenth-century musketeer and invention of the novelist Alexandre Dumas. Having escaped by burrowing a tunnel from his cell to the sea, Dantès returns to lord it over his friends and seek his revenge as the Count of Monte Cristo. So internationally successful has Dumas' story been for generations since its first publication in 1844, and so evocative of this island fortress, that the novel has become Île d'If's accepted emblem and *raison d'etre*, making it an uneasy point of comparison with islands of real exile such as Robben, Alcatraz and Devil's Island.

However, some of If's real captives were arguably even more colourful and unusual than its fictional hero. Tourists on the Monte Cristo trail leave unaware of the brief sojourn in 1516 of Europe's first rhinoceros. The pachyderm, a rare Indian species, was intended as a gift from King Manuel I of Portugal to Pope Leon X, and was being transported to Italy by the Portuguese navy. With a storm brewing the sailors decided to put in at If. By this stage the rhinoceros had already caused a stir and Albrecht Dürer was commissioned to record the

sight of an animal that few had ever seen at the time. Sadly, following its brief sojourn on If, the boat carrying the rhinoceros was wrecked in a storm in the Gulf of Genoa. The beast was eventually received by the Pope – stuffed and mounted.

Île d'If lies at the entrance to the Bay of Marseilles, part of the small Frioul archipelago, and in medieval times it acted as a last line of defence for that city. The fortress, with its three round towers of St Jaume, St Christophe and Mangouvert, was built by the French in 1524 initially to house the ordinary sinners of Marseilles. But the function soon expanded to include political dissidents, rebels and breakers of the taboos of French society, such as the serial recidivist Marquis de Sade. Prisoners were housed in cells on two floors; those on the upper deck with a window were known as "pistoles", after the bribe prisoners paid for a view during their sentence.

The island that Dantès describes as a "black and frowning rock" on his nocturnal arrival is in fact bright white, as if starched by the sun and salt. The mass seems to shift in the sea as its base is battered by the clear but turbulent waters whipped up by the mistral wind. Tourists wheel around it and feed off its legend – to quote the cryptic words of another Marseilles legend, Eric Cantona – as predictable as seagulls following a fishing trawler.

Île d'If, Marseilles, Bouches du Rhône, France **Longitude:** 5° 20' E **Latitude:** 43° 16' N **Area:** 3 hectares (7 acres) **Population:** None
Residents: Jean-Baptiste Chataud, Gaston Crémieux, Michel Mathieu Leconte-Puyraveau, Honoré Mirabeau, Marquis de Sade

ABOVE Some 470 dress shirts in an art installation at the Oerol Festival

Terschelling, Friesland, Netherlands **Local name:** Skylge, Schylge **Longitude:** 5° 19' E **Latitude:** 53° 25' N **Area:** 96 sq km (37 sq mi) **Highest point:** 31 m (102 ft) **Population:** 4,700
Principal town: West Terschelling **Native:** Willem Barentsz

Terschelling

WEST FRISIANS, NORTH SEA

In the famous offices of Lloyds of London hangs a bell recovered from HMS *Lutine*, a former French frigate captured by the Royal Navy, which in 1799 was drawn by the treacherous tidal stream off Terschelling and sank. It took with it all 240 passengers and crew, together with £1.2 million in gold bullion that had been on its way to Hamburg to support some German banks in an effort to prevent a worldwide financial crash. The gold was never recovered and became the subject of decades of Anglo-Dutch wrangling over salvage rights – a conflict that mirrored the two nations' fight for supremacy in Holland's more famous island assets in the East Indies. Following the installation of the bell in the headquarters of one of the world's largest shipping insurers, it was rung to signify to staff the fate of a ship: once if a ship was lost, and twice for a safe return. It is also rung in remembrance – on the death of Diana, Princess of Wales, on 9/11, the London bombings and, most relevant to the story of so many islands, the 2004 tsunami.

As readers of Erskine Childers' *Riddle of the Sands* will know, the waters around the Frisian islands, in the area known to sailors as German Bight, are treacherous in a unique and imperceptible way. The danger lies not in the currents or hidden rocks, but rather in the tides and a labyrinth of tidal trenches and islands in the sandbanks, which come and go, shift, or are covered and then uncovered. Terschelling and the surrounding islands are known as wadden islands, and the sea around them that rare natural phenomenon, the Wadden Sea. Here between land, wetland and sea, the defining line between *terra firma* and clear water is in constant motion. The phenomenon in fact stretches from the North Frisian islands up by Denmark and was created by huge storm tides between the tenth and fourteenth centuries. But it is here, particularly in the Vlie – the seaway between Terschelling and Vlieland – that it is most acute.

Wrecks abound, and the locals have made something of both a civilization and a recreation out of them over the centuries. Due to the shortage of trees on these enormous grassy sand dunes of islands, the masks and keels of wrecked ships made useful timber for houses. Nowadays locals also indulge in the risky sport of *wadlopen*, navigating the sandbanks on foot; at the right time it is possible to walk all the way from Terschelling to mainland Holland. *Wadlopen* can only be undertaken in the company of a licensed guide, partly because it is dangerous for those who do not know the routes and tides, but also to protect the unique flora and fauna of the shoreline.

Back on dry land, the village of West Terschelling is the main settlement, notable for its former Commodore's buildings and lighthouse. Every June a metropolitan crowd is attracted by the festival of Oerol (meaning "everywhere"), when the entire island turns into a giant open air theatre, with productions performed in impromptu amphitheatres in the dunes, grasslands and woodlands.

"One of the traditions of Terschelling is hanging around bars waiting for free drinks to come out."

Johnny Melville, comedian at the Oerol Festival

Menorca

BALEARICS, MEDITERRANEAN

Menorca's very name hints at its role as a junior partner to its larger Balearic cousin Mallorca, which lies just a short hop to the southwest. The "minor" quality of the island, however, is something more subtle: the relationship of the viola to the violin, inflected with a similar depth of feeling and dignified maturity. And Menorca has certainly never played second fiddle to its neighbour – during the Spanish Civil War Menorca was the only Balearic island to remain loyal to the Republican government, while the rest of the islands backed Franco.

One of the distinctive flavours of Menorca is the bitter edge of juniper in gin – a legacy of the island's involvement with the British, who intermittently took control here throughout the eighteenth century, arriving in the wake of the Phoenicians, Romans, Vandals, Moors, Aragonese and many others. British sailors introduced the joys of gin to the islanders, who developed their own version distilled from grapes (rather than grain) and flavoured with herbs. It is still produced by the Xoriguer distillery at the capital Mahón, and is often mixed with lemonade to create *pomada*.

The British influence lingers in other ways: Georgian townhouses in Villacarlos sport sash and bow windows; local folk dances include elements of the Highland fling; and the Menorca Cricket Club is known as "the other MCC". The *menorquí* language has adopted and adapted some quirkily English words. You can pour *grevi* (gravy) on your *bifi* (beef), and follow it with a slice or two of *plum queque* (plum cake). Horatio Nelson must have felt very much at home when he spent time at the Golden Farm mansion overlooking the great natural harbour of Mahón, the strategic incentive for the British, French and Spanish to wrest control of the island.

Although they were happy to borrow alcoholic recipes or sporting habits, Menorcans did not kowtow to any occupiers, and they are still likely to spray graffiti defiantly declaring *no som espanyols*, even though Spain has owned the island since 1802. Menorca's history stretches back before such transient visitors, proven by the island's extensive collection of prehistoric cave dwellings and megalithic monuments. The Naveta dels Tudons, just outside the second city of Ciutadella, is a funereal structure that resembles an upturned stone rowing boat; the village of Torre d'en Gaumes has T-shaped stones like Stonehenge, and affords views across the southern half of the island. Tourism has been controlled so the landscape has remained relatively unspoiled, and the creation of a UNESCO Biosphere Reserve has guaranteed protection of Menorca's gullies, caves, islets and wild olive groves.

"Good jams come in small pots."

Menorcan saying

Menorca, Balearic Islands, Spain **Alternative name:** Minorca **Longitude:** 4° 08' E **Latitude:** 39° 54' N **Area:** 668 sq km (258 sq mi) **Highest point:** 358 m (1,175 ft) Monte Toro **Population:** 88,000 **Principal town:** Mahón/Máo **Native:** Joan Riudavets Moll **Resident:** Admiral Cuthbert Collingwood

"The ever-changing Majorcan sky; the line drawn by a shooting star, and the sea, at night and during the day, always blue."

Joan Miró

Mallorca

BALEARICS, MEDITERRANEAN

Since the arrival on the island of package tourism in 1952, there have always been two Mallorcas: the Mallorca of the ultimate Anglo-German battleground for sun-loungers at dawn, and the secret Mallorca gloriously neglected by those put off by the island's package-tour reputation. It is true that on the golden strip and Easyjet mecca of Palma Bay, between S'Arenal and Magaluf, festooned like a German Ibiza with yellow signs announcing *Zimmer frei*, the proudly felt Spanish identity of Mallorca (or Mallorguí in the vernacular) seems submerged. But happily the high-rise development has been contained to this small area, and beyond the beach-loungers the island is rich with unexpected culinary treasures, artistic heritage, sacred sites and dramatic landscapes.

Civilization was founded here by the Romans (who called this largest of the Balearic islands after the Latin *maior*, meaning "larger"). The island's riches were built on trade in salt from the central plain of Es Pla, olives and wine. Following occupation by the Vandals and an enlightening period under the Moorish caliphate of Cordoba, the thirteenth-century reign of James I of Aragon left the most enduring mark. James laid the foundation stone of the cathedral of La Seu – built on the ruins of a Moorish mosque and on which Antonio Gaudí worked for thirteen years – which dominates the stylish and lively city of La Palma (or simply Ciutat ["city"], as it is known on the island).

His younger son, James II, commissioned the other principal architectural sites of the Gothic Almudaina Palace, next to the cathedral, and the Bellver castle where he entertained his political prisoners.

In the nineteenth century, the idyllic village of Valldemossa became the romantic hideaway in the mountains in which Frederic Chopin and George Sand conducted their love affair. Decades later the ochre-coloured, green-shuttered houses of Deia under the shadow of the Teix mountain became a colony for foreign artists. It was here also that Robert Graves wrote *Goodbye to All That*. More recently it has become a retreat for German millionaires such as Boris Becker, Claudia Schiffer and Michael Schumacher. The specialities of *sobrassada* (a raw cured sausage with paprika) and *ensaimada* (a generic yeast-based Spanish pastry but here made from pork lard instead of oil or butter) are enticing for all visitors.

Mallorca's countryside is defined by two mountain ranges, most notably the Serra de Tramuntana in the northwest, topped by the Puig Major. The island's most sacred site lies in a cleft in a rock at Lluc; here, a small statue of the Madonna known as *la maroneta* thrice miraculously returned after being removed. Beneath these rugged cliffs lie, in contrast to the exposed flesh of Magaluf, the more secretive bays and Roman and medieval ramparts of Pollenca and Alcudia and, offshore, the lesser-explored island jewels of Cabrera and Dragonera.

LEFT The view from Son Marroig near Deia

OVERLEAF The mountain village of Valldemossa

Mallorca, Balearic Islands, Spain **Alternative name:** Majorca **Longitude:** 2° 59' E **Latitude:** 39° 37' N **Area:** 3,640 sq km (1,405 sq mi) **Highest point:** 1,445 m (4,741 ft) Puig Major/Pico Mayor
Population: 790,800 **Principal town:** Palma de Mallorca **Natives:** Miguel Barceló, Maria del Mar Bonet, Ramon Llull, Jorge Lorenzo, Antonio Maura y Montaner, Carlos Moyà, Rafael Nadal, Junipero Serra **Residents:** Ola Brunkert, Frédéric Chopin, Robert Graves, Joan Miró, George Sand

Île St-Louis

RIVER SEINE, PARIS

Urban islands should always be this classy: right in the middle of Paris, girded by the waters of the Seine, the Île St-Louis is elegant, cultured and self-contained. It has been said that the island is like a small French village picked up and deposited in the centre of the French capital – but that is a trifle misleading. The streets of seventeenth-century townhouses are proudly urban. What gives the island its village atmosphere is its sense of identity and community, its profusion of small traders, and a charming collection of pâtisseries, fromageries and boulangeries past which the cavalry of the Republican Guard exercise their horses, adding the age-old clatter of hooves.

The Île was originally two smaller islands where cattle grazed. They were merged by an imaginative entrepreneur in 1614. This urban planning and property development eliminated the pastoral character, but whereas the neighbouring Île de la Cité became the site of impressive national edifices like Notre-Dame and the Palais de Justice, St-Louis was essentially residential. This is why many tourists miss a trick by not taking the time to amble across one of the bridges that tether the smaller island to its neighbour and the banks of the Seine. The six thousand inhabitants, or *louisiens* – no longer obliged to be Left or Right Bank – smugly call the rest of Paris *le continent*.

St-Louis' first denizens were nobles and financiers, who commissioned gracious residences, known as *hôtels*. Both the Hôtel de Lauzun and the Hôtel Lambert were designed by Louis le Vau, the architect who helped create the Palace de Versailles and the Louvre. His brother, François, was responsible for the island's main church, St-Louis en l'Île; its huge wooden door in a rather sombre exterior opens up into a fabulously Rococo interior. The *hôtels* have always attracted the bohemian as well as the wealthy. A roll-call of residents includes Charles Baudelaire, Jean Paul Gaultier, Paul Cézanne, Marc Chagall and Coco Chanel.

Amid the plane trees and grand façades stands an Île St-Louis institution. The Berthillon glacerie, founded in 1954 by Raymond Berthillon, is the Lourdes of ice creams and sorbets, where pilgrims can savour dozens of intense flavours, from wild strawberry, gingerbread and blood orange to the purist's nirvana, vanilla. So far the shop has not offered a sorbet based on the green *hashish*-flavoured jelly that was the *menu du jour* for Edouard Manet, Honoré de Balzac, Charles Baudelaire and fellow members of the Club des Haschischins at the Hôtel de Lauzun in the 1840s. In any case, the locals would say that their island offers its own sense of *bien-être*.

> "An oasis of solitude in the heart of Paris, which the river hugs in both arms as if protecting it against the encroachment of civilization."
>
> Théophile Gautier

OPPOSITE The famous Berthillon glacerie

OVERLEAF Île St-Louis

Île St-Louis, Paris, France **Longitude:** 2° 21' E **Latitude:** 48° 51' N **Highest point:** 27 m (89 ft) **Population:** 6,000 **Residents:** Charles Baudelaire, Guy Bedos, Jean-Claude Brialy, Paul Cézanne, Camille Claudel, Marie Curie, Théophile Gautier, Agnès Jaoui, James Joyce, Michèle Morgan, Georges Moustaki, Georges Pompidou, Jean-Baptiste Racine, Guy de Rothschild

Ibiza

BALEARICS, MEDITERRANEAN

Ibiza is many things: a place, a scene, an attitude; a type of music, a time of year, even a season. Every summer clubbers from all over the world descend on the island to indulge in weeks of ritual under the trance of electronic music being spun by spiritual missionary deejays. But anyone who thinks that the orgiastic clubbing culture with which the island has become so synonymous is an inconsiderate invasion of the modern world may not know that Ibiza has a long history of partying. The house music purveyed by Danny Rampling and Paul Oakenfold is only the latest form of the bacchanalian and pagan spirit that lies at the core of Ibiza culture and history.

Bes, after whom Ibiza is named, was the Phoenician god of pleasure, brought to the island by the Carthaginians, successors of the Phoenicians. With Bes came Tanit, the goddess of sex, and together they begat a whole culture. Successive civilizations, often exiles and fugitives, were unsurprisingly keen to absorb and expand the tenets of this liberal way of life, and it was not until the advent of Catholicism in mainland Spain that Ibiza's hedonistic ways were challenged. Even now the island retains a powerful sense of mysticism, be it in shrines to Tanit herself, the macabre forces of the Es Vedra rock, or the island's unique breed of dogs – said to be the model for the ancient Egyptian god of the underworld, Anubis.

A permissive way of life had been established and fuelled by an innate sense of isolation common to all islanders, but here with an added dose of Catalan separatism. It was one the Ibicencos were keen to protect. Thus Ibiza has always taken a dim view of edicts from mainland Spain and has long been a refuge for confused, fleeing, dreaming souls. On Ibiza you can be whatever you like as long as you respect your neighbour. This kind of *kibbutz* mentality and respect for individuality has attracted writers and artists, and was an obvious magnet for followers of the hippie movement. Each group has in turn been keen to pass on – even exaggerate – Ibiza's permissive creed.

It was normal, therefore, that a new form of music should make its way from Chicago in the suitcase of a chancer from Italy called Alfredo. He opened Ibiza's first after-show club, and unwittingly sparked the Balearic version of house music. With it came the trend for sunrise dance sessions at Space, foam-drenched closing parties at Pacha and Amnesia, and even live sex shows.

In recent times people have sounded the death knell for Ibiza now that clubbers have so many other destinations – Agia Napa, Mykonos, Thailand – to choose from. But Ibiza has always known how to reinvent itself. Nor is clubbing the all-pervasive or dominant phenomenon on "the white island" – so-called not after any nocturnal stimulant but due to the vast resources of salt that gave Ibiza its riches. Away from the fish 'n' chips of "San An", a quiet, impervious but fiercely defined sense of identity continues. It is easy to find isolation, untouched beauty and serenity for a more chilled form of meditation and self-liberation.

Ibiza, Balearic Islands, Spain **Local name:** Eivissa **Longitude:** 1° 27' E **Latitude:** 38° 54' N **Area:** 596 sq km (230 sq mi) **Highest point:** 476 m (1,562 ft) Pico de Atalayasa **Population:** 113,900
Principal town: Ibiza **Natives:** Al-Sabbini, Joan Castelló Guasch, Isidoro Macabich Llobet **Residents:** Mike Oldfield, Andy Taylor

"Ibiza seems to have done its best to live up to Bes, whether through the chaotic hedonism of dancing or the eternal sanctuary the place has provided for the troubled and the wandering across the centuries. It's an island of escape and an island of the night."

Stephen Armstrong, *The White Island*

ABOVE Es Vedra island rock

Formentera

BALEARICS, MEDITERRANEAN

Formentera is the wayward younger sibling of the Balearics. Along with Ibiza, the island is one of the subfamily of las Islas Pitiusas, or Pine Islands, and the aromatic savina is one of the few plants – along with monkey-puzzle trees and agaves that thrive in this stark but beautiful terrain. Hedonists thinking that they are better off hanging out in Ibiza, though, should know that beach cognoscenti consider Formentera's Ses Illetes a match for anything Ibiza has on offer at Playa d'en Bossa or las Salinas.

Although only a few kilometres separate the two islands, they could be a galaxy apart. There are megaliths at Ca na Costa that tell of age-old habitation, but settlers really only began to arrive in the late seventeenth century, led by Ibiza's Marc Ferrer (there are still many Ferrer descendants). Despite the flat, stony, windswept landscape, the settlers worked hard to harness the land's natural resources, digging out salt and scraping a living where they could establish some kind of cultivation on this straggly island, no more than 20 kilometres (12 miles) long and a handful wide.

Nothing much changed for three centuries, until the late 1960s when a vanguard of the curious gravitated here, intent on dropping out and tuning in. Bob Dylan was an early visitor, and French film director Barbet Schroeder used Formentera as a location for his 1969 movie *More*, which featured a soundtrack from the then relatively unknown Pink Floyd. By chance, the group had earlier brought Syd Barrett here, to Playa Mitjorn in the south, in a last-ditch but unsuccessful attempt to wean him off acid. Thirty years later the jagged landscape inspired Julio Medem to write *Sex and Lucia*.

Something of that 1960s hippie vibe persists, including gently ageing Floyd fans (David Gilmour bought a house here), and Formentera has kept traditional tourism at arm's length. That, of course, is its appeal. For those who have imbibed too large a dose of Ibiza's charms, Formentera is a convenient destination for recharging and recalibrating mind, body and soul, best worked out with a cycle ride past the stone walls that divide up the island. As word of mouth has travelled, however, the calibre of visitor has evolved. In the wake of Spain's King Juan Carlos, who was fond of tying up his royal yacht and adjourning for supper at the noted Es Moli dal Sal restaurant in the north of the island, an influx of visitors has taken the ferry over from Ibiza – there is no airport on Formentera – to chill out here and at restaurants like Juan y Andrea in Illetes, where *paella* and sea bass under the palms makes for a perfect detox.

> "There's no high-heel glamour here, just sand and sun. It's a hideaway where we can relax."
>
> Consuelo Castiglioni, fashion designer

Formentera, Balearic Islands, Spain **Longitude:** 1° 27' E **Latitude:** 38° 43' N **Area:** 83 sq km (32 sq mi) **Highest point:** 192 m (630 ft) La Mola **Population:** 6,900
Principal town: Sant Francesc Xavier **Native:** DJ Buty **Residents:** Consuelo Castiglioni, Philippe Starck

Canvey Island

RIVER THAMES

At the entrance to the Thames is an island that lies so low in the water it barely peeps over the surface. This is Canvey Island in Essex: a final, flimsy bastion before the onslaught of the often merciless North Sea. Although Dutch engineers shored up its defences in the seventeenth century, the ravenous waters often encroached. The most recent disastrous flood occurred in 1953, when the island was entirely swamped apart from one tiny area of raised ground surmounted by the Red Cow pub. With pragmatically sardonic humour, the locals renamed it the King Canute.

There is an older pub on Canvey, the Lobster Smack, which dates back to the early 1500s, a one-time haunt of smugglers, and later of Pip and Magwitch in Dickens' *Great Expectations*. When the tavern first opened its doors, the island was primarily populated by sheep – which still feature on its coat of arms – and had a thriving cheese industry. But although the marshlands were not the healthiest places (malaria was always a threat), Canvey enjoyed a remarkable turnaround in the Victorian era. A local businessman, Frederick Hester, took the seemingly reckless decision to turn the island's creeks and channels into a Venetian-style estuarine holiday resort, and promptly set about building palazzos and conservatories, and encouraging London pleasure-seekers to punt around the waterways as if they were on the Grand Canal or to ride the electric monorail he had installed. For a while, the *beau monde* descended on Canvey, until Hester overextended himself and went bust in 1905.

Seventy years, some Second World War pillboxes and one massive flood later, Canvey had its second great renaissance, courtesy of the legendary Dr Feelgood, whose no-frills, deliberately mono R&B presaged the arrival of punk on *Down by the Jetty* and the live Number One album *Stupidity*. Guitarist Wilko Johnson, vocalist Lee Brilleaux and their rhythm section of The Big Figure and John B. Sparks purveyed gritty tales and gruff, tough romances. Their very own delta blues captured life amid the mud, the marshes and the Shell Haven oil refinery: the front cover shot of their debut was taken right by the Lobster Smack.

There are now Dr Feelgood tours of the island. On a walk round the 23-kilometre (14-mile) seawall footpath, fans can also check out old thatched Dutch cottages, the Art Deco Labworth Café, the "upside down" houses (with sitting rooms upstairs) built after the 1953 flood, and spot oystercatchers and curlews.

As the late Lee Brilleaux pointed out: "Canvey was really a rural community in many ways. I grew up playing on the creeks, building pirate dens out in the marshes. We knew about tides, about birds and shellfish, alongside the bookies and the boozers."

ABOVE Art Deco Labworth Café

Canvey Island, Essex, England, UK **Longitude:** 0° 34' E **Latitude:** 51° 31' N **Area:** 18 sq km (7 sq mi) **Highest point:** 0.6 m (2 ft) **Population:** 37,500 **Principal town:** Canvey
Natives: Wilko Johnson, John Martin aka The Big Figure, John B. Sparks **Residents:** Lee Brilleaux, Dean Macey

"You can't pass through Canvey on the way to somewhere else.
You had to go over the bridge onto the island,
and there we all were, below sea level."

Wilko Johnson

"Look at her, snuggling into
the soft underbelly of England.
The little cutie. The little beauty.
Look at the shape of her. Pure diamond."

Julian Barnes, *England, England*

Isle of Wight

ENGLISH CHANNEL

For a certain stratum of the UK population, the Isle of Wight – separated from the mainland by the sliver of the Solent – is a time capsule of childhood, the year-in-year-out destination for holidays in the era before the seductive continental charms of Tuscany, the Dordogne or the Costa Brava beckoned. In the 1950s and 1960s, this superficially unpretentious island, only a short ferry trip for anyone who had a ticket to Ryde, had its own exotic appeal.

Although all the essential ingredients of a traditional British seaside holiday could be found in resorts like Ventnor, Shanklin or Sandown – dilapidated piers, fish and chips on the prom, sticks of rock, steep steps down to bucket-and-spade beaches, model villages and crazy golf – the Isle of Wight always offered something more. There was a hint of the unexpected. At the end of Sandown Bay, fossilized remains on the Dinosaur Coast tap into a prehistoric era. The jagged chalk stacks of the Needles, heading off into the sea at the very western tip, close to the coloured sand cliffs of Alum Bay, look like the spines of a submerged stegosaurus. And when the Doors, Hendrix, the Who and half a million fans flooded in for the Isle of Wight Festival in August 1970, the aura of respectable tourism was jolted once and for all.

It was the Victorians who made the Isle of Wight a tourist destination: Alfred, Lord Tennyson took a house on the Downs and invited chums like Charles Darwin and Lewis Carroll to stay. But the most famous Victorian to visit was Queen Victoria herself. Osborne House, which she and Prince Albert bought in 1845 and where she died over half a century later, still displays the opulence of the era, complete with horse-drawn carriages.

Osborne House lies just outside Cowes, the regatta capital of England, where each August Cowes Week fulfils its duties on the social calendar just after Glorious Goodwood. The soundtrack of the island shimmers with the tinkling of marina masts, and yachtswoman Ellen MacArthur has become an honorary native (the locals are known as "corkheads" after the caulk, or predominant chalk, of the local geology). The late film director Anthony Minghella was one such corkhead: his Italian parents founded a famous ice-cream company here in the 1950s, and alongside occasional excursions into the exotic – a garlic ice cream to tie in with the island's Garlic Festival – they produced new recipes for each of his movies, including a blend called Oscar Celebration to mark his award-winning success with *The English Patient*: passion fruit and champagne.

Isle of Wight, England, UK **Longitude:** 1° 17' W **Latitude:** 50° 41' N **Area:** 380 sq km (147 sq mi) **Highest point:** 241 m (791 ft) St Boniface Down **Population:** 132,800 **Principal town:** Newport
Natives: Uffa Fox, Vivian Fuchs, Marius Goring, Bear Grylls, Sheila Hancock, Robert Hooke, Jeremy Irons, Phill Jupitus, Mark King, Anthony Minghella, Brian Murphy, Horace Rawlins
Residents: Julia Margaret Cameron, Kenneth Kendall, Ellen Macarthur, Alfred Noyes, Bill Pertwee, J. B. Priestley, Algernon Swinburne, Alfred Tennyson, Alan Titchmarsh, Queen Victoria

ABOVE Nearly 1,700 boats compete in the 80-kilometre (50-mile) round the island race, here passing The Needles

OVERLEAF The beach at Shanklin

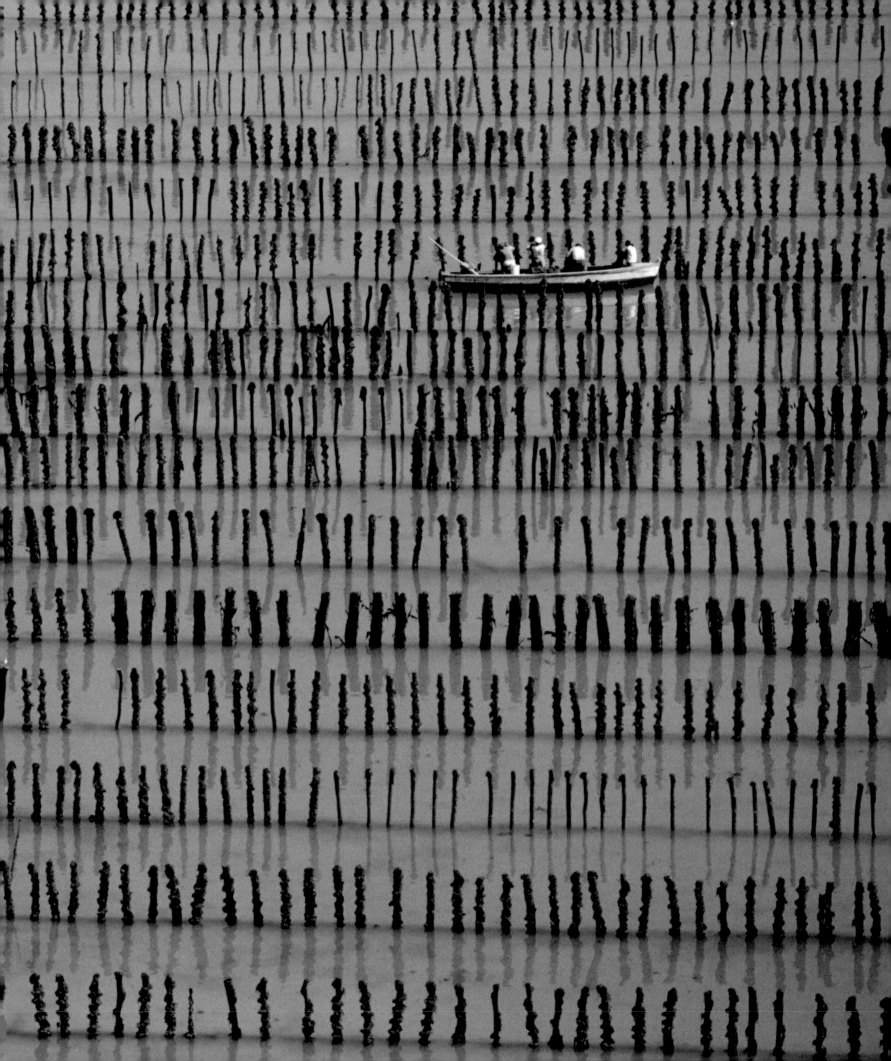

Île d'Oléron

ATLANTIC COAST, FRANCE

During the high summer months, the country roads leading towards the Île d'Oléron back up with bottlenecks as the lines of traffic jockey for position before crossing the only bridge on to the island. Once across its 3-kilometre (1.8-mile) span, the frenzy of the mainland dissipates and time appears to slow. Although located on the breezy, western Atlantic coast of France, the combination of mimosa, pines and tamarisk, and the families pedalling past in flip-flops, suggest a more Mediterranean feel and a sense of the French *grandes vacances*. At any moment you expect Jacques Tati to emerge from behind the carefully tended hedges and rows of hollyhocks.

The sandy beaches in the west of the island – Domino, la Perroche, la Rémigeasse – are an obvious attraction but because the Île d'Oléron is extensive (the second largest of France's immediately offshore islands after Corsica), there are plenty of secret corners to explore, ideally by bike since the terrain is so flat. For the less active, though, a little train putters north from St-Trojan-les-Bains through marshes and pine forests.

In the east of the island the predominant landscape is the broad expanse of oyster beds studded with the wooden *cabanes* of their owners. The *huîtres* of Oléron are justly renowned, and it is a shame if a visitor heads back across the bridge without tasting one of these delicacies. This is shellfish and seafood country: on *bouchots* (wooden stakes), mussels are carefully cultivated, and succulent langoustines are pulled from the waters. To wash all this down, other stretches of the island are covered in vineyards, producing crisp, dry white wine, or *pineau*, fermented from a blend of cognac and grape juice.

It is the mild climate, the long beaches, the salty air and the oysters that attract vacationers, rather than the island's history, although the main town, le Château d'Oléron, has a Cardinal Richelieu-commissioned citadel – still in extremely good condition. It stands on a fortified site that dates back to the Visigoths and Eleanor of Aquitaine, who lived here in the twelfth century. A later fortification, just off the island's eastern shore, is the squat rotund shape of Fort Boyard, which became famous in the 1990s for the game show of the same name that was filmed there. Napoleon had originally ordered its construction in 1801 against attack by foreign, especially British, ships. By the time it was completed around fifty years later, the fort was already redundant, but its presence seems to have worked in keeping out foreigners. Visitors to Oléron are almost all French and recently the islanders have even proposed a toll on the bridge to limit the numbers of their own compatriots.

> "An abundance of greenery, amazing flora, fields of poppies. It feels as though you're right in the heart of the countryside on the very edge of the sea."
>
> Mélanie Laurent, actress

OPPOSITE Mussel beds

BELOW The Chassiron lighthouse

Île d'Oléron, Charente-Maritime, France **Longitude:** 1° 18' W **Latitude:** 45° 55' N **Area:** 175 sq km (68 sq mi) **Highest point:** 34 m (112 ft) **Population:** 20,000
Principal town: Le Château d'Oléron **Native:** Pierre Bergé **Residents:** Eleanor of Aquitaine, Pierre Loti, Maurice Renard

"Peter played the mourning song of the Shetland fishermen…
Nothing can sing sweeter than a violin, and no music could have been
sadder than this lament for drowned men."

Mollie Hunter, *A Stranger Came Ashore*

Shetland, Scotland **Longitude:** 1° 23' W **Latitude:** 68° 38' N **Area:** 1,468 sq km (567 sq mi) **Highest point:** 450 m (1,476 ft) Ronas Hill, Mainland **Population:** 22,500 **Principal town:** Lerwick
Natives: Arthur Anderson, Tom Anderson, Aly Bain, Ian Bairnson, J. J. Haldane Burgess, Willie Hunter, Norman Lamont, Willa Muir, Robert Stout

Shetland

NORTH SEA/ATLANTIC

It is a measure of how insular the Shetlanders are that they call the largest of their some one hundred islands (only fifteen of which are inhabited) Mainland. The British Isles' most northern community, halfway to Iceland off the northeast of Scotland, they are proud of their remoteness and local identity; all "soothmoothers" – their derogatory word for outsiders – are regarded with a mixture of disdain, mirth and exclusionary elitism.

That the locals can get away with such attitude is not just because of a strong culture; it is also due to the islands' great prosperity – surprising perhaps for an island group with no apparent industry other than crofting and making jumpers from the abundant sheep – which is on a par with their Scandinavian neighbours further north and east.

The Shetlands boast thousands of Neolithic and other archaeological sites, recording the presence of the Picts, the founding civilization. Against northern cinemascope skies, and watched over by sentinel herds of the diminutive shaggy-maned local pony, their stone ruins form an eerie relief on these flat islands, often low but sometimes high with steep cliffs. The visitor is filled with a sense of the ancient and wise not dissimilar to that experienced amid the sands of Egypt. The Shetlands also have a strong link to the Viking civilization that gave the islands their name, Hjatland, meaning "hilt". From 1195 they were under the rule of Norway; after a long dispute over their ownership, and with the Viking economy in decline, they were eventually pawned to Scotland.

The Shetlanders always traded successfully with the Hanseatic League, but the islanders really hit the jackpot with the discovery of Britain's richest oil seam in the East Shetland Basin in 1970. Sullom Voe is still the United Kingdom's largest oil export harbour. The most spectacular showcase of the local Viking heritage (other than the dialect, which is re-establishing itself, and the fiddle music and sailors' jigs that are a mixture of Norwegian folk music and Scottish reels) is the annual post-Christmas festival of pyromania, drink and debauchery, Up Helly Aa (meaning "upending"). Make no mistake – however cold and windswept, the capital Lerwick is not a quiet place. If ever there was a way to break up the long winter days – which are contrasted in summer by the "simmer dims" – this is it. Led by the Guiser Jarl, an honour that can be bestowed just once on any Shetlander, the male islanders march through the town dressed up in horned helmets, armour and red beards, burn a longboat and then fall over each other cosily in a night of partying. It is a sort of Nordic Mardi Gras.

More serene pleasures to be enjoyed on the Shetlands are wreck-spotting and bird-watching. This archipelago, once described as a drowned jigsaw, is a cemetery of Second World War battleships, and home to a colony of some one million birds, including puffins, storm petrels, winter wrens and great northern divers.

LEFT Shetland farmhouses are based on Viking architecture

OVERLEAF The Up Helly Aa festival

Île de Ré

ATLANTIC COAST, FRANCE

Although the Île de Ré is not far north of the Île d'Oléron – and shares many of the same characteristics as its neighbour, particularly the flat, marshy landscapes and the fine ostreiculture – it has a completely different feel. Oléron is definitely a French family destination, and the roads running alongside its sandy beaches are full of campsites and neat villas. The Île de Ré is much less consciously designed for the ease of vacationing, but conversely, and precisely because of its rusticity, it has become the holiday choice of *le tout Paris*.

The likes of Vanessa Paradis and Johnny Depp, Princess Caroline of Monaco, Isabelle Adjani and Emmanuelle Béart have taken to hiding away on the island, but natives take great pleasure in being neither perturbed nor impressed by their famous guests. They have been joined by planeloads of British tourists, flying in to nearby La Rochelle on cheap flights, and invading the Île de Ré in a way their predecessor George Villiers, the first Duke of Buckingham, notably failed to do in 1627, when he was attempting to lift a siege at La Rochelle.

For long stretches of time the island was untroubled by unwelcome visitors, as the inhabitants concentrated on the year-round cycle of fishing, producing salt, cultivating mussels and oysters, or growing corn, potatoes and grapes. At the fortress in St Martin de Ré convicted felons would pass time while they waited to be dispatched onwards to French Guinea or New Caledonia: Alfred Dreyfus, following his great *affaire*, spent time there, as did Henri Charrière, better known as Papillon.

It was frankly a rather sleepy place, full of whitewashed fishing houses with turquoise and aquamarine shutters, where the quirkiest thing to happen was fitting the local donkeys with gingham bloomers to keep off the mosquitoes (they still sport them, for the tourists). What happened in the late 1980s to change this low-key lifestyle was the building of a rollercoaster of a bridge from La Rochelle, replacing the previous monopoly of the ferry. Now the population is boosted tenfold each summer.

It is a straight run off the bridge and along the length of the pleasingly lobster-shaped island, between the cornfields and salt marshes, through the little town of Ars-en-Ré, where the church steeple painted in horizontal black and white stripes acts as a landmark for passing sailors, and on to the lighthouse at the Cap des Baleines at its far end. After a climb of 257 steps you can look out at the rocky plateau where Atlantic whales came and beached themselves long before the celebrities ever did.

> "We'll drop anchor in the inky flask of a night pierced by the siren call of the lighthouse at the Cap des Baleines, reprising a love song from afar."
>
> Claude Nougaro, "Ile de Ré"

Île de Ré, Charente-Maritime, France **Longitude:** 1° 30' W **Latitude:** 46° 12' N **Area:** 85 sq km (33 sq mi) **Highest point:** 19m (62 ft) **Population:** 15,000 **Principal town:** St Martin en Ré
Residents: Henri Charrière, Alfred Dreyfus, Lionel Jospin

Mont St Michel

COUESNON ESTUARY

t is still inspiring to see the profile of Mont St Michel emerge on the horizon after driving through the fertile countryside on the cusp of Normandy and Brittany. Imagine the impact it must have had on the pilgrims in medieval times as they neared the end of their long trek to reach the island.

Thirteen hundred years have passed since Aubert, the bishop of nearby Avranches, saw a vision of St Michael while enjoying a nap in AD 708. He was inspired by this encounter to build a shrine to the saint and a monastery on a clump of granite in the estuary of the River Couesnon. The rock had already been used as a stronghold by the local Armoricans, but its new religious guise added to the mystique of this tidal island. Coming in at a brisk walking pace, the waters can still surprise the unwary, and signs warn of the dangers of the hidden quicksand, and of being caught unawares on the low-tide mudflats.

After becoming part of Normandy in the tenth century, the monastery stoutly resisted all assaults on the island by the English, who tried particularly hard during the Hundred Years' War, besieging the fortified mount in 1423–24; it was the only location in the region to survive the English onslaught. The shrine's lure for pilgrims eventually faded, though, and by the time of the French Revolution the monastery had closed, and the site was reclassified as a prison for political prisoners, a "Bastille of the sea".

Saddened that such a fine edifice had ended up as a jail, a group of concerned citizens – including Victor Hugo and Guy de Maupassant – campaigned from the 1830s onwards to preserve it as a national treasure. They succeeded, and Mont St Michel discovered a new lease of life as one of the great tourist attractions in France: it has consistently been one of the most visited sites in the country (Cornwall's St Michael's Mount is its mini mirror image across the Channel), and its silhouette has become one of France's most instantly recognizable icons, along with the Eiffel Tower and the Arc de Triomphe.

Passing through the first stretch of the main street curling up the side of the crag requires running a gauntlet of souvenir shops – though one could simply consider them natural descendants of the purveyors of pardons and relics of centuries past. Once beyond them, however, the spire-topped abbey-fortress (an active monastery once more), retains something of the "sublime quality" that Victor Hugo admired, and after climbing to the top pilgrims can fortify themselves in the island's restaurants with lamb raised on the estuary's salt meadows.

Mont St Michel, Manche, France **Longitude:** 1° 31' W **Latitude:** 48° 38' N **Highest point:** 60 m (200 ft) **Population:** 50

"The abbey, perched on its crag,
    has been raised far from the earth,
like some fantastical stately home,
    an amazing palace of dreams,
incredible, strange and beautiful."

Guy de Maupassant

Lindisfarne

NORTH SEA

> "Yet the island is holy. The way the tide without cease / Binds and liberates, tells me why heaven and hell / Are equally possible when world and spirit combine…"
>
> William Radice, *Green Red Gold*

One of many islands off the British coast with the sobriquet "Holy Island", Lindisfarne can probably claim to be truly the holiest Anglo-Saxon site in the British Isles. A tidal island, cut off twice a day by the rising North Sea, Lindisfarne is the English equivalent of France's Mont St Michel.

The monastery here was founded by St Aidan in AD 635 as a base for evangelizing in Northumberland and the rest of northern England, and is still a retreat for those who have revived interest in Celtic Christianity. The Lindisfarne Scrolls, the wondrous illuminated manuscripts made by the local monks, discovered here and which secured the island's religious and now tourist fame, are no longer here (they can be found in the British Museum in London). Nevertheless, thousands flock every year to cross the Pilgrim's Way, the low-tide sand crossing to the island, to visit the monastery and the priory in search of spiritual rehabilitation, and to find the same contemplative peace those first monks enjoyed centuries ago. It is still very much intact on this green but windswept isle. The peace, light and landscape also proved an inspiration to artists such as J. M. W. Turner. Many also are those who come for the excellent crab, be it in the sandwiches of twitchers or as titbits for the winter population of migratory birds, for whom this member of the Farne island group is a nature reserve.

Also intact and equally a tourist honey-pot is the famous Lindisfarne mead, which the resident monks prepared here for many years until forced to flee in an eighth-century Viking raid. They believed that any soul entrusted to God should be fortified with this elixir of herbs and fermented honey in order better to prepare them to meet their maker. The tradition passed into the custom, originally Norse, of giving newlyweds a drink of mead for a whole moon cycle after marriage in order to encourage fertility; from this we now have the term "honeymoon".

Elsewhere on the island the simple and archaic coexists with the sophisticated and urban. The landscape of the island is littered with lime kilns from the long-obsolete practice of lime-burning, and dotted with characteristic shed-like dwellings made from local fishing boats inverted and cut in half like a modern sculpture by Damien Hirst. In contrast, in 1901 the interior of the old Tudor fort was refurbished by Edwin Lutyens in the Arts and Crafts style, and its gardens landscaped by Gertrude Jekyll.

OPPOSITE The priory and Holy Island

Lindisfarne, Northumberland, England, UK **Alternative name:** Holy Island **Longitude:** 1° 48' W **Latitude:** 55° 41' N **Area:** 5 sq km (2 sq mi) **Population:** 160
Residents: St Aidan, St Cuthbert, Eadfrith

Jersey

CHANNEL ISLANDS, ENGLISH CHANNEL

The sign at Jersey airport bids visitors, or indeed returning locals conversant with the vernacular, **Seyiz les beinv'nus a Jerri**. A smattering of French and a knowledge of international airports around the world should make the welcome easy enough to decipher. But the sentence is as early a sign as you could want that, although Jersey is part of the British Isles, its roots lie in France. In fact the Jerriais dialect, sadly underused in officialdom and not taught in schools, is derived from old Norman French and as close as you can get to the language of William the Conqueror, France's sole successful subjugator of Britain in a thousand years.

The liberal feel and atmosphere of Jersey is also distinctly French but, much as the Isle of Wight recalls a previous England, it is a France of three decades ago – although more Hulot than Belmondo. Indeed, it is difficult for a certain generation of television viewers not to believe, as they walk down the seafront of the main and only real town of St Helier, that they will see the island's most famous fictional detective, Jim Bergerac, leather-jacketed and driving a Triumph Roadster in hot pursuit of some money-laundering building magnate. French too is the delicious gastronomy based around spider crabs, oysters and lobsters, and many unique ways of cooking the abundant local apples, including

bourdelots, apple dumplings or the local black butter made from apples and spices.

Beneath the out-of-season resort feel lies an affluence built on a modern service industry that has given Jersey one of the highest per capita gross domestic products in Europe. Jersey is a Crown protectorate but not part of either the European Union or the United Kingdom. The associated tax breaks, combined with the most hours of sunshine in the British Isles each year, make the island continually attractive to businesses as well as holidaymakers and retirees. The fruits of the island's prosperity are discreetly visible in mansions and villas that dot Jersey's interior, built into the *côtils* (steeply sloping fields) and Jersey cattle in the island's meadows – famous for their luscious thick cream. Almost half the island's population is not originally from Jersey, and Portuguese make up the second-largest minority group after the British.

Unfussed, liberal and surprising, Jersey lies between two heavyweight cultures but belongs truly to neither. Over the decades the island has sired an array of curious talents – from the erotic novelist Elinor Glyn, who pioneered the figure of the "vamp" to the original "it" girl, Lillie Langtry, whose oddball nature and lack of desire to fit the mould seems to personify the island itself.

OPPOSITE Beauport Beach

Jersey, Channel Islands, UK **Longitude:** 2° 07' W **Latitude:** 49° 11' N **Area:** 116 sq km (45 sq mi) **Highest point:** 149 m (489 ft) **Population:** 89,300 **Principal town:** St Helier
Natives: Elinor Glyn, Seymour Hicks, Lillie Langtry, Frederick Lonsdale, Harry Vardon, Wace **Residents:** Gerald Durrell, Victor Hugo, John Everett Millais, Walter Raleigh

"Jersey is an island. It's nine miles by five.
And if you drive very slowly, you can take
a whole *hour* to go right round it."

Jim Bergerac

"Deep inside many of us, there is a small corner
that remembers the comforting Enid Blyton stories
of our childhoods… That world may never have existed,
but you can find a very acceptable facsimile of it on Sark."

Andrew Gilligan, journalist

Sark

CHANNEL ISLANDS, ENGLISH CHANNEL

While many islands, by the very nature of their isolation, contrive to lose pace with time so that for the visitor they evoke a bygone age, it is usually only a matter of a few decades. Few islands so close to civilization can still conjure a golden age as far back as the 1920s. But with its horses (sixty-one of them, all registered), carts, tractor-trailer transport, little white cottages and tea houses each with a bicycle outside, life on Sark seems transplanted from the colour plates of an interwar boys annual. Not only are there no cars on Sark, there are also no civil servants and no police. On Sark they still use one pound notes and in some places even old hand-cranked phones. It is a picturesque and cultivated backwardness, deliberate and obstinate, that comes from being the last feudal state in Europe.

The tale of Sark is a classic piece of eccentric Victoriana belatedly clashing with the European Union. Until recently the entire island was owned by a former aircraft engineer, Michael Beaumont, who inherited the island from his grandmother. He was Grand Seigneur, or overlord, of Sark in both title and effect, with the right to enforce such laws as the requirement for each of his subjects to keep a musket. No one else was allowed to own land on the island and so the inhabitants of Sark were effectively tenants paying their lord a nominal feudal tax called a treizieme. But if it sounds dark and tyrannical, the reality was that Beaumont barely ruled at all and instead, aware of the globalized nature of the modern world, the locals complicitly perpetuated the medieval customs of their island.

It was the *Daily Telegraph*'s Darclay brothers, who had already bought the neighbouring island of Breqhou and fancied owning a piece of Sark, who first and successfully challenged the local overlord's ancient powers and privileges under the European Bill of Human Rights. And now Sark's inhabitants fear that creeping land ownership and the arrival here of the concept of holiday homes may lead to a change in culture and make-up of the island's population. They have to deal with democracy instead of relying on their local Chief Pleas parliament. Income tax is payable here, too, bringing an end to the so called "Sark lark" and consequently the tax evaders who set up "companies" on the island – whose headquarters were broken greenhouses – are no longer able to take advantage of the island's status.

For now, though, Sark still seems like a childhood adventure island straight out of Enid Blyton's *Famous Five*, the kind of place where paddling a small boat around its coves, crossing the precipitous causeway to neighbouring Little Sark, walking through the fields of fragrant foxglove and heather, or pottering in the rock pools of La Grande Grêve bay, the visitor might justifiably expect to uncover some portentous hidden entrance or treasure.

ABOVE La Grande Grêve Bay

Sark, Channel Islands, UK **Alternative names:** Sercq, Sèr **Longitude:** 2° 22' W **Latitude:** 49° 25' N **Area:** 5 sq km (2 sq mi) **Highest point:** 114 m (374 ft) Le Moulin **Population:** 580
Residents: David and Frederick Barclay, Sybil Hathaway

"The rock of hospitality and liberty,
this corner of ancient Norman soil,
the island of Guernsey, stern and gentle."

Victor Hugo

Guernsey

CHANNEL ISLANDS, ENGLISH CHANNEL

The French novelist Victor Hugo, who described the Channel Islands as "little pieces of France cast into the sea and picked up by England", had reason to be thankful for that quirk of history. Exiled from his homeland because of his opposition to Napoleon III, he retreated to Guernsey, to Hauteville House in the mellow capital of St Peter Port, for fifteen years.

Like all the Channel Islands, Guernsey (the second largest and most westerly of the group) exists in a kind of limbo between its nearest landmass France and its overseer Great Britain. It is a dependency of the British Crown, to which the island has stayed loyal since Norman times, (apart from during the English Civil War, when it sided with the Parliamentarians while Jersey supported the Royalists).

Frenchness is all around. The cattle that graze on Guernsey came from Normandy, when monks brought over their finest cattle. Their descendants still produce distinctively tasty beef and milk that is high in protein and creamy butterfat. The local patois, *guernésiais*, is a derivative of Norman French – though only two per cent of the islanders speak it fluently. The indigent *guerns* are also proud of the "Le" in their surnames (England footballer Matt Le Tissier, for example, or Ebenezer Le Page, hero of a classic novel of Guernsey life by G. B. Edwards).

Freshness is also prevalent. Air coming straight off the Atlantic, but warmed by the Gulf Stream, has turned Guernsey into an island of flowers – orchids and freesias especially – and with a lush hinterland of wooded valleys. The coastline is seductive, whether the little-known beauty of rocky Moulin Huet bay, beneath wild garlic-scented cliffs (a favourite landscape subject for Auguste Renoir), the sandy beaches of L'Eree or the surfing centre at Vazon Bay.

Guernsey is a relatively small island and its roads are narrow, so the penchant of the locals for owning four-by-fours (the island is reputed to have one of the world's highest cars-per-capita ratios) means a gentle meander along the back lanes is not always restful. The island's size gives rise to the usual interest in everybody else's business common to small communities, but equally means it is quite safe – any transgressors are promptly marched off to the local magistrate and their details plastered over the local press.

Skeletons from the past are marked on the island by burial mounds, menhirs and dolmens, traces of the Neolithic people who farmed here. Other ghosts date from the Nazi occupation of Guernsey during the Second World War (the only concentration camp on British soil was on the island), as the silent spectres of collaboration and fraternization still hover around the more tangible remains of bunkers and well-tended war cemeteries.

OPPOSITE The Pleinmont stone circle, commonly called the Fairy Ring

Guernsey, Channel Islands, UK **Alternative name:** Guernesey **Longitude:** 2° 35' W **Latitude:** 49° 26' N **Area:** 63 sq km (24 sq mi) **Highest point:** 110 m (361 ft) Hautnez **Population:** 65,600
Principal town: St Peter Port **Natives:** Roy Dotrice, G. B. Edwards, William Le Lacheur, Matt Le Tissier, George Métivier, Sarah Montague, Andy Priaulx, Warren de la Rue, James Saumarez
Residents: Victor Hugo, John Le Mesurier, Oliver Reed, Ronnie Ronald

Orkney

NORTH SEA/ATLANTIC

The islands of Scotland are magical and myriad, but conveniently fall into groupings. The Western Isles are heavily Gaelic, whereas the northern archipelagos, the Orkneys and Shetland, have remained primarily Norse. And while Shetland was obliged to rely on fishing to survive, the Orkneys had fertile land to cultivate, there's a saying that the Orcadians are "farmers with boats", the Shetlanders "fishermen with crofts".

Spraying north from the top northeast corner of Scotland, across the Pentland Firth from John O'Groats, the sandstone Orkneys are a repository of enigmatic Stone Age relics set in a low-lying network of nearly seventy islands. Seventeen are inhabited by humans, and all of them by a cavalcade of birdlife: vast colonies of skuas, puffins and kittiwakes, joined seasonally by avian tourists en route to southern sun.

The main island is helpfully called Mainland. Some of the finest stone circles and burial cairns in Britain stud its surface. Among these, Maeshowe is a magnificent chambered tumulus with a subterranean passageway lit by the sun at the winter solstice. The Ring of Brodgar is a dramatic circle of standing stones on an isthmus between two lochs; the creator of Rebus, Ian Rankin, who knows a thing or two about enigmas, has written about the "real sense of primal power and mystery" they still emit.

On Mainland, the houses of Orkney's capital, Kirkwall, cluster around a glorious Gothic cathedral – Britain's most northerly – and the ruins of the fine Bishop's and Earl's palaces. The cathedral, dedicated to the Norse Christian martyr St Magnus, is at the heart of the St Magnus Festival, founded thirty years ago by Peter Maxwell Davies, Master of the Queen's Music, a highlight of the long summer days. Maxwell Davies, an adopted Orcadian, draws on the sounds of sea and sky for his music, saying the islands are, appropriately, like "a cathedral, with music in three dimensions". The native poet George Mackay Brown was equally inspired by his homeland: his autobiography was called *For the Islands I Sing*.

The islands each offer their own melodic variations. Hoy, the second largest, riven with vales and edged by great cliffs, was made famous by the 1966 live telecast of an ascent of its sandstone smokestack-like pinnacle, the Old Man of Hoy. Papa Westray is home to the six-thousand-year-old Knap of Howar, the oldest extant house in northern Europe. On Lambholm, a delightful, minute chapel was built by Italian POWs in the Second World War, and in the anchorage waters of Scapa Flow – around which the central islands huddle – the German High Seas fleet was scuttled in 1919 and the HMS *Royal Oak* torpedoed in 1939. Not all the spectres of Orkney are prehistoric.

"The essence of Orkney's magic is silence, loneliness and the deep marvellous rhythms of sea and land, darkness and light."

George Mackay Brown

OPPOSITE The Old Man of Hoy

BELOW Atlantic puffin

Orkney, Scotland **Longitude:** 2° 54' W **Latitude:** 59° 02' N **Area:** 974 sq km (376 sq mi) **Highest point:** 401 m (1316 ft) Ward Hill **Population:** 19,800 **Principal town:** Kirkwall, Mainland
Natives: William Balfour Baikie, George Mackay Brown, Isabel Gunn, Magnus Linklater, St Magnus, Edwin Muir, John Rae, Robert Shaw, Cameron Stout, Hazel and Jennifer Wrigley
Residents: Peter Maxwell Davies, Jo Grimond, David Harvey, Eric Linklater

Anglesey

IRISH SEA

Such is the translation from the Welsh of Britain's longest place name, Llanfair-pwllgwyngyllgogerychwyrndrobwllllan-tysiliogogogoch, one of the first towns that greets visitors as they cross the Menai Strait, which separates Anglesey from the northwestern tip of Wales. It is a place where visitors come to have their photo taken by the sign at the North Wales Coast Railway station. They can even get a stamp of the name from the station tourist shop.

Would that the name was original, steeped in history and evocative of a bygone medieval and rural age, when locals knew every inch of their untouched landscape and communicated it to each other in terms like the Kalahari bushmen. In fact it was a publicity stunt from the industrial age of the 1850s, dreamt up by a cunning local cobbler from the town of Menai Bridge. The island had just been put on the map by the arrival of the railway and Telford's suspension bridge, and the village, which had hitherto only contained twenty letters (satisfied with Llanfairpwllgwyngyll) felt it would be a good ruse to detain tourists and passers-through if they could claim the longest place name in Britain. The idea seems to have worked. In recent years other towns, all of them Welsh and possibly with time on their hands, have tried to outnumber the fifty-eight letters of Llanfair PG (as most normal people refer to it) but none of them has received official recognition. It is an all rural war and merely confirms the peculiar, almost dyslexic, aptitude of the Welsh language (and Anglesey contains the highest percentage of native Welsh speakers) not just for high Scrabble scores but ridiculous-sounding names. Llanfair PG could so easily just have relied upon its fame as the birthplace in Britain in 1915 of that great purveyor of cakes, the Women's Institute.

More significant history on Anglesey (Ynys Môn in much more pronounceable Welsh) resides in the megalithic monuments, menhirs and druidic sites that cover its flat and low-lying landscape, as well as the Roman relics from Suetonius' invasion in AD 60 to subdue Boudicca. The island was described by Tacitus and Pliny but was assailed by pirates, Vikings and Saxons after the Romans left until it came under the rule of Edward I in the thirteenth century. The king commissioned the castle at Beaumaris, now a centre for local yachts. Writers have found Anglesey's landscape worn-down and depressing, Paul Theroux noting that "It was as if all the millions of lonely Irish people who travelled this way … had devoured the landscape with their eyes, looked upon it with such hunger that there was little of it left to take hold of and examine". But the coastline of cliffs and frothy beaches has long been declared an area of outstanding beauty, much to the appreciation of the local bitterns and peregrine falcons, and the puffins, razorbills, guillemots at the South Stacks cliffs.

OVERLEAF Anglesey and the Menai Bridge

Anglesey, Wales **Local name:** Ynys Môn **Longitude:** 4° 18' W **Latitude:** 53° 16' N **Area:** 715 sq km (276 sq mi) **Highest point:** 220 m (722 ft) Mynydd Twr/Holyhead Mountain **Population:** 66,800 **Principal town:** Holyhead **Natives:** Tony Adams, Dawn French, Hugh Griffith, Wayne Hennessey, Owain Tudor **Residents:** Aled Jones, Ian Kilmister aka Lemmy, Glenys Kinnock, Matthew Maynard, Naomi Watts

"St Mary's Church in the hollow of the white hazel
near to the rapid whirlpool and the church of St Tysilio of the red cave."

"The long, narrow island of Lundy sits in the water
like a half-submerged crocodile; an appropriately predatory analogy
given its long history as a base of pirates and smugglers."

Charles Connelly, *Attention All Shipping*

Lundy

BRISTOL CHANNEL

For such a small lump of granite sitting in the parochial and innocent-looking waters of the Bristol Channel 19 kilometres (12 miles) off the north coast of Devon, Lundy has an extraordinarily international history. The succession of pirate communities that once made the island their base for launching attacks on unwary passing vessels and storing their booty – French, English, Turkish, Spanish and Dutch – reads like a European Championship of piracy. And if Pirates of the Bristol Channel doesn't exactly role off the tongue or sound like a Hollywood blockbuster, it should not detract from the colourful and eccentric characters that led the mixture of ill-judged and swashbuckling escapades that define the island's history and which might just as easily be found in the pages of *Treasure Island*.

Perhaps the wildest and maddest of these were the Marisco clan who "governed" the island (and the seas around) for 150 years in the twelfth and thirteenth centuries. Their name lives on in the Marisco tavern, sole watering house on the island, full of the flotsam of notorious shipwrecks down the centuries. In 1238 William de Marisco was accused of plotting to kill Henry III, was drawn and quartered and his limbs dragged through Whitehall in London.

In the early 1800s Lundy (which derives its name from the Norse *lunde* meaning "puffin") was bought at auction by Sir Henry de Vere Hunt, whose son promptly lost it in a game of cards. It wasn't until 1834 that the island, famous only for its cabbage, finally fell into the hands of someone who wanted to make something of the place – a kingdom, no less, for one William Hudson Heaven, under whose watch the island became known as the Kingdom of Heaven. Heaven commissioned the grand Georgian mansion of Millcombe House as his residence, which greets visitors above the landing place.

This and the other buildings on the island, including the Old Light lighthouse (the world's tallest when it was built in 1819), the Marisco's 750-year-old keep and the ship-shaped Tibbets, have since the 1960s been administered by the Landmark Trust as holiday homes for hardy walkers and those in search of a romantic hideaway. They make the rough crossing on the HMS *Oldenburg*, complete with its original wood and brass fittings. Once there they can, from the top of the lighthouse, admire the views to the north of the Prescelly mountains in Pembrokeshire, bestride the green baize of the island's bridge table top, explore the fissures such as Quarry Beach, caused by the reverberations from the great 1755 Lisbon earthquake, and indulge in a spot of letter-boxing: orienteering around twenty-eight former smugglers' secret messaging points. One of them is hidden beneath the wreck of a crashed Second World War Heinkel bomber.

OPPOSITE The Island Ferry

Lundy, Devon, England, UK **Longitude:** 4° 40' W **Latitude:** 51° 10' N **Area:** 4 sq km (2 sq mi) **Highest point:** 144 m (471 ft) Beacon Hill **Population:** 20 **Resident:** William de Marisco

Caldey Island

BRISTOL CHANNEL

The Vikings named Caldey, just off the southwest Wales coast, "Kald-eye" – the cold island. Like many such isles, the isolation and hardship it offers have long been a lure to monks seeking a place of peace and prayer away from the daily hurly-burly. The monks who currently live on Caldey are Cistercians, whose devotions are particularly strict, since they not only observe the demands of poverty and chastity, but also that of silence between seven in the evening and seven in the morning. In the 1980s the monks' numbers had dwindled dangerously, but in recent years they have been joined by fresh adherents, and although the monastery buildings can only be visited by men, the island community has established itself as a tourist attraction, welcoming over sixty thousand visitors a year.

The religious history of Caldey and the founding of the monastery can be traced back to St Illtyd, a possibly Breton-born sixth-century abbot who spread the word of Christianity throughout South Wales, including this part of Pembrokeshire. The serene, pebble-floored church dedicated to Illtyd contains the Caldey Stone, with an inscription in the runic *ogham* lettering that dates from even earlier. On a nearby hill – everything on this island is close by – the rugged stone parish church of St David, the patron saint of Wales, has foundations equally old.

The original monastery was destroyed during the sixteenth-century Reformation, and the monks were expelled. The island was nursed back to economic and social health under a series of benevolent owners, including Thomas Kynaston and his son Cabot, who oversaw the development of limestone quarrying. In the early twentieth century, a fresh influx of Benedictine monks arrived, and by 1910 a new abbey had been constructed containing calm cloisters and a luminous oak-timbered refectory. The Benedictines later converted to Catholicism and sold the monastery to its current Cistercian occupants in the 1920s.

A ferry ride from Tenby, this world of charm and calm is not all monastic: the island has forty other inhabitants, a guesthouse, post office and its own fire engine. The only primary school was forced to close in 2000 after the intake dropped to a solitary pupil. There is a swimming pool off Priory Beach, and a bird and seal sanctuary on the neighbouring island of St Margaret's. And although the monks of Caldey seek a life of retreat, they are far from unworldly. A television was hired in for Pope John Paul II's funeral in 2005, and the monks conduct brisk business selling a range of Caldey produce, including butters, yoghurt, gorse, fern and lavender-scented perfumes, and Abbot's Kitchen chocolate – this last much recommended by serious cognoscenti.

OPPOSITE The Cistercian occupants of the monastery

Caldey Island, Pembrokeshire, Wales, UK **Local name:** Ynys Byr **Longitude:** 4° 41' W **Latitude:** 51° 38' N **Area:** 223 hectares (550 acres) **Highest point:** 56 m (164 ft) **Population:** 50 **Residents:** Brother David Hodges

"You could be here years, and be ranked with the seers,
and your chances would still be remote,
of learning the mystique of the Caldey boat."

Brother David Hodges, "Delayed By Rough Tides"

"Salt spray, seagulls, wild rocks and cavernous cliffs.
Beyond those mountains the dance halls of Douglas and
the dance-band leader in his faultless tails. An isle of contrasts!
A miniature of all the Western world."

John Betjeman

ABOVE The Douglas promenade

OPPOSITE The Beyer Peacock steam locomotive

Isle of Man, Crown Dependency, British Isles **Local name:** Ellen Vannin, Mann **Longitude:** 4° 30' W **Latitude:** 54° 15' N **Area:** 572 sq km (221 sq mi) **Highest point:** 621 m (2,037 ft) Snaefell
Population: 75,800 **Capital:** Douglas **Natives:** Barry, Maurice and Robin Gibb, Edward Forbes, Archibald Knox **Residents:** Jeremy Clarkson, George Macdonald Fraser, Neil Hodgson, Nigel Kneale,
Norman Wisdom

Isle of Man

IRISH SEA

Washed by the turbulent Irish Sea, the Isle of Man is geographically the centre of the British Isles. As the local saying goes, from its highest point at the top of Snaefell Peak you can see six kingdoms: England, Scotland, Ireland, Wales, Man and Heaven. But as with a number of islands around the British coast, including Sark and Jersey, Man is a law unto itself.

Technically a self-governing Crown dependency (Queen Elizabeth is, ironically, Lord of Man), Man has no capital gains tax, no stamp duty or inheritance tax and its own, lower rates of income tax – making it a favourite stand-in location for filmmakers. It also has its own laws, descended from the oldest continuous parliament at Tynwald established in AD 979: here, you can be charged with "furious driving", which is ironic considering there are no speed limits (or licensing laws) and that Man is also famous among petrolheads for hosting the Moto TT rally, now in its hundredth year. Homosexuality was illegal on Man on pain of birching until as recently as 1992. The symbol of the island is the triskelion, depicting three legs with spurred feet sometimes known as "the three legs of Man" which, according to the Manx locals, never kneel to England.

It is ironic, therefore, that the capital, Douglas, with its Victorian esplanades and horse-drawn trams is very much a bygone Little England. Man is believed to have been the inspiration for Rev W. V. Awdry's island of Sodor and the tales of Thomas the Tank Engine and friends. Douglas, meaning "the confluence of rivers" in the local Manx dialect, is a laid-back town where the expression *traa dy liooar* ("there's time enough") can often be

heard. The town contains a number of distinctly metropolitan items of architectural interest, including Frank Matcham's Gaicty Theatre and some early examples of Mackay Hugh Baillie Scott's Arts and Crafts style.

Man was the founder of the island games and has its own form of Irish hurling in the game of cammag. It has its own breed of cat, too – the tailless Manx.

These singularities together make up an intriguing, oddball island. Believed by locals to be the creation and realm of the Celtic sea god Manannan mac Lir, who would wrap the island in a misty cloak of defence (an excuse for the terrible local weather, no doubt), myth, legend and tales of the fairies, or "little folk", abound on Man.

St Helena

SOUTH ATLANTIC

Portuguese explorer João da Nova discovered St Helena in 1502, on Constantinople's saint's day of Santa Helena. The Portuguese and then Dutch used the island en route to and from Goa and the East Indies and, with the help of their goats, began a process of deforestation that rid the island of most of its wood and the endemic flora, including the strange cabbage tree and narcotic cactus pear, to be found on its central ridges leading up to Diana's Peak.

This lump of volcanic rock in the middle of the Atlantic Ocean would have remained as anonymous as it is distant from any mainland were it not for its most celebrated resident captive. Emperor Napoleon I of France spent the last years of his life here under a very civilized form of house arrest, from 1815 until his death in 1821.

Born on the island of Corsica, twice exiled to different islands (and long covetous of the island of Great Britain), Napoleon was one of history's greatest islomaniacs and serial island-hoppers. It is a measure of his personality and positive achievements that even in defeat he was treated with the respect and luxury accorded to a head of state. His large and rather fine quarters at Longwood House, with its ocean-view veranda of filigree balustrades, now arguably the best Napoleonic museum in the world, is a villa that might suit any modern-day magnate. Napoleon was even put up by the governor and his family on arrival, while his residence was appointed to the standard befitting a former head of state.

Fine too are the Georgian buildings of the capital, Jamestown, named after King James II, during whose reign the island was claimed by the British and where the island's fifty per cent black African population lives. Plantation House in particular looks like something out of Cecil Rhodes' South Africa – it was from here that the island's successive governors carried out jurisdiction over St Helena as well as Ascension and Tristan da Cunha islands. It would have been here also that governor Hudson Lowe, sent to St Helena not least for his fluency in French and Italian, would have enjoyed strained but respectful verbal and political chess with his exotic prisoner – the conversations of two captors of St Helena's isolation who have no choice but to be civil to each other.

OPPOSITE View over James Bay and Jamestown waterfront, from the top of Jacob's Ladder

St Helena, British Overseas Territory of St Helena **Longitude:** 5° 42' W **Latitude:** 15° 58' S **Area:** 122 sq km (47 sq mi) **Highest point:** 818 m (2,684 ft) Mt Actaeon **Population:** 3,900
Capital: Jamestown **Residents:** Napoleon Bonaparte, Dinuzulu kaCetshwayo

"It is not a pretty place to live.
I would have done better to stay in Egypt."
Napoleon Bonaparte

Mull

INNER HEBRIDES, SCOTLAND

The island of Mull has been on the itinerary of travellers since classical times. Somehow one imagines that these islands, tucked away off the western coast of Scotland, would have been a closely guarded secret known only to those in the immediate neighbourhood. But the Greeks certainly knew of Mull's existence, and there is a reference to "Maleus" in the writings of the first-century, Alexandria-based geographer and astronomer Ptolemy.

Most current visitors are drawn to the island's solitude and natural beauty, the very countryside that was on offer to Dr Johnson and James Boswell went they stopped off here in the 1770s. This landscape – "green, grassy island sparkling fountains, of waving woods and high tow'ring mountains", in the words of Mull's unofficial national anthem by Dugald MacPhail – is one of the best places to see otters in the British Isles, with red deer and stags bestriding the hillsides, ptarmigan nesting at ground level, and aloft a dynasty of majestic, rare golden and white-tailed eagles.

The human presence on Mull suffered heavily during the brutal Highland Clearances of the eighteenth century and the potato famine of the nineteenth. The current population of 1,900 or so is now boosted annually by an influx of summer residents – the locals sardonically refer to this as the "officer's club" – and hundreds of thousands of tourists. An odd phenomenon occurred during the early 2000s, when a BBC children's programme, *Balamory*, was filmed amongst the houses, painted in primary colours, along the harbour front of the island's pleasant capital Tobermory (the site of a nationally acclaimed fish and chip van). The island was inundated for a while by "toddler tourists", desperate to see the locations they watched on television.

Ben More, in the heart of the island, is the highest point in the Scottish isles (and a Munro, the term given to Scottish peaks higher than 914 metres or 3,000 feet). Around it lie moors and tumbling burns heading down to a coastline surrounded by small islands and perforated by caves. On the west coast, Mackinnon's Cave, visited by Dr Johnson, is one of the Hebrides' largest. Along the south coast lie the Nun's Cave, with age-old Christian carvings, and the eroded sea caves of the Carsaig Arches. MacCulloch's Tree, on the southern edge of Ardmeanach, known as the "wilderness", is a fifty-million-year-old, lava-engulfed fossilized conifer.

The relatively recent history of Mull is that of the Hebridean chiefs, who formed the Lordship of the Isles in the fourteenth century – the ferry to Tobermory from the mainland port of Oban passes Duart Castle, perched on a coastal crag, the imposing ancestral seat of the Clan Maclean, its history enough to fire any child's imagination.

> "Mull corresponded exactly with the idea which I had always had of it: a hilly country, diversified with heath and grass, and many rivulets."
>
> James Boswell, diarist

OPPOSITE Tobermory

Mull, Argyll and Bute, Scotland **Local name:** Muile **Longitude:** 5° 56' W **Latitude:** 56° 25' N **Area:** 875 sq km (338 sq mi) **Highest point:** 966 m (3,169 ft) Ben More **Population:** 1,900 **Principal town:** Tobermory **Native:** Colin MacIntyre, Dugald MacPhail

ABOVE The Old Man of Storr Quirang

"Speed, bonnie boat, like a bird on the wing,
Onward! the sailors cry;
Carry the bairn that's born to be King
Over the sea to Skye."

"The Skye Boat Song"

Isle of Skye

INNER HEBRIDES, SCOTLAND

The Isle of Skye is a distillation of Scottish Highland beauty as fine, golden and illusion-inducing as a dram of the local single-malt Talisker whisky. It is also an epicentre of Scottish history, or at least patriotic legend to rival the likes of Robert Bruce and William Wallace. For it was to Skye that in 1745 Prince Charles Edward Stuart, aka Bonnie Prince Charlie, came on his way to leading the Jacobite charge to overthrow King George II, restore the Stuart clan to the throne of England and safeguard Scottish Highland life. He was a Romantic fugitive with a £30,000 price on his head, a fearless warrior and Rome-educated heartthrob whom the Scots believed could save their homeland from the dastardly English and Protestant Tudors. For a while it looked like he might succeed – until he met his fate at Culloden.

Everybody needs a hero, and the Bonnie Prince fitted the mould. His story, however, is half history and half myth. On Skye, a gust of Atlantic gullibility has swept away the usual healthy scepticism of the Scots, and the island abounds with echoes and references to his passing, as rooted in certainty as the Hogwarts Express that snaked up the sinuous Highland coast to cross the Glenfinnan viaduct opposite the island. In St Kilmuir cemetery lies the grave of Flora MacDonald, who saved the young prince by dressing him up as her Irish maid and taking him across to Skye. She allegedly led him to Monkstadt House, now a roofless ruin but once home of Lady Margaret MacDonald, a Jacobite sympathizer. On their arrival, though, they discovered that one of the guests, Lieutenant Macleod, was head of the militia posted to the island to capture the prince.

Skye was the stronghold of the MacDonald clan. Their four castles of Armadale (now the Clan Donald centre), Dunscaith, Duntulm and Knock are just one part of the island's rich heritage of monuments, evocative of legends and a bygone era of red-bearded warring clans and monarchies.

That Skye, the Winged Isle and notional setting for Virginia Woolf's *To the Lighthouse*, should open the mind to flights of fancy is due to its landscape, which – as well as a coastline of peninsulas and the picturesque harbour of the capital, Portree – includes some of the most dramatic and challenging mountain terrain in Scotland. Legendary among these are the shrouded incisors of the Black Cuillin mountains, hewn from basalt and gabbro, and domain of the island's golden eagles. The mountains' sheer jagged rawness rather than their modest height – in particular the 11-kilometre (7-mile) traverse across all the peaks – makes them an ultimate mountaineering experience.

Skye, Highland, Scotland **Local name:** An t-Eilean Sgitheanach **Longitude:** 6° 10' W **Latitude:** 57° 15' N **Area:** 1,656 sq km (639 sq mi) **Highest point:** 993 m (3,258 ft) Sgurr Alisdair
Population: 9,200 **Principal town:** Portree **Native:** Myles MacInnes aka Mylo **Residents:** Ian Anderson, Sorley MacLean

Islay

INNER HEBRIDES, SCOTLAND

Whisky in its various manifestations, whether Kentucky bourbon, Irish or scotch, is an acquired taste. Some never get past their first experience of the "water of life". For connoisseurs, the whisky that comes from the Hebridean island of Islay demands one further leap of faith for the senses. The peaty aroma and taste is simply too medicinal for many. For a happy host of others, though, it is nothing less than ambrosial: the registered Friends of just one distillery, Laphroaig, number more than a quarter of million and rising, and each variety, including Ardbeg, Bowmore and Lagavulin, also has its faithful champions.

The secrets of whisky distilling arrived on Islay – pronounced "eye-la" – from Ireland, which can be seen looking west when the skies are clear. The Celts left other enduring traces, including one of the few intact Celtic crosses in the churchyard at Kildalton, but the locals took over the stills they brought with them, and used the mild climate, warmed by the Gulf Stream, and the natural resources at their disposal to refine their own variation. Above all, it is the peat of the south of Islay that is essential, both by flavouring the island's waters and as the source of the slow-burning fires that actually malt the barley (although whisky specialists also claim to detect the tang of heather and the iodine smack of seawater). To the peat, barley and yeast, the distilleries say they add one further ingredient: the people.

To the southwest of the wild, lesser-known island of Jura, Islay is known as Bànrigh nan Eilean, "Queen of the Hebrides", because of its fertile land, but the royal title is also a fitting nod towards Islay's role as the centre of the Lordship of the Isles in the fourteenth to sixteenth centuries. The Clan MacDonald was at the heart of that sometimes bloody period of history: the ruins of the Lords' administrative headquarters, the MacDonalds' powerbase, are on two islands or *crannogs* in Loch Finlaggan, and the Lagavulin distillery near Dunyvaig Castle was another former MacDonald stronghold.

Neither the island's current capital Bowmore, nor the other main township Port Ellen on the southeast coast, have more than a thousand inhabitants apiece. Islay is a pretty peaceable place with a virtually negligible crime rate: so much so that the probable murder of one of the islanders in the autumn of 2007 made national headlines. Usually the main disturbance to the quiet lives of the islanders – including the extensive communities of barnacle and white-tailed geese – is the gentle pop that marks the uncorking of another bottle of whisky, the clink of glasses, a satisfied inhalation of the rising flavours, and a toast of *slàinte mhath* – "good health".

ABOVE Washing the stills at Laphroaig distillery OPPOSITE The Needle OVERLEAF The Paps of Jura Mountains lying across the Sound of Islay

Islay, Argyll and Bute, Scotland **Longitude:** 6° 10' W **Latitude:** 54° 46' N **Area:** 620 sq km (239 sq mi) **Highest point:** 491 m (1,611 ft) Beinn Bheigeir **Population:** 3,500 **Principal town:** Bowmore
Natives: Donald Caskie, George Robertson

"Waters break on rocky shore,
sea winds sighing as of yore, sea birds
crying as they soar, over the mists of Islay."

"The Mists of Islay", traditional Scottish song

Rum, Highland, Scotland **Alternative name:** Rhum **Longitude:** 6º 20' W **Latitude:** 57º 00' N **Area:** 104 sq km (40 sq mi) **Highest point:** 812 m (2664 ft) Askival **Population:** 20
Principal settlement: Kinloch **Residents:** St Beccan, Sir George & Lady Monica Bullough

"A landscape born of fire, but shaped by ice, frost, wind and sea. For earth scientists, both lay and learned, Rum is a paradise."

Magnus Magnusson

Rum

INNER HEBRIDES, SCOTLAND

When in 1886 the wealthy Lancastrian textile magnate John Bullough bought this island in the Scottish Inner Hebrides – one of a group including Eigg, Muck and Carra sometimes nicknamed "the cocktail islands" – he added an "h" and changed its name to "Rhum", for he did not like the unruly sounding title he had just acquired of the Laird of Rum.

This was the first of a number of follies that hark back to an eccentric bygone age of Kind Hearts and Coronets. Bullough wanted an island on which to host extravagant private parties, so he cleared it of its original inhabitants and turned it into a hunting ground, populating it with game with which to entertain his guests. Shooting at prying boats was also encouraged, earning the island the sobriquet Forbidden Island. In 1900 he commissioned Kinloch Castle at the picturesque port of Loch Scresort on the northeast of the island as party venue, autumnal hunting lodge and family seat, allegedly paying the builders to wear kilts. In contrast to the black volcanic rock of the island, its imported red sandstone mass – to say nothing of its various neo-Gothic excrescences – is striking if a little wilful. The gardens contained warm pools complete with resident alligators and aviaries of hummingbirds. Inside, the castle has been kept as was and is a time capsule of Edwardiana, complete with Steinway piano.

Equally strange but of architectural note is the Greek-style mausoleum built on the west side of the island at Harris that John Bullough's son George commissioned to house his father's body on his death. This was the only piece of the island the Bullough family retained when it was bought by Scottish National Heritage in 1957. The Bulloughs even left their considerable cellar.

Rum now ranks as one of the most important of Scottish nature reserves, a centre for the reintroduction, monitoring and filming of sea eagles, red deer and otters – and unfeasibly large midges. Diamond-shaped and with a name possibly derived from the Gaelic for "ridge", the island presents a spectacular relief with barely any area of level land. At its centre lie the four knife-edge Cuillins hills, smaller versions of the famous tooth-shaped mountains on Skye, whose steepness and ruggedness have to be experienced to be fully appreciated. Their Norse names (Askival, Hallival, Trollaval and Orval), added to the spectacular local mist and rainfall, lend the island an extra air of daunting mystery.

OPPOSITE Kinloch Castle

Isles of Scilly

CELTIC SEA

> "The intensity of the sky, the white sand, and the rocks that stood up everywhere out of the sea, had a dream-like quality reminiscent of Salvador Dalí."
>
> Roger Deakin, *Waterlog*

On the southwest tip of the island of St Agnes, Britain's most south-westerly community (with the Turk's Head, Britain's most southwesterly pub) stands a tiny church, looking out over Hellweathers Rock. On the altar is inscribed the memorial: "To those who sailed from St Agnes to save those in peril on the sea." A set of fifty-five obstacles at the entrance to the English channel, 45 kilometres (28 miles) but three bumpy hours by boat from Land's End in Cornwall, shipwrecks abound on the shores and in the annals of the Isles of Scilly.

It is said that the wrecking of the HMS *Association* on its return from India – captained by Admiral Sir Cloudesley Shovell, who ignored his crew's advice and missed the channel by several kilometres – led directly to the establishment of the Board of Longitude, John Harrison's chronometers and the creation of Greenwich Mean Time. Losing an admiral to guesswork was considered by the Navy to be careless and a luxury they could ill afford.

A small cairn still lies by the Loaded Camel rock formation on the crescent beach at Porth Hellick on St Mary's, the largest of the five inhabited islands, marking the spot where Cloudesley crawled ashore.

There was a time when, in the kindest way possible, Scillonians prayed not for shipwrecks to occur but that in case they should, that they happen on Scilly's shores, bringing riches from across the seas to feather the locals' impoverished existence. Their prayers have been answered a number of times. In 1875 the German luxury liner *Schiller* came a cropper here, and more than half its 335 passengers are buried in the cemetery at Old Town. Most recently, in 1997, the *Cita* ran aground. Its containers floated ashore, in limbo, serving up a Whisky Galore of miscellany from tyres and clothing to electronics for the locals to swipe and keep or pawn.

With such wrecks come legends and the Isles of Scilly (calling them "the Scillies" will cause the local to frown) are the rumoured location for the Arthurian Atlantis of Lyonesse, birthplace of the knight Tristan. These islands inspire romantic flights of fancy. Indeed of Bryher, the wildest and most remote of the inhabited islands, the author Charles Connelly wrote: "It's the sort of place where the Romantic poets would have run around the cliff tops at night during thunderstorms wearing nothing but their nightshirts and gone off to write odes about it afterwards."

Many are those who have come to regard these islands as a second home, including former British prime minister Harold Wilson, who is buried in the graveyard of St Mary's. This is a cause for concern for born and bred Scillonians who fear damage to their unique heritage by two-week-a-year homeowners. But such is the rub of these alluring islands. Due to their position in the firing line of the Gulf Stream they benefit from a mild, subtropical climate unique in the British Isles. Palm trees abound, especially in the lush Abbey Gardens of Tresco, and the sea water looks positively Caribbean.

Isles of Scilly, England, UK **Local name:** Ynysek Syllan **Longitude:** 6° 22' W **Latitude:** 49° 56' N **Area:** 16 sq km (6 sq mi) **Highest point:** 44 m (144 ft) **Population:** 2,100
Principal town: Hugh Town, St Mary's **Resident:** Harold Wilson

Iona

INNER HEBRIDES, SCOTLAND

The tiny island of Iona, a fleck of land flicked out from the westernmost tip of Mull, is one of the great sites of Christian history. The exiled Irish prince and priest Calum, later known as St Columba, landed with twelve companions on Iona in AD 563, and for the next three decades dedicated his life to converting the pagans of Scotland and the north of England to Christianity. The spirit of the monastery he founded survives, even if the wattle and daub of the original was repeatedly destroyed by raiding parties of Norsemen in the centuries that followed.

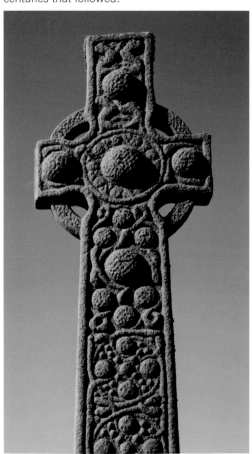

Columba may have been drawn instinctively to Iona. As many writers have observed, it is otherwise difficult to understand why he chose this unremarkable, far-flung corner of Scotland – rocky, austere, windswept, treeless. There must be something in Iona's pure air, for long before he arrived, the island was steeped in spirituality. It was known as Innis-nam Duridbneach, "Island of the Druids". One legend, preserved by oral tradition, even claims that Jesus visited the island. And it is said that seven years before the Day of Judgment the waters will submerge Ireland and Islay, but that Iona alone will swim.

Little remains from Columba's time. The frequent Norse raids destroyed much, and the saint's relics were removed. Martyr's Bay, on the east coast facing Mull, marks the scene of a massacre of nearly seventy monks in AD 806. However, the abbey built on this sacred soil in the early 1200s has survived (ruined in the eighteenth century, it was restored in the 1930s), and is one of the finest medieval ecclesiastical sites in Scotland. It stands proudly by the water's edge, against the stone heights of Dun I, the sole mountain on the island. The abbey was created for the Benedictines through the generosity of Reginald of Islay. Beneath its square tower, the communion table was hewn from local "Iona marble", a composite of Lewisian gneiss and limestone. The weathered, rose-tinted granite ruins of the Augustine nunnery of St Mary date from the same period.

As the religious importance of the island grew, Iona became a significant centre of pilgrimage. The ancient burial ground of the abbey, Reilig Odhráin, was the preferred resting place for Scotland's kings. No one knows for sure how many are interred here, but some estimates run as high as forty-eight Scottish kings (as well as eight Norwegian and four Irish), including Macbeth and his victim Duncan I. Nearly one thousand years later, in 1994, John Smith, Tony Blair's predecessor as leader of the Labour Party, was also buried here. His epitaph is drawn from the writings of Alexander Pope: "An honest man's the noblest work of God."

"To tell the story of Iona is to
go back to God, and to end in God."

Fiona MacLeod, aka William Sharp

OPPOSITE St Martin's Celtic Cross

Iona, Argyll and Bute, Scotland **Local name:** I Chailuim Cille **Longitude:** 6° 25' W **Latitude:** 56° 20' N **Area:** 9 sq km (3 sq mi) **Highest point:** 101 m (331 ft) Dun I **Population:** 125
Residents: St Columba, St Cuaran, St Finan, George MacLeod

"The Faroes are roughly halfway between
the Shetlands and Iceland, and legend has it
that they were created when God cleaned out
his fingernails after creating the Earth."

Charles Connelly, *Attention All Shipping*

ABOVE Tórshavn Marina

OPPOSITE A young supporter of the Faroe Islands' soccer team

Faroes, Denmark **Local names:** Faerøerne, Føroyar **Longitude:** 6° 47' W **Latitude:** 62° 00' N **Area:** 1,399 sq km (540 sq mi) **Highest point:** 882 m (2,894 ft) Slaettaratindur **Population:** 48,500
Principal town: Tórshavn **Natives:** Ian Hamilton Finlay, William Heinesen, Hans Jakob Jacobsen, Jørgen-Frantz Jacobsen, Teitur Lassen, Høgni Lisberg, Eivør Pálsdóttir, Rói Palursson, Sunleif
Rasmussen, Símun av Skardi **Resident:** Kristian Blak

Faroes

NORWEGIAN SEA/NORTH ATLANTIC

I f you took an extremely long run-up along the lengthy east coast of England and Scotland, and failed to put the brakes on as you left the mainland, the Faroes would be your next chance to touch down on solid land – around 350 kilometres (217 miles) later. There is nothing in between and precious little after the Faroes before Greenland. This remote geographical location caused the archipelago to spend millions of years in contented isolation before humans arrived, in the form of seventh-century Irish monks. They were followed by the Vikings: Norwegian kings took over the islands and in 1350 ceded them to Denmark as part of the treaty that united the two nations. The Danes still oversee the Faroes as an autonomous region.

The Danish connection has been vital to the survival of the islands. The Faroese have exploited the fish in the surrounding seas and the animals that live onshore. Indeed, the name of the islands is the local, old Norse, patois for "the islands of sheep", and mutton – in stews or dried strips – is a major ingredient in their cuisine. Pilot whales have been regularly culled, their meat and blubber a source of nourishment,

and even the local puffins occasionally grace Faroese tables. But for most other vittels – as well as a yearly grant – Denmark has been the provider. Thoughts of financial, if not national, independence have been fuelled by the prospect of oil revenues, but extensive explorations have failed to produce any significant finds.

The Faroese have, nonetheless, preserved their own identity. The Icelanders may rib them about their parochial rustic lifestyle, but their Norse roots run deep. Throughout the most intensive Danish rule, the Faroese language and the old stories were maintained through thousands of ballads, retold to the rhythms of unaccompanied ring dances. The music and the singing continues via a generation of young musicians – Eivør Pálsdóttir ("the Faroese Björk") and Teitur Lassen, among others.

The composer Sunleif Rasmussen described one of his earliest memories as the sound of water, the "endless rain" falling on the roofs of his home village. The roofs of Faroese houses are often covered in grass, a metaphor for the geology of the islands. These volcanic leftovers, slanting from western cliffs to eastern seafronts, also have only a slim covering of fertile soil. Trees are at a premium, although there is a profusion of wildflowers: the marsh marigold is the islands' national flower. Tórshavn, the main town on the island of Streymoy, has a suitably countrified feel and just a handful of pubs. Selling alcohol was only legalized in 1992, too late to celebrate the Faroes football team's famous victory over Austria two years earlier.

Hebrides

NORTH ATLANTIC

Collectively the Hebrides, especially the Outer Hebrides, have become a byword for the remote. The Vikings who probably gave them their name, originally Havbrobody, christened them "the islands on the edge of the sea". Lewis, Colonsay, South Uist, Barra, Harris – just some of their names, Inner and Outer – these are elemental places where the wind and sea rule, to say nothing of the clouds of midges. These islands are now the land of Gore-Tex rather than Harris tweed. And as fans of the radio shipping forecast litany will know, more often than not it is a case of "Hebrides, seven to eight, occasionally nine. Rain. Good."

One question the visitor has to ask when visiting the Hebridean island is "Will they be open?", especially if it is a Sunday. The inhabitants of many of the islands are traditional (and the further out the more so) –

a characteristic born of their God-fearing past – and the idea of working on the Sabbath provokes outrage. Equally polemical is the subject of building an airstrip to make the islands more accessible. Remoteness breeds a love of isolation and the islands can only tenuously be viewed as connected to Scotland.

Nowhere is the Hebridean sense of suspicion, Puritanism and miserliness better showcased than in the book by Sir Compton Mackenzie, *Whisky Galore*. It is much blacker in humour than the family favourite Ealing Studios comedy that it became. The book tells the story of the conflict of tradition, desire, thirst, whisky and authority that takes place in the fictional puritanical island communities of Great and Little Todday, when twenty-four thousand barrels of shipwrecked whisky washes up on their shores. The film was shot amid the white shell-sand and spongy grassland of Barra, and contains the immortal line, "It is a well-known fact that some men were born two drinks below par", that sums up the Scottish and Hebridean predilection for a dram of the local spirit.

The Hebrides are awash with Iron Age archaeological sites, but are otherwise notable for their absence of both trees and people. The low population might be typical of such a rural area in the twenty-first century, when people gravitate towards cities, but in the nineteenth century it was due to the enforced clearances. The tenant crofters were removed from their simple pebbledash houses and bungalows (still evident on the islands) by their wealthy London landlords in order to make way for grazing sheep.

Far more populous than people are puffins and a multitude of other seabirds that make their homes on the puzzle of cliff edges, dunes, and fjord-like lochs created by the huge Atlantic surf. Warmed by the Gulf Stream, the islands blaze with wildflowers in summer, while the waters beneath provide a haven for the endangered basking shark.

OPPOSITE Callanich stone circle

OVERLEAF Deserted crofters houses stand on Harta in the Outer Hebrides

Hebrides, Scotland **Local names:** Innse Gall Hebrides/ Na h-Eileanan Siar, Western Isles **Longitude:** 7° 00' W **Latitude:** 57° 30' N **Area:** 3,071 sq km (1,185 sq mi) **Highest point:** 799 m (2621 ft) An Cliseam, North Harris **Population:** 26,500 **Principal town:** Stornoway, Lewis **Natives:** Flora MacDonald, Alexander MacKenzie, Anne MacKenzie, Ken MacLeod **Resident:** Iain Crichton Smith

"To the west there is nothing. Except America."

Compton Mackenzie, *Whisky Galore*

"To the islanders their hard-won soil is
more precious than gold. They would not part with
a foot of their land, barren as it is, for any consideration."
Robert Flaherty

Aran Islands

GALWAY BAY/ATLANTIC

The Aran Islands form part of the final frontier of Europe, its very western edge, beyond which lies the immensity of the Atlantic and, beyond that, a New World. They were once described by the poet Seamus Heaney as "three stepping stones out of Europe". They have also offered a haven in times of turmoil in the rest of Ireland and Europe, and provided a sanctuary for Irish language and learning.

Set in the Bay of Galway, the Arans – not to be confused with the Scottish isle of Arran – are slabs of karst limestone, like the landscape of the Burren on the mainland rather than the granite of Connemara. They are crisscrossed by *boreens* – tiny lanes – and dry-stone walls enclosing minuscule fields, protecting the exposed soil. The wind and weather here can be savage, and unrelenting westerlies lash the outer edges of the isles. The fishermen in their traditional open canvas-covered *curragh* boats wisely avoided the west coast and put to sea in the east. However, although the storms are fierce, they are rarely freezing and so ice has not cracked the stones of many monuments and buildings on the islands. Among those that are still found here are round-towered early Christian churches, monasteries and the great prehistoric fortress of Dún Aengus on the largest island, Inishmore, a citadel so ancient that no one can precisely date

it, perched above plummeting cliffs that provided a natural defence. Dùn Dùbhchathair, the Black Fort, on the southern coast is even older.

Despite this fortification and an innate insularity, the Arans have had an impact on world culture completely disproportionate to their size and population. There was a period when their intense Irishness was seized on as a pure idyll, and its folk traditions romanticized by artists, writers and playwrights. James Joyce called it "the strangest place in the world". In the 1900s J. M. Synge was encouraged to visit the islands by W. B. Yeats, and wrote widely and warmly about them, drawing on these experiences for his masterwork, *The Playboy of the Western World*. In 1934 the American documentary-maker Robert Flaherty captured the islanders' harsh life in *Man of Aran*. More recently, and in a totally different way, the islands were the setting – dubbed Craggy Island – for the irreverent television sitcom *Father Ted*: the islands of Inishmore and Inisheer, the smallest of the trio, wrangle over which was the "real" Craggy Island and hold an annual football match to settle the dispute. The middle island, Inishmaan, quieter and less visited, is where J. M. Synge stayed: Cathaoir Synge ("Synge's Chair") was his favourite viewpoint – a rough semicircle of stones facing westwards across the rough seas...

OPPOSITE Inisheer Castle

BELOW Carrying a *curragh* to water from the shore of Inisheer

Aran Islands, County Galway, Ireland **Local name:** Oileáin Árann **Longitude:** 9° 38' W **Latitude:** 53° 06' N **Area:** 46 sq km (18 sq mi) **Highest point:** 123 m (404 ft) Dún Eochla **Population:** 1,400
Principal town: Kilronan, Inishmore **Natives:** Máirtín Ó Direáin, Liam O'Flaherty **Resident:** J. M. Synge

Skelligs

ATLANTIC

County Kerry is the land of the lakes of Killarney, a place where the Rose of Tralee (Ireland's Miss Congeniality) is elected each year, and where the Gulf Stream fosters lush green countryside. But there is nothing lush or congenial about the Skelligs – two islands off Portmagee, the fishing village at the end of one of the four fingers of southwest Ireland, clawing into the Atlantic. The Skelligs are pure drama.

On the rollercoaster ferry ride to the larger of the two islands, Skellig Michael, what looks like a snow-covered rock rises up. This is Little Skellig, and the snow is the guano of thousands of breeding gannets, which glide and soar on the thermals. The boat ploughs, yaws and pitches across the swell onwards to Skellig Michael, a pyramid of green. On arrival, after negotiating the transfer to dry land, visitors are greeted by a welcoming party of puffins, whose encouraging chatter pushes the fit and hardy to attempt the six hundred steps up the island's cone.

These thin, mossy steps were cut out by sixth-century monks, who chose Skellig Michael as a suitably inaccessible site for their retreat. Anyone who puffs up the ascent should bear in mind that each morning the monks had to come down to catch fish before breakfast – and then climb all the way up again. At the top, like a petrified aviary, half a dozen beehive huts (called clocháns), an oratory and a church huddle within a small, flat-walled space on the island's lower summit. Each dry-stone, corbel-roofed dwelling is just big enough to turn around in, but they are extremely snug and can withstand anything the Atlantic can throw at them. The view from the former self-sufficiency garden across Little Skellig to the coast of Kerry is awe-inspiring: on fine days uplifting, in wilder seasons thrilling.

In July 2007, Robert Bohane swam the 15 kilometres (9 miles) from Skellig Michael to the mainland, the first person to do so. Those of a slightly less adventurous character, however, can take time out from the main "tourist" trail on the island and climb up to the South Peak, where a standing stone perilously overhangs the ocean. Pilgrims would inch across this to plant a kiss and complete their mission.

Nearby, the ruins of a tiny hermitage commemorate a monk for whom the main compound was clearly too much fun. In "Skellig", Canadian singer-songwriter Loreena McKennitt imagines the solitary life of one of these loners. "Many a year was I perched out upon the sea," he remembers. "The waves would wash my tears, the wind my memory." Close your eyes as you stand by the clocháns on this outpost of Europe, and the elements will cleanse your soul.

"Magic that takes you out, far out,
of this time and this world."

George Bernard Shaw

OPPOSITE Little Skellig

Skellig Islands, County Kerry, Ireland **Local name:** na Scealaga **Longitude:** 10° 32' W **Latitude:** 51° 46' N **Area:** 25 hectares (61 acres) **Highest point:** 218 m (715 ft) Skellig Michael

"Our faith is our strength."

Motto of Tristan da Cunha

Tristan da Cunha

SOUTH ATLANTIC

There are a number of contenders for the crown of "the loneliest inhabited island in the world": Pitcairn, Easter and Christmas could all make a convincing case for the title. On a purely geographical basis, however, Tristan da Cunha, midway between South Africa and South America in the middle of the South Atlantic, wins hands down. Its nearest neighbour is St Helena, marooned 2,000 kilometres (1,240 miles) and then some to the north. Short of space travel, this is about as far from the madding crowd as you can get.

The first human known to have set eyes on this island gave it his name. Tristão da Cunha was a Portuguese sea admiral who led a 1506 expedition from Lisbon to India as part of the ongoing tug-of-war to control the spice routes. Lack of wind caused his ships to drift further south than the admiral had intended, and the fleet took some brief respite in the lee of this remote place, but could not land as the waters were too rough.

Dutch and French sailors reconnoitred the island over the next three centuries, and a group of Philadelphian sailors camped on it for nine months in 1790. The first true settler, however, was Jonathan Lambert from Salem, Massachusetts – a fugitive or pirate who landed here with two roguish chums in 1810. Later that decade the British annexed the island to keep an eye on Napoleon's St Helena, and Corporal William Glass founded a new community. There are still descendants of Glass on the island, and only a handful of other family names: the tight interrelation between these families has contributed to the unity of the population.

Their island is round, a volcanic cone rising so steeply from the sea that the crater at the top is never more than a few kilometres from the coastline. The houses in the township, known as the Settlement, shelter on a brief grassy pause between the cliffs and the central 2,000-metre (6,562-foot) peak. Its official name is Edinburgh, in honour of a visit by Queen Victoria's eldest son, the Duke of Edinburgh, in 1867; the current duke also dropped by in 1957.

When the volcano spewed out its black lava four years later, taking everybody – vulcanologists included – by surprise, the islanders were evacuated to the UK for a couple of years, abandoning their home to the shearwaters and albatrosses. When the island children wrote about their time in England, it was not the bright lights, shops or Changing of the Guard of London they remembered, but the River Thames, for they were, and are, water babies, who learnt as toddlers to row, sail and swim (though with care as the waters are shark-infested); Tristan da Cunha remains the deck beneath their feet.

Tristan da Cunha, British Overseas Territory of St Helena **Longitude:** 12° 20' W **Latitude:** 37° 06' S **Area:** 98 sq km (38 sq mi) **Highest point:** 2,062m (6,765 ft) Queen Mary's Peak
Population: 270 **Principal town:** Edinburgh of the Seven Seas aka the Settlement

Lanzarote

CANARY ISLANDS, NORTH ATLANTIC

In recent years, lager has been the drink most commonly associated with the Canary Islands; that and Union Jack flags and English breakfasts. But there was a time when "Canaries" was also the name of a fine dry dessert wine, pressed from the local malvasia grape that grows in the black volcanic earth of the eponymous islands. In its Elizabethan heyday Canaries, later known as Malmsey, was the drink of choice for the royal court, aristocrats, writers and merchants, and hailed by Shakespeare in *Henry IV* as "a Marvellous searching wine". The vineyards here are a surreal sight, rising up on the banks of Lanzarote's black mountains. They were never blighted by the phylloxera that devastated continental vines centuries ago, and now local viticulture is undergoing a renaissance, leading the push to turn the island into a sun-kissed oasis of windsurfing and wine.

Based around the region of La Geria, it is an artisanal low-volume wine production in keeping with the new breed of boutique accommodation springing up around the island. These are sensitively designed to incorporate the natural features of an abstract and striking landscape that is like a hotter version of Iceland: knobbly lichen-covered lava fields, bucolic valleys and many-hued volcanic pyramids, from ochre to chilli to saffron, piled up like a Moroccan spice-seller's stall. There are now luxury converted old haciendas and green-shuttered, whitewashed Arabic-style farmhouses. The finest example is the former house – more of a castle – and now museum-gallery at San José of the architect César Manrique, who set out the blueprint for the building regulations that have preserved the island's visage. Built on many levels into the rock, the lava fields seem to cascade down and spill through the windows, into the submerged theatre and nightclub and out into the cactus garden set out in a former quarry. In coffee-table book parlance it might be called "luxury troglodyte style". The actor Omar Sharif once owned a similar Bond-esque bachelor pad here, subsequently and perhaps uncharacteristically lost in a game of bridge.

Fish and chips are also increasingly off the menu around the island, and especially in the capital Arrecife. Restaurants along its castellated waterfront are now more likely to serve the local delicacy of *papas arrugadas*, salt-crusted wrinkly potato served in spicy sauce. Gales still batter the island, making it a windsurfer's paradise and the sun-seekers' charter flights still flock into Fuerteventura airport. But on touching down they find a unique island microclimate; just like the local wine, a finely preserved vintage just coming into its own. The island has well and truly moved on.

OPPOSITE The Harria Valley of 1,000 Palms

OVERLEAF Vineyard pits are protected by low crescent-shaped walls that serve to trap water to enable the vines to grow on the volcanic land

---

Lanzarote, Canary Islands, Spain **Longitude:** 13° 40' W **Latitude:** 29° 00' N **Area:** 846 sq km (327 sq mi) **Highest point:** 670 m (2,198 ft) Las Peñas del Chache **Population:** 135,200
Principal town: Arrecife **Natives:** Rosana Arbelo, César Manrique **Residents:** Princess Alexia of Greece and Denmark, José Saramago

"If Apple designed islands, they would look like this.
Lanzarote is an iLandscape of white villages set against black lava."

Sankha Guha

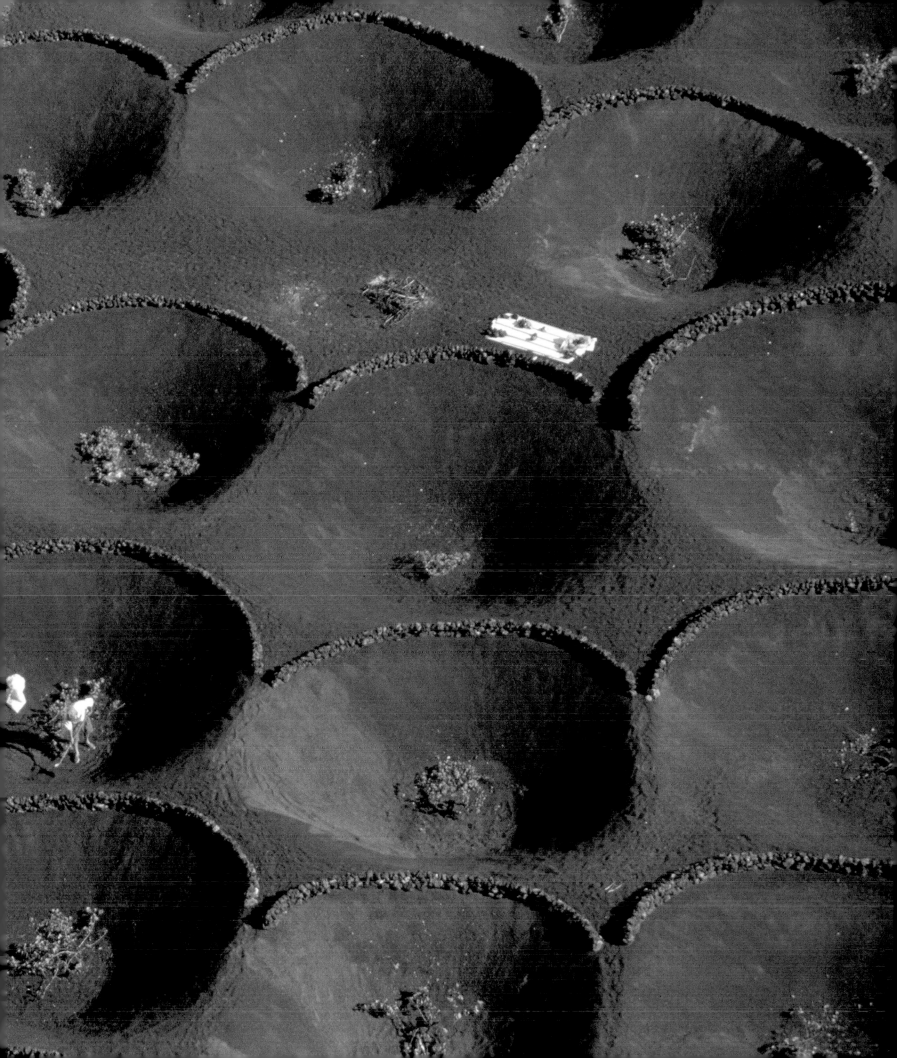

ABOVE Female green turtle (*Chelonius mydas*) heading back to sea after laying her eggs on the beach

Ascension Island, British Overseas Territory of St Helena **Longitude:** 14° 22' W **Latitude:** 7° 57' S **Area:** 88 sq km (34 sq mi) **Highest point:** 859 m (2,818 ft) Green Mountain **Population:** 1,100 **Principal town:** Georgetown

Ascension Island

SOUTH ATLANTIC

Together with Easter and Christmas, Ascension completes the trinity of islands named after Christian festivals whose poetic and symbolic names would seem to reinforce the crusading aspect of the early European explorers that christened them. In fact their names represent nothing more than the day they were discovered – in this instance in 1503 by the Portuguese explorer, Alphonse d'Albuquerque – a rare piece of humility on the part of a people used to naming parts of the world after themselves. That said, risen from the ocean, volcanic and cone shaped with the lush 90-metre (3,000-foot) Green Mountain at its centre, in the desolate middle of the southern Atlantic with nothing but water for miles around (and never a drop to drink), there is something epiphanous and salvational about the sight of Ascension.

Then, as now, the island offers a little-imagined, useful anchorage, victualling station and communications hub for transatlantic mariners. The early Portuguese imported and left goats to graze here as food and milk for future passers-by, and in pre-satellite days it was a vital cable node in the telegraph links between Britain and its colonial interests in South Africa.

Ascension was uninhabited until 1815 when, with Napoleon safely exiled on the nearest island of St Helena (albeit 1,200 kilometres/ 750 miles away), the British government took the precaution of garrisoning Ascension just in case the cunning French should plan a coup to release their former emperor. Thus began

Ascension's life as a military garrison, a naval establishment on land, or what the Royal Navy nicknames a "stone frigate". The island was a base for ships controlling the suppression of the slave trade in West Africa, leading to the erection of a now-incongruous mosque alongside the local Catholic and Anglican churches. In the Second World War the Americans built an airstrip on Wideawake Field, named after Ascension's most conspicuous bird, the sooty tern, nicknamed the "wideawake" because of its raucous call. During the Space Race the strip became an emergency landing strip for the Shuttle, then in the 1982 Falklands conflict Ascension was a vital stop for the British Task Force. Here they refuelled, convalesced and perhaps played a few holes on what the government website designates as one of the world's worst golf courses.

The terns, which nest in the ash-ridden western area known as "the fairs", are just one of a huge variety of land and seabird species native to the island, including boobies, frigates, boatswains, petrels and noddies, all of which are now flourishing under an RSPB programme to rid the island of predatory imported feral cats. Together with egg-laying giant green turtles, these birds supply the main income and tourist attraction for an island whose position just south of the Equator makes it warm all year round; that along with game fishing for marlin and barracuda and the enormous figures exchanged by philatelists for a prized Ascension Island stamp.

"HMS *Ascension*: a stone sloop
of War of the smaller class."

HM Royal Navy designation

Tenerife

CANARY ISLANDS, NORTH ATLANTIC

Like so many package-holiday destinations, it is temptingly easy to fly to Tenerife for a welcome dose of midwinter sun and barely budge from the hotel pool lounger, and then only to leave it for a pre-prepared outing involving tequila slammers and glass-bottomed boats. There is so much more to this Canary island (the largest of the group) than the resort metropolises of Playa de las Americas and Los Cristianos – both naturally located in the south of the island, where the sun is guaranteed. Since it only takes a day to drive round Tenerife at a relatively leisurely pace, lack of time is no excuse.

First stop on the itinerary should be the centre of the island, the great snow-clad, volcanic Mount Teide, Spain's highest peak, and the world's third largest volcano in volume after Hawaii's Mauna Loa and Mauna Kea. Teide, which last erupted in 1909, is surrounded by a collapsed caldera with a spooky lunar landscape that movie location directors have used for *Planet of the Apes*, *Star Wars* and a bowlful of spaghetti westerns.

Further north the climate is humid. There is even (and only whisper this to the sun-seekers) the possibility of rain. Consequently, the hilly lands along the top coast are fertile, the tomatoes are ripe and along the Orotava valley banana plantations are rife. The town of La Orotava itself is a restful oasis of historic buildings, with a wonderful botanic garden. Down on the coast, Garachico is a well-preserved Canarian village, but to see something of the original Guanche natives (whose language gave the island its name: *tene*, "mountain", and *ife*, "white") requires a hike into pine forests to the cave village of Chinamada, or an easier deviation to see the terraced stone pyramids at Güimar on the east coast.

Tenerife's capital, Santa Cruz, offers a different kind of escape from theme parks and "bifteck mit chips". The city's wide avenues have the colonial feel of a Latin-American capital: in its squares, tiled benches are cooling and calming. Not that all has been peace and quiet. The first shots of the Spanish Civil War were fired here: General Franco, then commander-in-chief of the Canary Islands, launched his coup from Santa Cruz in 1936. Horatio Nelson had earlier tried to raid the island after hearing that galleons loaded with bullion were moored at Santa Cruz. For his troubles and greed he took a direct hit of grapeshot on his right elbow, and his arm had to be amputated (he had already lost an eye besieging Calvi in Corsica). Today, however, the only explosions to be seen or heard are of colour and energy during the annual riot of fun that is Santa Cruz's three-week carnival each February.

> "Clad in your mail of ices, thigh of granite and thew of steel. Heedless, alike, of pomp or parting, Ah Teneriffe! I'm kneeling – still."
>
> Emily Dickinson

ABOVE The Carnival Queen contest in Santa Cruz de Tenerife

Tenerife, Santa Cruz de Tenerife, Canary Islands, Spain **Longitude:** 16° 35' W **Latitude:** 28° 15' N **Area:** 2,034 sq km (785 sq mi) **Highest point:** 3,717 m (12,195 ft) Mt Teide **Population:** 852,900
Principal town: Santa Cruz de Tenerife **Natives:** Natalia Bush, Óscar Domínguez, Pedro Guerra, Angel Guimerá, Rodrigo Moynihan, Leopoldo O'Donnell, Teobaldo Power, Caco Senante
Resident: Polo Orti

"Madeira is the home of wineries,
And extremely expensive embroidered fineries."

Ogden Nash

Madeira

NORTH ATLANTIC

North and slightly west of the Canary Islands, Madeira might seem a more obvious destination for the planeloads of tourists heading south to the suntraps scattered off the coast of Morocco. But the island has one significant disadvantage when compared to the likes of Gran Canaria and Tenerife: there are no sandy beaches; they are all volcanic and black. Neighbouring Porto Santo has all the sand.

So Madeira has stayed somewhat staid, preferred by honeymooners who want to spend a little time alone, and retirees who cannot bear the rowdy hordes of the Canaries. The senior citizens have always loved the fact that Madeira is a fantastic floral treat – it has been called variously "a floating plant pot" and "the island of eternal springtime". For those of a sedate age, the island is like Wisley or Kew Gardens with a suntan to boot: subtropical in climate, warmed by gentle zephyrs, with minimal temperature variation, and blessed with a rich volcanic soil that seems to welcome pretty much any vegetation.

Even the name of the island means "wood" in Portuguese, and that of its capital Funchal "fennel", which still grows wild on the island and flavours its traditional sweets. From the fifteenth to the seventeenth centuries, the elite of the islanders benefited from the export of sugar ("white gold") to Europe. The original coverage of laurisilva – a mix of laurel, cedar, broom and heather – is being carefully regenerated.

Madeira's reputation as a rambler's paradise is fully justified. To enhance its flora, the islanders constructed a system of *levadas*, irrigation channels bringing water from the north of the island to the more arid south. The maintenance paths for these waterways have created a pattern of easily mapped walks that bring visitors close to the local cultivators, whose work must necessarily be carried out by hand because of the steepness of the hillsides.

Funchal – red-roofed, colonially Portuguese, and the only town of any size – lies in a natural amphitheatre on the south of the island. There are oleanders, palms and silk cotton trees, but also the details of manmade glories in the local embroidery, black-and-white mosaics in the pavements underfoot, cedar ceilings in the cathedral, or the *azulejo* tiles and highly decorated columns in the church of St John the Evangelist. A cable car whisks visitors to the panorama of Monte, where a lunch of local scabbard fish can be followed by tea at Reid's (following Charles II's marriage to Catherine of Braganza, there has always been a strong British connection) or a glass of the fortified, port-like, Madeira wine. "Have some Madeira, my dear!"

OPPOSITE The harbour at Funchal

Madeira, Portugal **Longitude:** 16° 47' W **Latitude:** 32° 55' N **Area:** 741 sq km (286 sq mi) **Highest point:** 1,862 m (6,109 ft) Pico Ruivo **Population:** 240,800 **Principal town:** Funchal
Natives: Nadia Almada, Joe Berardo, Fátima Lopes, Cristiano Ronaldo **Resident:** André Antoine Bernard

Gorée

DAKAR, SENEGAL

> "I've always wanted to make the link between jazz and Gorée. For me this is where jazz started out from."
>
> Youssou n'Dour, *Retour a Gorée*

Gorée island is to France – if not all Europe – what Robben Island is to South Africa: a stain on its history, a reminder of and memorial to white man's inhumanity to black Africans. Today, it is a beautiful island steeped in pink bougainvillea draped over the balconies of purple-red fired-earth French colonial buildings, and complete with a solitary but pristine beach. Despite this, it is difficult to ignore the island's history. For returning African-Americans and modern-day politicians it has become something of a shrine.

Situated in the lee of the Cape Vert peninsula, off the bulge of Africa and that continent's nearest point to the Americas, Gorée was for three hundred years a centre for the triangular slave route between Europe, Africa and America. Thousands of black Africans were stored, bought and sold here – their varying ethnicities, build, strength and weight attracting different prices – before being dispatched principally to Louisiana, Haiti, Cuba and Brazil. The trade financed the opulence of French cities such as Bordeaux and, in particular, the more northern port of Nantes.

Some dispute the number of slaves, claiming Gorée was a far smaller centre than Zanzibar for example. They state that the island and the extant Maison des Esclaves ("Slaves' House") would have been too small for the storage of so many people, and that the green so-called Porte du Voyage sans Retour ("Gateway of No Return") under the French fort could never have been used by the ships since it is inaccessible from the sea. But these seem rather glib attempts to assuage guilt, especially as Zanzibar is better-known today as a honeymoon destination. The basics of what happened in Gorée's buildings are undeniable and their preservation in monuments a necessary symbol. Many French Africans, including the French rapper Booba, who sang "Gorée, c'est ma terre", regard it as a spiritual home. Popes and politicians, including Nelson Mandela, have come to pay their respects, and even George W. Bush managed to spend twenty maximum-security minutes here in an appeal for the African-American vote.

When the slave trade was suppressed in 1815 Gorée became a trade centre for beeswax, hide and grain. Now it boasts a hotel. Due to its form – a flat plain leading up to a steep basalt hill – the island takes its name from the southern Dutch island Goeree. After the Portuguese discovered it and built a church and cemetery here, the Dutch briefly claimed the island before turning their attention to the Cape. When the French colonized Senegal they adapted the name to mean "good harbour". An ironic title, finally Gorée is now a haven of good, celebrated in the natural sense of fun, and the rhythm and music of the Senegalese and Dakarois, for whom the island is now a weekend retreat from the capital.

Gorée, Dakar, Senegal **Local name:** Île de Gorée **Longitude:** 17° 23' W **Latitude:** 14° 40' N **Area:** 36 hectares (88 acres) **Population:** 1,100 **Principal town:** Gorée
Native: Blaise Diagne

ABOVE The long winding road through moss and lava

OVERLEAF The aurora borealis

Iceland, Republic of Iceland **Local name:** Ísland **Longitude:** 19° 00' W **Latitude:** 64° 45' N **Area:** 101,826 sq km (39,305 sq mi) **Highest point:** 2119 m (6952 ft) Hvannadalshnukar
Population: 307,260 **Capital:** Reykjavik **Natives:** Björk, Leif Fricson, Vigdis Finnbogadóttir, Eidur Gudjohnsen, Hermann Hreidarsson, Jon Ásgeir Jóhannesson, Jóhannes Kjarval, Halldór Laxness,
Jon Leifs, Magnus Magnusson, Múm, Hallgrímur Pétursson, Magnus Scheving, Sigur Rós, Jon Pall Sigmarsson, Jon Sigurdsson, Steinn Steinarr, Juliana Sveinsdóttir, Emiliana Torrini

Iceland

NORTH ATLANTIC

I n the 1990s the self-styled land of fire and ice, one of the world's youngest and most active volcanic islands and one that is therefore constantly evolving, underwent a serious re-branding. Once a place considered suitable only for heavy-duty ramblers with anoraks, its harbour capital, Reykjavik – whose name means "smoke city" on account of the atmospheric wisps of cloud in which it is regularly cloaked – became an alternative, winter and midnight-sun clubbing mecca. A freezing Ibiza. Hikers arriving to explore the great outdoors and in particular the Laugervegur trek, Iceland's equivalent of New Zealand's Milford Trail, were joined by urban weekend partygoers, among them famously Blur's Damon Albarn, looking to mix with the capital's newly trendy population of young blonds in shiny silver shellsuits fuelled by the local cumin-seed liqueur.

Suddenly Iceland's attributes, which had hitherto remained the secret of geologists and explorers prepared to go off the beaten track, became widely known. The government encouraged cheap flights between Britain and New York, including a stopover just long enough to take in Iceland's "golden circle" of highlights in the southwest of the island around the capital. These include the massive and powerful mud-golden waterfall at Gullfoss, the great Geysir which spouts like a whale every fifteen minutes, the continental rift and old parliament at Thingvellir and the famous Blue Lagoon, the sulphurous milky-blue water spa and hot spring.

Those who stay longer and venture farther afield will enjoy the elemental spectacle of a pubescent island wrestling with awkward geological hormones. In the eastern interior sits the glacier-topped volcano of Vatnajokull, on whose slopes Icelanders – lovers of SUVs, skidoos and all manner of all-terrain vehicles – tear around. But periodically the volcano has a fit and sends ice-cubes the size of houses down the river valleys, often wiping out parts of the ring road and bridges that circumnavigate the island.

On the north side of the island just beneath the Arctic Circle, the port of Husavik has turned itself from whaling port to whale-watching capital. In the fjords around here, in the deceptive warped light of the Arctic, dolphins frolic with minke whales. It is a landscape of snow-capped mountain ranges full of the folklore of fairies and the *fata morgana* mirage effect. As the mastermind of Iceland, Magnus Magnusson wrote, "It is a huge living island on which historians and 'storians alike can paint their perceptions of the past".

Iceland is a treeless island whose interior landscape is often considered close to that of the moon. The barren red crust in the centre, interrupted here and there by hot springs, sulphurous mud pools and glaciers, has been used as a lunar simulation ground for training astronauts. Like the rest of the island, it is a surreal place where the imagination can and frequently does run riot.

"The sun is a coin
on the loose,
spiralling down
around the Arctic rim;
the days
are strained and sieved
through the night,
and the nights arrive
with the days stirred in."

Simon Armitage and Glyn Maxwell,
Moon Country, Further Reports from Iceland

Cape Verde

NORTH ATLANTIC

Cesaria Evora, the "Barefoot Diva", is one of the great voices to have emerged from Cape Verde, a roughly semicircular archipelago of ten islands in the Atlantic ocean west of Senegal. The islands are rich in the sounds of music, and much of that music is laden with a sense of love, loss and longing because so many of the islanders are descended from the African slaves who were transported here to work on the sugar plantations. Almost every family has also had to wave a sad farewell to relatives travelling to find work elsewhere, in Portugal, Brazil and the United States. There are currently more Cape Verdeans based overseas than on the islands themselves.

The Cape Verde Islands (named after Senegal's Cap Vert) were uninhabited until Portuguese settlers arrived in the mid-fifteenth century. They quickly recognized the potential of the tropical climate and year-round sun, established the sugar-cane fields and shipped in slaves from continental Africa to provide the necessary workforce. Water is at a premium on these islands as there is little rain (most water still has to be imported), so the work was gruelling and unrelenting – as was the islands' later fight for independence, finally achieved in 1975.

For a long time Cape Verde was not even a blip on the tourist radar, but it has recently become a favourite of property advisers. They have excitedly flagged up its mix of sun and great beaches with eastern European apartment prices, and are keeping their fingers crossed that there will be a rush of potential purchasers and renters. The extra hours of flight beyond Madeira and the Canary Islands may yet prove something of a deterrent, though.

There is plenty of variety within the archipelago's islands for those who make the effort. Boa Vista has been compared to Mauritius for the quality of its beaches and the blue of its waters. São Tiago has wild mountains. Fogo is home to Praia, the capital set high on a plateau overlooking the coast, while São Vicente's port of Mindelo is the music capital. As well as the languid fado-like *morna* – "our version of the blues" in prime exponent Cesaria Evora's words – there is *batuque*, a slow, improvised vocal music originally sung by the native washerwomen. There is also the more upbeat, sensual accordion-fuelled *funaná*, originally from São Tiago (with something of New Orleans zydeco about it) and the Caribbean-influenced *zouk-love*. This blend of influences applies equally to the Cape Verde cuisine, whose trademark dish, *cachupa*, is a fish or meat stew with beans, maize and herbs – part gumbo, part *paella*, part *feijoada*, but above all, like the sublime music, uniquely Cape Verdean.

OPPOSITE The beach at São Vicente

Cape Verde, Republic of Cape Verde **Local name:** Cabo Verde **Longitude:** 24° 00' W **Latitude:** 16° 00' N **Area:** 4,033 sq km (1,557 sq mi) **Highest point:** 2829 m (9281 ft) Mt Fogo, Fogo
Population: 420,900 **Capital:** Praia, Santiago **Natives:** Maria Alice, Calú Bana, Frank Cavaquim, Cesaria Evora, Sergio Frusoni, Gardenia, Ildo Lobo, Manuel Lopes, Luis Morais, Manuel de Novas, Henrique Teixeira de Sousa, Eugénio Tavares, Titina, Antoninho Travadinha **Resident:** Mayra Andrade

"Cape Verde is my inspiration.
I always come back here.
This will be my home forever."
Cesaria Evora

"Nine volcanic islands strung out across three-hundred and seventy miles, like some fabulous necklace, half the Atlantic Ocean away."

Joanne Harris, novelist

Azores

NORTH ATLANTIC

To fans of the English country garden, the Azores may seem at first oddly familiar. Here, vast expanses of brilliant green roll out before the eye, bordered with pink and blue hydrangeas, rampant morning glory and colourful agapanthus, all divided into neat squares by snaking and undulating stone walls. But the sense of familiarity is jolted at every turn: the walls are made of basalt, the fields run down to black-sand beaches laden with turtles' eggs, and amid the emerald-coloured grass and woods lie vineyards, tobacco fields, and pineapple and tea plantations. These, and the endless horizon of blue sea, are constant reminders that here in the Azores one is situated perhaps not in the middle of nowhere, but certainly in the middle of the Atlantic Ocean.

The Portuguese archipelago is divided into three groups, with São Miguel in the east as the principal hub. Here the slow-paced capital of Ponta Delgada, with its marina, castle and cobbled, palm-lined streets of welcoming markets, friendly cafés and pungent with the smell of grilled sardines, is reminiscent of Madeira fifty years ago. The Catholic identity is obvious – there are statues of the Madonna and burning incense at every turn. Inland lie post-volcanic valleys of health-enriching sulphurous mud pools such as Furnas, where the local

speciality of *morcela* (blood sausage) is still baked underground. The famous twin lakes at Sete Cidadas, one blue and one green, fill a caldera around whose edges villages lie snugly tucked in by verdant cliffs, woods and fields.

To the south is Santa Maria and in the centre are Terceira, Graciosa, São Jorge, conical-shaped Pico and Faial, the latter known as the blue Island because of its hydrangea hedgerows hugging the volcanic moonscape that makes up the rest of the island. The town of Horta, a stopover and meeting point for transatlantic yachting fanatics (as well as many species of migrating cetaceans), has an incongruously international feel. Elsewhere, fifty years after the Capelinhos volcano erupted, the roofs of lava-submerged houses can still be seen jutting out, and at low tide the sea still sizzles from the dormant heat beneath.

Out west lie Flores and Corvo, also pockmarked with volcanoes, some dormant and still smoking. Suffice to say that the Azores is not a destination for beach bums, but rather an outpost for the curious and the active both of mind and body – as well as keen gardeners. As befits an archipelago that hints at an exotic version of the Garden of England, the weather is also suitably changeable, with four seasons often coming in one day.

OPPOSITE Furnas Valley in São Miguel

Azores, Autonomous Region of Azores, Portugal **Local name:** Açores **Longitude:** 27° 00' W **Latitude:** 38° 25' N **Area:** 2569 sq km (992 sq mi) **Highest point:** 2,351 m (7,713 ft) Pico Alto, Ilha de Pico **Population:** 238,800 **Principal town:** Horta, Faial **Natives:** Adam Lindsay Gordon, Christopher Hampton, Vitorino Nemésio, Álamo Oliviera, Pedro Resendes aka Pauleta, Mario Silva **Resident:** Fernando Pessoa

> "An island with so many beaches and a large and lengthy inland lagoon perfectly reflecting the forested dunes which surround it, smacks of excessive goodwill by the Creator."
>
> John Malathrones, *Brazil – Life, Blood, Soul*

Santa Catarina

ATLANTIC COAST, BRAZIL

Fans of the Brazilian telenovelas that dominate the television schedules from Punta Arenas to Mexico City, as well as much of Europe, will instinctively know the island of Santa Catarina. Its relaxed colonial towns, dunes, idyllic beaches and inland lakes such as Lagoa da Conceicão are often used as a backdrop for their continuous tales of love, jealousy, heartache and adulterous affairs. Brazil itself has a national love affair with the beach, and here on Santa Catarina it reaches its bikini-clad zenith. Even the more affluent *cariocas* of Rio tear themselves away from their beloved Copacabana and Ipanema strips to enjoy their summerhouses on the island and a game of beach volleyball or five-a-side on the caster-sugar sand of beaches with attractive names such as Joaquina or Canasvieiras. Others, such as Moçilambique, are surf paradises renowned for their tubular breaks, and host world surf championships. The seafood at the beachside restaurants, served to a chilled *bossa* beat, is known by Brazilians as some of the best in the country. On Santa Catarina everything one fantasizes about the Brazilian way of life is true.

The island lies off the southern Brazilian coast of the same name – an area of Brazil profoundly different from the megapoles of Rio and São Paulo. Settled principally by Germans in the 1850s, southern Brazil is less African, and more than a third of the locals can claim Germanic descent (think supermodel Gisele Bundchen). In 1839, during the Farroupilha Revolution, Santa Catarina even claimed independence and managed one year as a republic before being strong-armed back into the Brazilian empire. The island is an ecological reserve. The southern right whale comes here to mate and calve, and is now pursued by whale-watchers instead of being hunted. There is a ban on heavy industry and – a far cry from the city *favelas* – it is also blessed with a relaxed rhythm and a negligible crime rate.

That said, the island's capital, Florianópolis, nicknamed Floripa and split between the mainland and the island linked by the Hercilio Luz suspension bridge, is by European standards a Manhattan of skyscrapers and highways. Prior to the building of the Panama Canal it was a major port for ships from New York bound via the Cape for the gold rush in California. Santa Catarina was first claimed by the Spanish in 1542 before being passed to the Portuguese in the Treaty of Torsedillas, a Hispanic Yalta, at which the two colonial superpowers divided between east and west the continent over which they alone had dominion. It was the Portuguese, mainly from the Azores, who fortified the island and bequeathed it the battlements of Anhatomirim and Forte Sant'Ana, the Metropolitana cathedral and such pastel-coloured vintage colonial and Azorian jewels as Ribeirão da Ilha, especially the old port area formerly known as Santo Antonio de Lisboa.

Santa Catarina, Santa Catarina Province, Brazil **Local name:** Ilha de Santa Catarina **Longitude:** 48° 30' W **Latitude:** 27° 25' S **Area:** 523 sq km (202 sq mi) **Population:** 360,000
Principal town: Florianópolis **Natives:** João da Cruz e Sousa, Gustavo Kuerten, Victor Meirelles de Lima, Fernando Scherer, Rafael Verga

ABOVE Morro das Pedras Armacao Beach

ABOVE Devil's Island, as seen from Royale Island

Devil's Island, Îles du Salut, French Guiana **Local name:** Île du Diable **Longitude:** 52° 35' W **Latitude:** 5° 17' N **Area:** 14 hectares (35 acres) **Highest point:** 40 m (131 ft) **Population:** None
Residents: Henri Charrière, Alfred Dreyfus, Clément Duval

Devil's Island

ÎLES DU SALUT, FRENCH GUIANA

The Île d'If in the bay of Marseilles may have provided France's most celebrated fictitious prison-break adventure in *The Count of Monte Cristo*, but the sonorous name of Devil's Island, or Île du Diable, off the coast of French Guiana has earned its place in the spine-chilling pantheon of forbidding prisons, largely through the daring exploits of a small-time villain of the Paris underworld, Henri Charrière – nicknamed Papillon because of the butterfly tattoo on his chest – wrongly convicted of killing a pimp.

Opened as a penal colony by Napoleon III in 1852, Devil's Island quickly became one of the most infamous prisons in history. Lying just 11 kilometres (7 miles) off the mainland and the outermost of the Îles du Salut, it was said to be disease-infested, inescapable due to its steep cliffs, rough seas and the strong currents below. Few who were sent there ever returned alive. It was the destination for anarchists such as Clement Duval and France's worst thieves and murderers.

But the island's notoriety was cemented by the 1895 *affaire Dreyfus*. Dreyfus was a Jewish captain in the French Army, convicted of pro-German sympathies and of passing French artillery secrets to the Kaiser's growing military. Dreyfus was tried, convicted of treason and dispatched to Devil's Island. Meanwhile his family and the liberals, republicans and left-wing intellectuals of French society fought against his conviction, against the Third Republic old establishment, charging them with anti-Semitism and eventually flushing out the real culprit – a French Army colleague of Dreyfus. The innocent captain was eventually released. The Dreyfus affair gave rise to one of the most celebrated French quotations: on 13 January 1898, the novelist and liberal social progressive Émile Zola penned an impassioned exposé on the affair to President Félix Faure, which covered the entire first page of the maiden issue of the newspaper, *l'Aurore* ("Dawn"). The journalist Georges Clemenceau added the famous headline "J'accuse!"

Seventy years later Henri Charrière published his gripping account of a decade of derring-do, serial Houdini-esque escape from various of the Guiana penal colonies, and life as a fugitive and lover among the natives, culminating in his escape from Devil's Island by diving into the waves with nothing but a raft made of coconuts. It read like a fantastical action adventure, and some challenged whether it was he who lived each episode or whether he simply compiled the stories of other inmates. Either way, it was a bestseller and in 1973 it was made into a film starring Steve McQueen and Dustin Hoffman.

Nowadays the *Papillon* trail attracts pilgrims to this rocky, palm-covered Caribbean island. Since the penal colony closed in 1952, it has been given over to the Guiana Space Center, full of astronomical measuring apparatus near France's principal space port at Kourou on the mainland. Whenever there is a rocket launch the islanders still have to escape – albeit via controlled evacuation and not on coconut rafts. *Plus ça change…*

"Strange things happen to the head here.
Put all hope out of your mind. And masturbate as little as possible.
It drains the strength."

From the film *Papillon*, based on the book by Henri Charrière

> "Newfoundland is both the beginning and the end,
> the alpha and omega, the gateway to and the outer barracks
> of a country, a continent, a New World."

Will Ferguson, *Beauty Tips from Moose Jaw*

Newfoundland

NORTH ATLANTIC

Many islands have their own unique plants and animals, sightings of which cause great excitement among locals and visitors alike. But few can claim the wondrous and infinitely varied natural visitor to Newfoundland. Here the draw is not some rare whale, as it could be, but the arrival of giant icebergs, complete with internal waterfalls, which float into the tiny "outport" harbours, as the fishing villages around the island are known. On Newfoundland, iceberg-spotting is a local sport.

As the sight of these wandering clouds of ice suggests, benign in the surroundings of a humble fishing port, the province of Newfoundland is a quirky place. Already its position – nudging up against the wet snout of Labrador, in its own time zone half an hour ahead of the rest of Canada – sets it apart from the rest of North America. To the ear of those that locals call "come-from-aways", the Newfie accent is closer to Irish or original London cockney than Canadian. Locals speak of "oy toyd" (high tide), needing to go for "an art hoperation" (a heart operation) and spatter their speech with estuary double negatives. These roots, together with the shipping news-style wet weather, have combined and come through in a mordant sense of humour and irony innate to all Newfies that seems designed to mock unlikely and foolish visitors. Take the place names: Blow Me Down, Heart's Desire and Witless Bay, or the Baie d'Espoir (Bay of Hope) named originally by French fishermen and then

changed by the English to Bay Despair. One of the waterfalls at the island's many inland fjords is called Pissing Mare Falls. And it is surely cockney craftiness that inspired many locals to place their "mother-in-law" doors above ground with no steps leading up to them, so they could avoid tax on the grounds that the house was still under construction.

In truth, Newfoundland is an island in transition. Depleted Atlantic fish stocks have caused a ban on the customary cod fishing and reduced the permitted quotas of other fish to such an extent that the outlook seems bleak for the island's traditional livelihood. Adaptable as they are, though, Newfies are now turning to tourism and seeking to attract the Iceland brigade. With the UNESCO-listed Gros Morne national glacier park, a landscape of fjords and chimney-like rock formations carved by sea, wind and ice – to say nothing of visiting icebergs – they have the geology to match. Coffee shops and museums dedicated to the discovery of America and the beginning of the British Empire are now sprouting up in downtown St John's, while a number of the island's fifty-five lighthouses have been converted into upmarket bed and breakfasts.

Fish, however, is still firmly on a menu definitely not designed for vegans. The most famous dish is Jiggs Dinner – roast moose and vegetables – which is also now sold (probably as a joke) as a local delicacy in hampers by the roadside and, should the taste not suit, washed down with the local *screech* firewater.

OVERLEAF Spring icebergs at Saint Lunaire

Newfoundland, Newfoundland and Labrador, Canada **Alternative names:** Terre-Neuve, Talamh an Éisc **Longitude:** 55° 00' W **Latitude:** 49° 00' W **Area:** 10,883 sq km (4202 sq mi)
Highest point: 814 m (2,671 ft) Lewis Hills **Population:** 466,200 **Principal town:** St John's **Natives:** Christa Borden, Johnny Burke, Alex Faulkner, Ann Harvey, Cathy Jones, Tommy Ricketts, Joey Smallwood, Kim Stockwood, Marie Toulinguet, Shannon Tweed, Mary Walsh

Falkland Islands

SOUTH ATLANTIC

Back in 1770, Samuel Johnson looked on with an amazement and disbelief not dissimilar to that of Britain and the rest of the world two hundred years later (and after some thirty-five years of Empire-shedding), as the British government sent its fleet to the opposite side of the Atlantic to defend ownership of a few far-flung islands "which not the southern savages have dignified with habitation". "To proportion eagerness of contest to its importance," Johnson wrote, "seems too hard a task for human wisdom."

In Johnson's day this move almost provoked outright war with the Franco-Spanish alliance. The English and French had both claimed the islands, unaware of each other's landings. When John Strong arrived on a 1690 expedition to the Cape he named the islands after his patron, Viscount Falkland, even though maps of the day referred to them as the Sebald Islands after the Dutchman Sebald de Weerd who had first happened upon them. Quite independently, some Breton fishermen all the way from St Malo had arrived on the islands and christened them the Iles Malouines. When France ceded them to the Spanish they inherited the name as Las Islas Malvinas. The Spanish eventually bowed to Britain's claim over the Falklands, but since declaring independence in 1816, Argentina – who administered the islands on behalf of Spain – has wanted Las Malvinas back. In 1982 the military junta of General Galtieri invaded them to arouse patriotism and deflect attention from the economic crisis at home. The move prompted Margaret Thatcher to dispatch a Task Force to win back the islands; after two bloody months, they succeeded. True to the history of islands with no heroes to conquer or regimes to change, and where hitherto the only event of note was a name change, no mention of Las Malvinas was allowed in the surrender document. Naturally, however, all Falklanders have the right to Argentine citizenship.

The inhabitants of the Falklands, divided into "kelpers" (ancestral), "islanders" (those born there) and "belongers" (those who have obtained citizenship), are fiercely patriotic and loyal to the Crown. The capital, Stanley (twinned with Whitby), and the other towns of the two principal islands, East and West Falkland divided by the Falkland Sound, abound with corrugated iron rooftops of kit houses, flagpoles and car bonnets emblazoned with the Union Jack. Locals live off a growing economy of war tours around the white-grass battlegrounds such as Goose Green and Mount Pleasant, English-language teaching to South Americans, visiting cruise ships, sheep-farming, sea-trout fly-fishing and observing the abundant wildlife, which includes such birds as petrels and albatross, seals and sea lions and five different species of penguin, from frog-hopper to king – all British subjects, of course.

ABOVE Magellanic penguins

OPPOSITE Port Howard, the oldest farm on the island

Falklands, British Overseas Territory **Alternative name:** Islas Malvinas **Longitude:** 59° 00' W **Latitude:** 51° 30' S **Area:** 12,173 sq km (4,699 sq mi) **Highest point:** 705 m (2,313 ft) Mt Usborne, East Falkland **Population:** 3,100 **Principal town:** Stanley

"What continuance of happiness can be expected
when the whole system of European empire
can be in danger of a new concussion,
by a contention for a few spots of earth,
which, in the deserts of the ocean,
had almost escaped human notice"

Samuel Johnson, *Thoughts on the Late Transactions Respecting Falkland's Islands*

Barbados

NORTH ATLANTIC/CARIBBEAN

"Barbados or Little
England was the
oldest and purest of
England's children,
and may it always be so."

George Lamming, *In the Castle of My Skin*

Heading westwards across the Atlantic, Barbados is the first of the Caribbean islands to emerge on the horizon, set slightly apart from the outer curve of the Lesser Antilles. It is significantly distinct in this region by virtue of being a limestone coral island: all the other islands are the fallout of volcanic activity. There are no towering pitons, just a gentle rise to the highlands of the centre, dubbed Scotland by homesick Celtic settlers. And in general Barbados escapes the worst of the Caribbean hurricanes.

The first shipload of Brits, aboard the *William and John*, arrived in 1625, anchoring off the west coast of the island near the present location of Holetown. Within less than twenty years they had been joined by twenty-five thousand fellow settlers, and by the 1640s these incomers had focused on the cultivation of sugar as the perfect crop – Charles Kingsley called the island "that prosperous and civilized little cane-garden". That decision led to Barbados becoming a much-valued jewel of the British Empire, and the island remained in British hands until 1966. Despite Martinique's location a couple of hundred kilometres away, the direction of the wind discouraged any attacks by the French to acquire Barbados's riches. There is a heavy residue of Caribbean-flavoured Britishness. Afternoon tea is taken to the sight and sound of hovering hummingbirds and darting honeycatchers. For the Brits there is a reassuring familiarity to the place names: Hastings, Dover, Clapham. Cricket is a huge part of Bajan life: this is the island of Garfield Sobers and Frank Worrell, Malcolm Marshall and Desmond Haynes.

Traces of the sugar industry are now largely historical, although rum is still produced; the Mount Gay distillery is the best-known of the island's brands. Planters' homes include the seventeenth-century Jacobean houses of St Nicholas Abbey and Drax Hall (both intact thanks to that low hurricane count) and the more predictable colonial-style Sunbury House. Workers survived in the coral "chattel houses", some of which still stand. Although most of the five hundred windmill towers where the sugar cane was ground have long since been converted, the Morgan Lewis mill, its four sailpoles silhouetted above a central cone of stone, has been carefully preserved.

Barbados – the name, bestowed by Portuguese sailors, means "the bearded ones" and is possibly a reference to the local fig trees, whose aerial roots dangle down – tends to corral its visitors on the "Platinum" west coast, while the local Bajans head to the rugged eastern coastline, cooled by the trade winds and pounded by the Atlantic, where Bathsheba is a world-renowned surfing beach. Bridgetown, the small capital, has a collection of bright colonial buildings around the old parade ground, Garrison Savannah. Despite the tea and cricket, however, Barbados is moving on from its colonial past. The 1813 statue of Lord Nelson has been removed and his former site, Trafalgar Square, renamed National Heroes Square.

ABOVE The main street of Speightstown

OVERLEAF Beach cricket at Bathsheba

Barbados **Longitude:** 59° 30' W **Latitude:** 13° 10' N **Area:** 430 sq km (166 sq mi) **Highest point:** 336 m (1,102 ft) Mt Hillaby **Population:** 279,000 **Capital:** Bridgetown **Natives:** Grantley Adams, Errol Barrow, Edward Kamau Brathwaite, Sarah Ann Gill, Gordon Greenidge, Desmond Haynes, Wes Hall, John King, Malcolm Marshall, Rihanna, Garfield Sobers, Clyde Walcott, Everton Weekes, Frank Worrell, Edwin Yearwood **Residents:** Bussa, Alison Hinds, Oliver Messel, Rupee

Tobago

CARIBBEAN

Trinidad and Tobago are twinned like one of the Caribbean's great double acts, like Sly and Robbie, Greenidge and Haynes, rum and coke. But although they are next-door neighbours, the two islands are in fact the region's Odd Couple. Their union was a political marriage enacted at independence in 1962. Trinidad is surprisingly industrial (it has cruelly been called "Walsall with palm trees"), noisy, claimed by Columbus for Spain, strongly Catholic, hence its great carnival. Tobago is less developed, rural, British, Protestant. The big celebrations here take place at Easter, including goat races in the village of Buccoo – goat curry is a local speciality, along with rice and pigeon peas, pig foot souse and mango chow.

Tobago, the smaller and more easterly of the two, is in many ways a microcosm of what first-time visitors imagine a Caribbean island to be: frequently deserted beaches, an unspoilt rainforest with stunning wildlife. Because Tobago – and in this way it *is* like Trinidad – is a breakaway chunk of South America it has inherited and attracts a particularly rich selection of flora and fauna, especially its birdlife. Alongside hummingbirds, banaquits and warblers are the rare black-headed, blue-crowned mot mots and white-bearded manakins. The cry of the turkey-like cocrico, Tobago's national bird, echoes through the forests, while offshore frigate birds patrol for fish.

The island changed hands between the colonizing powers many times. The capital of Scarborough – home to four-fifths of Tobago's population – was variously called Lampsinsburg by the Dutch and Port Louis by the French, before the British took a firm grip as part of the negotiations of the 1814 Treaty of Paris. Scarborough, a rambling town, spreads up and over the slopes surrounding its cove, a harbour from which the Sea Cat ferry eases out at first light on its way to Port of Spain. High up in the hills above, guesthouses tucked away in the forest have views over the port's twinkling lights (in truth it is far more attractive at night than by day).

Although the island's internal roads are sometimes challenging, and a four-wheel drive often a necessity, the journey around Tobago tracks the northern ridge of mountains and runs up through the rainforest towards the fishing village of Charlotteville – a peaceful contrast to the popular Pigeon Point Beach in the west – and the diving coves of Man o'War Bay and Pirate's Bay. Here, blennies and squid swim beside parrotfish, angelfish, turtles and barracudas; further away are hammerheads and morays. This is a secret corner of the island, where the mood is mellow and visitors can stand on the pier to watch the evenings ebb away with a bottle of Stag or Carib. The fish to accompany the beer is, of course, freshly caught.

> ## "If there is no room in heaven send me back to Tobago."
>
> Local saying

Tobago, Republic of Trinidad and Tobago **Longitude:** 60° 40' W **Latitude:** 11° 10' N **Area:** 300 sq km (116 sq mi) **Highest point:** 567 m (1,860 ft) Pigeon Peak **Population:** 54,000
Principal town: Scarborough **Native:** Dwight Yorke **Resident:** Winston Bailey aka Shadow

> "I have travelled the globe. I have seen the Canadian and American Rockies, the Andes and the Alps and the highlands of Scotland, but for simple beauty, Cape Breton outrivals them all."
>
> Alexander Graham Bell

Cape Breton

NORTH ATLANTIC

Someone once pointed out that Nova Scotia looks like a lobster, and if you study the map for a while you can see exactly what they meant. Spread out on the platter of the Atlantic Ocean off Canada, the lobster's claws are formed by the island of Cape Breton, joined to the main body by a causeway across the Strait of Canso.

Geologists believe that this strip of land was once connected to Norway and Scotland, so it is particularly appropriate not only that the region is "New Scotland", but also that in the early nineteenth century, a bevy of Scots – some fifty thousand of them – arrived on Cape Breton, driven from their homeland by the scourge of the Highland Clearances, "encouraged" to move away to allow the lairds to introduce more profitable sheep farming. This Gaelic Scottish heritage is still very much a proud part of Cape Breton's character, not least in the fiddle music

OPPOSITE The fall colour reflects on Jigging Cove Lake

BELOW A Canadian coastguard lighthouse

of the island and the low-stepping dances that accompany them, both transported through time from Scotland two hundred years ago. Performers such as Natalie MacMaster and the Rankin Family have taken this music to an audience far beyond fans of folk.

The emigrant Scots chose a wonderful destination – one originally home to the Mi'kmaq, settled by the French as Île Royale, part of Acadia (the Acadian heritage and their own violin music lives on in the fishing village of Chéticamp). Rocky coastlines, rolling farmlands, glacial valleys, the Bras d'Or saltwater lake complex – Cape Breton frequently makes the top five of the world's most beautiful islands. One of its highlights is the Cabot Trail, a highway slicing into the rugged northern coastline and rising up to the northern highlands, the plateaus of tundra that form the highest point in the Atlantic region. The route is named after John Cabot, the great fifteenth-century explorer and navigator, who encountered the island in June 1497. Another visionary – and a Scot – Alexander Graham Bell came to Cape Breton in 1885 and built himself a summer home (Beinn Bhreag, or "Beautiful Mountain") at Baddeck, now the start of the Cabot Trail, where he continued his investigations into telephony, hydrofoil technology and the development of a precursor to the iron lung.

Coal was a major part of Cape Breton's economy from the 1830s onwards, and the mining communities provide the setting for Ann-Marie MacDonald's bestselling novel *Fall on Your Knees*. Fishing is also big business on the island – whether inland on the salmon runs of the Margaree River, or offshore for the local fishing fleets. Appropriately, the lobsters are delicious.

Cape Breton, Nova Scotia, Canada **Alternative names:** Île du Cap-Breton, Eilean Cheap Breatuinn, Únamakika **Longitude:** 60° 45' W **Latitude:** 46° 10' N **Area:** 10,311 sq km (3,980 sq mi) **Highest point:** 532 m (1,745 ft) White Hill **Population:** 147,500 **Principal town:** Sydney **Natives:** Aselin Debison, Ashley MacIsaac, Natalie MacMaster, Rankin Family **Residents:** Alexander Graham Bell, Mary Jane Lamond, Alistair MacLeod, Buddy MacMaster

"Every global writer in the end has to write 'Paris' as if
the Parisian Experience is superior to being in a village in St Lucia.
This is a wrong idea. Cathedrals aren't greater than the village shrine.
The subliminal urge is to return to your home, especially if it is an island."

Derek Walcott

ABOVE The Almond Morgan Bay Resort on Choc Bay   OPPOSITE First Communion   OVERLEAF A cruise ship beneath the Pitons

St Lucia **Longitude:** 60° 57' W **Latitude:** 14° 00' N **Area:** 620 sq km (239 sq mi) **Highest point:** 959 m (3,146 ft) Mt Gimie **Population:** 170,000 **Capital:** Castries
Natives: Arthur Lewis, Joseph Marcell, Darren Sammy, Dunstan St Omar, Joseph Sylvester, Derek Walcott

St Lucia

CARIBBEAN

The Trojan Wars seem a long, long way from the classically Caribbean beaches of St Lucia, but the island has often been called "the Helen of the West Indies", a reference not to any Greek history, but to the ping-pong ownership of the island played out between France and Britain. St Lucia changed hands fourteen times between the pair before the British finally won out in the territorial tug of love by gaining control in 1814.

Given that history, it is not surprising that the French managed to establish a lasting influence. The islanders are predominantly Roman Catholic, there is a local Creole, and many of the island's townships bear French names – Soufrière, the capital Castries and Marigot Bay down in the south – and St Lucia's trademark twin peaks are the jungle-clad Grand and Petit Pitons. These spiky, vertiginous highpoints on the edge of the west coast are scaled by most visitors only in their imagination, as the trails are extremely steep and there is a constant threat of landslides.

The British-ness is, oddly, a little less overt. Cricket is extremely popular here, but Darren Sammy was the first islander to make the West Indies team when he joined the one-day side in 2004. Three years later, Freddie Flintoff's ill-advised late-night pedalo outing from Rodney Bay helped scupper the England team's chances in the Cricket World Cup.

Some compare the shape of this Windward Island – between Martinique and St Vincent – to an avocado or a mango. The latter is a particularly appropriate comparison for anyone who has savoured a fresh mango and guava juice for breakfast here. A drive across the island from south to north through the mountainous, rainforested centre passes the fields of bananas that fill the gap left by the end of the sugar plantations in the 1960s; most islanders are descended from the slaves imported to work the sugar cane. The main road swings away from the east coast at Dennery Bay, leaving behind a rarely visited northeast coast of heavy surf, to head for the hill-ringed port of Castries, birthplace of poet and playwright Derek Walcott, one of St Lucia's two cherished Nobel Laureates (the other was the economist Sir Arthur Lewis).

Here on the west coast, alongside the Pitons, are clapboard houses, cocoa plantations, lush botanical gardens, and what the brochures call "the world's only drive-in volcano". It is not drive-thru however; but park up, and you can inhale, if you feel you must, a lungful of sulphurous fumes and admire the most recent crater, made when a local guide slipped and fell into the bubbling mud. Thankfully he survived to tell the tale.

Martinique

CARIBBEAN

If you are listening to a radio in one of the northerly resorts on St Lucia, a deft twiddle of the dial will catch the radio stations of Martinique, 50 kilometres (30 miles) north. In one fell swoop you are immersed into *la vie française*, a quirk of history, since Martinique, like St Lucia, was wrangled over in the eighteenth century by France and Britain – this time the French won out. Fort-de-France, the island's capital, is considered by many to be the epicentre of Frenchness in the Caribbean. Lying on a bay on Martinique's west coast, its spillover suburbs clambering up the lush hills behind, Fort-de-France has something of Marseilles about it: flower-decked balconies, quayside cafés, the tang of a post-prandial Gitane.

In fact, Martinique could as easily have been a part of Spain: Christopher Columbus sailed past in 1493, calling the island after St Martin, and making a note that it was "the most beautiful country in the world", but his Spanish masters did not follow up the opportunity. And so the French took over from the Carib islanders, who had previously ousted the native Arawaks. However, for some Martinique is a little bit *too* French. They complain that the island is full of roundabouts, that it is just like the Paris suburbs, and moan about the *bétonisation*, or concreting-over, that stepped up a level once Martinique became a DOM (overseas department) in 1946.

Thankfully the concrete has not really encroached on the beauty that caught Columbus's eye. To the east, on the Atlantic coast, are steep coves and surf-lashed beaches. The north is green, mountainous and wild, home to the still-active volcano Mount Pelée, which last erupted in 1902, wiping out the town of St-Pierre, once known as the "Paris of the Lesser Antilles". Only one of St-Pierre's twenty-five thousand inhabitants survived, it is said: a drunk locked up in the town jail. An earlier, social, upheaval occurred in 1789 – a rebellion by sugar-plantation slaves. Resentment against the slavers ran deep and as late as 1991 a statue on Fort-de-France's grassy Savane, celebrating the birth on the island of Napoleon's Empress Joséphine (to a wealthy family of Creole planters) was decapitated. A leading abolitionist, Victor Shoelcher, provided one of the capital's other landmarks: the elaborate building containing his library was built by the Eiffel company and shipped over in 1890.

The sugar plantations have now disappeared, although one of the rattlesnakes that previously slithered through the sugar-cane fields appears on the island's flag, and some of the world's best rum comes from Martinique. A shot of Rhum Clément or La Mauny, with a backing track of *zouk* music, is the perfect end to a Martiniquais day.

ABOVE A Martiniquais woman wears a dress made from local French-language newspapers

OPPOSITE Mount Peleé

Martinique, Département d'outre-mer, France **Longitude:** 61° 00' W **Latitude:** 14° 40' N **Area:** 1,130 sq km (436 sq mi) **Highest point:** 1,397 m (4,583 ft) Mt Pelée **Population:** 401,000
Capital: Fort-de-France **Natives:** Joséphine de Beauharnais, Mario Canonge, Aimé Césaire, Patrick Chamoiseau, Frantz Fanon, Édouard Glissant, Joseph Zobel **Resident:** Paul Gauguin

"Martinique is France.
Arriving from Trinidad you feel you have crossed
not the Caribbean, but the English Channel."

V. S. Naipaul

Mustique

GRENADINES, CARIBBEAN

It was Princess Margaret who really brought the Grenadine island of Mustique into the global consciousness. When she married the photographer Antony Armstrong-Jones, Lord Snowdon, in 1960, the island's owner Colin, Lord Glenconner, gave her a ten-acre plot of land on Mustique as a wedding present. The villa she commissioned, Les Jolies Eaux, became her home away from home, especially when the marriage began to unravel (Snowdon did not like the island, and dubbed it "Mistake"). The photos of her attending or hosting parties, dressed in her Mustique ensemble of kaftan, headscarf, sunglasses and straw hat, became an iconic image, linking the island to glamour and celebrity.

In her wake came rock stars and fashion designers – among them David Bowie, Mick Jagger and Tommy Hilfiger – who acquired some of the ninety or so villas on the island, many of which were designed, like Les Jolies Eaux, by the British stage designer Oliver Messel (Snowdon's uncle) between 1960 and 1978. They have been joined by a new generation of owners: the seriously new money of hedge-fund managers and IT and telecommunications honchos. All the owners concur that Mustique should retain its special quality: cynics would say that this is simply elitism, but they also care about both the ecology and natural state of the island – even if they do not always agree on how best to achieve that.

Mustique is tiny, only 3 by 5 kilometres (1.8 by 3 miles). There are no real roads but tracks best negotiated by the tanked-up golf carts called mules or on foot, especially on rainy days. The destinations are the island's tennis courts, soccer matches (including the annual locals vs visitors), regular barbecues, weekly cocktail parties and beaches by turquoise waters – Macaroni Beach is one of the finest. Many families have come to winter here year in year out, and despite the high celebrity/wealth factor, there is nevertheless a strong feeling of community.

Of course, the pleasant lifestyle needs a workforce to make it all happen, and many of the staff – like the daily supplies of food and drink – have come from St Vincent, since there are no indigenous islanders. For those of us who don't have a million, let alone a billion, to spare, the Mustique experience can be sampled courtesy of a hotel and guest house: one is based in a converted eighteenth-century coral warehouse and sugar mill harking back to a time when European planters settled here. A must-do is an evening at Basil's Beach Bar, the Bondesque shore-side venue and Mustique institution, where the lobster salad dressing is a closely guarded secret.

> "Mustique isn't smart, though some pretty smart people live there. Nearly everyone who arrives is amazed that it's so simple."
>
> Patrick Lichfield

OPPOSITE Basil's Beach Bar

Mustique, St Vincent and the Grenadines **Longitude:** 61° 11' W **Latitude:** 12° 52' N **Area:** 6 sq km (2 sq mi) **Highest point:** 151 m (495 ft) **Population:** 500 **Principal settlement:** Lovell Village
Residents: Bryan Adams, Basil Charles, David Bowie, Felix Dennis, Tommy Hilfiger, Mick Jagger, Princess Margaret, Colin Tennant (Lord Glenconner)

Trinidad

CARIBBEAN

"When the steelband
play, on Carnival
Day, Hear the rhythm,
the lovely rhythm.
Make you feel to jump
up, So you start
to sway."

Aldwyn Roberts, aka Lord Kitchener, "Pan in Harmony"

Go down to St James in Port of Spain, the capital of Trinidad, on a Sunday evening. Stop outside Smokey & Bunty's, perhaps the island's most legendary bar, and negotiate your way across the road, squeezing between the low-slung cars pumping out rap, cruising the streets looking for action or just limin', and you find open-air stalls, temporarily erected in the darkened shop fronts, serving some of the most exquisite *roti* (flour pancakes filled with curry) outside the Indian subcontinent. Along with *callaloo*, a soup made from the leaves of the dasheen plant, and *mauby*, a drink like root beer, the *rotis* contribute to Trinidad's distinctive flavour.

Nearly forty per cent of Trinidadians consider themselves Indian – specifically East Indian – in origin, a further ten per cent or so are mixed Indian/African, known as *dougla*. They are descended from indentured Indians, who along with Lebanese, Syrian and Chinese workers arrived on the island when slavery was abolished in the early 1800s. They give this rather un-Caribbean island a very individual character. In fact, Trinidad often feels very different from the rest of the Caribbean – its westernmost finger is separated from a peninsula of the Venezuelan mainland by a narrow strait, the two fingers reaching towards each other, Sistine Chapel style. There is oil and gas to exploit, and swathes of industrialized areas. Trinidad is not an oasis of beach houses, hammocks and cocktails, although there are unspoilt beaches, and marvellous natural landscapes to explore, including Trinidad's own islands like Chacachacare and Gasperee ("down the islands"), mangrove and freshwater swamps, mud volcanoes, tar pits, and the rainforest and waterfalls of the Northern Range, all with a cavalcade of exotic flora and fauna.

Port of Spain, tucked underneath the northwestern tip of the island, is, as its name promises, a major harbour. Christopher Columbus, arriving in his fleet of three ships, saw, according to one version of events, a cluster of three hills that prompted him to call the island after the Spanish word for "Trinity". The British acquired the island in the late 1790s, and there is fine colonial architecture, particularly an Edwardian collection of residences, government and school buildings known as the Magnificent Seven. They stand alongside the Queen's Park Savannah, a huge expanse of grassland reached by walking up from the busy quaysides of the port through squares and narrow streets, rising up and away from the promenade named after Brian Lara, one of Trinidad's finest cricketers – some would argue *the* finest.

Each February the Savannah is also the location of the competitions that are part of the massive, boisterous Trinidad carnival, and temporary stands are raised to allow enthusiastic crowds to watch the parades and steelbands competing. Here also you can see performers of calypso, that mix of musical poetry and often astringent social commentary that is one of the island's great cultural inventions.

OPPOSITE Carnival time in Port of Spain's Queen's Park Savannah

ABOVE Nariva Swamp, a protected area on the island

Trinidad, Republic of Trinidad and Tobago **Longitude:** 61° 25' W **Latitude:** 10° 30' N **Area:** 4,828 sq km (1,864 sq mi) **Highest point:** 940 m (3,084 ft) El Cerro del Aripo **Population:** 981,600
Principal town: Port of Spain **Natives:** Stephen Ames, Ian Bishop, Ato Boldon, Sharlene Boodram, Hasely Crawford, Daren Ganga, Geoffrey Holder, Brian Lara, Hollis Liverpool aka Chalkdust, Trevor
McDonald, Shiva Naipaul, V. S. Naipaul, Billy Ocean, Sundar Popo, Aldwyn "Lord Kitchener" Roberts, Jason Scotland **Residents:** Robert Lechmere Guppy, Peter Minshall, Derek Walcott

"The surf in the moonlight, the whistlings of the more distant shores;
the strange music that is born and is muffled under
the folded wing of the night, like the linked circles that are
the waves of a conch, or the amplifications of the clamors under the sea."

Saint-Jean Perse, *Pictures for Crusoe*

Guadeloupe

CARIBBEAN

So rich and important did Guadeloupe's French owners consider this tiny possession in the Caribbean to be, they were willing to relinquish to Britain their claims to the vast terrain of Canada in order to keep it. Along with Martinique, the colony's plantations yielded a vital source of sugar and represented a rare French corner of a foreign field in a part of the world principally carved up between the Spanish, British and Dutch. The lines of riches this butterfly-shaped island has bequeathed to France has continued into the post-slavery, post-colonial era, with Guadeloupe siring an impressive lineage of literary and artistic achievement and a fine sporting pedigree, disproportionate for this small piece of the Earth.

Despite various tugs of war with the British and locals in a post-French Revolution era when there was little sense of *fraternité* and *liberté*, Guadeloupe is still technically French, a *département outre-Atlantique*. The taste buds are constantly assaulted by the smell of coffee and freshly baked croissants and baguettes.

In the towns the look and layout is distinctly Gallic and neoclassical: the central *place de ville* and *mairie*; the early capital of Le Moule with its old fort, cathedral and customs house. For French football fans this is just as well, since four members of their 1998 World Cup-winning squad – Messrs Henry, Thuram, Saha and Gallas – could have claimed Guadeloupe parentage and made up the backbone of a pretty mean team for the island. In 1960 the Guadeloupe poet Saint-John Perse, who wrote under the *nom de plume* Alexis Léger and frequented the literary circles of luminaries such as André Gide and Paul Valéry, was awarded the Nobel Prize for Literature. And the island moves to the rhythms of a wide variety of dances and musical forms, notably the quadrille, a forerunner of square-dancing, and the zouk, ballad-like zouk-love and kompa in which many local artists have obtained international recognition.

Guadeloupe's original inhabitants called their island Karukera – "the island of beautiful waters", and whales, seahorses, turtles and would-be Jacques Cousteaus enjoy in abundance the pristine waters of the nature reserves named after the famous French diver off the west coast of the island. The water inland is also spectacular, with the steep inclines of Grande Terre laced with waterfalls. Columbus, who first saw the island, referred to "the land where the water falls from the sky". He also gave the island its name, after the town of the same name in Extremadura, Spain.

Guadaloupe has all the typical Caribbean attributes of palms, beach chic, diving and secluded alcoves for tall, elegant sailing boats, especially on the offshore boutique idylls of the undulating Les Saintes, the former leper colony of La Desirade and Marie Galante. But with its Gallic *laissez-faire* and artistic heritage, the colourful dresses and scarves of its women, the Creole and French cuisine celebrated yearly in the Fête des Cuisinières, and in the limey tang of its powerful rum-based punches, the island butterfly has bright, very rare and distinct markings that a lepidopterist would treasure.

OVERLEAF Local cooks gather for mass during the Fête des Cuisinières

Guadeloupe, Département d'outre-mer, France **Longitude:** 61° 35' W **Latitude:** 16° 20' N **Area:** 1,373 sq km (530 sq mi) **Highest point:** 1,484 m (4,869 ft) Soufrière **Population:** 420,000
Principal town: Basse-Terre **Natives:** Joseph de Bologne, Maryse Condé, Patricia Girard-Léno, Alexis Léger aka Saint-John Perse, Serge Nubret, Marie-José Perec, Mikaël Piétrus, Lilian Thuram

Grenada

CARIBBEAN

It is often said that variety is the spice of life. Grenada is the isle of that variety of spices, infinitely diverse and aromatic, the enrichment of worldwide cuisine and the livelihood of its inhabitants. Grenada's volcanic soil is some of the most fertile on Earth, and the original source of flavourings that are the holy grail of gourmets and television chefs: nutmeg (Grenada is the largest exporter of the spice after Indonesia), cinnamon, allspice, ginger, cloves, mace and many more. Grenada and her string of fruity consorts, the Grenadines, is the Zanzibar of the Caribbean.

This fertility is matched by the resourcefulness of Grenada's inhabitants, who have had to rebuild their island from nothing twice in the last fifty years. After nearly half a century's grace the island bore the brunt of two major onslaughts from the alphabet roulette of hurricanes. First in 2004 Hurricane Ivan, a category-four storm, literally flattened ninety per cent of the spice plantations and the human habitation on the island, sending a debris of trees, telegraph poles, hotels, boats, cars and even grand pianos into the Caribbean Sea. Just as the Grenadans were picking themselves up, along came Emily in 2005. With man and nature consorting in a hard-work ethic, the locals have rebuilt much of the island and the spice economy incredibly quickly, with the destroyed nutmeg forests and banana plantations already on the point of maturity and ready to bear fruit.

It is no surprise that such fertility should have been greatly coveted by the colonial powers. As with much of the region, it was Columbus who christened the island, originally Concepcion and then Granada. The French took over in 1650, changing it to "La Grenade" and exterminating the indigenous Kalinago people, the last twenty of them jumping off the cliff at Sauteurs rather than face government by the French. They founded the capital at Fort Royal, which changed to St George as the English, in ascendancy on the seas, wrested the island from the French at the 1762 Treaty of Paris, which carved up the Caribbean between the warring powers of Britain, France and Spain.

The twentieth century brought independence to the point of being a Commonwealth realm, but not without civil war, military dictatorship and, in 1983, invasion by the US army, worried about the Grenadan government's collusion with the serial threat of Cuba.

It is the remaining French influence on Grenada that gives the island its spicy charm. Whether that be in the cuisine – similar to that found in New Orleans and typified by "oildown", a dish of meat and vegetables cooked in reduced coconut milk – the names of beaches such as Grand Anse that list-makers are apt to place in the world's top ten, or the tradition of storytelling and in particular of the *ligaroo* or *loup-garou* (werewolf). Post Ivan and Emily, the locals have a few first-hand spirit stories to tell of their own.

LEFT Workers sorting nutmeg nuts

OPPOSITE St George's Bay

Grenada **Longitude:** 61° 40' W **Latitude:** 12° 10' N **Area:** 310 sq km (120 sq mi) **Highest point:** 840 m (2,757 ft) Mt St Catherine **Population:** 92,800 **Capital:** St George's
Natives: Tubal "Buzz" Butler, Slinger Francisco aka Mighty Sparrow **Resident:** Peter de Savary

"I love visiting the island.
Maybe someday I'll visit some of
the other beautiful islands
of the Caribbean, but for now
Grenada is the place."

Lewis Hamilton, racing driver

"It is no secret that the twin islands
enjoy an international reputation as
one of the most exotic and romantic pieces
of real estate on the planet."

Sir Viv Richards

Antigua

CARIBBEAN

While Lord Horatio Nelson was stationed here for three years from 1784, charged with patrolling the Caribbean to protect British interests from the independent-minded colony of the United States, he made no secret of his desire to get away. But it was not an aversion to turquoise waters, palm trees and coconut-milk cocktails. These were the days before tourists and Nelson was simply not the sun-lounging, go-slow type. Besides, he would far rather have been back in the Mediterranean fighting the French.

Nelson's former dockyard is one of the epicentres of life in St John's, the capital of Antigua. Abandoned in 1899 it was refurbished in 1950s and now presents an elegant waterfront ensemble of inns, boutiques, markets and a museum to the island's nautical history. The other hub of Antiguan life is the cricket ground, named after the island's most famous native, the master-blaster batsman Sir Viv Richards, captain of the all-conquering 1980s West Indies cricket team, whose glare and attitude was equally "up an' at 'em" but whose relaxed gum-chewing swagger – a signature of the island – was the very opposite of the Nelsonian stiff upper lip.

Antiguans like to boast that their island has 365 beaches, one for each day of the year. These are found all round the island in secluded coves formed by arms of the sea at the foot of Antigua's high, rocky coastline. Unlike many of its lush Caribbean cousins, Antigua is flat, with no rivers or natural springs, and almost treeless. Its wildlife is consequently more scarce: offshore Bird Island is home to the rarest snake in the world, the Antiguan Racer.

Efficient desalination provides the island with the water that nourished the sugar plantations on which Antigua's initial riches were founded. Discovered by Columbus and named after a church in Seville, Antigua (and neighbouring Barbuda, which together comprise this Commonwealth nation) in the seventeenth century became a British possession and centre for the sugar trade. The fine plantation buildings and stone mills at Betty's Hope – named after the governor's daughter – as well as the poignantly named settlements of Freetown and Liberta, are reminders of this profitable but slave-driven era.

Apart from for the usual attributes of laid-back Caribbean life, people come to Antigua for its water-based activities. The wind is a feature of the island and the towns of English Harbour and Falmouth a favourite for world-class yachtsmen, especially during the internationally renowned Antigua Sailing Week. Every so often the wind gets up a little too strong, however. In 1996 Hurricane Louis chose Antigua as the place to vent its wrath, ripping off the roofs of the hotels and shanty towns of St Johns – now, happily, restored – as fearsomely as a Curtly Ambrose bouncer through an English batsman.

LEFT English Harbour

Antigua, Antigua and Barbuda **Alternative name:** Wadadli **Longitude:** 61° 50' W **Latitude:** 17° 00' N **Area:** 281 sq km (108 sq mi) **Highest point:** 402 m (1,319 ft) Boggy Peak **Population:** 69,000 **Principal town:** St John's **Natives:** Curtly Ambrose, Ridley Jacobs, Jamaica Kincaid, Viv Richards, Richie Richardson, Andy Roberts **Residents:** Giorgio Armani, Calvin Ayre, Alphonsus "Arrow" Cassell, Eric Clapton, Ken Follett, Robin Leach, Horatio Nelson

Montserrat

CARIBBEAN

Montserrat is a Caribbean island version of Pompeii. For centuries a lush, fruit-laden idyll where in more recent times the world's rock glitterati came to record their albums, the fates were not kind to this tiny member of the Leeward Isles. In 1989 the island was nearly flattened by Hurricane Hugo, then in 1995 the volcano that dominates the island's relief and landscape, and which had lain dormant for some four hundred years, gave an opening salvo before venting her full wrath and destroying half the island in 1997.

The airport, ferry port and many villages virtually disappeared and the pretty Victorian capital of Plymouth was all but buried under 15 metres (50 feet) of lava. The area is black and still redolent of the suffocating smell of sulphur. Guided tours can be taken to view the top of the steeple of a church and, ironically, the buried graveyard. There is a branch of Barclays bank with just a sign visible saying "Accounts", as if this Act of God had settled some form of debt. There are submerged tennis courts, and shops with groceries on their shelves exactly where they were. It is like Pompeii but without the bodies, since most of the population were able to flee in time.

Consequently, Montserrat is an island of two halves and two colours – green and black. Plymouth lies in the southern Exclusion Zone while in the northern half life has been slowly returning to normal. A new port has been built, a new capital is under construction and a new air link is being planned. The north is a verdant landscape of palms, rubber and vanilla plants, and mango and breadfruit trees sing with the calls of the national oriole bird and the so-called "mountain chicken", which is actually a local frog (and a local delicacy).

The original Montserrat population was of Irish descent and the island is sometimes referred to as the "Emerald Isle of the Caribbean". Back in 1632 Catholics found here a refuge from neighbouring islands such as St Kitts, where their faith was not respected. They were scattered when the volcano blew and have since been replaced largely by immigrants from Guiana, Trinidad and Dominica. It's been a while since Paul McCartney and the Stones came through to record at Sir George Martin's famous Air studios on the island. But on the sole sand strip of Rendez-Vous Beach, the new locals still celebrate St Patrick's day – albeit with a cool can of Carib lager rather than stout. The shamrock is the stamp visitors receive in their passport and the Harp of Erin flies in the Montserrat flag.

Montserrat is a Caribbean paradise with a difference: an unusual, duotone island of mixed moods. Quite like Madame Soufrière, as the locals call the volcano that is at once their patron and their destroyer, it sits there, still smoking, like some capricious diva liable to fly off the handle at any moment.

"When God gives you lemons, you make lemonade.
He gave us a volcano, so we're selling volcano tourism."

Ernestine Cassell, Montserrat Director of Tourism

OPPOSITE Dust cover from the erupting Soufrière volcano

ABOVE Rural homes near Montserrat mountain

Montserrat, British Overseas Territory **Longitude:** 62° 10' W **Latitude:** 16° 40' N **Area:** 102 sq km (39 sq mi) **Highest point:** 915 m (3,002 ft) Chance's Peak **Population:** 4,500
Principal town: Plymouth **Natives:** Alphonsus "Arrow" Cassell, Kulcha Don, E. A. Markham **Resident:** George Martin

St Kitts and Nevis, Federation of St Kitts and Nevis **Longitude:** 62° 40' W **Latitude:** 17° 20' N **Area:** 261 sq km (101 sq mi) **Highest point:** 1,156 m (3,793 ft) Mt Liamuiga, St Kitts
Population: 42,700 **Capital:** Basseterre, St Kitts **Natives:** Joan Armatrading, George Astaphan, Henri Christophe, Kim Collins, Alexander Hamilton, Desai Williams

St Kitts and Nevis

CARIBBEAN

S t Kitts was named after the old-fashioned nickname for Columbus's namesake and patron saint, Christopher. It is the medieval equivalent of calling the island you've just discovered and mapped St Chuck or St Bob. But it is an informality that more than suits the breezy, down-to-earth and relaxed air of life on the island. Across the water and sounding like some naughty brother lies Nevis – named not, as some accounts relate, after a ring of cloud (or *nicbla* in Spanish) that surrounded its cone-shaped volcanic peak but after Nuestra Señora de la Nieves, Our Lady of the Snows, the liturgical feast for the dedication of the eponymous basilica on the Esquiline Hill in the Rome of Columbus's native Italy.

Together comprising the smallest nation in the Americas, St Kitts and Nevis have been conjoined in one way or another, either as a nation or as pawns locked in the battle between two colonizing nations, since Britain and France arrived here in the early seventeenth century. The British turned St Kitts into the capital of their sugar empire in the West Indies, wiping out the indigenous Kalinago people (some say in pre-emption of suffering the same fate at their hands) and importing sugar-cane plantations and slaves to work them. Vestiges of that inhumane era constitute the two islands' finest architectural heritage, in particular in Brimstone Hill Fortress, the crumbling Fort Charles on St Kitts and the Georgian buildings of Nevis's principle town, Charleston. In its heyday under British rule the two islands were among the

richest in the Caribbean. This attracted frequent visitations from pirates, attacks from the covetous French (which a young Horatio Nelson stationed here managed to repel) – and is partly to be thanked both for the high local literacy rate and the prosperous trade in offshore financial services that has taken the place of the sugar cane, which nobody bothers to harvest any more other than to convert into biofuel.

The mountainous and tropical rainforested interior of both islands is too steep for habitation, so life revolves around their edges – and that means on the beaches, be they the gently sloping sands of South Friar's Bay on Kitts or the 6.4-kilometre (4-mile) golden crescent of Pinney's beach on Nevis. Wherever you are there is always music, which runs as thick in the blood here as the local cocktail of Cane Spirit Rothschild with a "sting" of the local Ting lemonade. It is music in great variety and usually high volume. The islands dance to a calypso beat but salsa, soca, steelpan and many forms of jazz are also consumed and performed live all over the islands and especially at all-comer open-mic sessions. Though less well known than Port of Spain's, carnival on St Kitts is a highlight in the Caribbean calendar, the streets of Basse Terre vibrating with the glucose energy of dances of the flesh and doomsday, and the sight of masks and towering *moko jumbies*, "ghosts of god" on stilts. And in the summer, two Dixieland street bands, competing to be king of the islands, spar each other with their own local music festivals.

> "His Royal Highness has told me that if I am not married this time we got to Nevis it is hardly probable he should see me there again."
>
> Horatio Nelson in a letter to his betrothed, Fanny Nesbit

OPPOSITE The Rawlins Masquerade Dance Troupe, performing at the annual festival, which celebrates the emancipation of slaves in the 1830s

St Barts

CARIBBEAN

It does seem rather odd to come across a sliver of Sweden in the middle of the Caribbean. On Saint-Barthélemy, familiarly known to both the truly chic and the would-be chic as St Barts or St Barth (the choice seems quite random), there is a bracing dash of Nordic *froideur* amid the prevailing French panache. It is a remnant of one of those multiple twists and turns that have punctuated the game of Caribbean diplomacy. In 1784 King Louis XVI handed this Leeward island to his royal chum King Gustav III of Sweden, in exchange for some trading rights in the port of Gothenburg. For nearly a century the Swedes had the run of the place.

Their influence remains most evident in the capital of Gustavia, where Swedish and French street names rub shoulders on the signposts. Despite a devastating fire in 1852, examples of Swedish architecture can still be found, not least in its three forts and the houses ranged along the harbour side.

As with so many of the Caribbean islands, it was Columbus who not only had the honour of being the first European to set eyes on the place (in 1496), but who also took responsibility for naming it: this time after his sibling Bartolomeo, a cartographer. French settlers, fisherfolk from Brittany and Normandy, first established a foothold on the island after buccaneers had dispersed the Carib natives. Many of the current islanders can claim a direct ancestry with those seventeenth-century forefathers. Because St Barts is low on water, and its soil is agriculturally impoverished, slavery figured minimally in the island's history, and consequently there is a very noticeable preponderance of white faces, blond hair and blue eyes. Some residents even speak a local dialect related to old Norman, and on festive occasions in coastal villages like Corossol elderly women sport traditional, starched white *quichenotte* bonnets.

Nowadays the fashion choice of preference is designer label. In the 1970s the small, volcanic, hilly island – only twenty-something square kilometres – was discovered as a wintertime tourist destination. Ever since celebrities, mainly of the A to A-plus variety rather than from the lower echelons of the breed, have holed up here, attracted not so much by the interior (which pales in comparison to, say, St Lucia), but by twenty to thirty fabulous white beaches. They can choose between popular St-Jean, secluded Colombier, topless Grande Saline or the surf at Le Toiny. The cuisine on the island is gourmet French, with a splash of Caribbean – although there has been a belated resurgence of the Swedish connection, especially amongst Americans of Swedish descent...

"What I didn't know about St Barts
was the Swedish connection.
Sitting in the Select Bar one lunchtime,
I looked up and saw a photo of the King of Sweden.
Then I noticed some Swedish posters and flags.
Outside, it was France, by the sounds and sights.
What was going on?"

Hunter Davies, writer

OPPOSITE French and Swedish street signs in Gustavia

ABOVE Gustavia Harbour Fort overlooking the city

St Barts, Collectivity of Saint Barthélemy, France **Alternative names:** Saint Barthélemy, Saint Barth, Saint Barths **Longitude:** 62° 50' W **Latitude:** 17° 50' N **Area:** 21 sq km (8 sq mi)
Highest point: 286 m (938 ft) Mt du Vitet **Population:** 8,450 **Principal town:** Gustavia

> "And the governments rule in French and Dutch, but that doesn't mean much… Whatever they say or do, one S'Maatin people forever we will be."
>
> Ruby Bute, "One S'Maatin People"

Sint Maarten/St-Martin

CARIBBEAN

ABOVE Hotels lining the coastline

The most frequently repeated, but nonetheless worthwhile, fact about the island of Sint Maarten/St-Martin is that it is the smallest land mass split between two nations: the Netherlands and France respectively. As an island it is not unique in this Hispaniola further west in the Caribbean is divided between the Dominican republic and Haiti – but what is special is the level of friendly cooperation that has always surrounded the partition of Sint Maarten/St-Martin. There was none of the bitterness inherent in the dissections of Cyprus, for example, or Ireland.

It was all very civilized and perfectly amicable, as is proven by the very name of the Treaty of Concordia of March 1648, which marked the decision a century and a half after Christopher Columbus had identified the island and named it after St Martin, just like Martinique. There is a colourful tale about how the French and the Dutch actually settled on the border, involving a representative from each side perambulating around the island simultaneously in a race to claim their sector. The Frenchman, fuelled by *un bon vin rouge*, lasted the course, it is said, but the Dutchman rather overdid his gin consumption… The border – not marked by any fences or border crossings – does indeed meander rather drunkenly through the dry land like wonky stitching on a baseball. And whatever the truth of the story, the Netherlands certainly ended up with much less than half the island (although they make up more of the population). It was, however, the part they most wanted: the southern section with its salt flats.

To this day, the two cultures have existed alongside each other quite merrily. For the Dutch, Sint Maarten is the largest of the three islands that make up this northerly cluster of the Dutch Antilles, along with small, secluded Saba and unhurried Sint Eustatius; there is also the more southerly trio of the ABC islands Aruba, Bonaire and Curaçao. The Dutch sector's capital Philipsburg, pinioned on a strip of land between the Great Bay and the Great Salt Pond, has most of the nightlife, while the French side – a sub-prefecture of Guadeloupe, with Marigot as the main town – is seen, almost inevitably, as slightly more chic. The predominant mood of the island is sun, sea, surfing and yachting, and there has been a hefty amount of hotel and villa development around the coastline on both sides (planes landing at Princess Juliana Airport scoot right over the heads of of beachgoers on the neighbouring Maho Beach). Just inside the French part stands the highest point on the island, Pic Paradis, while straddling the border is Mount Concordia, the site of the historic treaty signing. One oddity: neither French nor Dutch is the main language on the island, but English.

St Maarten, Eilandgebied Sint Maarten, Netherlands/St Martin, Collectivité de St-Martin France **Longitude:** 63° 00' W **Latitude:** 18° 00' N **Area:** 87 sq km (34 sq mi)
Highest point: 414 m (1,358 ft) Pic Paradis **Population:** 71,000 **Principal towns:** Philipsburg, Marigot **Resident:** Ruby Bute

Prince Edward Island

GULF OF ST LAWRENCE

"A summer twilight
    when the dew is
falling and the old, old
    stars are peeping
out and the sea keeps
    its nightly tryst with
the little land it
    loves. You find your
soul then."

Lucy Maud Montgomery

Welcome to *Anne of Green Gables* country. In 1908, Lucy Maud Montgomery – a native of Prince Edward Island, which lies in the gulf of St Lawrence north of Nova Scotia and next to New Brunswick – published the book that introduced the world to Anne Shirley. This is the tale of an eleven-year-old, red-haired, feisty orphan girl who comes to live with a couple on the island and discovers, with good humour, the trials and tribulations of adolescent self-identity. It was Montgomery's first book, an immediate publishing success, and created one of the best-loved characters not just in Canadian fiction but across the globe. Seven further titles about Anne followed.

Mark Twain wrote to Montgomery to say that Anne was "the dearest and most loveable child in fiction since the immortal Alice". Various television and movie interpretations later – including an *anime* version from Japan,

where Anne is particularly popular – there is a thriving tourist trail on Prince Edward Island, or PEI as it is familiarly called. The white-painted, and, yes, green-gabled farmhouse at Cavendish that was one of the principal inspirations for the books, is an obvious and charming destination. Scattered around are woods and hollows featured in the books that fans of the high-spirited heroine can visit, including Idlewild, Anne's "romantic spot", from which the Scottish indie band took their name.

If, heaven forbid, Anne's upbeat adventures have not captivated visitors to Prince Edward Island, they can simply enjoy a relaxed pastoral way of life on the beaches or among the red-clay roads and rolling hills of this "Gentle Island". The Mi'kmaq natives had a suitably soothing name for PEI: Abegweit, or "the island cradled in the waves". The Prince Edward now honoured was Queen Victoria's papa, Edward Augustus, Duke of Kent: the British had taken over the island from French Acadia in the 1760s.

The 12-kilometre (7-mile) bridge that links the island, Canada's smallest province, to the mainland is called Confederation Bridge. This is a reference to the 1864 conference held in the elegant, colonial-style capital Charlottetown, which initiated the process that created the confederation of Canada. On the journey across there is plenty of time for new arrivals – visitors "from away" as they are called locally – to feel their blood pressure subside. And to let their gastric juices prepare for the seafood delights that lie ahead: great lobster and mussels, but above all oysters. Clean, cold and perfectly salted waters, rich in plankton, mean that PEI is one of the world's great oyster-growing regions. The fruits of the sea – bearing names like Malpeque, Raspberry Point, Colville Bay – are tasted and appreciated with all the religious reverence accorded to great clarets and cognacs.

ABOVE The French River lighthouse

Prince Edward Island, Canada **Alternative names:** Île-du-Prince-Édouard, Eileann a'Phrionnsa **Longitude:** 63º 20' W **Latitude:** 46º 20' N **Area:** 5,660 sq km (2,185 sq mi)
Highest point: 152 m (499 ft) Springton **Population:** 139,100 **Principal town:** Charlottetown **Natives:** Albert Arsenault, Angèle Arsenault, Timothy Chaisson, Lennie Gallant,
Tara MacLean, Lucy Maud Montgomery, Nancy White **Residents:** Stompin' Tom Connors, Don Messer

Bermuda

NORTH ATLANTIC

Bermuda's Latino name, its sunshine, palms and beaches, and a vague sense of where it must be – to say nothing of the cut of its shorts – give it all the associations of a Caribbean island. It is striking, therefore, to find it so far east of the American seaboard, as far into the Atlantic Ocean as St Helena is from the other direction.

Comprising 138 islands, Bermuda lies at the western fringe of the fabled Sargasso Sea, full of the sargassum seaweed in which newborn sea turtles are thought to hide from predators. Mariners consider these to be strange waters, where it is often possible to experience a total lack of wind. This has long given Bermuda an aura of mystery – even Columbus spoke of seeing "strange and dancing lights in the horizon" – and ultimately led to several shipping and aviation accidents and disappearances (in some of the busiest shipping lanes in the world) being attributed to paranormal forces. A famous geometry was established between Florida, Puerto Rico and Bermuda into which ships and aircraft were liable to disappear without trace. But this has long been attributed to H. G. Wells-inspired fantasy on the part of Hollywood.

One very real wreck Bermuda can be thankful for is that of the *Sea Venture* (allegedly the inspiration for Shakespeare's *The Tempest*), captained by George Somers, who promptly claimed the islands for Britain. He used the native cedar trees to build another ship, the *Deliverance*, a replica of which stands proudly in the northern town of St George. He also founded an industry and a colony, and today the oldest continually occupied British territory in the New World, often referred to as the Gibraltar of the West.

As the closest British possession to America, tensions ran high over Bermuda following US independence, and the island played a key role in the American Civil War when anti-slavery Yankees blockaded cotton shipments to Lancashire – obstacles that were overcome by Confederate runners. The island was the location for Winston Churchill's Conference in 1953, directed at easing tensions between the United States and Russia at the start of the Cold War.

Bermuda has a proud British and Victorian history, visible in the World Heritage sites of Fort Scaur, St Peter's church and the large mansions that are now shops and museums in St George. Despite the creeping reggae influence and the sunny primary colours of this tropical island, however, it is a highly sophisticated place where people come to work, not holiday on the South Shore beaches or at Jobson's Cove. The capital, Hamilton, is a multi-billion dollar financial centre, and more than half the companies that quoted on the Hong Kong stock exchange are incorporated here. Bermudans regularly top the league of per-capita gross domestic product.

Chief among the service industries in which Bermuda specializes is insurance – ironic considering the number of vessels the island's strange siren pull is supposed to have consumed. Since 1846 there has been a perfectly good lighthouse made entirely of cast iron to steer people away. Nowadays, in the obligatory teashop, the nearest thing to a Bermuda Triangle is the "house special" sandwich made of local salmon, tuna and shrimp.

> "'There are black people with names like Bascomb who speak Savile Row British, and there are white folks who sound like they come out of a ghetto in Jamaica.'"
>
> Peter Benchley, *The Deep*

OPPOSITE The replica of the *Deliverance* in St George

OVERLEAF Boats moored in Riddles Bay

Bermuda, British Overseas Territory **Alternative names:** The Bermuda Islands, The Somers Isles **Longitude:** 64° 45' W **Latitude:** 32° 18' N **Area:** 53 sq km (21 sq mi) **Highest point:** 76 m (249 ft) Town Hill **Population:** 66,200 **Capital:** Hamilton **Natives:** Clyde Best, Diana Dill, Shaun Goater, David Hemp, Dwayne Leverock, Heather Nova, Mary Prince, Gina Swainson **Residents:** Silvio Berlusconi, Michael Bloomberg, Collie Buddz, Michael Douglas, Glyn Gilbert, F. Van Wyck Mason, Ross Perot, Robert Stigwood, Mark Twain

Puerto Rico

GREATER ANTILLES, CARIBBEAN

"A kind of lost love-child, born to the Spanish Empire, and fostered by the United States."

Nicholas Wollaston, writer

ABOVE The final of the "Salsa Open" competition at Hotel San Juan
OPPOSITE El Yunque rainforest

While next-door Cuba continues to resist all US influence, Puerto Rico is where conquistador old colonial Hispanic architecture meets the American mall, fast-food joint and brown-bag grocery store. There are more Puerto Ricans in New York City than in Puerto Rico itself (or PR as it is sometimes known) – they are the self-styled Nuyoricans who hanker after the mother country but just can't bring themselves to go back – and more than a hefty dose of NYC in Puerto Rico. It is symbolic of the on-off, symbiotic relationship the island has historically had with the United States, still the case many decades after *West Side Story*, that leads to its continued, rather indefinite political status as something between a state and a semi-autonomous country.

Wandered in from the city of St John without a dime, Puerto Ricans are sometimes described as the workforce of America, doing the blue-collar jobs that make the great metropolises go round. This fact dates back to the 1950s' Operation Bootstrap, when America made huge investments into the country's industrial infrastructure, especially petrochemical and pharmaceuticals, the legacy of which is the bizarre meeting of sleepy, rural Hispanic and modern American that defines the island. Until that moment there had been a lull of activity and purpose dating back to when Columbus nicknamed the island La Llave de la Américas ("the key to the Americas") and his successors subsequently commissioned the impressive sixteenth-century wall and fortifications of El Morro in the capital port of San Juan to ward off the intrusions of the British and Dutch.

The Spanish influence is at its prettiest in the old quarter of San Juan and also the southern central town of Ponce, laid out in sloping cobblestone grids of single-floor, high-ceilinged Andalucían houses with flower-enlaced balconies and dark, heavy imperial doors.

This is the birthplace of the salsa – the original hot sauce to spice up any party – and the sexy percussive rhythm, complete with *jibaro* (hillbilly) cowbells, along with a mishmash of other Afro-Hispanic-American hybrid musical styles such as the *bomba y plena*, to which the happy people of this island, all flowery shirts, haircream and Cuban heels, tick. The legacy of Tito Puente reverberates throughout the island, either in modern exponents of the traditional form such as Willie Colón or in the "living la vida loca" pastiches of that famous *boricua* (Puerto Rican), Ricky Martin.

Sport as well as music is a religion on Puerto Rico. The island has sired more boxing champions than any place outside the US, a string of Hall of Fames heroes of the baseball World Series, and a battery of champion chickens, heroes of the cock-fighting that is both legal here and avidly followed.

But Puerto Rico is not just a port of strategic naval or human riches. Its nature is a mountainous goldmine of rainforest (rich in endemic flora and fauna such as the island's mascot, the coqui chirping frog), desert, beaches and caves with subterranean rivers and spectacular bats, as well as stalagmites and stalactites made from the karst rock. Offshore lie the little-explored gemstones of Vieques, Culebra and Mona islands, the last a mini Caribbean Galapagos. It seems unthinkable that the characters from *West Side Story* could ever have doubted their homeland. Contrary to Sondheim's lyrics they should in fact have boasted "We are the kids from *boricua*!"

Puerto Rico, Commonwealth of Puerto Rico, Semi-Autonomous Territory of the United States **Longitude:** 66° 30' W **Latitude:** 18° 15' N **Area:** 8,870 sq km (3,424 sq mi) **Highest point:** 1,338 m (4,390 ft) Cerro de Punta **Population:** 3,990,000 **Capital:** San Juan **Natives:** Ramón Emeterio Betances, Julia de Burgos, Juan Morel Campos, Orlando Cepeda, Roberto Clemente, José Feliciano, Gigi Fernández, José Ferrer, Wilfredo Gómez, Giovanni Hidalgo, Raúl Juliá, Rafael Hernández Marín, Luis Muñoz Marín, Ricky Martin, Rita Moreno, Luis Muñoz Rivera, Willie Rosario, Félix Trinidad

"It was a lightning blow, those white sand tongues against the crystalline sea, the pelicans, the inhabitants… from that began my Venezuelan adventure."

Vincenzo Conticello, founder of first foreign *posada* on Los Roques

Los Roques

CARIBBEAN

Venezuela is a nation obsessed with beauty pageants. Venezuelans are the largest per-capita consumers of cosmetics and avid fans of the annual search for Miss Universe, a competition for which they have supplied more than their fair share of winners. If there was to be a beauty pageant among islands, this little-known archipelago of fifty islands, cays and islets off the north coast of Venezuela would challenge any of the traditional pearls of the world's seas and oceans.

Their name, "the rocks", is testament to the simplicity of that beauty. The islands are remarkably untouched by human trappings or any artificial embellishment. There is a law against further development of the islands, now a nature reserve, and this has left a delightful dusty and deserted feel. There is just one village, Gran Roque, with a few stuccoed inns in faded pastel colours and a church whose entrance stands right on the waterfront and whose stone floor is covered in sandy footprints. Time elsewhere in Venezuela is a topical issue, with President Chavéz moving the clocks forward half an hour to make Venezuelans feel more energized by the morning light. But life on Los Roques will not be rushed. There are few restaurants, no discos and certainly no vehicles. If Caracas, 130 kilometres (80 miles) to the south and the rest of the country is in its own time zone, the Los Roques archipelago, spread across its own private sea and reached by ancient DC3, lives in the Caribbean of forty years ago, at the dawn of tourism to the area.

Of course, like any decent rocks, these islands have exerted a siren call on some. Before Columbus, fishermen came here to catch the queen conch. But unlike so many islands, Venezuela's ownership, decreed in 1589 and confirmed by the statue of Simón Bolivar in the centre of Gran Roque, has been undisputed. Nor have these flat islands of cacti, sea grape trees, thorny scrub and mangrove forests been mined for anything other than the salt from their inland marshes, which is much to the benefit and delight of the unblemished coral reef, the resident populations of pelicans and boobies, large iguanas and frigate birds.

That the call of Los Roques has extended beyond in-the-know Venezuelans is down to a few Italians who have made the islands their home since the 1960s and set up what little infrastructure is geared towards tourists. They own most of the pretty *posadas* and these, together with the risottos and espresso bar, make this corner of the Caribbean a refreshing Little Italy.

Life on Los Roques demands that the visitor leave behind material possessions and thoughts such that they may feel they have happened upon a secluded commune from the pages of Alex Garland's novel, *The Beach*. The benefit is the opportunity to cast away and be the only soul on your own private key, with no one else around other than a soothing anchor of pared-down Italianate civilization. On Los Roques, being a desert-island castaway is a case of bohemian cappuccino-style self-sufficiency.

Los Roques, Federal Dependency of Venezuela **Longitude:** 66° 45' W **Latitude:** 11° 51' N **Archipelago area:** 2,212 sq km (854 sq mi) **Highest point:** 130 m (427 ft) El Faro **Population:** 1,200
Principal settlement: Gran Roque

Bonaire

NETHERLANDS ANTILLES, CARIBBEAN

When the conquistadors toured the Caribbean in the sixteenth and seventeenth centuries picking up colonies, they referred to Bonaire, with some trepidation, as "la isla de los gigantes" ("the island of giants"). To the diminutive Spaniards the aboriginal Caiquetos, an Arawak people, seemed startlingly and disconcertingly tall for potential subjects. It was fitting, therefore, that despite being claimed for Spain by the Italian Amerigo Vespucci (who gave his Christian name to the Americas), in 1633 Bonaire fell into the hands of those equally tall folk from northern Europe, the Dutch.

Curiously they retained the positively un-Dutch-sounding name (pronounced correctly as per the Spanish "bon-eye-re") and its even less Dutch-sounding neighbour Klein Bonaire, and the island is still part of the Kingdom of the Netherlands. Although Spanish, English and the indigenous Papiamentu are widely spoken, Dutch is the official language. Visitors are greeted everywhere with the words "Bon Bini!" meaning "Welcome!" and signs in a strange Teutonic-Hispano-African patois such as "Aki ta Bende Kuminda Krioyo" ("Creole food sold here").

The Caiqueto heritage is still proudly visible in rock paintings and petroglyphs all over the island and especially in Spelonk, in Onima and in Lac Bay for those who fancy a culture break from the windsurfing for which this crescent beach is known. But the real attraction of Bonaire is its unparalleled diving, as boasted on the majority of licence plates on the island, which read "Divers' Paradise!" Much of the boomerang-shaped island's coast is a marine sanctuary where the major draw are the seahorses. On land, the fauna comes in the form of bright-green iguanas and pink flamingos, which tiptoe delicately through the brackish waters of the island's inland and coastal plains.

These plains are home to Bonaire's historic asset – salt – on which were built its first riches, but not without leaving a stain on its past. Industrial-sized piles of white salt are a defining feature of Bonaire's coastal landscape. But the Dutch also set up plantations on the island, where the aboriginal and imported slaves were forced to work and then retire at night to stone quarters no taller than waist-high. Rows of these bare cairns still stand like gravestones as memorials outside the town of Rincon.

Bonaire is making the most of its natural gifts, indigenous culture and past – even the German internment camps from a brief spell under German occupation in the Second World War are now hotels (for Germans). A lesser-known destination, outside the hurricane zone a short hop from Venezuela, it makes a gentle escape, as easy – as they call this alphabetic trio of islands including Aruba and Curaçao – as A, B, C.

Bonaire, Netherlands Antilles **Longitude:** 68° 15′ W **Latitude:** 12° 10′ N **Area:** 288 sq km (111 sq mi) **Highest point:** 239 m (784 ft) Brandaris **Population:** 14,000 **Principal town:** Kralendijk **Native:** Angel Salsbach **Resident:** Don Stewart

"Bonaire is to conservation what Greenwich is to time."
Captain Don Stewart, environmentalist

Mount Desert

ATLANTIC COAST, MAINE

The French explorer Samuel de Champlain was responsible for mapping much of the northeastern coast of North America. On one visit Champlain worked his way down from Nova Scotia towards Martha's Vineyard and Rhode Island. In September 1604 he landed, or ran aground, on what is now known as Mount Desert Island, the largest island off the coast of Maine, and the second largest on the Eastern Seaboard (after Long Island). This was sixteen years before the Pilgrim Fathers on board the *Mayflower* made their landing at Plymouth, and New France, rather than New England was the discovery of the day. Although Monts Déserts became Mount Desert, the emphasis still falls with Gallic flair on the final syllable of Desert.

The barren, rocky nature of the island, which had led Champlain to name it Monts Déserts in the first place, meant that initially few were drawn to settle here and the island existed for the next century and a half in a kind of no-man's land between the French territories to the north and the burgeoning English presence to the south. There was a brief flurry of activity when Antoine Laumet, the self-styled Sieur de la Mothe Cadillac, based himself on the island in the 1680s, but he quickly moved on to achieve lasting fame as the founder of Detroit.

What pushed Mount Desert forward was the arrival of a group of painters in the mid-nineteenth century, who discovered what was to them a rugged rustic idyll populated by farmers, lumberjacks, quarrymen and fishermen who had gravitated to the island. Thomas Cole, founder of the Hudson River School of painters, and his protégé Frederic Church were entranced by the rugged wilderness, and through their landscapes Mount Desert was introduced to a clan of wealthy vacationers. By the turn of the century it was a massively popular retreat for the Vanderbilts, Carnegies, Astors and their coterie, who spent time on elegant "cottage" estates: Mount Desert's luxurious heyday lasted until the end of the Second World War. A 1947 fire destroyed many of the estates, but some still stand, often converted into classy guesthouses, and the island is patterned by hiking and cycling paths along the network of horse-carriage roads constructed in the 1900s by John D. Rockefeller Jr.

Three million visitors pile into Mount Desert each year, but luckily there is plenty of space outside the few townships like Bar Harbor, where a folksy, tie-dye, late-1960s mood persists. Within the Acadia National Park are lakes, pools and boulders left behind by the glacier that created the island, vertiginous trails like the Precipice and the Beehive, and the ever-popular sunset seen from the top of Mount Cadillac, the highest point on the eastern coastline of America.

> "The summits of the mountains are all bare and rocky. I name it Île des Monts Déserts."
>
> Samuel de Champlain

OPPOSITE Autumn colour at Somesville

Mount Desert Island, Maine, USA **Longitude:** 68° 20' W **Latitude:** 44° 21' N **Area:** 280 sq km (108 sq mi) **Highest point:** 466 m (1,529 ft) Cadillac Mountain **Population:** 10,000
Principal town: Bar Harbor **Residents:** Brooke Astor, Natalie Clifford Barney, Barbara Bel Geddes, John D. Rockefeller Jr, Martha Stewart, Caspar Weinberger, Marguerite Yourcenar

> "Willemstad. The toy-like prettiness of the town makes you gasp. Ridiculous little classical porches, window-frames decorated with bold slap-dash festoons of colour, an air of mock grandeur."
>
> Christopher Isherwood

Curaçao

NETHERLANDS ANTILLES, CARIBBEAN

Curaçao is a toponym that everyone other than the strictly teetotal will have encountered at some point in their journey across the barstools of international drinking. The sharply orange liqueur – created by marinating in alcohol the peel of the Laraha orange, which is much too bitter to eat – comes in a variety of colours, but by far the best known is blue curaçao. It is a staple of many classic cocktails but also, alas, of far too many brain-damaging mixtures concocted in the early hours of the morning on a stag or hen weekend.

The island where the liqueur was created, and which provides its name, is the C of the three ABC islands off the north coast of Venezuela. Curaçao – the name possibly derived from *coração*, the Portuguese for "heart" – is the largest of the six Dutch Antilles; the other three fall within the Windward Islands. It is a long, scrawny strip of arid land that tilts towards Venezuela like a ship holed on its landward side. Although populated by a diverse mix of people – a blend of Afro-Caribbean with strains of East Asian, Portuguese and Sephardic Jews – the main cultural influence is Dutch, not least in the capital Willemstad.

When the town's houses were built in the seventeenth century, the settlers took as their template their homes back in the Netherlands, the tall, gabled shapes of Antwerp, Delft or Amsterdam, and simply transplanted them to the Caribbean, making no allowance for the different climate. Verandahs and terraces to provide some shade from the sun were only added much later. The walls and façades of Willemstad are painted in bright, childlike hues of blue, pink and yellow, apparently because one-time governor Vice-Admiral Albert Kikkert complained that white paint gave him migraines.

Most of the interest in Curaçao lies in Willemstad, which is divided in two by a channel leading to the natural inland harbour of Schottegat; the Queen Emma pontoon bridge occasionally and laconically swivels to let boats pass. The oldest active synagogue in the western hemisphere, the Mikvé Israel-Emmanuel, dates from 1732. The town used to be a centre for money-laundering, though the financial loose ends of being a tax haven are being tidied up, and the main revenue outside tourism comes from oil. Visitors do not often stray from the town since the interior is still pretty dry and uneventful – there is little rain on the island and only cacti thrive – although there are coves and diving sites (including a protected underwater park) around the coast for those who prefer healthy activity to kicking back in a Willemstad restaurant with a good *rijstaffel* and a shot of curaçao.

Curaçao, Netherlands Antilles **Longitude:** 69° 00' W **Latitude:** 12° 10' N **Area:** 444 sq km (171 sq mi) **Highest point:** 375 m (1,230 ft) Christoffelberg **Population:** 138,000
Principal town: Willemstad **Natives:** Izaline Calister, Cola Debrot, Daniel De Lion, Andruw Jones, Randall Simon, Dinah Veeris **Residents:** Kizzy Getrouw, Tula

ABOVE Willemstad waterfront

"Fireland then is Satan's land, where flames flicker
and fire flies on a summer night, and, in
the narrowing circles of Hell, ice holds the shades
of traitors as straws in glass."

Bruce Chatwin, *In Patagonia*

Tierra del Fuego

ATLANTIC/PACIFIC

As the crudite Chatwin tells us in his famous account of travels to Patagonia in search of the giant sloth, Tierra del Fuego is where the Italian renaissance poet Dante Alighieri located the bottom of his Hell, the foot of the mountain of Purgatory and the climb to redemption.

It would certainly have seemed the end of the world, if not as infernal, to the first explorer and his crew who found themselves here in 1520 while searching for the southern passage. This was Portuguese explorer Ferdinand Magellan (in the service of the Spanish crown), who gave his name to the Strait that provided his own redemption around Cape Horn. Despite the cold, the explorer remarked upon the fire rather than the ice of the landscape, naming the land after the bonfires he could see, lit by the local Fuegians of the Yamama tribe to warm themselves against the low temperatures (he mistook them as natives preparing to ambush him). Magellan actually only saw smoke and returned to the Spanish court with tales of the Tierra del Humo, but King Charles V felt the name lacked drama (he knew there was no smoke without fire) and rechristened the tail shaped flick of land at the bottom of darkest South America Tierra del Fuego.

When Charles Darwin passed through in 1830 on the *Beagle* voyage, he brought two Fuegians back with him. They became celebrities in Britain, obtaining an audience with the king and queen. Now there remains just one native speaker of the Yaghan language – the younger generation prefers the Spanish vernacular.

"Fireland" remained under Spanish control until 1984, when Argentina, derobed of the Falklands, claimed the east, governed from the frontier city of Ushuaia and Chile claimed the west, governed from Río Grande. The two nations disputed territorial rights to both land and water down to the Mitre Peninsula – the physical end of the continent. Meanwhile, European immigration to this part of the world, including many missionaries, ensures a local demographic make-up as varied as Welsh and German, with the red hair and physiognomy to go with it.

The magnetic pull of Tierra del Fuego has ensured that it is a mecca for latter-day adventurers – extreme sportsmen, lovers of the remote and outward bound – and more sedentary cruise ships. The Antichthon of Pythagorean times, marked on maps simply as "fogs", is now a place where extreme fishermen can trawl for brown trout (for release only) on the banks of rivers clad in the world's southernmost conifers, beach strawberry and calafate berry bushes, under wheeling condors and amid the calls of parakeets, hummingbirds and owls.

OPPOSITE Roca Lake

Tierra del Fuego, Patagonia, Argentina/Chile **Longitude:** 69° 06' W **Latitude:** 54° 34' S **Area:** 48,100 sq km (18,567 sq mi) **Archipelago area:** 73,746 sq km (28,470 sq mi)
Highest point: 2,488m (8,163 ft) Monte Darwin, Chile **Population:** 115,300 **Principal towns:** Porvenir, Puerto Williams, Ushuaia **Natives:** Lucas Bridges, Orundellico aka Jemmy Button
Resident: Julius Popper

"We were drifting through a beautiful reedy world …
green and orange reeds, great unending beds of them
pierce the surface … in places families have made their homes on
floating islands of reeds, their little huts built in wood and straw …
it was strange chugging past their little settlements,
huts groaning slightly in our wake."

Matthew Parris, *Inca-Kola*

Uros Islands

LAKE TITICACA

L iterally afloat on the surface of the lake at the top of the world, the Uros Islands are the world's highest. At 3,812 metres (12,506 feet) up on the Bolivian altiplano, Lake Titicaca joins the nations of Peru and Bolivia. Between them live the Uros people, a pre-Incan civilization that belongs to neither country and has for centuries made the waters of the lake their home. They live here on some forty islands made entirely of totora, a strong local reed with whose deep and dense roots the islands are also anchored to the lake bed. A water-based republic living on islands built on reed stilts, the Uros is a mini, natural Venice.

The Uros originally built their islands as a defence – the largest of the islands has a watchtower also made entirely out of the same reed – to which they could retreat from life at the shores of the lake. With the arrival of the Incans they might have been justified in their fear, but the new lords of the altiplano simply asked the Uros to pay taxes. Today they have just to contend with the attentions of tourists, who embark at the Peruvian port of Puno, and the odd naval manoeuvre of that great maritime nation, landlocked Bolivia.

The community of Uros is made up of a few hundred individuals. Over the centuries they intermarried with the Aymara people with whom they shared Titicaca's shores, so that their own language has all but disappeared. They are by no means a backward or hermetic people, though, and they have fully embraced the modern world. Many of their boats, or balsas, also made of dried totora reed, have motors, their houses have solar panels, televisions and radios, and there are schools on the islands themselves. A toothy, smiling and hospitable people, dressed in colourful ponchos and floppy reed hats, they perpetually chew the totora much as the Quechua of Peru chew the coco leaf. They live on their islands, constantly patching them up like birds feathering a nest, making a living from fishing for catfish (or the local ispi and carachi fish), and the weaving and embroidery of rugs that they sell to travellers after sharing a brew of totora tea.

In the 1980s archaeologists claimed to have discovered Wanatan, an ancient city of the pre-Incan Tlahuanaco civilization at the bottom of Titicaca. This claim attracted teams of divers, including Jacques Cousteau, but they could only find some pieces of pottery. There is also ongoing talk of Incan gold in the depths – the lake is fundamental to the creation myth of the Incan civilization, in which the Children of the Sun arose from its waters. But these are greedy rumours and, anthropologically at least, in the Uros people and their island homes – marvels of herbal architecture a great human treasure lies already tangible on the surface.

OPPOSITE Uros children play on a boat

BELOW Cabins on the floating islets

Aruba

LESSER ANTILLES, CARIBBEAN

There have been moments in Aruba's history when the islanders thought they were going to be very happy indeed. Ever since the islands had become known to European explorers, there were rumours that there was gold to prospect on the island, inspired by claims that its name "Aruba" might have originated from the phrase *oro rubí*, or "red gold", accredited to the Spanish conquistador Alonso de Ojeda, who landed here in 1499. Although that derivation is decidedly unreliable, there was absolutely no doubting the fact that gold was discovered for real in 1824, by a twelve-year-old boy called Willem Rasmijn, who was herding his father's sheep across a dried-up creek in the island's heartland.

A genuine gold rush ensued, settling into a successful mining industry that lasted until Aruba's stocks had been fully exhausted in the 1910s (a number of ruined gold mills and mines can still be seen). The following decade a different kind of gold was discovered, this time of the black variety, and oil provided the main economy on the island for another half century – at one point a refinery established at San Nicolas by an Exxon subsidiary was one of the largest in the world. When Exxon wound down the refinery in the 1980s, a new source of income was required, and attention turned to the possibilities of tourism.

Aruba, the smallest of the ABC islands and the most westerly, is only 40 kilometres (25 miles) from Venezuela. Down in the deep south of the Caribbean, it is well out of the way of hurricanes, and sun is virtually guaranteed. Along the leeward coast, resorts have sprung up to make the most of the climate and the highly rated white sands of the Druif, Eagle and Palm beaches. Like the other ABC islands, the water-parched *cunucu*, or interior countryside, does not appeal to many, although there are Arawak drawings, giant lizards and wind-sculpted rock formations for those who do venture inland.

The capital Oranjestad is architecturally not a patch on the eighteenth-century Old Dutch charm of Willemstad, and the quarters that look as if they might be equally authentic are often modern recreations. The town is really a starting point for sun-seeking, for diving around the coral reefs off the southern shore or for the top-notch – and world-renowned – windsurfing at Fisherman's Huts.

In a throwback to the mining days of the nineteenth century, Aruba has created a less demanding way of stumbling across a fortune: the lure of the gold on offer at the island's dozen or so casinos entices a stream of high rollers to travel from the United States and try their luck at a Vegas blessed with great beaches.

"One happy island."

Aruba's national motto

OPPOSITE Casibari Rock, Paradera

OVERLEAF Palm Beach, Aruba

Aruba, Netherlands Antilles **Longitude:** 69° 58' W **Latitude:** 12° 30' N **Area:** 193 sq km (75 sq mi) **Highest point:** 189 m (620 ft) Mt Jamanota **Population:** 69,600 **Principal town:** Oranjestad
Natives: Ruby Bute, Susan Cagle, Ivan Jansen, Eugene Kingsale, Sidney Ponson

Nantucket

NORTH ATLANTIC

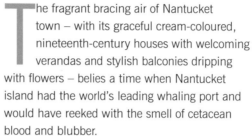

The fragrant bracing air of Nantucket town – with its graceful cream-coloured, nineteenth-century houses with welcoming verandas and stylish balconies dripping with flowers – belies a time when Nantucket island had the world's leading whaling port and would have reeked with the smell of cetacean blood and blubber.

Siasconset (abbreviated locally to Sconset), the eastern point of this half-moon-shaped island off Cape Cod, is America's nearest point to the finisterres of Spain and Portugal, making it a perfect station for processing Atlantic whales. It was from here that Ishmael set forth on the *Pequod* in search of Moby Dick in Herman Melville's classic novel of the same name. Of Nantucket Melville writes: "Two thirds of this terracqueous globe are the Nantucketer's. For the sea is his; he runs it, as Emperors run empires."

Whaling is now consigned to a fine museum topped by a whale-shaped weathervane. Before whaling moratoriums were introduced Nantucket was devastated by the Great Fire of 1846, causing much of the population to flee. Thus the island remained undeveloped until the middle of the twentieth century, allowing the community of resident locals to avoid the overdevelopment experienced by their neighbours across the Nantucket Sound on Martha's Vineyard. Chain stores are outlawed (except Ralph Lauren, which got in before the ban).

The island was once a refuge for Algonquin Indians retreating from the Europeans settling in Cape Cod. They named the island, possibly meaning "in the middle of the waters", as well as christening its features with picturesque appellations. Nowadays it is a summer colony or retreat – the population in summer is five times that of the residents – and vacationers come to enjoy the empty expanse of Coatue beach, kayaking in the Wauwinet Straits, the ponds of Hummock and Miacomet, and the undulations of the Popsquatchet Hills.

Real-estate prices on the island have rocketed, as New Yorkers and Bostonians have rushed to snap up holiday homes on this quaint summer idyll. It hasn't always been a bed of roses, as Nantucket has suffered the environmental impacts of many shipping disasters – notably the wrecking of the *Argo Merchant* in 1976, which unleashed one of the largest oil spills in history. But the descendants of Thomas Mayhew (to whom the British had ceded the island) might regret that their ancestor sold the island back in the early nineteenth century for the pittance of thirty pounds and two beaver hats – one for him and one for his wife.

"You could cut the brackish winds with a knife
Here in Nantucket, and cast up the time
When the Lord God formed man from the sea's slime
And breathed into his face the breath of life,
And blue-lung'd combers lumbered to the kill.
The Lord survives the rainbow of His will."

Robert Lowell, "The Quaker Graveyard in Nantucket"

OPPOSITE Center Street

Nantucket, Massachusetts, USA **Longitude:** 70° 05' W **Latitude:** 41° 16' N **Area:** 129 sq km (50 sq mi) **Highest point:** 33m (109 ft) Folger Hill **Population:** 9,500 **Principal town:** Nantucket
Natives: Abiah Folger, Maria Mitchell, Lucretia Coffin Mott, Joseph Gardner Swift **Residents:** Frank and Kathie Lee Gifford, Theresa Heinz and John Kerry, Tommy Hilfiger

Martha's Vineyard

NORTH ATLANTIC

Martha's Vineyard, Massachusetts, USA **Longitude:** 70° 38' W **Latitude:** 41° 25' N **Area:** 232 sq km (90 sq mi) **Highest point:** 95 m (312 ft) **Population:** 14,900 **Principal town:** Edgartown
Natives: Caleb Cheeshahteaumauk, Christopher Rebello **Residents:** Thomas Hart Benton, Judy Blume, Art Buchwald, Walter Cronkite, Evan Dando, Spike Lee, David Letterman, David McCullough, Mike Nichols, Carly Simon, William Styron, James Taylor

"Don't worry, we'll bury him. On the Vineyard."

Judith Jacklin Belushi, widow of John

ABOVE Gingerbread house, Oak Bluffs

OPPOSITE Edgartown lighthouse

Following his death in the Chateau Marmont on Sunset Boulevard, John Belushi's body was brought back from West to East, to the island where he had a holiday home. He was buried beneath a suitably larger-than-life stone slab with the single word BELUSHI chiselled into it, in a cemetery straggling down a gently wooded slope near Chilmark, on the southern shore of Martha's Vineyard.

Belushi was just one of many celebrities to summer there. James Cagney had bought a farm on this triangular island in the 1930s. The Kennedy clan spilt over from their Hyannisport complex on Cape Cod, 11 kilometres (7 miles) to the north; they were followed by James Taylor and Carly Simon, and a bevy of writers, television hosts, filmmakers and politicians, all part of the diaspora from the mainland that boosts the island's winter population of fifteen thousand fivefold.

But out of season – once the yachting fraternities have hauled anchor and the beautiful people have taken the ferry back from Vineyard Haven – is the best time to see the island, especially during the fall, when fading reds and browns dapple the gentle hillsides, and there is the strongest sense of time standing still. Here, something of 1950s America still persists.

In Oak Bluffs the mood harks back even further, to the 1890s, when a group of zealous Methodists from the main town of Edgartown – "down island" in Vineyard-speak – would head inland each summer to hold prayer meetings. Initially they pitched a handful of tents. Over the years the tents multiplied and then became wooden cottages, tiny gingerbread houses with filigree decorations (a style known as "Carpenter Gothic") surrounding a circular tabernacle and bandstand.

At the time Martha's Vineyard was withering. In the footsteps of the explorer Bartholomew Gosnold, who named the island in 1602 after its wild grapes and, depending on which version you choose, a saint, his daughter, or his mother-in-law, the island had prospered from whaling. Nearby Nantucket supplied the boats, Martha's Vineyard the captains and crew: the houses of leafy, elegant Edgartown still sport widow's walks. But the discovery of petroleum reduced the demand for whale oil, and the island's decline was only rescued by tourism.

Somehow Martha's Vineyard has continued making the news – Edgartown is instantly recognizable to anyone who has watched *Jaws* – though it was not always positive. In 1969 Teddy Kennedy swam back to Edgartown after his accident on Chappaquiddick. Thirty years later his nephew John Jr's plane plunged into the waters off the Aquinnah cliffs, the former Gay Head, home of the descendants of the island's original inhabitants, the Wampanoag tribe.

Hispaniola

GREATER ANTILLES, CARIBBEAN

The city of Santo Domingo on Hispaniola is the oldest European settlement in the New World. It was here, on his second voyage, that Columbus founded the first Spanish colony and patriotically christened the island "La Espanola" – "the Spanish Isle". The local *tainos*, as they called themselves (meaning "good and noble") even helped him build his first fort. Thus began a tortuous history on a harsh island of mountain ranges below sea-level depressions, crocodile-infested saline lakes and treeless savannah.

Over the subsequent centuries the Spanish grew careless about protecting the shores of this large island, concentrating themselves in the south-east around Santo Domingo while pirates and other empires became first curious and then covetous of this undefended island. In 1665, Louis XIV claimed the island for France and after a few decades of wrangling the historic intermarrying allies of France and Spain reached a settlement. In 1697 a divorce was signed granting the western third to France – which became Haiti – and the east to Spain, which became the Dominican Republic. The two sides engendered very different nationalities, fates and livelihoods.

Haiti saw the rise of some of the most brutal dictators the world has ever seen. In 1791, two years after the Storming of the Bastille, Toussaint Louverture, the Black Napoleon, conducted a slave's revolt and was the first subject to overthrow colonial rule. He appointed himself *de facto* emperor and tried to reunite the island. Then, for much of the twentieth century, Haiti came under the despotic rule of the Duvaliers, Papa Doc and then his son, Baba Doc and their terrifying private army of Tonton Macoutes. Haiti is still one of the most volatile states and its capital Port-au-Prince one of the most no-go cities in the world. This legacy of dictatorship has left their part of Hispaniola island denuded by deforestation and the Haitians among the poorest people on Earth, seeking solace in voodoo Christianity and a reassuringly vibrant music scene dominated by the rhythms of *kompa* jazz.

After a promising start under the watch of their founding father Juan Pablo Duarte, after whom Hispaniola's highest peak is named, and who commissioned America's first cathedral, their Hispanic neighbours in the newly declared Dominican Republic fared little better. In the early twentieth century they suffered the dictatorship of Rafael Trujillo, who ordered the "Parsley Massacre" genocide of ethnic Haitians, judged on whether or not they could pronounce the Spanish for parsley (*perejil*) with a rolled "r". He at least was a fan of the arts, stealing an improbable background role in the famous airport scene of *Casablanca* and being an enthusiastic supporter of the Dominican Republic's signature music and dance – the merengue. Since his assassination in 1961 this half of the island, like the music founded in the Vega Real (Royal Meadow) of Cibao, the fertile bread-basket of this diminutive republic has flourished and become a confident, hopeful and developing nation. All the while, across the Cordillera Central, Haiti bleeds under uneasy UN supervision. Such grand beginnings, such grand dreams – but five centuries on, two very different sides of the same post-colonial coin.

LEFT Market stall in Haiti

OPPOSITE Yaque del Norte river valley in the Dominican Republic

Hispaniola, Dominican Republic/Haiti **Alternative name:** Isla de Santo Domingo **Longitude:** 71° 00' W or 70,40 measure on map (71,20) **Latitude:** 19° 00' N ditto **Area:** 76,480 sq km (29,521 sq mi) **Highest point:** 3,087 m (10,127 ft) Pico Duarte **Population:** 18,070,000 **Capitals:** Santo Domingo, Port-au-Prince **Natives:** John James Audubon, Nemours Jean-Baptiste, Francisco Cabrera, Juan Pablo Duarte, François "Papa Doc" Duvalier, Wyclef Jean, Dania Ramírez, Oscar de la Renta, Francisco del Rosario Sánchez **Residents:** Henri Christophe, Jean-Jacques Dessalines

"I left Haiti when I was nine years old …
but I always say that the music I make is a reflection
of what I remember from my childhood there."

Wyclef Jean

Chiloé

PACIFIC COAST, CHILE

Chiloé is an archipelago shrouded in mists and mythology. About three-quarters of the way down the long coast of that extraordinarily thin country, Chile, and just on the cusp of Patagonia, these islands have carved out for themselves a nature and a personality that the locals like to think is very separate from the mainland.

The myths date back to pre-colonial times, told by the Mapuche people who merged with the original Chonos islanders. The Mapuche brought dark tales involving wizards clad in jackets made from the flayed skin of virgins, legends involving fights between good and bad serpents. They told each other about lost cities, about Trauco, the dwarfish but superpowered satyr, Fiura, a gruesome coquette, and Caleuche, a ghostly, doom-laden ship – all perpetuated through songs and dances that are still performed. Many of these myths personified life on Chiloé; folklorists point out that the legend of Trauco, the troll-like seducer, was actually a convenient way for families to explain unwanted pre-marital pregnancies.

This clutch of volcanic islands, based around the main Isla Grande, is divided from Chile by the conjoined glacier-formed gulfs of Corcovado and Ancud. The tides pouring in simultaneously from the northern and southern openings of the two gulfs set up whirlpools and powerful riptides that even local boatmen find challenging.

The first European to brave the crossing was Alfonso de Camargo in 1540; the territory of Nueva Galicia was established two decades later.

Jesuit priests landed and found themselves corralled on Chiloé when they were barred from the mainland after Chile became a republic in 1818. They left their mark not just spiritually but visually, in a hundred or so churches, constructed in a Bavarian style (where many of the Jesuits and other settlers hailed from), with wooden shingle exteriors and clock towers. On the shoreline the architecture of the fishing houses is equally distinctive, perched on *palafitos*, wooden stilts. The fish and shellfish the residents catch is blended with chicken, sausage, potato, peas, onions – whatever is to hand – and covered with rhubarb or fig leaves to create *curanto*, the local signature dish, cooked for hours, traditionally in a deep hole in the ground.

Chiloé has been praised as one of the planet's best-preserved islands because of its isolation, its unspoiled forests and protected churches. But its artificially created salmon-farming industry currently ranks second in the world, and talk of a bridge link to the continent has alarmed those who want to retain Chiloé's character and folklore. They are putting their faith in Trauco, Fiura and their mythical chums to dispel the modernizers and preserve the archipelago's quirky charm.

> "The island of Chiloé is celebrated for its black storms and black soil, the thickets of fuchsia and bamboo, its Jesuit churches and the golden hands of its woodcarvers."
>
> Bruce Chatwin

OPPOSITE The priest of Tenaun village

OVERLEAF A view from the island of the majestic Andes

Chiloé, Los Lagos, Chile **Local name:** Isla Grande de Chiloé **Longitude:** 73° 50' W **Latitude:** 42° 30' S **Area:** 8,394 sq km (3,240 sq mi) **Highest point:** 823 m (2,700 ft) Cerro Cap Maldonado
Population: 154,700 **Principal town:** Castro

Manhattan

NEW YORK

"This rock island,
this concrete Capri."

Cyril Connolly, critic

Everyone has their private sense of Manhattan, even if they have never been there, such is the prevalence and power of the New York borough's imagery received worldwide. For some it is the literary, satirical world of Dorothy Parker and cronies at the Algonquin round table, for others the psycho-sexual world of Woody Allen. For some, Broadway and Sinatra's showbiz city that never sleeps, for others the world of Seinfeld or the set of *Friends*. For some a city of bagels, once-over-easy fried eggs and the ethnic ghettos Chinatown and Little Italy; the jazz of Harlem; the home of Pop Art and famous galleries. And for some it is a consumer heaven, of shopping at Bloomingdales or Tiffany's or trading down on Wall Street.

Manhattan is just one part of a famous city, but it is the only part that many people ever see; the financial, cultural and commercial centre of America. Manhattan is the world paradigm of a modern city centre. On an island.

An 11 September it was, in 1609, when Henry Hudson sailed through the Narrows between Staten Island and Brooklyn and claimed Manhattan for the Dutch East India Company. The island took its named from the Lenape Indian language *mannahata*, meaning "island of many hills" and, acquired for an apocryphal $24, in 1625 became Fort Amsterdam, which later became New Amsterdam, a major centre for the Dutch fur trade. In a prescient transaction the British acquired New Amsterdam from its governor, Peter Stuyvesant, in return for a fetid corner of South America – Surinam. Renamed after the Duke of York and Albany, at that time Manhattan's future could scarcely have been imagined.

After the devastating Great Fire of 1776 Manhattan was transformed by the trade opened up by the Erie Canal and by immigration of Europeans for whom New York was the gateway to the American dream. The island went vertical. Emerging from the tunnels underneath the Hudson and East rivers, the eyes are pulled breathtakingly upwards, the view stretched as if reflected in an elongating mirror. "Mannahata" became again an island of many hills, now the peaks of skyscrapers: the Singer, Chrysler and Empire State buildings, and the smaller Flatiron. Art Deco, neo-Gothic and Americanist they are some of the most iconic buildings of the modern world and part of a much-imitated skyline.

Some of the world's most famous streets – the Avenues, Lexington, Madison and Fifth, and streets east and west – give rise to those lilting Manhattan incantations to cab drivers "West 42nd and Fifth, please". It is a grid encompassing resonant neighbourhoods such as Brownstone, bohemian Greenwich and the East Village, the clubbing post-industrial Meatpacking District, intellectual Upper West and affluent Upper East side, gay Chelsea and the acronyms of TriBeCa and the original SoHo. All names to conjure with and lapse into movie speech.

Whichever is your Manhattan it has an unmistakable livery: the yellow of the taxis; the blue and white of the NYPD; Airstream silver of the subway; and the atmospheric, pop-video dry-ice effects of its steam vents. Another 11 September felled not just two iconic tower blocks but, briefly, an entire island's swagger and self-confidence. But from a new year zero and with a reassessed sense of its position, the core of the Big Apple is once again at the heart of the world.

OPPOSITE Heading towards the Flatiron building

OVERLEAF Entering Manhattan over Brooklyn Bridge

Manhattan, New York, New York, USA **Longitude:** 73° 59' W **Latitude:** 40° 44' N **Area:** 59 sq km (23 sq mi) **Highest point:** 87 m (284 ft) Bennett Park **Population:** 1,611,500 **Natives:** Lauren Bacall, Humphrey Bogart, James Cagney, Washington Irving, Roy Liechtenstein, the Marx Brothers, Herman Melville, Henry Miller, Eugene O'Neill, Al Pacino, Norman Rockwell, Theodore Roosevelt, Sonny Rollins, Jonas Salk, Gloria Vanderbilt, Edith Wharton **Residents:** Woody Allen, Truman Capote, Alistair Cooke, John Lennon, Samuel Morse, Dorothy Parker, Andy Warhol, Tom Wolfe

"Chapter One. He was as tough and romantic as the city he loved.
Beneath his black-rimmed glasses was the coiled sexual power of
a jungle cat. I love this. New York was his town, and it always would be…"

Isaac Davis, *Manhattan* by Woody Allen

Ellis Island

NEW YORK HARBOR

"Give me your tired,
your poor,
your huddled masses
yearning to
breathe free."

Emma Lazarus, poet

Beneath the benign, unflinching gaze of the Statue of Liberty, the buildings of Ellis Island cluster. Whereas Liberty herself, a generous gift from the people of France in 1886, is a noble symbol of freedom – America's very own Marianne – Ellis Island represents the sharp end of practical reality, a factory for humans built to process the flood of immigrants who hungered to follow the dream.

Mind you, not all the wannabe Americans who docked in New York Harbor were obliged to enter through the portals of Ellis Island, the "front doors to freedom". Those travelling in the first- and second-class accommodation offered by Cunard or White Star could relax in their cabins while their papers were discreetly checked by officials onboard. It was the swilling hordes in steerage who were deposited on to the quayside, and herded in trepidation through a warren of corridors and anterooms to be examined by the doctors, clerks and tallymen who would decide their fate. For those who failed, the Island of Hope became the Island of Tears, the mainland so tantalizingly close.

First to be processed on New Year's Day 1892 was Annie Moore, a colleen from County Cork celebrating her fifteenth birthday who – doubtless chosen in the late nineteenth-century equivalent of a photo-opportunity – was presented with a gold coin before she headed west. A statue on the island captures her holding a battered suitcase and clutching her hat to her head. In her wake came twelve million more; some forty per cent of the current American population, so it is said, are directly descended from an Ellis Island alumnus.

As immigration from the Old World swelled, the federal government had picked Ellis Island as a suitable venue for controlling arrivals. Previously known by the Mohicans as Kioshk or Gull Island, it had later been variously a source of shellfish, a site for gibbets and a fortified military base. At the time Annie Moore was processed, the rather elegant buildings of Ellis Island – described as like a "watering place hotel" – were built of Georgian pine. They burned down five years later, and new brick and limestone halls were raised in 1900, their style reflecting the great American railway terminals, underlining the industrial efficiency of their task and impressing the new arrivals.

By the 1920s the flood declined, and quotas were put in place. After acting as a holding pen for wartime aliens, the island ceased all activity in the 1950s and the fierce harbour weather battered its fabric until its rehabilitation as a heritage centre, a sanitized museum with little hint of the clamour that H. G. Wells noted on a visit, the hum of hope emitted by the "dingy and strangely garbed, wild-eyed aliens".

OPPOSITE The Statue of Liberty gazes down on Ellis Island

"The clear light and the multi-coloured ice
in all its shapes and textures were mesmerizing.
In the sun the ice sparked like a kaleidoscope."

David Hempleman-Adams, explorer

Baffin Island

BAFFIN BAY

onsidering this is the fifth largest island on the planet, half as big again as a country the size of Germany, Baffin Island is still only known by true island cognoscenti. A slab of land perched off the top right-hand corner of northern Canada, Baffin is part of the infant province of Nunavut, only officially created in 1999; Iqaluit – a township previously called Frobisher Bay, in the island's southern reaches – was selected as the provincial capital.

Despite its vast size, there are hardly any humans on the island – only eleven thousand in total, of which eighty per cent are Inuit, a race so in tune with their natural surroundings that they instinctively know the noise an ice cliff will make when its lip is about to break away. Nature is king in Baffin. On an island that mostly lies above the Arctic Circle, ice glimmers and glisters; tundra stretches unceasingly towards sheer mountainous cliffs and deep fjords; water is a constant presence in all its many guises – fast-flowing rivers, still lakes and swamps, gently rippling streams. In the brief window offered by the summer months, wildflowers and berries erupt across liberated meadows.

And in this natural theatre of dreams roam Arctic foxes and wolves, lemmings, caribou and polar bears (Nunavut licence plates are

polar-bear shaped). Seasonal visitors include seals, terns and Canada geese. Humans are not always welcome guests in this environment and must take their chances in a climate where the weather can change in an instant from gentle to savage, and where danger lurks behind the beauty of the landscape. The Inuit, who need no lessons in fieldcraft and handle such risks with pragmatic humour, encountered Europeans on a regular basis from the 1570s onwards, though the great Viking explorer Leif Eriksson possibly landed en route to Newfoundland five hundred years earlier. One of the early visitors was the English navigator William Baffin; later Scottish settlers followed, drawn by the prospect of whaling and fishing.

Heading out of the few townships on the island, and into the wilderness, the most authentic transport are the *qamutik*, wooden dog-drawn sleds which were once made by laying fish on sealskin and letting the whole freeze into a rigid frame, with antler or bone runners (motorized skidoos offer a modern alternative to dog-power). Fishing, trekking and kayaking are most visitors' chosen activities, though that hardy breed of BASE jumpers are focused on the near vertical cliffs of mounts Odin and Asgard – the latter known to most of us as the location for the "Union Jack" ski-jump-cum-parachute leap at the start of *The Spy Who Loved Me*, performed by stuntman Rick Sylvester for a consideration of $30,000.

OPPOSITE Auyuittuq National Park

RIGHT Nunavut villager fishing for Arctic charr

Baffin, Nunavut, Canada **Alternative names:** Île de Baffin, Qikiqtaaluk **Longitude:** 75° 00' W **Latitude:** 68° 00' N **Area:** 507,450 sq km (19,588 sq mi) **Highest point:** 2,147 m (7,044 ft) Mt Odin
Population: 11,000 **Principal town:** Iqaluit **Natives:** Kenojuak Ashevak, Zacharias Kunuk, Annabella Piugattuk, Aqpik Peter, Toonoo Sharky

Bahamas

ATLANTIC

As locals are apt to point out, there are three seasons in the Bahamas: last summer, this summer and next summer. A short hop across the Straits of Florida, these islands are an extension of the sunshine state. There are seven hundred in all, and more than two thousand cays of powdery white sand, folded like double cream into a turquoise sauce, strung out in a 1,000-kilometre (650-mile) line down through the northern Caribbean. Many of them are just shallow reefs and sandbars that form a labyrinth precarious to navigate by ship. Indeed, the early Spanish explorers – Columbus was the first, reaching the outer island of San Salvador and thinking it was the East Indies – christened this seascape the *baja mar* or "shallow sea", from which is derived the islands' modern name. The waters here are strewn with the wrecks of ships snagged, beached and sunk in the Bahamian shallows.

Less than one per cent of the islands are inhabited, but each group has its own distinct character. The tiny central island of New Providence is the hub, with the Bahamian capital of Nassau – a laid-back town of considerable colonial charm. This is as urban as the Bahamas get, never more so than when downtown Nassau comes alive with Junkanoo, the local Mardi Gras celebrated from the day after Christmas to New Year. At this time, the locals dance through the streets to *goombay* music and gorge themselves on fried fish. Next door is Paradise Island, linked by two bridges and famed for the sands of Cable Beach, where incongruous resorts have mushroomed amid the tangle of palms and mangroves. The gaudiest of

these is the Atlantis hotel-cum-mall, complete with underwater aquarium shopping experience, where it is not clear whether the sharks are inside or outside the goldfish bowl.

The so-called "out" islands of Abacos and Andros offer fishing and a wilder, more jungle-like experience, as well as diving off the famed plunging reef TOTO (tongue of the ocean) – the Bahamas has the largest coral reefs of the Northern Hemisphere. The quaint retreat of Eleuthera is named after the Greek word for "freedom", as sought by the Eleutheran Adventurers from England in the seventeenth century, who came and settled here to express their religious freedom and left behind an ambience of "New England in the tropics".

More remote still is the seductively named Stocking Island, with its underwater caves and strange sea life. The stromatolites here – large humps partly buried below water – can only otherwise be found in Australia's Shark Bay. Finally, and most British of this former British colony, the designer seclusion of Harbour Island is characterized by gingerbread houses with stained-glass windows and retreats, created by interior designers such as India Hicks.

Celebrities first came here in the wake of Ernest Hemingway. He came to enjoy the solitude, earthiness and game fishing off the smaller northern Biminis and Berrys. But he moved on, decrying the Pandora's box he had opened – his pared-down life and writing style a far cry from the jet-skis, piña coladas and fawning entourage attending to the would-be Pirates of the Caribbean, filmed off Grand Bahama.

ABOVE Investigating a cushion sea star   OPPOSITE Fly fishing for bone fish   OVERLEAF One of the seven hundred small Bahama Islands

Bahamas, Commonwealth of the Bahamas **Longitude:** 76° 00' W **Latitude:** 24° 15' N **Area:** 13,878 sq km (5,357 sq mi) **Highest point:** 63m (206 ft) Mt Alvernia, Cat Island **Population:** 299,700 **Capital:** Nassau **Natives:** Kirkland Bodie, Ronnie Butler, Ian Hamilton Finlay, Shawn Forbes, James Gambier, Alphone "Blind Blake" Higgs, Shakara Ledard, Charles Allen Smith, Joseph Spence, Tonique Williams-Darling **Residents:** Jimmy Curry, Arthur Hailey, Persia White, Duke and Duchess of Windsor

"Where the world is spinning on greased grooves."

John Steinbeck, *Cannery Row*

ABOVE Aerial view of a fishing village

"Soon the crab pot breaks the water's surface,
Glistening in the light of the red-balled sun,
And it's full of white-bellied 'Jimmy Crabs',
Looks like a good crabbing day's just begun."

Jennings Evans, "A Day in the Life of a Smith Island Crab Potter"

Smith Island

CHESAPEAKE BAY

Time and tide have always been uppermost in the minds of Smith Islanders. Now time is running out for the crab potters and oystermen who have farmed the waters offshore for centuries. Tide, on the other hand, is very much running *in*, as those same waters continue to rise and threaten the very existence of the island.

Smith Island (really a collection of small islands) lies in Chesapeake Bay, the long sliver of estuary water pinioned between the mainland mass of Maryland below Baltimore and Annapolis, and the great pincer claw of the Delmarva Peninsula. The shoreline of Chesapeake Bay is a haunting location in its own right, a place full of marsh grass, mud flats and waterfowl, where the shingle houses, skiffs and crabbing contests seem little-changed from decades past. And Smith Island, the only inhabited island in the bay, is even more of a time capsule.

The water people who live and work on the island are the descendants of English colonists who arrived in the seventeenth century from Cornwall and Devon via Virginia. They liked what they found. One of the first Brits to arrive, Captain John Smith, wrote that "Heaven and earth seemed never to have agreed better for man's commodious and delightful habitation". He actually called the island the Russel Isles (a later landowner also called Smith provided its current name). It soon became clear that the easily eroded and frequently swamped soil

was not particularly good for grazing cows or farming, so the settlers turned to the Bay to provide their subsistence.

Isolated and independent – with no town council, mayor or city taxes – the Smith Islanders retained the inflections of their original West Country burr in their still-evolving Tidewater English accent ("brown" sounds more like "brain"), along with some archaic vocabulary and phrasing, "a-going" and "a-coming". It is a dialect as rich as the local ten-layer, cream-filled chocolate cake.

Oysters were shipped in their millions to the big cities, and the island families sat beside their crab shanties waiting to catch exquisite soft-shell crabs – female blue crabs known as "peelers" who, between May and September, shed their shells and must be captured at that precise moment. But this is a disappearing craft. Fewer and fewer watermen have the energy to undertake the hard work required to dredge up a living.

No one knows quite how long the island has left to survive. Here now, waders are essential; picket-fenced front yards are frequently awash in the three tiny communities, Ewell, Rhodes Point and even more remote Tylerton, only accessible by boat ("a backwater's backwater"). Whole islets, which once had hotels and schools, have already disappeared, and the otters, swimming foxes and terrapins in the wildlife refuge may end up being Smith Island's final residents.

Smith Island, Maryland, USA **Longitude:** 76° 02' W **Latitude:** 37° 58' N **Area:** 12 sq km (5 sq mi) **Highest point:** 2m (5 ft) **Population:** 360 **Principal settlement:** Ewell **Native:** Jennings Evans

Jamaica

GREATER ANTILLES, CARIBBEAN

"Jamaica is
    the loudest
island in the world!"

DJ Spooky

Regardless of its great history and natural charms, Jamaica is remarkable for the huge impact its music has had on the rest of the world – a diaspora of rhythm that has pulsated in ever-widening ripples from the heart and soul of the Caribbean. The reggae explosion, fronted internationally by Bob Marley and the Wailers, is but one – if the best-known – sonic boom; before reggae there was mento and ska, and latterly dancehall and dub have influenced world music. The great mobile sound systems of Duke Reid and Coxsone Dodd, and the innovative techniques of DJs like Lee "Scratch" Perry, one of the begetters of rap and hip hop, altered the way we even listen to music.

The island, 150 kilometres (96 miles) south of that other great Caribbean music machine Cuba, has a lush landscape as varied as its music. Xaymaca, its Arawak name, means "land of wood and water". Behind the capital Kingston rise the Blue Mountains, shrouded in the near-constant mists that give them their distinctive

hue, and the clouds of ganja smoke exhaled by the spiritual Rastafarians who have retreated to these hills, as their once-enslaved ancestors, the self-liberating Maroons, did before them. Up here in the mountains, botanists, ornithologists and lepidopterists are spoilt by the range of species, and coffeephiles can hunt down rare aromas in the plantations.

The hard-core tourists are based along the north coast – Ocho Rios, and, of course, Montego Bay – which means the southern coastline either side of the wetlands of the Black River is often overlooked. Bays like Bluefields and Treasure Beach are relatively unvisited. The south coast is also where Kingston sits – a microclimate all its own in this actually rather straight-laced island, a harder, tougher, often suspicious environment unrelieved by the Blue Mountain breezes, a city trying hard to rid itself of a Yardie, high-crime reputation. Much of Kingston is modern – earthquakes, fire, hurricanes and town planners have razed most of the British colonial character (the island's former capital Spanish Town is the place to visit for Georgian architecture).

Jamaica's cultural mix is energetic, a mash-up of imports and exports: its cuisine of jerk chicken, patties and rice'n'peas is as widely known as its music. Alongside the Afro-Caribbean majority are significant minorities of Chinese, Indian and Arab Jamaicans – Leslie Kong, who produced Desmond Dekker, Jimmy Cliff and Marley was Chinese; Lee Gopthal, founder of Trojan Records was Indian. Other incomers who helped spread the awareness of Jamaica were Noël Coward at Firefly and Ian Fleming at Goldeneye (both houses near Ocho Rios) – Fleming named James Bond after the author of what he called "one of my Jamaican bibles": *Birds of the West Indies*. And Chris Blackwell, a white Jamaican, the owner of Island Records, has long been a diligent champion of the finest of Jamaica's many voices.

ABOVE Bog Walk Gorge

OVERLEAF Diving at Pirate's Cave in Negril

Jamaica **Longitude:** 77º 30' W **Latitude:** 18º 10' N **Area:** 11,420 sq km (4,408 sq mi) **Highest point:** 2,256 m (7,402 ft) Blue Mountain Peak **Population:** 2,651,000 **Capital:** Kingston **Natives:** Beenie Man, Jimmy Cliff, Carole Joan Crawford, Desmond Dekker, Clement "Sir Coxsone" Dodd, Marcus Garvey, Chris Gayle, Gregory Isaacs, Ben Johnson, Grace Jones, Bob Marley, Lee "Scratch" Perry, Asafa Powell, Shabba Ranks, Lady Saw, Shaggy, Tanya Stephens, Courtney Walsh, Willard White **Residents:** Andrew Salkey, Chris Blackwell, Noël Coward, Ian Fleming, Errol Flynn

Cuba

GREATER ANTILLES, CARIBBEAN

Cuba is a figurative as well as physical island. It is the last surviving bastion of true Communism (as opposed to dictatorships that abuse that doctrine) – that twentieth-century ideological experiment that elsewhere has been discredited. Here, under the Caribbean sun, it shows no sign of changing with the secession already in place in view of Fidel Castro's failing health. It is no wonder, really, for it is not the communism of grey apartment blocks, snow, fur hats, red cabbage and vodka. It is a communism of faded Hispanic colonial buildings, beaches, bikinis, Hemingway's mojitos and cigars. An altogether happier concoction.

The romance and Baudelairian *nostalgie de la boue* of the place is overwhelming but deceptive. Although the historic centre of Havana has been shored up and given a lick of pastel paint, elsewhere the colonial buildings are in a perilous state of decay. The signature *botero* Cadillacs from the 1950s are naturally photogenic, evoking the age of Elvis when parked up in lines in the central plaza or bouncing past

with a Cuban elbow leaning casually out of the window. But they are slow, polluting and falling apart, yet vital to a population that cannot afford or obtain any other form of car. Havana is a sensuous place of dancing and music, which moves to the rhythm of the salsa and the *son de cuba* famously exported by Ry Cooder and the Buena Vista Social Club. It is also the place of the poverty-driven, promiscuous under-age sex and prostitution depicted in Gutiérrez's *Dirty Havana* trilogy.

The Cubans, at least of Havana, are a sinuous, swaggering people, confident to the point of arrogance and happy to take the best of what their newfound, post-Buena Vista tourist industry brings them of the outside world, but boasting allegiance to the regime that maintains their singularity. They are faithful to their Fidel (and his many doubles), proud of the Che that sold a million T-shirts in London's Carnaby Street, and feign a sense of revolution now under the inertia brought on by the Caribbean sun. From Pinar del Rio in the west to the colonial treasure of Trinidad in the southeast,

amid sugar-cane and tobacco fields, and the bungalows with verandas and rocking chairs, the countryside is devoid of conventional advertising. Instead it is full of freshly painted communist propaganda signs shouting *Luchar!* ("Fight!") or *Siempre Invencibles* ("Always Invincible"), while in real life a lazy tractor driver dozes off in the foreground. Pupils in Cuban schools wear red pioneer kerchiefs and the Cubans are proud of their claimed one hundred per cent literacy rate, even though there are not enough jobs in which to apply it. It is a form of Cuban *jihad*. Appropriate then that Cuba is also home to that other island of islands and law unto itself – Guantanamo Bay.

The Caribbean's largest island, blocking the entrance to the Gulf of Mexico, Cuba has always been a flashpoint and thorn in the side of the United States, never more so than during the 1963 nuclear missile crisis that nearly brought the world to its knees. Despite this, it remains tantalizingly original, a purveyor of Monte Cristos to the world of luxury and as elusive as any one of its champion boxers.

ABOVE Young "pioneers" return home after school in Havana   OVERLEAF The *son de cuba*

Cuba, Republic of Cuba **Longitude:** 79° 27' W **Latitude:** 21° 00' N **Area:** 110,860 sq km (42,792 sq mi) **Highest point:** 1,974 m (6,476 ft) Pico Turquino **Population:** 11,230,300 **Capital:** Havana **Natives:** Alicia Alonso, Desi Arnaz, José Raúl Capablanca, Fidel and Raúl Castro, Celia Cruz, Gloria Estefan, Ibrahim Ferrer, Andy García, Celina González, Rubén González, Pedro Juan Gutiérrez, Rita Marley, José Marti, Raúl Martinez, Arnaldo Tamayo Méndez, José Méndez, Dámaso Pérez Prado, Silvio Rodríguez, Teófilo Stevenson **Residents:** Alejo Carpentier, Che Guevara, Ernest Hemingway

"He is the true prototype of the British colonist …
the whole Anglo-Saxon spirit is Crusoe:
the manly independence, the unconscious cruelty,
the persistence, the slow yet efficient intelligence,
the sexual apathy, the calculating taciturnity."

James Joyce

Juan Fernández Islands

SOUTH PACIFIC

The Juan Fernández Islands will be forever linked with the legend of Robinson Crusoe. Two of the four islands of this small archipelago in the South Pacific, several hundred kilometres from the Chilean coast, were even renamed in 1966 to fit the legend in an effort to drive tourism towards this otherwise barely inhabited possession.

When the Spanish explorer Juan Fernández discovered the islands in 1574, he named them prosaically according to how close they were to the coast: La Isla Más a Tierra (the nearest), La Isla Más Afuera (the furthest away) and Juananga and Santa Clara in between. But in 1966 the outer and inner became nothing less than Robinson Crusoe Island and Alejandro Selkirk Island after the Scottish sailor Alexander Selkirk, commonly thought to be the inspiration for the original castaway in Daniel Defoe's bestseller about survival on a desert island.

Selkirk was a buccaneer who in the early 1700s joined the explorations of William

Dampier aboard the vessel *Cinque Ports*. After a number of storms had taken their toll on the fleet, they put in at Juan Fernández to undertake repairs. When Dampier gave the order to set out again, Selkirk was not satisfied of the seaworthiness of the *Cinque Ports* and tried to form a rebellion to stay behind. But none of his crew stood with him and so – more Clouseau than Crusoe – he chose to remain on his own, abandoned in the middle of the Pacific with nothing more than a musket, some gunpowder, a knife, carpenter's tools and a Bible. The original reality TV show. He was convinced that another ship would come by and pick him up, but in the event this took four years. He had to hide from two Spanish ships since, as a Briton and a privateer, he would have been lynched. He was eventually rescued by Captain Woodes Rogers, aboard the *Duke* (coincidentally, the navigator of the *Duke* was William Dampier).

It is Rogers' 1712 account of Selkirk's story of survival – eating goats and living in a hut

made of the local pimento trees – that Defoe appropriated for his novel. He embellished it quite a bit on the way, too. Unlike Selkirk's stay of just four years – a mere weekend – Crusoe was marooned for twenty-eight years. Little description is given to the island; there is no mention of the Antarctic flora of forest ferns, its local species of fur seal, or the local hummingbird, the Juan Fernandez firecrown. In fact, a passage that refers to the island's location at the mouth of the river Orinoco would suggest Defoe's inspiration was more Tobago than La Isla Mas Afuera.

Pirates ruled the waves here for centuries before the islands saw action as a penal colony and then in the First World War with Admiral Spee, who congregated the kaiser's fleet here before crushing the British Navy at Coronel. Above all, though, these islands are interesting for their sheer remoteness and aura of Crusoe that no other island escape can claim.

OPPOSITE San Juan Bautista village

Juan Fernández Islands, Valparaíso, Chile **Local name:** Islas Juan Fernández **Longitude:** 79° 49' W **Latitude:** 33° 42' S **Area:** 181 sq km (70 sq mi) **Highest point:** 1,650 m (5,413 ft) Los Inocentes, Alexander Selkirk Island **Population:** 630 **Principal town:** San Juan Batista, Robinson Crusoe Island **Resident:** Alexander Selkirk

Cayman Islands

CARIBBEAN

"'The bankers here are extremely quiet. They make the Swiss look like blabbermouths.'"

John Grisham, *The Firm*

OPPOSITE A snorkeller holds a conch in the waters of Stingray City

The Caymans are all about bankers, turtles and divers. The bankers created their own financial district in Grand Cayman, the largest of the three Cayman Islands, because of the advantageous taxation arrangements, and the fact that it is a distinctly attractive alternative to Wall Street in the depths of winter.

There has long been an enjoyable legend that the Caymans were granted tax-free status by King George III, when islanders rescued the crew and passengers (including a royal prince) from a shipwreck offshore in 1794. Sadly the truth is more prosaic. When the one-time thriving industry of turtling entered a terminal slump, a change of economy was required, and from the 1960s onwards the provision of financial services was an ideal option. There are over 250 banks licensed on Grand Cayman. Hence the popular image of besuited financiers, clutching briefcases and gabbling into mobile phones, perched on stools in beachside bars alongside the ultra-white sands of Seven Mile Beach.

Thankfully the turtles are still part of the Cayman culture, and the only commercial turtle farm in the world is at North West Point on Grand Cayman. In fact the islands – which nestle in the southern lee of Cuba – were originally called Las Tortugas (the Spanish for "turtles") by Christopher Columbus in 1503.

Their current name is also taken from natural history, courtesy of Sir Francis Drake who, eighty years later, named them after the "caymana" crocodiles he saw there.

Snorkelling and scuba enthusiasts come here for the superb diving in clear waters alongside great vertical walls of coral reef. The Bloody Bay wall on Little Cayman is a mile deep, but its top is only 20 metres (65 feet) from the surface so that even inexperienced divers can float over the drop-off. At Stingray City and the shallower Sandbar off Grand Cayman, hundreds of stingrays come looking for food: on the dive boats the guides dole out handfuls of squid, which surround the snorkellers, in a unique alternative to swimming with the dolphins.

Little Cayman and Cayman Brac are much smaller and quieter than Grand Cayman, which has a noticeably British feel. The islands were ceded to England by Spain in 1670, along with Jamaica, and became a British Overseas Territory in 1962. The island clasps the mangrove-flanked lagoon of North Sound; the capital George Town is on a strip of land between the lagoon and the Caribbean. And just for fun there is Hell, the name of a field of limestone formations by the Grand Cayman town of West Bay, which makes maximum capital out of offering the chance to "send a postcard from Hell".

Cayman Islands, British Overseas Territory **Longitude:** 80° 30' W **Latitude:** 19° 40' N **Area:** 262 sq km (101 sq mi) **Highest point:** 43 m (141 ft) The Bluff, Cayman Brac **Population:** 46,600 **Principal town:** George Town **Resident:** Dick Francis

"I stand on the firm-packed sand.
Free, by a world of marsh that borders a world of sea."

Sidney Lanier, "The Marshes of Glynn"

Golden Isles

ATLANTIC COAST, GEORGIA

Where Georgia squeezes down to the Atlantic coast between South Carolina and Florida, a string of barrier islands run south from the antebellum delights of Savannah towards the alligators lurking in the freshwaters of the Great Okefcnokee Swamp. Of these eleven islands, four are described communally as the Golden Isles of Georgia, a reflection of their once gilt-edged reputation as one of the most exclusive hideaways in America – and outside the United States, the serenity of this world of moss-strewn live oaks, marshy crecks and white beaches, animated by the flash of bluebirds and herons, remains a delicious secret.

The era when the great, good and incredibly rich discovered their delights began in the 1880s. A group of millionaires purchased Jekyll Island and created a club described a couple of decades later as "the richest, most exclusive and most inaccessible club in the world". Jekyll became a playground for the likes of the J. P. Morgans and the Pulitzers, the Rockefellers and Vanderbilts, where they could winter in their elegant "cottages"; these and the grand Jekyll Island Club can now be stayed in by lesser mortals. The club members moved on after the 1940s – allegedly scared off when U-boats sank a number of oil tankers off the Georgia coast, and hysterical rumours spread about saboteurs and assassins being deposited on the island. On Sea Island, two islands to the north, an Ohio car executive, Howard Earle Coffin, had built the Cloister Hotel in 1928. Another top-end destination, it was the location for the G8 summit of 2004.

The largest of the Golden Isles is St Simons, connected to the mainland by a causeway. The original inhabitants, Guale and Mocama Indians, had been turfed off by first Spanish and then British settlers. In 1742 British troops ambushed an invading Spanish force, winning the Battle of Bloody Marsh and guaranteeing British control over Georgia. Along the length of the island are the ruins of the cotton-plantation buildings that they constructed – during this colonial period, John Wesley and his brother Charles, the founders of Methodism, visited as Anglican missionaries. The current religion on St Simons is that of the five-iron: Sea Island Golf Club, opened in 1927, is a star attraction – the seventh hole on its Seaside course was voted by *Golf Digest* one of the world's finest.

Although purists argue that it is technically not one of the Golden Isles, Cumberland Island, south of Jekyll, is a magical garden of magnolias, oaks, pines, salt marshes and dunes, occupied by armadillos, sea turtles, a hundred or so Wildlife Service rangers … and not much else. Cumberland received a brief burst of news coverage in 1996 when John Kennedy Jr married Carolyn Bessette in the log cabin African Baptist Church, with a reception in the local Greyfield Inn. After the guests departed, the armadillos, wild turkey and oystercatchers just carried on where they had left off.

OPPOSITE Sand dunes at Jekyll Island beach

Golden Isles, Georgia, USA **Longitude:** 81° 23' W **Latitude:** 31° 10' N **Area:** 260 sq km (100 sq mi) **Highest point:** 4 m (13 ft) **Population:** 14,400 **Principal town:** St Simons
Natives: Robert S. Abbott, Jim Brown **Residents:** Charles and John Wesley

Key West

FLORIDA KEYS

"It's the best place
I've ever been, anytime,
anywhere, flowers,
tamarind trees, guava
trees, coconut palms."

Ernest Hemingway

The spiny tail of the Florida Keys pokes out into the Caribbean for 200 kilometres (125 miles), its islands like eight hundred mini vertebrae. Key West, the island at their very far end, can consequently claim to be the "southernmost city in the continental United States of America". This sense of being far-flung, but not *too* far, has attracted a wide selection of alternative lifestylers (Key West was one of the first US cities to actively foster gay tourism), who like to group themselves beneath the banner of the self-styled "Conch Republic".

Robert Frost once said of Key West: "What a beautiful island it is. I wish it could be a little more isolated, though." In fact, the island could only be reached by boat until the 1910s, when the Florida Overseas Railroad constructed by Henry Flagler joined it to the mainland. Perhaps surprisingly, despite its previous isolation Key West had already prospered: by the end of the nineteenth century it was the most populated and the wealthiest city in Florida. There had been influxes of immigrants from the Bahamas and Cuba, some of whom had grown rich on the proceeds of cigar-making, salt production and salvage acquired from picking over the carcasses of nearby shipwrecks. Appropriately, the name Key West is most likely to be an Anglicization of *cayo hueso*, the Spanish for "bone key, or island". Its ownership had been somewhat convoluted during the early 1800s, until the US Navy commander Matthew C. Perry physically claimed it for the United States in March 1822.

Key West's grid of laidback streets is an attractive network of cafés, art galleries and shrines to its notable residents. John James Audubon worked on his seminal book *The Birds of America* here; the Little White House was a retreat for Harry S. Truman. The list of writers who have plied their trade on the island is a lengthy one – ranging from poet Richard Wilbur and Pulitzer Prize-winner Alison Lurie to Tennessee Williams. And top of the pile is Ernest Hemingway, who combined the two great Key West traditions of game fishing and writing.

Hemingway spent ten years on the island, mainly at 907 Whitehead Street. He wrote *To Have or Have Not*, and fell for his third wife Martha Gellhorn at Sloppy Joe's, the bar that is still going strong (though it has since moved premises) and sensibly making the most of the Papa Hemingway connection, as does much of Key West. Carl Hiaasen, a resident of Islamorada, back along the keys, has a typical darkly comic view: "Key West trades in on the name 'Hemingway'. You can't take a leak without seeing Hemingway this and Hemingway that. And the irony is, if Hemingway were alive today he'd take a blowtorch to Duval Street...".

OPPOSITE Sunset near Key West

Key West, Florida, USA **Longitude:** 81° 48' W **Latitude:** 24 ° 33' N **Area:** 19 sq km (7 sq mi) **Highest point:** 5 m (16 ft) Solares Hill **Population:** 25,500
Natives: Lincoln Perry aka Stepin Fetchit, David Robinson **Residents:** Elizabeth Bishop, Annie Dillard, Robert Frost, Ernest Hemingway, Alison Lurie, Richard Wilbur, Tennessee Williams

> "Both in space and time, we seem to be brought
> somewhat near to that great fact, that mystery of mysteries,
> the first appearance of new beings on this earth."
>
> Charles Darwin

Galapagos Islands

PACIFIC

Although the Galapagos Islands are still an Eden of ecological delight, the first visitors to this remote archipelago had mixed feelings. A thousand kilometres west of the coast of Ecuador – the country to which they belong – there were never any aboriginal peoples on the islands: the first recorded sighting in 1535 was inadvertent, by Fray Tomás de Berlanga, the Bishop of Panama, who was trying to reach Peru when his ship got blown off course. A relieved crew sighted an island, where they found seals, turtles, iguanas "like serpents", and giant tortoises a man could ride. Subsequent Spanish visitors often referred to the islands as the Islas Encantadas, but the enchantment may have been more evil than beneficent: Herman Melville described them as "five and twenty heaps of cinders".

Charles Darwin, the onboard naturalist of the HMS *Beagle*, arrived in 1835. From then on the extraordinary natural life of these volcanic, relatively barren islands, would get a much wider press. The Galapagos had remained a kind of "evolutionary laboratory" because of both their remoteness and lack of humans – even after being discovered, few were interested in settling here – and climate. The Equator bisects the northern end of the largest of the Galapagos Islands, Isabella or Albemarle (most of the main islands have both Spanish and English names, the latter inherited from buccaneers and explorers). But the effect of the Humboldt current creates a dry, moderate climate, coupled with a marine effect called "upwelling", which pushes rich nutrients to the surface.

The wildlife is extraordinary. There are comedic blue-footed boobies, huge albatrosses and frigate birds, the now-famous finches that helped Darwin form his revolutionary theory of evolution. Little Galapagos penguins potter and dive, the only penguins in the tropics. Giant loggerhead turtles and hammerhead sharks swim offshore. Marine iguanas casually sun themselves on the rocks, completely blasé in the presence of human visitors who they seem to be studying with equal curiosity. And everyone remembers the giant tortoises, lumbering across the landscape like gently perambulating hillocks, including the oldest of the lot, "Lonesome George".

There are many surprises: the realization that the colony of flightless cormorants or algae-grazing iguanas you have just seen is pretty much the entire existing global population, or the fact that there are actually some significant townships on the islands. In fact, the increasing local population, the impact of ever-growing tourist levels, even if they are corralled on to walking routes, and the threat of disease imported by animals smuggled in from the mainland are all cause for concern. If the Galapagos (the name is from the Spanish *galápago*, referring to a "saddle" or "turtle") are to retain their integrity, ensuring a positive balance between human intervention and nature is absolutely critical.

OVERLEAF Craters on Santiago Island, one of the Galapagos Islands

Gálapagos Islands, Ecuador **Alternative names:** Archipiélago de Colón, Islas de Colónumio **Longitude:** 90° 33' W **Latitude:** 0° 40' S **Area:** 7,880 sq km (3,042 sq mi)
Highest point: 1,707 m (5,600 ft) Volcán Wolf, Isabela **Population:** 20,000 **Principal town:** Puerto Ayora, Isla Santa Cruz

Easter Island

SOUTH PACIFIC

The island that Polynesians call Te Pito O Te Henua ("the navel of the world") is often seen as a metaphor for the likely fate of our planet: once a fertile earthly paradise, but abused to such an extent that its inhabitants are being driven to extinction.

The Pacific Ocean's most isolated outpost, Easter Island lies over 3,220 kilometres (2,000 miles) from anywhere and even then the nearest landfall is Tahiti, hardly a hub of civilization

Known by Polynesians as Rapa Nui, meaning "The Great Rapa" after a mythical Tahitian sailor, the island takes its western name from its discovery on Easter Day in 1722 by the Dutch Admiral Jacob Roggeveen, or Isla de

Pascua since its annexation by Chile in 1888. It was inhabited well before then as its famous petroglyphs testify. Who has not wondered at the colossal statues, or *moai*, some three hundred of them discovered scattered around the island's circumference (they were in fact re-erected by archaeologists)? Like sentinels, sphinxes, lighthouses or lorelei they gaze out to sea, omniscient but unseeing, mystical yet questioning; as Neruda put it: "the universal interrogation which passes beyond the limits of the island to the very heart of man and his absence." No one knows the significance of the statues, but they were most likely a symbol of social stature among native families. Nowadays they are so iconic you can buy facsimiles of them on eBay.

The identity of Rapa Nui's early inhabitants has been the subject of hot debate. The veteran Norwegian explorer-cum-raft builder Thor Heyerdahl spent two years on the island in 1955–56 to come to the conclusion (since

disproved) that they were of Peruvian descent. According to his balsawood experiments the Peruvians could have sailed here by raft, and Heyerdahl may have been bewitched by the statues whose strangeness and size is certainly the equal of many Incan structures. At the non-scientific end of the spectrum there is no shortage of purveyors of romantic and science-fiction theories, notably Erich von Däniken, whose novelistic theories on alien links to the *maoi* have all too broad a following. Today, however, the consensus is that an ancient Polynesian people settled here as early as AD 380. They would have found a triangular rock covered in *hauhau* trees, which they cut down to make boats to fish for food. When they ran out of trees they began to eat their animals and eventually, it is thought, each other. At the time of their discovery in 1722 these natives would not have known that other human beings existed and would have been susceptible to imported diseases, which probably finished them off.

"The tremendous, pure heads, long in the jaw and lugubrious, with jawbones of giants, erect in the pride of their solitude – those presences, preoccupied, arrogant presences"

Pablo Neruda, "The Separate Rose"

OPPOSITE Giant *moai* overlooking the ocean

Easter Island, Overseas Territory of Chile **Local names:** Isla de Pascua, Rapa Nui **Longitude:** 109° 23' W **Latitude:** 27° 07' S **Area:** 164 sq km (63 sq mi)
Highest point: 507 m (1663 ft) Maunga Terevaka **Population:** 3,800 **Principal town:** Hanga Roa **Native:** Santi Hito **Resident:** Claudio Cristino

"A long narrow island… It is mountainous
and stands high and sheer from the blue water."

John Steinbeck, *The Log From the "Sea of Cortez"*

Espíritu Santo

SEA OF CORTEZ

John Steinbeck was one of the earliest ecotourists to land on the island of Espíritu Santo. Marine biology was one of the novelist's passions, and he was great friends with Ed Ricketts, a biologist and ecologist (who was also the inspiration for the character Doc in Steinbeck's *Cannery Row*). Together they undertook a six-week journey in 1940 around the Gulf of California, also known as the Sea of Cortez – that long spindly bay between mainland Mexico and Baja California – looking for specimens.

The Isla Espíritu Santo lies towards the southern end of Baja California, and Steinbeck later wrote that he and Ed Ricketts had stopped off on the island to contrast the fauna there with a secluded bay near the seaside town of La Paz on the mainland: they lifted boulders, caked in seaweed, to reveal a profusion of the greenish-yellow sea cucumbers and giant brittle stars they were particularly interested in.

The marine life they uncovered was but one tiny part of a wonderful though fragile ecosystem located on and around the island. The great Jacques Cousteau described the Sea of Cortez as "the world's greatest aquarium" because of the number of species it contains. Espíritu Santo – with a mix of canyons, coves, tropical and arid forest, mangrove lagoons, and desert scrub populated by rare cacti – was acquired in 2003 by the Mexican government, with the assistance of international conservation bodies, to preserve the island's ecology and to protect it from the possibility of development.

Their intervention has ensured that Espíritu Santo is as it has always been – no marinas, no hotels, just a few campsites where groups of the eco- and island-friendly can stay and commune with nature. There is a blend here of the natural and the spiritual, and it is no surprise to learn that some of the trips on offer combine the physical (a course in sea kayaking) with the transcendent (daily yoga practice). The wildlife is the biggest draw: the opportunity to join sealion pups for a swim, to see manta rays close up, to view the island's endemic animals, including the black-tailed jack rabbit and ground squirrel. There are quirky, spiky boojum trees (an English name taken from Lewis Carroll's "The Hunting of the Snark"), and tall, ribbed cardon cacti, on top of which perch turkey vultures.

There are even beaches. One, Ensenada Grande, on Isla Partida – the neighbouring lump of land attached to Espíritu Santo by an isthmus at low tide – was voted one of the world's best beaches in 2007 by *The Travel Magazine*: the nomination described the waters around Espíritu Santo in a memorably islomaniac phrase: "so turquoise it's like swimming in a bottle of Curaçao".

OPPOSITE Boojum tree

Isla Espíritu Santo, Baja California Sur, Mexico **Longitude:** 110° 20' W **Latitude:** 24° 28' N **Area:** 81 sq km (31 sq mi) **Population:** None

Santa Catalina

PACIFIC COAST, CALIFORNIA

"Twenty-six miles out across the sea, Santa Catalina is a-waitin' for me, Santa Catalina, the island of romance."

Glen Larson and Bruce Belland, "26 Miles"

"26 Miles (Santa Catalina)" was the B-side of a single released in 1957 by the Four Preps, a clean-cut vocal harmony group. Its lyrics, about the "tropical trees" and "salty air" of Santa Catalina, the island closest to metropolitan Los Angeles, helped the record reach Number 2 on the US charts and reminded Californians of a certain age of the island's heyday in the 1920s and 1930s.

There are eight Channel Islands off the coastline of California, four bunched together close to Santa Barbara, the others, including Santa Catalina, the only inhabited island of the eight, scattered erratically further south. Facing the Palos Verdes peninsula, south of the great beaches of LA, Santa Catalina was home to Pimuvit natives when Juan Rodríguez Cabrillo arrived in 1542, claiming the island for Spain and naming it San Salvador after his ship; sixty years later he was followed by Sebastián Viscaino, who renamed it after Saint Catherine.

But neither explorer stayed. Santa Catalina became a haven for smugglers as the island was incorporated first into Mexico and then the United States, later passing through the hands of a variety of owner/developers. A couple of them tried to turn the island into a Mediterranean-style resort, and the sister of one plucked the name Avalon from Tennyson's Arthurian poems for the main town. But it was not until William Wrigley Jr, of the chewing-gum family, bought Santa Catalina in 1919 that there was a serious upturn in interest. The island became a popular location with Hollywood directors. Steamships brought film stars of the era to Wrigley's gorgeous circular Art Deco Casino in Avalon, the island's main landmark, not a gambling place, but a high-ceilinged, Tiffany-chandeliered ballroom and luxurious cinema. Both are still in use and, with the nearby pleasure pier and mosaic-covered fountain, and some old-style ice-cream parlours, give Avalon a period, slightly faded, feel.

Santa Catalina, California, USA **Alternative name:** Catalina Island, Catalina **Longitude:** 118° 25' W **Latitude:** 33° 23' N **Area:** 192 sq km (74 sq mi) **Highest point:** 648 m (2,126 ft) Mt Orizaba
Population: 3,700 **Principal town:** Avalon **Native:** Gregory Harrison **Residents:** Zane Grey, Tom Mix, Marilyn Monroe, William Wrigley Jr

Santa Catalina – locally known simply as Catalina – is a weekend (and a world) away from LA, with little traffic, rocky peaks and a nature conservancy covering much of the island, containing rare foxes, reintroduced bald eagles and, in a very Hollywood twist, the descendants of a herd of bison introduced for the movie *The Vanishing American*, written by sometime resident Zane Grey. Offshore glass-bottomed boats make the most of the clear waters (in which, alas, Natalie Wood drowned in 1981) where forests of giant kelp rise 30 metres (100 feet) or more from the sandy sea floor and at night phosphorescent flying fish take flight.

William Wrigley also owned the Chicago Cubs and newsreels of them at spring training on Santa Catalina were one memory that Bruce Belland of the Four Preps drew on for the lyrics to "26 Miles". As Belland pointed out, the distance from the island to LA is actually only 22.3 miles, but it just didn't scan…

ABOVE Buffalo grazing on the island

TOP Avalon Harbor and Casino

Alcatraz
SAN FRANCISCO BAY

"Cold steamy air blew in
through two open windows,
bringing with it half a dozen times
the Alcatraz foghorn's dull moaning."

Dashiell Hammett, *The Maltese Falcon*

The power of Alcatraz is proof of the glamour that pop culture has bestowed upon the underworld and in particular the gangster Prohibition era. Alcatraz the island is inseparable from Alcatraz the prison and, most famously, guardian of America's number-one gangster icon, one-time furniture dealer and inmate number AZ85, Alphonse "Scarface" Capone.

A Hollywood prison, Alcatraz is where gangland meets the movies. Known by inmates as "the Rock" the name Alcatraz is appropriately exotic, lazy and cool. It would sit well in the mouth of a De Niro. In fact the name refers to one of the island's former natural attractions. In 1775 a passing Spanish Lieutenant, Juan Manual de Ayala, was struck by the large number of pelicans that had colonized the island and so christened it "isla de los alcatraces" after the Spanish word for "pelican". More than a hundred years later, in 1934, the island became a maximum-security roost for another sort of bird, among them jailbirds Robert "Birdman" Stroud and George "Machine Gun" Kelly. Before that the island hosted the West Coast's first lighthouse before becoming the first American coastal fortress, initially built to guard San Francisco's gold-rush riches. Alcatraz then saw action in the American Civil War but only the prison's former powerhouse building, which was adapted from the north battery remains. In fact Alcatraz island was heavily re-sculpted, as the design for the prison took shape and subsequently evolved. It is hard to believe it was originally a humpbacked landmass.

Alcatraz's history does not finish with the prison's closure by Attorney General Robert F. Kennedy in 1963 – an event that was, for those prison workers and families who had been brought up there, like shutting down their country. In 1969 the island was colonized by a group of Indians under the leadership of a Mohawk, Richard Oaks, campaigning for Indian land rights. After two years of physical and political resistance they were evicted – but not before President Nixon had made significant concessions to the First Nations Indian community in America.

Millions of tourists each year take the launch across the bay to Alcatraz, seduced by the island's battleship profile, the echo of its infamous inhabitants and its legendary impenetrable security. Warden James A. Johnston's proud introductory phrase to new inmates was: "None has ever escaped from Alcatraz and none ever will." Out of fourteen documented escape attempts involving thirty-six men, only five are unaccounted for, including Frank Morris. All of these (unless you are Clint Eastwood in the 1979 movie *Escape From Alcatraz*), are presumed to have drowned in the bay's freezing waters and treacherous tidal pools.

Alcatraz's twenty-five acres are now a National Park and far more profitable for its ex-prison chic than as a functioning prison. Every July it even hosts an aquathlon, where swimmers pit themselves against the waters in the breaststrokes of the criminals who went before them; whether this takes place in mockery or in tribute is not clear.

Alcatraz, San Francisco, California, USA **Longitude:** 122° 25' W **Latitude:** 37° 50' N **Area:** 8 hectares (20 acres) **Highest point:** 40 m (130 ft) **Population:** None **Residents:** Clarence and John Algren, Arthur "Doc" Barker, James "Whitey" Bulger, Al Capone, Clarence Carnes (The Choctaw Kid), Meyer "Mickey" Cohen, Philip Grosser, Ellsworth "Bumpy" Johnson, Alvon "Creepy" Karvis, George "Machine Gun" Kelly, Frank Morris, Robert Stroud (the Birdman of Alcatraz)

Vancouver Island

NORTH PACIFIC

"I love being on
Vancouver Island.
Of all the places
I've travelled,
I still feel it's the most
beautiful place
I have ever been.
I still need to go
home and walk in
the woods and be
in the mountains."

Diana Krall, singer

Although sharing its name with the city in whose harbour mouth its southern tip begins, Vancouver Island is not just some weekend, outdoor and offshore retreat for Canada's West Coast city slickers. It is an island-world apart – and a huge one at that – with a paradoxical universe, capital and distinct identity all its own.

Shaped like one of the grey whale mothers that migrate past its western shores, calf in tow and in fear of attack from raiding orcas, Vancouver Island is at once an eco-reserve and a centre for logging. Part of the wet and rugged mountainous west coast is cordoned off as the Pacific Rim National Park, home to the island's dense population of cougars and black bears, gravel rivers full of Pacific salmon and steelhead, and old-growth forests of some of British Columbia's most signatory trees: the Douglas Fir, the red and yellow cedar, oak and maple, and hemlock, huckleberry and blueberry bushes. Many of these towering, thick Ozymandian trunks are half as old as time, while others lie blanched like the skeletons and carcasses of dinosaurs, felled by the wind and broken by the pacific rollers that pummel the golden western sands. Storm-watching is a local sport on Vancouver Island, especially at the Wickanninish Inn on the point of Chesterman beach or further north from the bohemian artists colony and surf and kayaking summer resort of Tofino on the Clayoquot Sound.

Yet nearby, daily, old and new trees are being felled for the paper and pulp industries, the older wood prized for its higher quality timber. Logging and matters ecological are the subject of huge debate and tension on the island, appropriate for the city of Vancouver where the Greenpeace movement was born. But it is a debate between a modern ecological sensitivity and an old nation whose tradition is built on the exploitation of nature, be it furs or fir trees.

As garrisons on the fringes of so much mountain and forest sit a number of settlements. On the east coast, facing inland, is the lively if surreal town and BC Ferries port of Nanaimo, famed for its watering holes, music heritage and the curious sport of bathtub racing that has earned the place the nickname "Hub, Tub and Pub City".

Meanwhile the island's capital, Victoria, on the southern point and all navy-spruce white verandas, tea shops and flowers (and monuments to Her Highness), is a quaint, model-village version of imagined Victorian English life straight out of Miss Marple, but with seaplanes constantly landing and taking off to add a spot of local frontier flavour. The creation of this capital is an act of nostalgia, looking back with the ordered mind and clean lines of hindsight at the British beginnings of the Canadian nation – Captain Vancouver was a midshipman in Captain Cook's fleet when he claimed the island for the Crown in 1778. But in its artifice it is, ironically, the antithesis of the jumbled, musty attic of St John's over the other side on Newfoundland where the British-Canadian story really began.

OPPOSITE A kayaker close to a killer whale

OVERLEAF Clayoquot Sound

Vancouver Island, British Columbia, Canada **Longitude:** 125° 57' W **Latitude:** 49° 57' N **Area:** 31,285 sq km (12,076 sq mi) **Highest point:** 2,200 m (7,218 ft) Golden Hinde **Population:** 734,900 **Principal town:** Victoria **Natives:** Pamela Anderson, Cameron Bright, Anne Cameron, Emily Carr, Nelly Furtado, Diana Krall, Lynn Patrick **Residents:** Jennie Butchart, Kim Cattrall, Elvis Costello, Atom Egoyan, Robert Dunsmuir

"It is a matter of supernatural indifference to me
whether you contaminate the natives, or
the natives contaminate you."

Captain Bligh in *The Mutiny on the Bounty*

Pitcairn

SOUTH PACIFIC

The name and fame of Pitcairn has a unique mystique and romance; a vague sense of a tropical desert-island idyll discovered by swashbuckling rebel adventurers who settled it to found a Utopian mixed-race society. It is one of the famous stories in maritime history: the year is 1790 and the HMS *Bounty* is under the command of Captain Bligh, pushing his underfed and under-resourced crew to the limits to speed their trans-Pacific voyage home. The crew, led by Fletcher Christian, form a mutiny and together with a group of Tahitian men and women they have picked up en route, cast off their captain and escape to the isolated rock of Pitcairn. Here they set fire to the *Bounty*. Over centuries they form a close, interbred society and dialect all their own.

Nowadays, for all the passing cruise tourists in thrall to the story, Pitcairn (named after the midshipman Robert Pitcairn, who first sighted the island in 1767) is perhaps also a prisoner and victim of its own bizarre origins. In the twenty-first century human life on the island has been analyzed like some zoological experiment. With virtually no new arrivals in two centuries, modern Pitcairners are essentially all descendants of the original settlers. Steve Christian, the island's lord and mayor, is a direct descendant of Fletcher Christian himself – and this, an uncomplicated lifestyle, combined with physical Polynesian values where girls are deemed to have reached maturity as early as ten or eleven, means that what the Western world calls adultery, incest and under-age sex had become commonplace. In the words of Christian's wife, Olive: "We thought sex was like food at the table – it's hot stuff."

This is the last British territory in the Pacific, though – a colony since 1838 – and thus answerable to the very long arm of British law.

In 2004 Christian and several other central male figures in the Pitcairn community found themselves in the dock facing 96 charges of rape and sexual abuse dating back to the 1960s. Judges and a whole court were flown in from French Polynesia, and Christian and the others were convicted. But most of the close-knit though feuding islanders viewed this intervention as an invasion of their privacy, claiming that it was a family matter. Christian is still revered as the *de facto* king of this bizarre island kingdom. It is ironic that Marlon Brando, who played Bligh in the memorable film of the story, ended up marrying the lead Tahitian actress.

The reality of this metaphor for paradise is somewhat different, although some lateral thinking may be required. Pitcairn is more *Lord of the Flies* or the latest reality TV show. Visitors who climb the Hill of Difficulty up to the settlement of Adamstown above Bounty Bay (where the wreck of the ship was discovered in 1957) will find a solitary palm tree – no beaches or coral reefs, no sewerage or phone reception and one shop which opens for an hour three times a week. As the famous anthropologist Desmond Morris put it: "There's virtually nothing to do. They fish and get food and sing songs and have sex."

BELOW The island descendants of *Bounty* commemorate this famous English ship each year

Pitcairn, Pitcairn Islands, British Overseas Territory **Longitude:** 130° 06' W **Latitude:** 25° 04' S **Area:** 5 sq km (2 sq mi) **Highest point:** 347 m (1,138 ft) Goathouse Peak **Population:** 50
Principal settlement: Adamstown **Residents:** John Adams, William Brown, Fletcher Christian, William McCoy, Isaac Martin, John Mills, Matthew Quintal, John Williams, Ned Young

"The cloudless days are calm, pearl-grey and brooding in tone. The islands seem to drowse and float on the glassy water."

John Muir, "Wrangell Island and Alaska Summers"

Wrangell Island

NORTH PACIFIC

There is plenty of room for confusion when it comes to Wrangell Island – part of Alaska, and hence the United States – because there is also a Wrangel Island (spelt with only one l) which is part of Russia. Both, just to add to the potential for a mix-up, are named after the same person: Baron Ferdinand von Wrangel, a nineteenth-century Estonian-born Russian explorer and admiral.

Thankfully these two islands are at least a couple of thousand kilometres apart: the Russian island languishing in the freezing Arctic seas north of the Chukchi Peninsula in Siberia, its American cousin located in the middle of the Alexander Archipelago, which hugs the panhandle of Alaska as it runs south alongside British Columbia.

Wrangell has become a destination island as a stepping stone to the wild and remote landscape of the Tongass National Forest, seen as one of the great final frontiers. The United States bought Alaska from Russia in 1867; Baron Ferdinand had been Russia's governor in the area during the early 1830s. He was fiercely opposed to any sale of this vast area, with its plentiful natural resources, but eventually – for $7.2 million – Russia preferred to take the money to prevent the danger of Great Britain, its main rival in the Pacific, acquiring the territory by force.

There was gold in these parts. The 1890s rush to Klondike in the Yukon is one of the best known, but thirty-five years earlier there had been similar excitement about the Stikine River, which emerges from the mainland near Wrangell Island. A prospector called Alexander "Buck" Choquette struck lucky in 1861. Fort Wrangell, previously a tiny fur-trading settlement, was transformed into a boomtown, steamboats were commissioned to deliver supplies, and canoes steered by local Tlingit guides brought the miners to the goldfields on the Stikine. When the furore moved on to the Klondike, Wrangell was still able to join in by offering itself as a safe way to get there (this was a somewhat overinflated piece of self-publicity by the Wrangell inhabitants).

The gold rush has subsided, but there are still garnets to be found in the Stikine River, a majestic, blue-green, glacial body of water. And Fort Wrangell, now called Wrangell City, has retained something of that frontiersman feel as a base for rafting or kayaking journeys, or a stop off for naturalists on the trail of the great blue herons that gather in the Zinovia Strait separating Wrangell from Etolin Island to the west. There are also strong traces of Tlingit culture – literally, as you can take rubbings from images of owls and whales etched into boulders at Petroglyph Beach just near the township, where there are copses of ornately carved totems.

Wrangell Island, Alaska, USA **Longitude:** 132º 33' W **Latitude:** 56º 28' N **Area:** 544 sq km (210 sq mi) **Population:** 2,400 **Principal town:** Wrangell City

Tahiti

WINDWARD ISLANDS, SOUTH PACIFIC

"Tahiti accepts France's adoration with a slight yawn and with the bored air of a great and spoiled beauty."

George Mikes, writer

Tahiti has become a word that single-handedly suggests a particular kind of South Pacific exoticism, the island, in Charles Darwin's phrase, "to which every voyager has offered up his tribute of imagination". The images it summons up are an amalgam of beautiful flower-bedecked, hip swaying dancers, racing canoes, sumptuous fruit and a languidly erotic freedom; much of that is still on view, especially for the tourist trade, though there are those who consider that the Polynesian fantasy the island offers is nothing more than a Disney-like mirage. This is not the real Tahiti, they say. To discover that you must flee the hotels and the bars of the capital Papeete, leave behind the ukuleles, black-pearl vendors and garlands of *tiare* flowers and flee to the volcanic mountains at its centre.

Tahiti is the largest – and the most populous – island in sprawling French Polynesia, one of the Society Islands, halfway between California and Australia; it is formed from two islands joined by a narrow isthmus. The interior of the main island, Tahiti Nui, is dominated by the peaks of Mount Orohena (2,241 metres/7,352 feet) and her only slightly less towering sister, Aorai. Up in these lush heights, among waterfalls and grottos, in the valley of the Papenoo River are the settlements that existed before Europeans arrived, with its relics of the ancient Polynesian religion.

As well as its inner beauty and coastal charms – the less-visited south around Teahupoo, on the smaller Tahiti Iti, is a favourite with surfers – Tahiti is a starting point for outward exploration to the French Polynesian islands, especially the honeymooner favourites of Moorea, Raiatea or Bora Bora. They are best visited by yacht or local boat, as did in times past Robert Louis Stevenson, Herman Melville and W. Somerset Maugham. The first European to visit these parts was the Englishman Samuel Wallis in 1767. French explorer Louis Antoine de Bougainville (of bougainvillea immortality) was a close second the following year.

The reports that they sent back to Europe created a favourable impression of paradise on Earth: an extremely pleasant climate; noble, good-looking islanders; no diseases. No coincidence that when the HMS *Bounty* left the island, the crew promptly mutinied.

Of all the foreign visitors Paul Gauguin was the most notorious, a purveyor of the idyll, even though he saw that by the time he came to Tahiti in 1891 the colonial influence of the West was already taking hold: the French wrested control in the mid-1800s (Tahiti is still a semi-autonomous French territory). Gauguin seemed to believe his own myth – fathering a child by a local teenage concubine-muse – and his mythmaking lives on. Rupert Brooke, though, affected comic outrage at his paintings: "Gauguin *grossly* maligned these ladies," he wrote. "Oh, I know all about expressing their primitive souls by making their bodies squat and square. But it's blasphemy."

Tahiti, French Polynesia, Collectivité d'Outre Mer, France **Longitude:** 149° 27' W **Latitude:** 17° 37' S **Area:** 1043 sq km (403 sq mi) **Highest point:** 2241 m (7352 ft) Mt Orohena

Population: 178,100 **Principal town:** Papeete Residents: Jacques Boullaire, Paul Gauguin, James Norman Hall, Bobby Holcomb, François Ravello, Victor Segalen

Bora Bora

LEEWARD ISLANDS, SOUTH PACIFIC

Bora Bora is the geological equivalent of Winston Churchill's riddle wrapped in a mystery inside an enigma. At the island's heart are jungle-clad peaks, the legacy of an extinct volcano. Around them are the blue waters of a lagoon, dotted with islets, ringed in turn by a palm-fringed outer circle of coral reefs – one of the best ways to see the island is from a helicopter. An emerald, Bora Bora is called, set in turquoise, one of the world's most famous islands and high on the list of destinations for honeymooners of the celebrity, well-heeled or starry-eyed variety (or all three): Nicole Kidman and Keith Urban, and Ashiwarya Rai and Abishek Bachchan just two of the couples who have chosen it as a post-nuptial destination.

The natural beauty of Bora Bora, which lies in the Leeward group of the French Polynesian islands, lives up to the hype. James Michener considered it the most beautiful island he had ever seen. The three mountains – Hue, Pahia and the highest, Otemanu – are lofty turrets keeping guard over the aquamarine lagoon below. The water over which the resort bungalows hover is crystal clear, an underwater photographer's paradise. Onshore, hibiscus, plumeria and gardenia add their own splashes of colour to the palette on display.

For many people, simply being on Bora Bora is enough, and they feel little need to do much else than salve their souls with a little R&R soothed by the clement, cooling trade winds. The more active can take a motorized outrigger canoe into the heart of the lagoon to look for sharks and stingrays, or watch the annual Hawaiki Nui Va'a open-ocean canoe races. Since the main road around the island is only 25 kilometres (15 miles) or so, a cycle ride is a carbon-neutral option: there are coconut plantations to visit as well as the ancient *marae* temples and Ofai Honu, a carved turtle stone that local legend claims mated with a nearby cliff and produced the island's first chief. The "guns of Bora Bora" are the rusting, left-over cannon from the US Army's stay in the Second World War; the rumour is that when peace came, some soldiers had to be forcibly repatriated.

The continuing construction of resort hotels – even when designed with impeccable taste – has put a strain on the island's resources, especially its water supply. Travellers who came before the rush (Captain James Cook was the first westerner to set foot on Bora Bora in 1777) fear that the quest for money, especially the American dollar, may harden the attitude of the locals even though the tourism provides them with regular work. Even paradise has a downside.

OPPOSITE Green sea turtles

OVERLEAF A reef circles the island, with Mount Otemanu in the centre

Bora Bora, French Polynesia, Collectivité d'Outre Mer, France **Longitude:** 151° 45' W **Latitude:** 16° 30' S **Area:** 40 sq km (15 sq mi) **Highest point:** 727 m (2,385 ft) Mt Otemanu **Population:** 8,800 **Principal settlement:** Vaitape

"So stunning,
there are really no adequate words
to describe it."

James A. Michener

Kodiak

GULF OF ALASKA

Kodiak is the name of an archipelago – an archipelago that, joined with the rest of the Aleutian chain, stretches in a necklace all the way across the sub-Arctic north Pacific Gulf of Alaska, as far as the evocative Russian peninsula of Kamchatka. It is also the name of an island – an island in terms of Alaskan scale but a landmass the size of which might elsewhere qualify as a nation. It is also the name of the resident endemic beast and lord of the island – the great Kodiak brown bear.

Most people come here to enjoy a Kodak moment – to snap one of the largest and most impressive land mammals on Earth, 3 metres (10 feet) tall when standing. But some come to shoot them not with a camera but with a gun, paying anything up to fifteen thousand dollars for the dubious honour. These magnificent beasts have long had a bounty on their heads, eliminated as a form of pest control and sought after for their pelts and as trophies. It was hardly a level playing field, with hunters and poachers taking to the air to shoot them lest they be mauled in a confrontation on the ground. Happily, bear control ended in 1960 since when, with the establishment of the Kodiak National Island Refuge in the southwest, the population has thrived with only limited and controlled hunting allowed. The figure is supposed to be 160 per year, and mostly male bears. For those who have never had the privilege of setting eyes on a Kodiak bear, though, this is 160 too many.

Since the first Russian explorers arrived here with Grigory Shelikov, Kodiak the island has been a hunter's land for bears and man alike. Both are drawn to and compete for the king and silver salmon that run in Kodiak's big rivers, notably the Karluk and Ayakulik and the gravelly bays and sounds, including Ugak and Three Saints Bay. Following the Alaska Purchase of 1867, in which the island passed to Alaskan control, sitka deer and snowshoe hare have been imported for the enjoyment of hunters, and they can be spotted frolicking nervously in the heavily forested north and treeless southern plains of the island. The other native Kodiak animal – and altogether more prickly adversary (and delicacy) – is the king crab, a curious asymmetrical derivative of the hermit crab.

Like much of Alaska, Kodiak is not man's dominion, and any settlement is something of a frontier post or garrison. What urban life exists here centres around Kodiak town. There is no need for another name. The First Nation natives for whom the island is ancestral home were the Koniaga, who – fittingly for an island of evolutionary offshoots – became known for their practice of bringing the most handsome male offspring up as concubines to be married to wealthy men as companions. It seems a curiously effeminate practice in a land of such ursine strength.

Kodiak, Alaska, USA **Longitude:** 152° 45' W **Latitude:** 57° 30' N **Area:** 9,293 sq km (3,588 sq mi) **Highest point:** 2,047m (6,716 ft) Mt Katmai **Population:** 13,500 **Principal town:** Kodiak **Native:** Jason Everman

"A reader shouldn't be surprised that I describe Kodiak as the finest place where thousands of pleasures would wait for us. It's unpleasant to be in a sea in cold autumn and to fight with winds and waves incessantly. At last you get so bored that even the most desert and wildest island will seem paradise."

Nikolai Resanov, Russian explorer

ABOVE An old Russian Orthodox church near Karluk lagoon

LEFT Kodiak brown bear

"The trembling blue plane of the Pacific.
The moss-covered cliffs and the cool rush
of Manoa Falls, with its ginger blossoms and
high canopies filled with the sound of
invisible birds. The North Shore's thunderous
waves, crumbling as if in a slow-motion reel.
The shadows off Pali's Peaks; the sultry,
scented air."

Barack Obama, *Dreams of My Father*

Hawaii

HAWAIIAN ISLANDS, NORTH PACIFIC

Hawaii is a state of mind, a lifestyle, and of course a style of shirt. Breezy, alternative and laid-back to horizontal, when we think of chucking it all in and beginning another, more stress-free life it is to an imagined Hawaii and its beach life that our mind wanders. And for those moments when we want to express the bright, hula-dancing party side of life – or simply dress up as Magnum PI (minus the Ferrari and moustache) – most of us call on the trusty *aloha* shirt in our wardrobe, the parrot-patterned garment sporting Polynesian motifs, first sold by an enterprising Chinese merchant in 1930s Waikiki.

Hawaii is also a state of America – the southernmost and fiftieth state, as in the title of the long-running detective series, *Hawaii Five O*; an archipelago of many hundred islands spread out over 2,400 kilometres (1,500 miles) and, after Easter Island, the furthest from any landmass in the world; and the name of an individual island, otherwise known as "the Big Isle".

Today, parts of Hawaii are definitely an island-world of wraparound shades sponsored by Burton, O'Neill and Sex Wax. But "Owyhee", meaning "homeland" in the Polynesian vernacular, is also an archipelago with a history and culture all of its own. Captain Cook and his crew were the first Europeans the natives saw, in 1778. Cook named these volcanic lands the Sandwich Islands after his patron the 4th Earl of Sandwich. It was here also that he met his maker. Just decades later a dynasty arose that would make Hawaii a kingdom. Under British "protection" the Kings Kamehameha ruled Hawaii for most of the nineteenth century.

Remarks of surfing can be found in Cook's reports of his time on Hawaii, and it is clear that as a means of transport it was already then part of the Hawaiian way of life. Here all forms of boat or canoe are sacred to an isolated people who arrived by, depended on and consequently worship the three "w"s – wind, waves and wings. It was not until the 1930s that it became a sport for the masses, with Duke Kahanamoku widely considered as its original dude.

The British influence subsists in the flag and elements of the Creole pidgin – the prefix "auntie" or "uncle" is used to denote a friend – much of which has also found its way into surf slang. But Hawaii rapidly transformed itself like no other isolated spot, moving on from trade in sandalwood, sugar and fruit to carve its way into the twentieth century on a Pacific breaker of tourism. Filmmakers such as Steven Spielberg love Hawaii for its Jurassic landscape of volcanoes – some of them still smoking – and lush, shampoo-advert valleys dripping with flowers and waterfalls. Mauna Kea is from its base on the sea floor to summit the tallest mountain in the world.

But most people come to Hawaii as if to a glade in the forest of their urban mind, to find the sun within and do very little at all except kick back and, where it might raise an eyebrow elsewhere, pull on that flowery shirt with comfort and impunity.

Hawaii, Hawaii, USA **Alternative name:** The Big Island **Longitude:** 155° 30' W **Latitude:** 19° 30' N **Area:** 10,433 sq km (4,027 sq mi) **Highest point:** 4,205 m (13,795 ft) Mauna Kea
Population: 148,700 **Principal town:** Hilo **Natives:** Rodney A. Anoa'i aka Yokozuna, Kamehameha the Great, Robert Kiyosaki, Bob Shane **Resident:** Keiko Bonk

Maui

HAWAIIAN ISLANDS, NORTH PACIFIC

When King Kamehameha I stood upon the heights of Maui and watched the masts of Captain Cook's ships approach in 1778, two worlds were about to irrevocably collide and a new Western voice would be added to the oral history of Maui, the *mele* that preserved the lore and legend of the island.

The most elemental of all the traditional tales related how Maui, an adventurous deity – the island is the only one of the Hawaiian chain named after a Polynesian god – created the islands by hoisting them from the sea bed via a rope-and-pulley system suspended from the heavens (geologists may interrupt at this point to murmur that Maui is the top layer of magma piled up on the ocean floor). The god decided that the sun was passing too quickly overhead and slowed it down with a web of ropes: the volcano that forms the immense main bulk of the island, Haleakala, means "House of the Sun".

Maui is the second largest and most elemental of the Hawaiian islands, two landmasses joined by a lava isthmus, and consequently known as the "valley island". Although surfing, diving – and most recently kite-surfing – are all part of its culture, the natural world is Maui's strongest calling card. Haleakala itself, which forms eastern Maui in its entirety, is one of the largest dormant volcanoes on the planet, with a vast array of terrains and climates.

The top of Haleakala, 3,055 metres (10,023 feet) high, is a popular destination for those *malihini*, or guests, prepared to rise early enough to catch the sunrise. If they look down into the volcano's crater, they will see lashings of the sunflower-related silversword (probably even more characteristic of Maui than the *lokelani* rose, the island's official flower), and a landscape barren enough to have been used by the moon-landing astronauts for a practice run. Rising from Pai'a is the Hana Highway, a testing and exhilarating drive winding up around Haleakala via hairpin bends and narrow bridges.

The smaller nodule of Maui, West Maui, is less dramatic, but can offer the attractions of Lahaina. Whereas the island's main towns of Wailuku and Kahului have a little too much of the condo and mall, Lahaina has a relaxed bohemian air, with a boardwalk, bars and art galleries, and an ancient banyan tree. The town was once the playground of Maui's royalty, many of whom are buried in the deeply revered Wainee cemetery. The *nene* or Hawaiian goose, the state bird, is notoriously shy, but offshore from Lahaina there is an annual arrival of less-retiring humpback whales, here to breed during the winter months. A classic T-shirt reads "Don't hassle the humpbacks", a slogan that could apply equally to the twin volcanic humps of Maui.

"Aloha – love,
I love you,
my love to you.
It is a positive
affirmation of the
warmth of one's
own heart-giving."

Jack London

OPPOSITE Humpback whale

Maui, Hawaii, USA **Longitude:** 156° 20' W **Latitude:** 20° 48' S **Area:** 1,888 sq km (729 sq mi) **Highest point:** 3,055 m (10,023 ft) Haleakala **Population:** 118,000 **Principal town:** Kahului
Natives: Richard and Sol Ho'opii **Resident:** W..S. Merwin

"If more politicians were surfers
then we'd have a cleaner and better world."

Kelly Slater

Oahu

HAWAIIAN ISLANDS, NORTH PACIFIC

f the state of Hawaii is the home of surfing and beach life, then its third largest island, Oahu, is its epicentre. Gilding the edges of this small volcanic rock lie some of the most famous and evocative stretches of sand in the world. In the Hall of Fame of world beaches Waikiki, whose name means "sprouting water" on account of the natural springs that once rose here, is right up there with Bondi and Copacabana. As the comedian Ken Dodd once joked: "Honolulu – it's got everything. Sand for the children, sun for the wife sharks for the wife's mother..."

Crowned by the volcanic crater of Diamond Head, the island and state capital's answer to Rio's Sugar Loaf, Waikiki bends round the coast in front of the capital city with the name that suggests that surely life can't be taken too seriously – Honolulu. It was here that King Kamehameha III of Hawaii moved his country's capital in 1845, and his magnificent 'Iolani royal palace still stands as the only royal building on American soil. The seafront had become tatty over the years but has recently been given a facelift much like many of the sun-worn residents of a town where a tuck might equally be a term used by surfers or plastic surgeons.

As much as Waikiki is famous, it is a sedentary urban beach in front of an urban sprawl of hotels. It is round to the relative wilderness of North Shore that, by common consent the world's best surfer, Kelly Slater and disciples flock for Hawaii's national sport. Here

at Pipeline Beach, "the yardstick by which all breaks are measured", surfers with eyes creased and deep set from watching for waves, tackle the most challenging and consistent waves on Earth. Meanwhile, under the trees on Sunset Beach next door, other dudes and their entourages might gather round with a ukulele or guitar and enjoy a picnic and piña colada sundowner.

As much as Hawaii represents the lighter side of life, Oahu was also the scene of one of America's darkest moments. Here, on the morning of 7 December 1941, the Japanese imperial forces launched a surprise attack on the US fleet moored in Pearl Harbor, killing over two thousand soldiers and many civilians, and formally levered the United States into the Second World War.

Oahu's sunny disposition and coastal life could conceal the wondrous landscape of lush forested mountains set out in two parallel spines that define its relief and are laced with waterfalls and teeming with exotic wildlife. It is a landscape some locals (many of them surfers like Jack Johnson, the stormrider turned folk singer) are concerned for and actively, through founding their own environment foundations, seek to protect from overdevelopment. The island's natural features have played a starring role in many feature films and television series, including, in the Ka'a'wa Valley, a part as the unnerving home for the passengers of the fictional Oceanic flight 815, which "crashed" on Mokuleia beach west of North Shore. There are far worse places to be "lost".

OPPOSITE Surfers at Waimea Bay

ABOVE Diamond Head

Oahu, Hawaii, USA **Local name:** O'ahu **Longitude:** 157° 58' W **Latitude:** 21° 28' N **Area:** 1,545 sq km (596 sq mi) **Highest point:** 1,225 m (4,020 ft) Mt Ka'ala **Population:** 876,100
Principal town: Honolulu **Natives:** Hiram Bingham, Tia Carrere, Yvonne Elliman, Jack Johnson, Israel 'Iz' Kamakawiwo'ole, Joseph Kekuku, Nicole Kidman, Konishiki aka the Dumptruck, King Ben Nawahi, Barack Obama, Maggie Q, Michelle Wie **Residents:** Marie Helvin, Dwayne Johnson aka The Rock, Ray Kane, Jack Lord, Ferdinand Marcos, Bette Midler, Tau Moe, Sun Yat-Sen

Cook Islands

SOUTH PACIFIC

"A grandeur surpassed by few other islands in the Pacific.
    Glory after glory of hibiscus, and orange trees rich in promise;
bronze-red blossoms of the tulip tree, purple sprays of bougainvillea,
    and purple petals of banana flowers lifting to release whorl
after whorl of fingered fruit."

Robert Gibbings, *Over the Reefs*

LEFT A woman from the northern Mariana islands dressed for a festival

It seems only fair that Captain James Cook, the north Yorkshire lad who spent years charting the Pacific and was the first non-native to encounter so many of its islands, should be honoured in the naming of land somewhere in those parts. Sure enough, he was the first European to explore this South Pacific archipelago of fifteen major islands in 1773 – although he was not the first to sight them: over a century earlier the Spanish navigator Alvaro de Mendaña had noted their existence. Cook did not have the hubris to name them after himself, but called them the Hervey Islands as a tribute to Augustus Hervey, the Earl of Bristol, a Lord of the Admiralty. Fifty years later it was the Russian cartographer Johann von Krusenstern who took it upon himself to rename them after Cook.

The Maori Polynesians who inhabited the islands were not particularly enthralled to welcome an influx of outsiders. When the crew of the *Cumberland* landed on Rarotonga in 1814, there was fierce fighting with fatalities on both sides, and the unfortunately named Ann Butchers, consort of the *Cumberland*'s captain, was eaten by the islanders; cannibalism was taken off the menu when Christian missionaries arrived on the islands a decade or so later.

When France took control of the Tahitian sector of Polynesia, the chiefs, or *ariki*, of the Cook Islands grew alarmed, and asked Great Britain to protect them. After some protracted political shenanigans, the islands were eventually annexed by New Zealand in 1900. To this day there is a constant two-way traffic between the two places: Cook Islanders have emigrated in droves to NZ to earn money for their families back home; the return flights transport hordes of Kiwis heading off on holiday.

Within this archipelago, in the heart of the South Pacific, a range of geological ages and styles are jumbled up. Mangaia is the oldest of all the Polynesian islands; stunningly beautiful Aitutaki is a Bora Bora-style lagoon atoll; Atiu a raised volcanic island. Rarotonga ("Down South"), formed from the residue of a mighty volcano, is the main island yet still not much more than thirty kilometres (nineteen miles) in circumference. Pukapuka, the most isolated of the group, way off to the northwest, is closer to Samoa than Rarotonga and has its own customs, a distinct language and a variant of cricket (called "kirkiti") that requires a three-sided bat.

Creeping westwards towards the International Date Line, the Cook Islands actually seem to exist within their own very special time zone, or perhaps that should be "timeless" zone. There is not much to do apart from chill out and relax – exactly why so many New Zealanders head this way – and the motto displayed on the Cook Island car licence plates is a description of the benefits of a slower pace of life. "Kia Orana", they say: "May you live long."

Cook Islands, self governing in free association with New Zealand **Longitude:** 160° 00' W **Latitude:** 17° 00' S **Area:** 236 sq km (91 sq mi) **Archipelago area:** 1.8 million sq km (694,800 sq mi) **Highest point:** 652 m (2,139 ft) Te Manga **Population:** 21,800 **Principal town:** Avarua, Rarotonga Island **Natives:** Will Crummer, Teata Makirere, Jake Numanga, Turepu Turepu **Resident:** James Chalmers

"Ua ou sau nei ma le mea atoa
Ma lo'u malosi ua atoatoa
Ia e faatafa ma e sósó ese
Leaga o lenei Manu e uiga ese
Le Manu Samoa! Le Manu Samoa!"

"Here I come completely prepared
My strength is at its peak
Make way and move aside
Because this Manu is unique
The Manu Samoa The Manu Samoa!"

The *Siva Tau*, Samoan war dance and rugby *haka*

Samoa

SOUTH PACIFIC

For centuries following first contact in the 1700s, Europeans and Americans regarded the Samoans as warlike savages. But this judgement seems rather ironic given that at the dawn of the twentieth century they were at each other's throats in an eight-year triangular war between Britain, America and Germany (as if any of them had a right) over whose subjects the Samoans should be. Fortunately nature intervened and the military storm that had been brewing in the southern Pacific, with three fleets converging on each other and all sides arming the Samoans themselves, was met by an even fiercer storm that all but destroyed the primed ships and, overnight, all bets were off. The Treaty of Berlin divided up the country – formed of the two principal islands of western Upolu and eastern Savai'l – between German Samoa and American Samoa. Only for the First World War to spark off in Europe, proving yet again who were the savages and aggressors.

Strength is a revered value in Samoan society. Physically these are some of the most impressive specimens of the human race. When in the eighteenth century the French explorer Antoine de Bougainville first came across them he remarked on the Samoans' spectacular seafaring ability – referring not to longitudinal savvy but principally to their immense power at rowing – and christening their land The Navigator Islands; a name by which they were known until the Berlin agreement.

Remarkably and exemplarily for people of such power, the Samoans are also a gentle, spiritual and religious people who have absorbed the Christianity bequeathed by missionaries into their own mythology of gods. Communal life is very important and founded on the notion of *fa'aaloalo* (respect) and with, in the towns and villages as well as the capital of Apia, *fales*, a type of house with no walls but with just coconut-palm blinds for separation a common sight. Even when revolting against maltreatment at the hands of New Zealand, their new lords by the end of the Great War, the Samoan "Mau" movement was specifically non-violent, even though in 1929 it led to the shooting of many Samoans during a demonstration on what is now remembered as Black Saturday.

Instead the Samoan strength, which seems to be a human metaphor for the power of a mountainous volcanic landscape towered over by Mount Maunga Silisili, is channelled into sports such as sumo wrestling, and in particular rugby. Had half this island nation remained German they would surely have been a competitive, resilient and sporting race, but would they have gone on to produce such stars of the oval ball as Va'aiga Tuigamala, just one of many Samoans this small but often giant-killing nation has lost to the New Zealand game? There can be few more fearful sights than the Samoan fifteen, all bronzed muscle, piercing eyes and geometric painted tattoos, lining up for the *siva* war dance before each international game.

OVERLEAF Sunset in Samoa

Samoa, Independent State of Samoa **Longitude:** 172° 00' W **Latitude:** 14° 00' S **Area:** 2,944 sq km (1,136 sq mi) **Highest point:** 1,858 m (6,096 ft) Mauga Silisili, Savaii **Population:** 179,000
Principal town: Apia, Upolu **Natives:** Olo Brown, Opetaia Foa'i Brian Lima, Tau Moe, Maa Tanuvasa **Resident:** Robert Louis Stevenson

Index

Picture Credits

Acknowledgements

For all their help in sharing island-hopping memories, observations and suggestions, the authors would like to thank: Frédérique and Titi Alvarez, Gordon Baker, Anne-Laure Bates, Graham Beirne, Didier & Catherine Bernard, Emily Buchanan & Gerald Slocock, Margot Carmichael, John Cork, Margaret Crawford, Andrew & Lisa Dodd, Arthur & Esther Dodd, Kevin Duncan, Mark & Olga Gibbon, Pam & John Gibbon, John Glen, Letecia Griffith, Lucinda Hawksley, Charlie Jenkins, Lesley McVey, Nick Mason, Helen Monroe, David Owen, Charlotte Parry-Crooke, Reg Potter, Mark Puddy, Sarah Taylor, Elsa Turceininoff and Libby Weir-Breen. Many thanks to the Palazzo crew, captained by Colin Webb – more than ably supported by Sonya Newland and Terry Jeavons – who nobly steered the book to completion through the usual crosswinds and high seas. As ever, thanks for their patience to our travelling companions: Wan, Wan Mae & Mei Mae, and Merida, Oliver & Gigi. A swift doff of the cap to the rendezvous for our summit meetings, The Island in Kensal Rise, and to Nick Hornby for creating one of our favourite islands quotes, uttered by Hugh Grant as Will Lightman in *About A Boy*: "In my opinion all men are islands. And what's more, now's the time to be one. This is an island age. You can be sun-drenched, tropical, a magnet for young Swedish tourists. And I like to think that perhaps I'm that kind of island. I like to think I'm pretty cool. I like to think I'm Ibiza."

First published in Great Britain in 2008 by
PALAZZO EDITIONS LTD
2 Wood Street
Bath, BA1 2JQ
www.palazzoeditions.com

Art Director: Terry Jeavons
Managing Editor: Sonya Newland

ISBN 978-0-9553046-6-8

Design / layout © Palazzo Editions Ltd, 2008
Text © 2008 Philip Dodd and Ben Donald
Photographs © see picture credits page 511

The moral right of each of the Authors has been asserted.

A CIP catalogue reference for this book is available
from the British Library

This book can be ordered direct from the publisher.
Please contact the Marketing Department, but try your bookshop first.

Printed and bound in Singapore by Imago

1 3 5 7 9 10 8 6 4 2